The Pedagogical Concern

An Analysis of the Sanskrit Vicārasāgara of Vāsudeva Brahmendra Sarasvatī

The Pedagogical Concern

An Analysis of
The Sanskrit Vicārasāgara
of Vāsudeva Brahmendra Sarasvatī

S. Bhuvaneshwari

DK PRINTWORLD
Publishers of Indian Traditions

Cataloging in Publication Data — DK
[Courtesy: D.K. Agencies (P) Ltd. <docinfo@dkagencies.com>]

Bhuvaneshwari, S., 1976- **author.**
The pedagogical concern : an analysis of the Sanskrit Vicārasāgara of Vāsudeva Brahmendra Sarasvatī / S. Bhuvaneshwari.
pages cm
Includes bibliographical references (pages).
ISBN 9788124608180

1. Niścaladāsa, -1863. Vicārasāgara. 2. Niścaladāsa, -1863 – Translations into Sanskrit – History and criticism. 3. Sarasvatī, Vāsudeva Brahmendra – Criticism and interpretation. 4. Advaita. 5. Upanishads – Criticism and interpretation. I. Title.

DDC 181.482 23

ISBN 13: 978-81-246-0818-0
First published in India in 2015

Printed and published by:
D.K. Printworld (P) Ltd.
Regd. Office : *Vedaśrī*, F-395, Sudarshan Park
(Metro Station: Ramesh Nagar)
New Delhi – 110 015-11
Phones : (011) 2545 3975, 2546 6019; *Fax* : 2546 5926
e-mail : indology@dkprintworld.com
Web : www.dkprintworld.com

In loving memory of

Professor. S. Revathy
(1959-2014)

An inspiring teacher and
a loving guide, friend and philosopher

जिस रीतिसें जिज्ञासुकूं अद्वैत बोध होवै तैसें बुद्धि की स्थिति करै ॥

— *Hindi Vicārasāgara, Taraṅga 5, ṭīkā 247*

यया प्रक्रियया जिज्ञासोरद्वैतबोधो भवति तस्यां प्रक्रिययां तस्य बुद्धिः स्थिरीकर्तव्या ।

— *Sanskrit Vicārasāgara, Taraṅga 5, āvartta 260*

By whichever pedagogical measure the seeker of truth gains non-dual knowledge; by that pedagogical device the mind of the seeker is to be made firm.

Foreword

THE desire to seek happiness is basic in all individuals, but the ability to recognize what makes one happy, and the means of attaining it are rare. While some seek money, fame and power, hoping that these will lead to happiness, others may choose to renounce worldly life in the hope of attaining peace. Restlessness in individual lives is unavoidable since alternating joy and sorrow make peace and tranquillity, a distant dream. To overcome this endless plight one should ponder over the nature and purpose of one's existence, and engage in *ātmavicāra.* The Upaniṣads are the sources of highest knowledge and it is divine grace that fosters the desire to pursue this knowledge that leads to liberation. The premise of the teachings in the Upaniṣads rests on the ability of human understanding to strive for enlightenment. In this context, the role of preceptors who can unravel the goal of life and guide one towards attaining it becomes very significant. Great preceptors like Ādi Śaṅkara have analysed, interpreted and explained the hidden meanings in the Upaniṣads wherein is contained the esoteric and useful information about life here and hereafter and of the path to liberation. The teachings of Advaita that emanated from Ādi Śaṅkara have reached several preceptors of Advaita, to be interpreted and explained in various ways. These preceptors, however, were cautious in maintaining preferences but no exclusions. Their views were centred around promulgating that *Brahman* alone is real; the world is false and the individual self is no other than *Brahman.* In other words, in their teachings the core remains to be the same while the periphery keeps changing. In fact, this paved the way for diversified views within Advaita. Therefore, the philosophy of Advaita may be characterized as pointing to unity in diversity. This is precisely the lesson that Niścaladāsa and Vāsudeva Brahmendra Sarasvatī have impressed upon in their work *Vicārasāgara.* Of these two writers the former wrote the original work in Hindi, while the latter trans-created it in Sanskrit with the needed additional notes. Sureśvara, a noteworthy preceptor of Advaita, observes:

यया यया भवेत्पुंसां व्युत्पत्तिः प्रत्यगात्मनि ।
सा सैव प्रक्रिया ज्ञेया साध्वी सा चानवस्थिता ॥

> Modes of interpretation with regard to the nature of self are manifold in order to suit the intellect of pupils; and they are all treated to be valid.

Niścaladāsa adheres to this principle and, therefore, has taken a novel approach and classified the seekers of knowledge or aspirants of liberation (*adhikārī*) as *uttama, madhyama* and *kaniṣṭha* in resonance with their level of understanding. This shows the concern and large-heartedness of the preceptors in their fellow beings. It redounds to the credit of Vāsudeva Brahmendra to have made it available in Sanskrit for those unfamiliar with Hindi.

In the contemporary scenario there is a growing interest among young scholars in Indian philosophy and it is a matter of real gratification. Indian philosophy has at last come to be valued for its own sake. This reawakened interest in the subject is sure to lead to a deeper understanding of its knowledge. I am sure that Niścaladāsa's *Vicārasāgara* and Vāsudeva Brahmendra's trans-creation thereon have given a right direction to the future reconstruction of philosophic thought in India by means of this novel approach.

Dr S. Bhuvaneshwari has thoughtfully chosen this topic for her research to fulfil the need of the hour. The treatment of topics is exhaustive, and she has set forth the great variety of solutions of nearly all the philosophic problems clearly and carefully. The book is well written in six chapters and it gives a remarkably clear and comprehensive account of Niścaladāsa's views. The book contains diagrammatic representations and flow charts. The get-up, it is scarcely necessary to add, is excellent. I hope we can expect many more publications of this kind from Dr Bhuvaneshwari.

I heartily recommend this publication to all those who are desirous of acquainting themselves with the essentials of this important system of thought. I wish her all success.

Chennai

S. Revathy
Professor, Department of Sanskrit
University of Madras

Preface

THE text *Vicārasāgara* authored by Niścaladāsa (eighteenth-nineteenth century CE) in one of the regional dialects of Hindi is well known for its unique approach in imparting the teaching of Advaita to different kinds of aspirants. Pītāmbar (nineteenth century CE) has provided notes (*ṭippaṇīs*) again in regional dialect of Hindi. This text has been well-received throughout India through its translations in regional languages like Telugu, Tamil and Bengali, including a translation into Sanskrit by Vāsudeva Brahmendra Sarasvatī (nineteenth-twentieth century CE). The present study is based on this Sanskrit version of *Vicārasāgara*. The Sanskrit *Vicārasāgara* was popularized in the city of Chennai by (Late) Kalyanasundara Sastrigal, one of the editors of this text in the 1990s. It has also been systematically taught in Sanskrit by Swami Paramarthananda Sarasvati, in Chennai, during the period from 21 February 1997 to 5 August 2005, in 307 classes (each class exactly of a duration of one hour). He continues to teach the same in English (from 17 December 2011 onwards).

This book has been developed based on the classes conducted by Swami Paramarthananda in Sanskrit. The result of this study is the identification of the importance of the triple concept, viz. pedagogy, language and interpretation as demonstrated in the text *Vicārasāgara*. This study is a gradual shift from the student-based pedagogy to the pedagogical concern of the teacher as exhibited in the text *Vicārasāgara*. The position of the Sanskrit version as a "trans-creation" and that of Vāsudeva Brahmendra as a "trans-creator" has been amply justified in order to arrive at a double-layered "pedagogical concern" found in the Sanskrit *Vicārasāgara*. The first layer of concern can be discerned from the trans-creator Vāsudeva Brahmendra, who had taken up a stupendous task of "translating" the Hindi work into "simple" Sanskrit, with appropriate modifications to cater to the readers with a knowledge of Sanskrit language. The second layer of concern is revealed in the work through a dialogue between the *guru* and the different *adhikārī*s, viz. *uttama, madhyama* and *kaniṣṭha,* through which the teaching of Advaita is unfolded depending upon the need of the seeker. The present study is an earnest attempt to extract this double-layered pedagogical concern, a study of which serves as a model to be adopted in our modern education system. It also attempts to genuinely venture into a "textual study" to highlight "pedagogy" as an important element in the "Philosophy of Education" or rather an "Education of Philosophy".

The present study is developed through six chapters wherein I have given a title (in Sanskrit) to each chapter based on the predominant aspect discussed in that particular chapter. In the first introductory chapter "Upodghāta", we shall find a detailed discussion on the life and works of the author Niścaladāsa, *ṭippaṇīkāra* Pītāmbar and the trans-creator Vāsudeva Brahmendra. The triple concept of pedagogy, language and interpretation as found in the *Vicārasāgara* is examined with suitable examples. The contribution of Vāsudeva Brahmendra in his Sanskrit *Vicārasāgara* is discussed with instances and also the reasons for choosing the same for the present study are amply justified. The concept of *adhikārī*-based pedagogy has been briefly explained.

The second chapter "Adhikārisvarūpaprakaraṇa", begins with a survey of the nature and classification of *adhikārī*s as found in the tradition of Advaita. In this survey a slow emergence of *adhikārī*-based pedagogy is highlighted. The perspectives of Niścaladāsa and Pītāmbar on the nature and classification of *adhikārī*s are studied from the original *Vicārasāgara* and that of Vāsudeva Brahmendra from the Sanskrit *Vicārasāgara.* Thereafter, the difficulty in defining and classifying the *adhikārī*s in *Vicārasāgara* is pointed out and the proposition to treat the text *Vicārasāgara* as pedagogic centric is enunciated.

In the following chapters 3-6, the content of *Vicārasāgara* has been restructured in terms of employment of pedagogical tools by the *guru,* catering to an *adhikārī.* Thus, the related questions and discussions as found in different *taraṅgas* of *Vicārasāgara* are pooled in and presented in a cohesive manner so as to arrive at the core of the text *Vicārasāgara* as that with a "pedagogical concern".

We shall find the discussion on the nature of knowledge based on the dialogue between the *guru* with *uttama* and *kaniṣṭha adhikārīs* in the third and fourth chapters "Jñānasvarūpa-prakaraṇa" and "Jñānapratibandhanivṛttiśca". In the fifth chapter "Upāsana-svarūpa-prakaraṇa" the role of meditation and its efficacy as a means to gradual liberation are highlighted. The final chapter "Mokṣasvarūpaprakaraṇa" deals with the nature of liberation.

I wish to record that the Sanskrit *Vicārasāgara* has been taken up for research as suggested by my Vedānta Guru, Swami Paramarthananda Sarasvati who is drawn to this work that provides well-defined concepts of Advaita in simple language. I take this opportunity to thank Swami Paramarthananda Sarasvati for his kindness, compassion, grace and unlimited blessings showered on me.

I wish to acknowledge all those who were instrumental in completing my thesis. First, I thank the University of Madras for permitting me to pursue my research work in the Department of Sanskrit. I also wish to thank the authorities of the University of Madras for providing the University Research Fellowship (URF) for the period 2009-10. My thanks are also due to the University of Madras for granting permission for the publication of the thesis.

I thank Shri Siniruddha Dash, Head of the Department of Sanskrit, University of Madras for his kind support and encouragement. My sincere thanks are due to Smt. S. Revathy, Professor, Department of Sanskrit, University of Madras, for her supervision, encouragement, constant guidance and ready help throughout the study. I also wish to thank her for readily accepting to write a foreword for this book. Dr. S. Revathy was a well-known erudite scholar of Advaita Vedānta and Navya-Nyāya. It is most unfortunate that her passing away recently (on 5 February 2014) has created an irreparable loss in the field of Sanskrit studies and research.

My thanks are also due to all the faculty members of the Department of Sanskrit for their encouragement. I wish to thank all the administrative staff of the Department of Sanskrit for their ready support.

It is vital to thank many students of Swami Paramarthananda from whom I have immensely benefitted. As it is difficult to thank every one of them, I take the privilege to mention a few. I am grateful to Shri V.J. Mohan, who sponsored the CDs of Swamiji on the classes of Sanskrit *Vicārasāgara*. I thank Smt. Sarala for giving me the original and the (modern) Hindi translation of the *Vicārasāgara*. My sincere gratitude and thanks are due to Shri Ramaseshan, discussion with whom has enriched me in many ways. I would like to sincerely thank Shri S.B. Raman, who on the request of Swamiji readily arranged for my visit to the Vāsudeva Brahmendra's Library at Mayilāḍuthurai. I am indebted to Smt. Jaya Srinivasan for her patience and kind cooperation in going through the manuscript of the book and providing valuable suggestions.

I personally thank the team at Mayilāḍuthurai for their kindness and support in culling out the information on the life and works of Vāsudeva Brahmendra. My heartful thanks are due to Smt. Annapurani Krishnamurthy, who accommodated me in her "traditional" home during my stay at Mayilāḍuthurai. I am grateful to Shri M. Gopalan, for permitting me to access the handwritten manuscripts of Vāsudeva Brahmendra at the Library, Mayilāḍuthurai.

I specially thank Shri Francis X. Clooney of Divinity School, Harvard University for going through the first and third chapters of the thesis and for providing his valuable comments.

My thanks are due to Shri Allen Michael, Research Scholar,

Harvard University for going through the revised dissertation material and for providing his feedback and valuable suggestions.

I also wish to thank Smt. Padma Malini S., Retired Lecturer, Department of English Language, Stella Maris College, Chennai for going through the first three chapters of the book and providing her comments.

I thank the Librarians of the Adyar Library, Kuppuswami Sastri Research Institute and Ramakrishna Mutt. My special thanks are due to the Curator Shri R. Chandramohan of GOML for his ready help in tracing the record of the manuscripts of Vāsudeva Brahmendra handed over to GOML in the year 1958.

In this connection, I fondly remember my favourite teacher, (Late) Smt. Saroja Krishnamurthy, Lecturer, Department of Sanskrit Language, Stella Maris College, Chennai who constantly encouraged me to excel in my studies and it is unfortunate that she did not live to see this day of my life.

I wish to offer my sincere thanks to Shri Susheel K. Mittal, Director of D.K. Printworld for his kind acceptance to undertake the publishing of my study and for the neat execution carried out by his team.

The text *Vicārasāgara* contains the essentials of Advaita from the times of Ādi Śaṅkarācārya to the author's own time (nineteenth century CE); thus it demands a sound knowledge of the basic concepts of Advaita Vedānta. The objective of the present study is to cater mainly to the needs of the students of Philosophy in general and sincere seekers of knowledge in particular.

With *Nārāyaṇa smṛtis*.

Chennai, Makara Saṁkrānti, 2015 **S. Bhuvaneshwari**

Contents

Abbreviations

Aa	*Ātmabodha*
AB	*Aparokṣānubhūti*
AM	*Advaita Makaranda*
AU	*Aitareya Upaniṣad*
BG	*Bhagavad-Gītā*
BGŚB	*Bhagavad-Gītā Śāṅkara Bhāṣya*
BP	*Bhāgavata Purāṇa*
BS	*Brahma-Sūtra*
BSŚB	*Brahma-Sūtra Śāṅkara Bhāṣya*
BU	*Bṛhadāraṇyaka Upaniṣad*
BUŚB	*Bṛhadāraṇyaka Upaniṣad Śāṅkara Bhāṣya*
BUŚBV	*Bṛhadāraṇyaka Upaniṣad Śāṅkara Bhāṣya Vārttika*
CU	*Chāndogya Upaniṣad*
CUŚB	*Chāndogya Upaniṣad Śāṅkara Bhāṣya*
DDV	*Dṛg Dṛśya Viveka*
HV	Hindi *Vicārasāgara* of Niścaladāsa
IU	*Īśa Upaniṣad*
KP	*Kūrma Purāṇa*
KS	*Kāmasūtra*
KU	*Kaṭha Upaniṣad*
KeU	*Kena Upaniṣad*
KeUŚB	*Kena Upaniṣad Śāṅkara Bhāṣya*

MaU	*Māṇḍūkya Upaniṣad*
MaK	*Māṇḍūkya Kārikā*
MaKŚB	*Māṇḍūkya Kārikā Śāṅkara Bhāṣya*
MU	*Muṇḍaka Upaniṣad*
MUŚB	*Muṇḍaka Upaniṣad Śāṅkara Bhāṣya*
MS	*Manusmṛti*
NS	*Naiṣkarmyasiddhi*
PANV	*The Philosophy of Advaita* as expounded by Niścaladāsa with special reference to his *Vṛttiprabhākara*
PD	*Pañcadaśī*
PK	*Pañcīkaraṇa*
PU	*Praśna Upaniṣad*
SD	*Saddarśanam*
SS	*Sūtasaṁhitā*
SU	*Śvetāśvatara Upaniṣad*
SV	Sanskrit *Vicārasāgara* by Vāsudeva Brahmendra
SKS	*Saṁkṣepaśārīraka*
TU	*Taittirīya Upaniṣad*
TUŚB	*Taittirīya Upaniṣad Śāṅkara Bhāṣya*
VC	*Vivekacūḍāmaṇi*
VCD	*Vicāracandrodaya*
VP	*Vedānta Paribhāṣā*
VS	*Vedāntasāra*
VVS	*Viśuddhavedāntasāra*
VV	*Vākyavṛtti*

1

Introduction (Upodghāta)

INDIAN philosophical systems are nurtured through a rich literary tradition and an institution of education. The various philosophical literatures are enlivened through teaching by committed teachers of a particular system. In this dual flow of "literature" and "teaching", "literature" brings out the intellectual acumen of an individual, while "teaching" includes transferring the traditional science of interpretation of the texts to the following generation. In the School of Advaita Vedānta, spearheaded by Ādi Śaṅkarācārya and continued by other preceptors, we find an amalgamation of both writing and teaching that has been adhered to as late as the twentieth century. The purpose of writing a text varies depending on the type of readers, say, a seeker of knowledge of Advaita, the seekers of other philosophical systems, and a new entrant into a philosophical discussion and so on. A text may or may not cater to all kinds of readers since a reader is distanced from the author in place and time.

In the tradition of teaching, there is a direct philosophical discourse between the teacher and the taught, where a teacher always addresses a heterogeneous group. The onus is on the teacher to communicate the highest truth catering to the different levels of students. A teaching that reaches out to different minds and the same written for the posterity is a rare combination in the live tradition of Advaita Vedānta. In this context, we name a late-eighteenth–early-nineteenth century mendicant, Niścaladāsa, who not only devoted himself to teaching the masses but also presented the experience of his teaching in his (magnum opus) *Vicārasāgara* in Hindi. The uniqueness of this work lies in the dissemination of Advaitic knowledge to different kinds of aspirants adopting suitable pedagogical tools. Niścaladāsa's *Vicārasāgara* that has received attention from the scholars and the laity alike is commented upon in the form of *ṭippaṇī* in Hindi by one Pītāmbar. It has been adapted and translated into various languages including Sanskrit. Its Sanskrit translation by Vāsudeva Brahmendra Sarasvatī (hereafter VB) forms the base for the present study. We shall first briefly deal with the life and works of Niścaladāsa, Pītāmbar and VB followed by an analysis of the triple concept, viz. "pedagogy", "language" and "interpretation" based on the text *Vicārasāgara* in order to arrive at the "pedagogical concern" exhibited in this text.

1.1 Life and Works of Niścaladāsa (CE 1791–1863)

From the early fourteenth up to late eighteenth century CE, north India witnessed an upsurgence of Bhakti cult. During this period, there emerged many saints, mystics and religious reformers like Kabīr, Nānak, Mīrābāī, Sūrdās and Tulasīdās. The philosophical teachings were presented to the masses in regional dialects. During the late sixteenth century CE, one of the most important mystic-reformer named Dādū Dayāl,[1] born in Rajasthan, popularized the couplets of Kabīr and others, blended with the essence of Advaita Vedānta. Dādū's teachings in the form of couplets attracted the common mass in large numbers. Later, his followers claimed to have taken to what came to be known as the Dādū-panth (Dādū's way). We find a meaningful continuity of the tradition of Dādū-panth in a mendicant scholar from Haryana, called Niścaladāsa, a great Advaitin of the religious monk-order. Niścaladāsa is said to be born in 1791 in Dhanana village, Jhajjar district, Haryana.[2] He belonged to the Jāṭ community and his

[1] Farquhar 1920: 341-46.

[2] The biographical details are from Kishoredas Svāmi's (Modern Hindi) *Vicārasāgara*, Śrī Sādhubelā Udāsīna Āśram, Bombay, 1992. For further details on life and works of Niścaladāsa see Allen 2013.

father was a farmer. He lost his mother at a very early age. His father who developed an intense dispassion towards worldly life took his son to Delhi. The father and son served the saints in an *āśrama* at Delhi and learnt the teachings of *Dādū Vāṇī*. The boy was directly under the care of Śrī Alakrāmjī. Seeing the boy's interest and immense dedication, Śrī Alakrāmjī, accepted the boy with his father's permission, as his disciple and named him Niścaladāsa. At the age of 15, he was sent to Varanasi for further studies of scriptures.

He lived in a Dādū Maṭha at Varanasi and continued learning from scholars. He studied Advaita under Svāmi Kīkārāmjī. He returned to Delhi around the age of 34-35 and, staying in a village named Kihaḍaulī, he spread the teaching of the scriptures. He is said to have been the preceptor of King Rāmsiṁha of Būndī. Later, he found that the common man had difficulties in understanding the nuances of grammar, logic and other philosophical teachings presented in Sanskrit. For the benefit of the masses he decided to write the essentials of Advaita found in Sanskrit classical works in the regional dialect. It is believed that Niścaladāsa wrote the two prominent works, viz., *Vicārasāgara* and *Vṛttiprabhākara* at the request of King Rāmsiṁha of Būndī. He refers to the place of the composition of *Vicārasāgara* as a village to the west of Delhi.[3] He continued teaching for a very long time to all those who sought to learn from him. He passed away in the year 1863. His two main disciples were Dayārām and Muktārām who continued the tradition of teaching Advaita to the masses.

Based on the handwritten manuscript of Hindi *Vicārasāgara* dated CE 1849 and its first publication with the *ṭippaṇīs* of Pītāmbar in CE 1874, an edition of it by Svāmi Dvārikādās Śāstrī was published (without *ṭippaṇīs* of Pītāmbar) by Svāmi Niścal Dās IInd Centenary Committee, Varanasi in 1989. The text was again published along with Pītāmbar's *ṭippaṇīs* by Khemraj Shri

[3] दिल्लीतैं पश्चिमदिशा कोस अठारह गाम।
तामैं यह पूरो भयौ किहडौली तिहि नाम॥ — *HV* 7.115

Krishanadas, Bombay in 1994. The popularity and importance of *Vicārasāgara* can be discerned from the later writings based on this work and from its translations and adaptations into various other languages. The two well-known minor works based on *Vicārasāgara* are *Vicārasāgaradarpaṇa* by Svāmi Manohardās, published by Śrī Akhila Bhāratīya Vedānta Pracār Maṇḍal, Advaita Āśram, Ajmer and *Vicārasāgara-praśnottarī* by Svāmi Siddhanātha, published by Siddhāśrama, Rishikesh, 1957.[4] Pītāmbar, who wrote *ṭippaṇīs* for *Vicārasāgara*, was highly influenced by the style and presentation of *Vicārasāgara*. He wrote an independent work in Hindi titled *Vicāracandrodaya*[5] as a preliminary text to *Vicārasāgara*. *Vicārasāgara* has been adapted into various regional languages like Tamil, Marāṭhī, Gujarātī and Bengalī besides Sanskrit and English.[6]

---

[4] *PANV*.

[5] For details see Bhuvaneshwari 2013.

[6] a. The English translation by Lālā Sreeram titled *Vichārasāgara*: *The Metaphysics of the Upanishads*, was published by Munshiram Manoharlal Publishers, Delhi, in 1885 and in 1994.

b. A brief English translation of the crux of *Vicārasāgara* entitled *Vicārasāgara*: *The Ocean of Enquiry* by A. Siva Rao, ed. E.R.S. Mead, Theosophical Society European Section, Departmental Papers, Theosophical Publishing Society, London, was published in 1894.

c. The Telugu *Vicārasāgara* by O.Y. Doraisamaiah was published by Satvasādhani Kāryasthānam, Chennai-puram (year of publication not mentioned).

d. The Tamil *Vicārasāgara* by A. Siva Rao was published by Kumbhakona Brahmajñāna Sangha, Kumbhakonam, in 1893 and again in 1904.

e. Ramaṇa Maharṣi brought out a condensed version of the Tamil *Vicārasāgara* under the title *Vicārasāgara Sāra Saṁgraham* published by Ramaṇa Āśrama, Tiruvannāmalai, in 1909.

f. Ramaṇa's condensed version in Tamil has been translated into English titled *Jewel Garland of Enquiry* (renamed the Tamil version as *Vicāramaṇimālai*), and this was first published by Ramaṇa Āśrama, Tiruvannāmalai, in 1977.

g. The Sanskrit *Vicārasāgara* by Vāsudeva Brahmendra Sarasvatī edited by Panchapagesha Shastrigal and Varahur Kalyanasundara Shastrigal was published by Śrī Vāsudeva Brahmendra Sarasvatī Svāmigaḷ Library Committee, Mayilāḍuthurai, in 1964, 1986 and a reprint in 2012.

→

IMPORTANCE OF THE TEXT *VICĀRASĀGARA*

The greatness (*mahimā*) of the text *Vicārasāgara*, says Niścaladāsa is that it is like the unfathomable ocean since it contains the "waters" of Vedic teaching in the form of (Advaita) Siddhānta.[7] This is explained by Pītāmbar in his *tippaṇī*; "since it is vast like an ocean (*sāgara*), the text is titled as *Vicārasāgara*. The letters employed in the text from the beginning till the end, in its totality, form an introduction (*bhūmikā*) likened to a land. This land is filled with waters in the form of (Advaita) Siddhānta of the Veda. The seven chapters are like waves (*taraṅga*). The use of *chandas* (poetic metre) in the text is compared to the aquatic creatures and the terse portions are said to rise like the sharks. The elegantly presented *chandas* are like the precious pearls and the portions where the Absolute Pure Reality is revealed are like the priceless gems. The description of the qualities (*sādhanā*) is comparable to fourteen gems (includes *bahiraṅga* and *antaraṅga sādhanās*).[8] The inquisitive mind of the seeker of liberation resembles a boat accelerated by the repetition (*abhyāsa*) of Advaitic concepts that is likened to the gentle breeze. The *guru* who is established in the Truth (*brahmaniṣṭha*) is like a ferryman who helps others to abandon the dreadful land (*kudeśa*) likened to bondage and guides to reach the other shore, to the land of paradise (*sudeśa*), i.e. liberation. The study of this text *Vicārasāgara* with intense faith (*śraddhā*) culminates in the attainment of the result (*phala*) of liberation.[9] VB while describing the significance of the word *sāgara* also explains the importance of the word *vicāra*. He says that the dialogue between the teacher and the seeker is in the form of

---

← h. The (Modern) Hindi *Vicārasāgara* by Kishoredās Svāmi was published by Śrī Sādhubelā Udāsīna Āśram, Bombay, 1992.

i. The (Modern) Tamil *Vicārasāgara* was published by Śrī Vāsudeva Brahmendra Sarasvatī Svāmigaḷ Library Committee, Mayilāḍuthurai, in 2007.

[7] भन्यो वेद सिद्धांत जल जामें अतिगंभीर ।
अस विचारसागर कहूं पेखि मुदित हैं धीर ॥ — *HV* 1.6

[8] For details on *sādhanās* see Section 2.6 of Chapter 2.

[9] *HV* 1. *ṭippaṇī* 4.

inquiry into the nature of Truth (*vāda*), discussion (*carcā*) and derivative conclusions (*nirṇaya*). The inquiry is taken up by a seeker with a desire to know the Truth, the discussion is in the form of the presentation of the view of the opponent (*pūrvapakṣa*) followed by the teaching of the Advaita system (*siddhānta*) and finally the conclusion is in the form of the logical presentation of the subject matter by utilizing the sixfold indicators (*upakrama*, etc.).[10]

Niścaladāsa mentions the purpose of writing the Advaitic teaching in Hindi:

> There are many works like Sūtra, Bhāṣya, Vārttika that discuss the teachings in various ways but still I proceed to write for the benefit of *manda adhikārī*, i.e. those who find it difficult to grasp the teaching from such texts.[11]

He also mentions that:

> There are works in regional dialect too but the study of *Vicārasāgara* helps in removal of all doubts.[12]

He explains in his *ṭīkā* to the above *dohā* that other works in regional dialect do not analyse the Advaitic teaching completely and some are even defective due to improper analysis. But *Vicārasāgara* undertakes elaborate analysis and deals with every aspect of the Advaita School. He proclaims the benefit of reading his text *Vicārasāgara*:

> Those for whom grammar is difficult and Sanskrit language is unknown should read this text (*Vicārasāgara*) and obtain the absolute peace.[13]

---

10 *SV*, p. 7.

11 सूत्र भाष्य वार्तिंक प्रभृति ग्रंथ बहुत सुरबानि।
तथापि मैं भाषा करूं लखि मतिमंद अजानि॥ — *HV* 1.7

12 कविजनकृत भाषा बहुत ग्रंथ जगत विख्यात।
बिन विचारसागर लखै नहिं संदेह नसात॥ — *HV* 1.8

13 बिन व्याकरन न पढि सकैं ग्रंथ संस्कृत मंद ।
पढै याहि अनयास हीं लहैं सु परमानंद॥ — *HV* 7.114

But he says the qualifications and guidelines according to the tradition of Advaita are to be followed, i.e.:

> One who has acquired the fourfold qualification, who listens from a *guru* will attain liberation.[14]

He emphasizes the importance of a *guru* in gaining knowledge[15] and he wants to prove the reliability on the text *Vicārasāgara* and therefore he enumerates the sciences mastered by him. He says:

> Niścaladāsa has learnt Sāṁkhya, Nyāya, Vyākaraṇa, Advaita and has taken the effort to know the essence of the Vedas.[16]

That this text *Vicārasāgara* originally written for readers of Hindi language and not for readers exposed to Sanskrit language is emphasized in his explanation of the tradition of language. He says:

> The short letters elongated and long letters shortened are not defective since it is the tradition of (Hindi) language.[17]

His conviction in the knowledge of Advaita is declared by him in the concluding couplets of *Vicārasāgara* and he also records his reverence to the Dādū-panth.[18]

---

14 पेख च्यारि अनुबंधयुत पढै सुनै यह ग्रंथ।
ज्ञानसहित गुरुसें जु नर लहै मोछको पंथ॥ — *HV* 3.1

15 बिन गुरुभक्ति प्रवीनहु लहै न आतमज्ञान। — *HV* 3.7

16 सांख्य न्यायमैं श्रम कियो पढि व्याकरण असेष।
पढे ग्रंथ अद्वैतके रह्यो न एकहु सेष॥
श्रमतैं अवगाहन किये निश्चलदास सवेद॥ — *HV* 7.111-12

17 लघु गुरु गुरु लघु होत है वृत्ति हेतु उच्चार।
रु ह्वै अरुकी ठौरमैं अबकी ठौर वकार॥
संयोगौ क्ष न क पर ख न नहीं टवर्ग णकार।
भाषामैं ॠ लृ ॡ ह्र नहीं अरु तालव्य शकार॥ — *HV* 7.401

18 ज्ञानी मुक्ति विदेहमैं जासौं होय अभेद। दादू आदूरूप सो जाहि बखानत वेद॥
नामरूप व्यभिचारिमैं अनुगत एक अनूप। दादूपदको लच्छ्य है अस्तिभातिप्रियरूप॥
— *HV* 7.116-17

Niścaladāsa's other important work[19] *Vṛttiprabhākara* deals with Advaitic epistemology. It challenges some of the basic epistemological arguments as found in Dharmarāja's *Vedānta Paribhāṣā*. This text has also received the attention of scholars. There are two expositions of this work in Hindi. They are:

1. *Vṛttiratnāvalī* by Pītāmbar, ed. Camanlāl Gautam, Bareilly, Sanskrit Sansthān, 1974.
2. *Svāmi Śrī Niścaladās Viracit Vṛttiprabhākara* by Camanlāl Gautam, Bareilly, Sanskrit Sansthān, 1974.

There is a translation of *Vṛttiprabhākara* into Tamil by Kuppusvāmi Rāju alias Brahmānanda Svāmi, published by Ripon Press, 1901. The same author has translated the *Vṛttiratnāvalī* also into Tamil.[20] The *Vṛttiprabhākara* has received the attention of academicians too and the same has been studied in the dissertation titled *"The Philosophy of Advaita as Expounded by Niścaladāsa with Special Reference to His Vṛttiprabhākara"* by R. Kamal.[21] The epistemological exposition in the *Vicārasāgara* is based on the *Vṛttiprabhākara*.

1.2 Life[22] and Works[23] of Pītāmbar (CE 1846/47–1899/1900)

Pītāmbar, the *ṭippaṇīkāra* of *Vicārasāgara*, is a prolific writer and a preceptor who has substantively contributed to the school of Advaita Vedānta. Born in 1846/47, in a small village named "Anjar" in the city of Kutch (Gujarat), he was the second son of Paṇḍit

---

[19] Niścaladāsa's other important work is *Yuktiprakāśa*, an interesting work written in Hindi in which the Advaitic concepts are examined through illustrations (*dṛṣṭānta*) and the principles deduced from those illustrations (*dārṣṭānta*). Niścaladāsa has also written commentaries on *Īśāvāśyopaniṣad* and *Kaṭhopaniṣad* in Sanskrit (only in manuscripts), a gloss for *Mahābhārata* in Sanskrit and a treatise on *Āyurveda* (both of which are said to be lost now).

[20] *PANV*.

[21] See *PANV*.

[22] *VCD*, pp. 39-84.

[23] For a list of published and unpublished works of Pītāmbar see the preface to *HV*, p. 13.

Puruṣottama and Vīravatī. At the age of five, the boy could easily recite the *subhāṣitas* taught by his father. At a very early age he learnt Devanāgarī and spent his time amidst the monks in the temple who recited the scriptures periodically. At the age of eight, the boy was formally initiated into the scriptural studies by way of the sacred thread ceremony. For twelve years he led a life of a *brahmacārī* engaging in the study of Upaniṣads and *Gītā* under the tutelage of Bāpū Mahārāj. He married at the age of twenty but left the family to pursue advanced scriptural study. He lived in the Majjala village in the *āśrama* of Śrī Rāmaguru. At the age of thirty he went on a pilgrimage and mastered various sciences under different teachers. He learnt astrology from Svasvasāpati Devacandra, grammar from Labdhivijaya and advanced grammar from Padmavijayī. He lived in Bhuj for some years and mastered all the sciences. He engaged himself in learning *Rāmāyaṇa* from Śrī Rāmacaraṇadās. He shortly returned to his native village on the request of his mother. Fortunately his study of scriptures did not diminish. Great scholars and mendicants visited his home from whom he learnt the Vedānta. After some time he went to Bombay with his father. In Nāsik he studied *Bhāgavata* and mastered Sanskrit under the guidance of Sūryarāmaśāstrī, disciple of Nārāyaṇaśāstrī.

Having developed an intense liking for Vedānta he then studied *Pañcadaśī* under Śrī Rāmagiri. He met Bāpū Mahārāj again and learnt other Vedāntic works. He then returned to his native village and conducted discourses on Vedānta to the public. He was visited by Rāma-caitanyāśrama and Bāpūjī Varma from whom he learnt *Upadeśasāhasrī, Naiṣkarmyasiddhi, Tattvānusandhāna, Vicārasāgara,* etc. In 1868, he was blessed with a male child. After three months, his father passed away. He then visited Bombay, where Śrī Viṣṇudāsa, one of the disciples of Niścaladāsa and Śrī Trilokarām were present. Amidst these saints, Pītāmbar spent 19 months in Bombay. During this time, he was deeply engrossed in the works of Niścaladāsa, namely, *Vṛttiprabhākara* and *Vicārasāgara.* He also learnt *Ātmapurāṇa* from Jayakṛṣṇa, Nyāya from

Bhīmācāryāśrama and advanced Vedānta from Gaṅgāsaṅg. In 1870, in Kāśī, he was involved in a philosophical debate and won the hearts of scholars assembled. Later he compiled this debate in a work titled *Praśnottarakadamba*. Much later, on the request of his disciples he wrote many works. He travelled widely, teaching and propagating the essence of Vedānta.

PĪTĀMBAR'S CONTRIBUTION TO VICĀRASĀGARA

Pītāmbar's main contribution to the text of *Vicārasāgara* lies in his 598 (45 + 553)[24] *ṭippaṇī*s elucidating various Advaitic concepts as found in the main work and also referring to other popular Vedānta works in Hindi. It is believed that Niścaladāsa did not write *ṭīkā* to the benedictory verses presented in five *dohā*s and this was prioritized by Pītāmbar who wrote both *ṭīkā* and 45 *ṭippaṇī*s exclusively for these first five couplets. He shows the absence of defects in the form of over-applicability, partial-inapplicability and total inapplicability in the definition of the Self revealed through the benedictory verses. In his 45th *ṭippaṇī* to the fifth verse we come to know for definite the influence of Dādū order on Niścaladāsa. According to the Dādū-panth the *Nirguṇa-Brahman* is referred to by the name *Rām*. While revealing the attributeless nature of the Self in the benedictory verses, Niścaladāsa uses the expression *bhajata rāma niṣkāma*. In the *ṭippaṇī*s to the first five couplets, Pītāmbar gives references to the later chapters of the text thereby indicating the content or the subject matter of the text revealed through the benedictory verses.

Now we shall briefly survey some of the salient features as found in the (553) *ṭippaṇī*s of Pītāmbar. He enumerates the Vedāntic works in Hindi indicated by Niścaladāsa in his *ṭīkā*. In *ṭippaṇī* 9, he refers to the six famous works, viz., *Ṣaṭpraśnī*, *Śatapraśnī*, *Jñānamañjarī*, *Jñānacūrṇa*, *Vedāntasāra* and *Pañcīkaraṇa* in Hindi of Manohardās. In *ṭippaṇī* 11, he refers to the works of Mānakdās as *Mānakabodha* or *Ātmavicāra*, and also mentions the

---

[24] Number of *ṭippaṇī*s from *taraṅga*s 1-7 in *HV* are 1-45 and 1-59, 60-123, 124-32, 133-214, 215-341, 342-473 and 474-553.

commentary *Sāroddhāra* to *Mānakabodha* by Mūlcandjñān. In *ṭippaṇī* 14, he defines *śraddhā* in two ways: first, *śraddhā* as the vessel for churning the other disciplines and second, *śraddhā* as the fruit of the tree of disciplines. He then mentions that both these aspects are discussed in the first *ratna* or chapter of *Bodharatnākara* and in *Bālabodha Ṭīkā* as its first instruction to the disciple. In *ṭippaṇī* 157, he gives the reference to the theories of error discussed in *Vr̥ttiprabhākara*, chapter 7, which is not dealt with in detail in *Vicārasāgara*. Some of the Sanskrit works mentioned are Vidyāraṇya's *Pañcadaśī* (*ṭippaṇī* 187), Purāṇas (*ṭippaṇī* 215), Śrī Harṣa's *Khaṇḍaṇakhaṇḍakhādya* (*ṭippaṇī* 216), anecdotes from *Mahābhārata* (*ṭippaṇī* 236), and references from Upaniṣads and Śaṅkara's works. He refers to his own *ṭippaṇī* to *Pañcadaśī* 7.102 in the *ṭippaṇī* 522 of *Vicārasāgara*. In *ṭippaṇī* 530, Pītāmbar quotes a verse in Sanskrit[25] and mentions that it was composed by a *paṇḍit*. This he quotes in connection with varied scriptures that directly serve as the means of knowledge and some other works that indirectly lead to knowledge. This verse is a reverberation of the idea presented in *Vicārasāgara* that all scriptures are instrumental in uplifting the individual being.

1.3 Life and Works of Vāsudeva Brahmendra Sarasvatī (CE 1848(?) – 1931)

VB, the translator (trans-creator) of the Hindi *Vicārasāgara* into Sanskrit, the author of the present study, has served as a major support to popularize *Vicārasāgara* among the scholars. He was born in Pañcanadakṣetra (now called Tiruvaiyyāru, Tanjavur district) on the banks of the River Kāverī, 7 miles north to Tanjavur, in a brāhmaṇa family of the Triliṅga community. He took to the mendicant order from Kr̥ṣṇānanda Sarasvatī[26] at the age of 25 after handing over the family responsibilities and a young son to the care of his dedicated wife. He stayed with his *guru* for over twenty-one years at the Gaṇapati Agrahāram (a village on the banks of the River Kāverī, about 8 miles east from his birthplace). After the

[25] भक्तिज्ञाने यत्र विष्णोर्यत्र वेदाः परा प्रमा। मतानि तानि सर्वाणि जीवोद्धारस्य हेतवः॥

[26] See Sarma 1980: 396.

passing away of his *guru*, he lived in several villages on the banks of Kāverī and reached Māyūram (about 35 miles east of Gaṇapati Agrahāram) in the Tanjavur district. He lived there for over seventeen years in a *maṭha* by the side of Śrī Viśvanāthasvāmi Temple on the south bank of the River Kāverī. At Māyūram (or Mayilāḍuthurai), VB expounded the Vedāntic teaching to the public. Many benefited from his teachings and among them were Viśvanātha Śāstrī[27] and others. During this time VB collected many works both printed and in manuscript form and was a towering personality in popularizing Vedānta.[28] He maintained a library which is said to have contained more than thousand printed works and about 600 manuscripts. He copied a number of rare works in his own hand neatly and legibly that were studies in Vedānta, Purāṇa, Yoga, Stotra, Mīmāṁsā, Nyāya, etc. After handing over the library to his able disciples he proceeded to the Gaṇapati Agrahāram and in about six months he shed his mortal coil on 21 January 1931. He is said to have been more than eighty years. An account of his life is found in print in these works.[29]

The Library[30] of VB was maintained in the name "Śrī Vāsudeva Brahmendra Saraswathy Swāmi Library Association, Māyāvaram". The rules of the committee were reformulated on 24 July 1943, presided by one A. Saptarṣi Iyer. The six life members of the library committee were A. Veṅkaṭarāmaiyyar,

---

27 In his magnum opus *Gītāmṛtamahodadhi*, Viśvanātha Śāstrī dedicates a few verses eulogizing his *guru* Vāsudeva Brahmendra. Refer URL: www.krishnamurthys.com.

28 A list of 597 works as entered in the register of Śrī Vāsudeva Brahmendra Saraswathy Swāmi Library accessed by me on 8 July 2009 is provided in my thesis.

29 a *Śāstrasiddhāntaleśatātparyasaṁgrahaḥ* (*SSLTS*), in the Introductory note by Vaidyanātha Śāstrī in Sanskrit. (published in 1926).

b *Brahmāhnikam*, in the Preface by Kṛṣṇa Śarma in Sanskrit (published in 1932).

c Sanskrit *Vicārasāgara*, in the Preface by Pañcāpageśa Śāstrīgaḷ in Sanskrit with an English translation (1st edn., 1964 and 2nd edn., 1986, repr. 2012).

30 These details are based on my field visit to Mayilāḍuthurai on 8 July 2009.

M.R. Bālasubramaṇiayyar, A. Sapatarṣi Iyer, V. Veṅkaṭarāma Śāstrīgaḷ, Brahmaśrī Nidur Kṛṣṇa Dīkṣitar and Brahmaśrī K.N. Mahāliṅga Dīkṣitar. Another set of members revisited on 18 April 1984 to amend the existing rules of the library. Currently the library is named "Śrī Vāsudeva Brahmendra Sarasvatī Library Committee" with a new set of members.

According to the "Visitor's Book", maintained during 1949 to 1985, we come to know that the library was well-maintained by a set of dedicated disciples of VB. It was a centre of religious activity with lessons conducted on Vedānta in the mornings and in the evenings. The handwritten works of VB were well-maintained and priority was given to encourage the study of texts in Sanskrit. There is also a mention of the performance of important Vedic rituals in the *maṭha* by the disciples. The visitors have expressed wonder on the massive collection of rare and important works on various subjects. The list of works contained in the library is found in an undated register in the library now. I learnt that the large collection of the library was well-maintained for quite some time by one Gurumūrti Śāstrī, who also delivered discourses on Advaita regularly.[31]

About 519 palm-leaf manuscripts collected by VB have been handed over to the Government Oriental Manuscripts Library, Madras (GOML) during the month of July 1958. The list has been recorded by GOML on 30 December 1959.[32] There is a mention in the preface to the Sanskrit *Vicārasāgara* that about twenty manuscripts were handed over to the Annamalai University, Chidambaram in March 1959.[33] There is no trace of other

[31] This information I gained from Shri A.S. Rāmanāthan of Mayilāḍuthurai, whose father Shri R. Subrahmaṇya Iyer was a disciple of Vāsudeva Brahmendra.

[32] I have noted the accession number along with the titles of the 519 manuscripts from the GOML register on 17 September 2009 and the list is provided in my thesis.

[33] I personally visited the Manuscript Library, Annamalai University, Chidambaram on 21 January, 2010. The concerned authorities could not locate the relevant records.

handwritten manuscripts and collected printed books of VB in the library. Presently, there are about twenty-six handwritten manuscripts found in the library.[34] The library currently possesses about thirty printed books in Grantha, Tamil, Sanskrit and Telugu, but all are in a decrepit condition. The library currently is not opened to the public and is poorly maintained. However, the present committee members hope to re-build the lost glory of this great tradition.

VB seems to have been highly influenced by Rāmacandrendra Sarasvatī who is said to have compiled the 1,008 *mahāvākyas* from the 108 Upaniṣads under the title *Mahāvākyaratnāvalī* for easy recitation by all. In the same light VB has compiled important and valuable teachings of Advaita Vedānta from various texts. He has also condensed and translated many works for the benefit of the masses. Some of his works are yet to be identified. The essence of the three published works is discussed here which reveals his competence to "condense", "compile" and "translate" works of Advaita.

ŚĀSTRASIDDHĀNTALEŚATĀTPARYASAṀGRAHAḤ (SSLTS)

It is a prose condensation of the well-known work *Śāstrasiddhāntaleśasaṁgrahaḥ* of Appayya Dīkṣita in Sanskrit. This was first published by one T. Veṅkaṭakr̥ṣṇaiyya of Chatrapur, Gañjam district during the lifetime of VB. The second edition available now was published in 1926. A Sanskrit introduction by Pūrṇānandendra Sarasvatī to the second edition gives an account of the subject matter of this work. It highlights the importance of *śravaṇa* and the pedagogy to be adopted to impart the knowledge of Advaita to the three kinds of aspirants, namely, *manda*, *madhyama* and *uttama adhikārī*s (this does not refer to the classification of aspirants in the text *Vicārasāgara*). The text contains four chapters (*paricchedas*) as in the Appayya's work covering all the topics in a nutshell. VB commences the text with a *namaskriyā*

[34] A list of paper manuscripts as on 8 July 2009 is provided in my thesis.

type of benediction invoking the blessing of his *paramaguru*. He mentions the purpose of writing this text as any other traditional author and that it is meant for his own conviction (*mamahṛdaya-naiścalyakṛte*). The text is in the form of questions and answers where the question raised covers each aspect of Advaita and the varied viewpoints of preceptors of Advaita are presented as the answers in lucid Sanskrit language of not more than five or six sentences. *Pariccheda* 1 defines the metaphysical categories and the epistemology of Advaita Vedānta. *Pariccheda* 2 deals with the supremacy of the scriptures, the ontology of the world and the nature of happiness experienced. *Pariccheda* 3 takes up the discussion on the nature of aspirant and the means to liberation. *Pariccheda* 4 deals with the nature of destruction of ignorance and its residue and the nature of liberation.

BRAHMĀHNIKAM

VB has compiled the teachings of Advaita in this work in 467 verses sourced from the primary and secondary Advaitic texts. It was first published by Engineer Naṭeśa Śarmā who lived in Madurai and who was an ardent disciple of VB. The book published in 1932 contains a preface in Sanskrit by Kṛṣṇa Śarmā who was a teacher at that time in the Municipal High School, Māyūram. This work is an anthology of verses from *Yoga-Vāsiṣṭha*, *Sūta Saṁhitā*, Purāṇas, *Bhagavad-Gītā*, *Pañcadaśī*, Upaniṣads and other Prakaraṇas. The intention is to get rote the selected verses on Advaita and for effortless reflection on its meaning. The verses include description of the nature of *Brahman*, *māyā*, *Īśvara*, *jīva*, the ephemeral world and liberation.

VICĀRASĀGARA

The third published work of VB is the Sanskrit translation of Niścaladāsa's Hindi *Vicārasāgara*. There is no clue as to how he obtained the Hindi *Vicārasāgara* and how he set to translate (trans-create) this work into Sanskrit. However, it appears that by the time the original work was received by VB, *Vicārasāgara* was a popular text that has reached the southern tip of India. At the end of the Sanskrit *Vicārasāgara* VB mentions his objective to "translate" it into Sanskrit.[35]

1.4 The Triple Concept in Vicārasāgara[36]

From the interpretation of *Prasthānatraya* (Upaniṣads, *Bhagavad-Gītā* and *Brahmasūtra*) in the form of commentaries and from the varied Prakaraṇas we come to know that a seeker is defined, according to Advaita, as one who possesses the fourfold qualities (*sādhanacatuṣṭayasampatti*). Such a one is classified as *uttama adhikārī*, an ideal seeker to receive the identity-knowledge (*aikyajñāna*) through *mahāvākya*. The *uttama adhikārī* gains the non-dual knowledge and enjoys liberation while living (*jīvanmukti*). A second kind of classification of a seeker is based on the intellectual calibre and they are categorized as *uttama, madhyama* and *adhama*. Here again, the *uttama* gains the highest knowledge, whereas the *madhyama* and the *adhama,* who have not elevated themselves to that of the *uttama*'s calibre, do not enjoy the benefit of knowledge.

Niścaladāsa differs from this conventional method of classification of seekers and categorizes *adhikārī*s (*sādhana-catuṣṭayasampannāḥ*) into three as the *uttama*, the *madhyama* and the *kaniṣṭha*. Thus, the text *Vicārasāgara* is devoted to an *adhikārī* for knowledge of Advaita with finer classification of the *adhikārī*s. In his art of communicating to the different aspirants we can identify that Niścaladāsa amalgamates the three important features of imparting knowledge and that is "pedagogy", "language" and "interpretation".

I propose to define pedagogy and its relation to language and interpretation in the following manner:

---

[35] *SV, āvarta* 538. Here a verse reads as "one will go to hell if the scripture is not studied in Sanskrit language" — this is only in its figuartive sense and should not be read literally. VB's idea is to make the Hindi work available in Sanskrit to benefit those who do not know Hindi.

[36] The triple concept is derived from the original *Vicārasāgara* of Niścaladāsa and any additional or different approach taken by VB is mentioned in relevant places.

> Pedagogy is an art of conveying a philosophical disposition adopting ingenious methods catering to the mind of an interrogative seeker of Truth.

Pedagogy by itself is not an independent tool of communication but is an inseparable component that operates "language" on one hand and utilizes the method of "interpretation" on the other. While pedagogy takes care of the "kind" of aspirant addressed to, the elucidation of language takes care of the "comfort" in the regional language (or the accepted language of the masses) and the conceptual interpretation takes care of presenting a "consistent" subject matter of a philosophical school. Thus, they are mutually interrelated and form a core unit that is vital in imparting the knowledge of Truth. This idea is represented in *fig.* 1.1.

In our study, we shall focus on the *pedagogy* factor which is one of the important elements of communicating the philosophical truth to a specific *adhikārī*. Now, we shall trace this "triple concept beginning from pedagogy as found in the text *Vicārasāgara*".

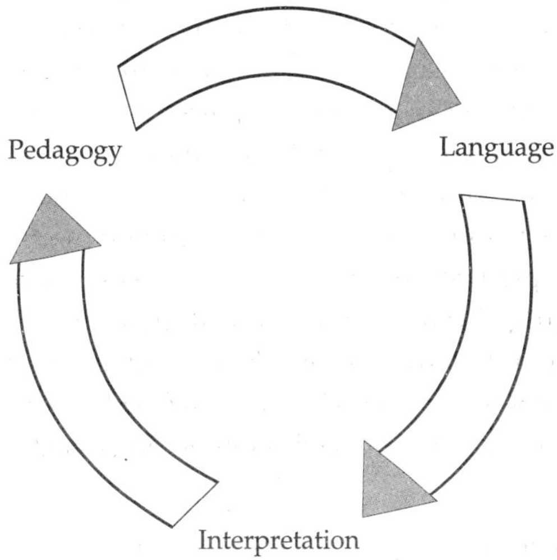

fig. 1.1: pedagogy and its relation to language and interpretation

PEDAGOGY

Niścaladāsa has ingeniously used the method of imparting knowledge to different aspirants since his writing is specifically for the masses. He divides the chapters into seven *taraṅga*s (waves) wherein the first two *taraṅga*s are devoted to establish the fourfold factors required to commence a text (*anubandhacatuṣṭaya*). The third *taraṅga* deals with the characteristic features of a Vedānta *guru* and the disciple. In the fourth *taraṅga*, he introduces three kinds of aspirants through a parable. He narrates that there was a king by name Śubhasantati who had three sons: Tattvadṛṣṭi, Adṛṣṭi and Tarkadṛṣṭi. The name of each character introduced by the author is self-explanatory. When the king expressed his desire to retire to the forest to seek salvation, the three sons demonstrated their yearning for absolute happiness and they abandoned the kingdom and roamed in the forest in search of a *guru*. They found a *guru*, and their interactions with their *guru* are presented in the fourth, fifth and sixth *taraṅga*s. The king's episode is described later in the seventh *taraṅga*. The dialogue between the *guru* and the first son Tattvadṛṣṭi classified as the *uttama adhikārī* occurs in the fourth *taraṅga*. The second son Adṛṣṭi categorized as *madhyama adhikārī* sets his arguments in the fifth *taraṅga* and the third son Tarkadṛṣṭi who is introduced as the *kaniṣṭha adhikārī* seeks clarification in the sixth *taraṅga*. Thus, the three *taraṅga*s are classified based on the teaching imparted to the *adhikārī*s who in the course of the dialogue are classified as *uttama, madhyama* and *kaniṣṭha*. The seventh *taraṅga* begins with an account of *jīvanmukti* and *videhamukti* and presents the independent mode of reasoning (*manana*) adopted by *kaniṣṭha adhikārī*. It also describes the path taken by King Śubhasantati. Niścaladāsa does not classify Śubhasantati under any type of *adhikārī*, and in my present study, I have positioned Śubhasantati as *manda-madhyama adhikārī*.[37] He is identified as *manda* because though he possessed the qualities[38]

---

[37] For details on classification of *adhikārī*s see Section 2.9 of Chapter 2.

[38] *HV* 4, *caupāī* 4, *dohā* 5-8.

to be a spiritual aspirant, he did not possess them in full measure.[39] He is identified as *madhyama* because he took to the path of meditation. Niścaladāsa mentions the attainment of *kramamukti* by Adṛṣṭi whereas Śubhasantati is said to have attained *brahmaloka*. The text does not give further details with regard to the liberation of Śubhasantati (and attainment of *brahmaloka* alone is not considered as liberation in Advaita school). Hence, in my present study I have maintained the difference between Adṛṣṭi and Śubhasantati. Thus, the pedagogical study here refers to four kinds of aspirants as discussed in *Vicārasāgara*.

The means to liberation according to Advaita Vedānta is knowledge. Without deviating from this basic tenet, Niścaladāsa imparts the same principle in different ways to different aspirants. Thus, the teaching contained in Chapters 4-6, that are based on the *adhikārī*, gives tremendous scope for the study of pedagogy as adopted by Niścaladāsa. The feature of pedagogy is emphasized here as *Vicārasāgara* is an outcome of the teaching of Advaita to various kinds of seekers, thus, catering to everyone with varied aptitude. We shall focus on this feature of pedagogy in our later chapters based on the Sanskrit *Vicārasāgara*.

LANGUAGE

Now, we shall see the role of language. The most striking feature of *Vicārasāgara* is its presentation to the masses in their language, namely Hindi, prevalent during the time of Niścaladāsa. He composed the abstract Advaitic teaching in lucid couplets that could be sung, like that of *Rāmāyaṇa* of Tulasidās. Niścaladāsa's metrical compositions include *dohā, caupāī, soraṭhā, kavitā* and *ardhadohā*. The crux of Advaita is beautifully presented in an *ardhadohā*, viz.: *sat cit ānanda eka tū brahma ajanma asaṅga* (*HV* 6.9). The different *chanda*s used are *indava, kūṇḍaliyā, savaiyā, śaṁkara, ardhaśaṁkara* and *sārdhaśaṁkara*. The whole work in metrical form consists of 534 couplets and 527 prose *ṭīkā*s. The couplets along with his *ṭīkā* are the complete texts of *Vicārasāgara*. Some are of

---

[39] *HV* 7, *ṭīkā* 499.

the opinion that the *ṭīkā* and the *ṭippaṇī* were written by Pītāmbar, on the ground that the use of language in the *ṭīkā* and *ṭippaṇī* are similar, and the couplets alone form the original text of Niścaladāsa. Here, we take to the view that the couplets along with the *ṭīkā* comprise the original *Vicārasāgara*, since the style of presentation is: the couplets introduces the concept and the *ṭīkā* explains and elaborates the presented concept. Pītāmbar's contribution is in the form of *ṭippaṇī*s alone. Niścaladāsa has given out the teaching from the *Prasthānatraya* and other Vedāntic works in Sanskrit, thus, the "language" factor includes elements of translation (Sanskrit to Hindi here).

INTERPRETATION

The third important factor in the "triple concept" mentioned above is "interpretation". While dealing with the texts on Advaita, Niścaladāsa by way of interpreting the concepts, presents his view on various issues of Advaitic thought. He employs the traditional method of interpretation, viz. the method of co-presence and co-absence (*anvaya-vyatireka*), the method of discrimination (*viveka*), and the method of acceptance and negation (*adhyāropa-apavāda*). The inseparable layers of "interpretation" and "pedagogy" can be seen in his teaching pertaining to a particular aspirant. The *kaniṣṭha adhikārī* (in *taraṅga* 7) arrives at non-duality as the central teaching of all branches of knowledge and different systems of philosophy through his independent process of *manana* and further he approaches other preceptors seeking clarification. Niścaladāsa through the words of other preceptors ascertain that non-duality alone is the central teaching of not only all branches of knowledge but also of the different systems of philosophy. However, when the *manda-madhyama adhikārī* (in *taraṅga* 7), in another context questions the purport of different systems of philosophy, here the *kaniṣṭha adhikārī* who is the *guru* states that one should not expose oneself to all the systems, but commit only to the system of Advaita, which alone leads to salvation as desired by this seeker. Both the conclusions are presented with adequate reasons.

In another instance, when the desire for liberation is expressed by the *uttama adhikārī* (in *taraṅga* 4), Niścaladāsa in the words of the *guru* says, "the very idea of liberation as attainment of absolute happiness and removal of sorrow is due to delusion". Here, the theory of error is taken up for analysis. For the *kaniṣṭha adhikārī* (in *taraṅga* 6), the ontology is explicated and the falsity of not only the bondage but also the falsity of the scriptural knowledge is pointed out. In explaining the nature of liberation to the *kaniṣṭha adhikārī* (in *taraṅga* 6) it is said that the false duality is resolved by the false knowledge of non-duality. Whereas, the liberation expounded to the *madhyama adhikārī* (in *taraṅga* 5) (and the *manda-madhyama adhikārī* in *taraṅga* 7) is interpreted within the realm of empirical reality, wherein meditation is presented as the means to reach *brahmaloka,* the end. Thus, we find a "pedogogical-interpretation" in *Vicārasāgara* that is modified to suit the need of the aspirant in front. At this juncture it is important to note that through the text *Vicārasāgara,* the position of Niścaladāsa in the tradition of (post-Śaṅkara) Advaita (as of *Vivaraṇa* or *Bhāmatī*) cannot be determined unambiguously. The objective of the author is to present the various methods of teaching as found in the tradition of Advaita and the intention is not to establish any sub-school of Advaita. Thus, Niścaladāsa can be well considered as a great synthesizer of the Advaitic teachings.

It is doubtless that Niścaladāsa is highly influenced by Vidyāraṇya, especially through the work *Pañcadaśī.* He carries forward the conceptual presentation of Advaitic thought as in *Pañcadaśī* throughout *Vicārasāgara.*[40] We also find, while he agrees

[40] It is crucial to note here the influence of Vidyāraṇya on Niścaladāsa. We find many of the Advaitic concepts explained in *Vicārasāgara* are in accordance with Vidyāraṇya's *Pañcadaśī.* Vidyāraṇya, the mendicant of the fourteenth century CE, who headed the Śṛṅgerī Maṭha as the 12th pontiff was a vibrant personality and a prolific writer. Of his many works like *Jīvanmuktiviveka, Vivaraṇaprameyasaṁgraha, Anubhūtiprakāśa,* etc. *Pañcadaśī,* a work with more than 1,500 verses, is the prominent one in the Advaitic literary tradition. *Pañcadaśī* is known for its clear exposition of various Advaitic concepts in a well-structured language. It is one of the most influential works of post-Vidyāraṇya Advaitic school that has attracted those who specifically took to the writing of independent →

with most of the post-Śaṅkarites, he places on record his differing views on certain concepts especially those different from that of

← works. Niścaladāsa is not an exception in this regard, who has developed some of the key arguments in his *Vicārasāgara* based on *Pañcadaśī*. Pītāmbar and Vāsudeva Brahmendra also have cited many cross references and parallel ideas from *Pañcadaśī*, which they have indicated in their *ṭippaṇīs*. *Pañcadaśī*, as the title suggests is a work consisting of fifteen chapters that can be classified into three sections with five chapters in each section, namely, Vivekapañcaka, Dīpapañcaka and Ānandapañcaka. We shall see a few instances from *Vicārasāgara* that replicates the ideas as found in *Pañcadaśī*.

In the fourth *taraṅga*, the teaching is directed towards the *uttama adhikārī*. Niścaladāsa refers to Vidyāraṇya's *Kūṭastha-dīpaprakaraṇa* (chapter 8) to reveal the nature of witness-consciousness in his *ṭīkā* 4.144. Here, Niścaladāsa wants to show that the illumination of object, knowledge and knower is not an action by the witness-consciousness. The nature of self is presented classifying Consciousness as *kūṭastha*, *jīva*, *Īśvara* and *Brahman* comparing them to the pot-space (*ghaṭākāśa*), the water-space (*jalākāśa*), the cloud-space (*meghākāśa*) and the total-space (*mahākāśa*) respectively. Niścaladāsa carries on this discussion in *ṭīkā* 4.159-72. This classification is popularly referred to as *citcāturvidyā prakriyā*, that is a pioneering attempt of Vidyāraṇya in his *Pañcadaśī*, *Citradīpaprakaraṇa* (chapter 6, verse 18) that is explained to gain the direct knowledge of the Self.

In the context of revealing the nature of *jīva*, VB quotes Vidyāraṇya's definition of *jīva* from *Dvaitavivekaprakaraṇa* (chapter 4, verse 11). In the description of the nature of *Īśvara*, VB quotes Vidyāraṇya's presentation of varied views on the nature of *Īśvara* as in *Citradīpaprakaraṇa* (verses 120-22). VB adds an additional note for further clarification for the comparison of *Īśvara* with cloud-space in his *ṭippaṇī* [see *SV*, p. 102].

The exposition of the seven states of the reflected consciousness is discussed in *ṭīkās* 4.177-83 by Niścaladāsa, which is found in *Pañcadaśī Tṛptidīpaprakaraṇa* (chapter 7, verse 33). In *ṭīkā* 4.203, Niścaladāsa mentions the name of Vidyāraṇya as one who opposed the Avacchedavāda. The relevant reference is not found in the text nor in the *ṭippaṇīs*. We find Vidyāraṇya's refutation of Avacchedavāda in the *Kūṭasthadīpaprakaraṇa* (verses 27-31).

The fifth *taraṅga* consists of the teaching to the *madhyama adhikārī*. The three orders of reality are described, in the description of empirical reality in *ṭīkā* 5.233, neither Niścaladāsa mentions Vidyāraṇya's work as a support nor is it found in Pītambar's *ṭippaṇī*, but VB quotes the *Citradīpa-prakaraṇa* (verses 13 and 14) as supportive argument to show that *Īśvara-sṛṣṭi* is of the empirical order of reality.

Also, in *dohā* 5.152, Niścaladāsa describes the origination of the world without any order as in dream citing the instance of mirage-water. Pītambar does not →

Sarvajñātman and Dharmarāja Adhvarīndra.[41] In the course of his dissemination of the Advaitic teaching, Niścaladāsa presents his novel, unique and thought-provoking deviation from the traditional line of thinking. We shall examine some of these with relevant examples.

His conviction, that a seeker of knowledge will benefit directly on hearing (*śravaṇa*) the *mahāvākya*, is explicitly presented in the first *taraṅga*.[42] He says that as even the Vedic instructor utters "you are *Brahman*", on hearing the same the seeker directly gains the knowledge and expresses "I am *Brahman*". He exhibits a stronghold on *śābda-aparokṣa-vāda*, the direct knowledge of Self as *Brahman* on hearing the *mahāvākya*. Through the parable of *bharchu* in the fifth *taraṅga*,[43] he reveals that if one is unable to gain the

← further explain this couplet, but remarks that this couplet is (self-explanatory) clear. But, VB, explains further with relevant quotations from the Upaniṣads and also quotes *Tṛptidīpaprakaraṇa* (verses 171-73) and other works.

In *ṭīkā*s 5.253-57, Niścaladāsa elucidates the process of creation. While describing the evolution of the subtle universe, he uses the onomatopoeic words to reveal the quality of the five elements. This description, we find in Pañcabhūta-vivekaprakaraṇa of *Pañcadaśī* (chapter 2, verses 3-5).

In *ṭīkā* 5.316, Niścaladāsa distinguishes *jīva-sṛṣṭi* from *Īśvara-sṛṣṭi* and mentions that such a classification is done by Vidyāraṇya. However, we do not find the relevant portion quoted either in the text or in the *ṭippaṇī*s. We find this description in the Dvaitavivekaprakaraṇa (verses 38-66).

The *kaniṣṭha adhikārī* interacts with the *guru* in the sixth *taraṅga*. In *ṭīkā* 6.443, the application of *bhāga-tyāga lakṣaṇā* to the four *mahāvākya*s is given by Niścaladāsa. While Pītambar refers to his Hindi commentary on Mahāvākyaprakaraṇa (chapter 5) of *Pañcadaśī*, VB quotes the eight verses of Vidyāraṇya's Mahāvākyaprakaraṇa in his *ṭippaṇī*.

In the seventh *taraṅga* while describing the nature of a *jīvanmukta*, Niścaladāsa shows that an enlightened person is not subject to rules and regulations and he quotes *Tṛptidīpaprakaraṇa* as a reference in this context and the *ṭippaṇīkāra*s provide the verse numbers (143-62). These are instances which show how Niścaladāsa supports his arguments by drawing heavily on Vidyāraṇya's *Pañcadaśī*.

41 For details on his views against Dharmarāja see Niścaladāsa's *Vṛttiprabhākara*.

42 त्वं ब्रह्म ऐसा आचार्यनें उच्चारण किया जो वाक्य ताका श्रोताके कर्णसें संबंध होते हि मैं ब्रह्म हूं ऐसा अपरोक्षज्ञान श्रोताकूं होवै है। — *HV* 1, *ṭīkā* 20

43 सो जन दुख भुगतै सदा है न ब्रह्मको ज्ञान ॥ — *HV* 5, *dohā* 121

direct knowledge of *Brahman*, it is not the defect of the teaching, but the obstacle is in one's own mind. Hence, he favours the view on the rise of direct knowledge of *Brahman* on hearing the *mahāvākya*, thereby he supports the *Vivaraṇa*'s standpoint. In this context, he does not take up the discussion of *Bhāmatī*, neither does he reject the view of *Bhāmatī* that considers the possibility of rise of knowledge in *nididhyāsana* and not *śravaṇa*. But here, Niścaladāsa places a Vedānta *ekadeśī* as the opponent, who is identified by Pītāmbar, the *ṭippaṇīkāra* as Vidyāraṇya and his followers.[44] According to this *ekadeśī*, *śravaṇa* gives indirect knowledge and the obstacles like *asambhāvanā* and *viparīta bhāvanā* are removed through *manana* and *nididhyāsana*, after which there is the rise of the direct knowledge.[45] Niścaladāsa refutes this view by stating that which is obstructed need not be far away (indirect) and this he explains through the example of the "tenth man".[46] Here, though Niścaladāsa does not resort to any other supportive source, we find Sureśvara explicitly stating in his *Naiṣkarmyasiddhi*[47] the rise of the direct knowledge of *Brahman* through *śravaṇa*. However, in the sixth *taraṅga*,[48] Niścaladāsa refines the definition of the nature of *Brahman*-knowledge and takes the support of Sureśvara[49] to claim that even *śravaṇa* is not the cause of *Brahman*-knowledge. It is to be remembered here that the different standpoints found in *Vicārasāgara* is a pedogogical device catering to various aspirants.

---

44 सिद्धांतके एकदेशकूं आश्रय करिके स्वतन्त्र अधिक अर्थका निरूपण जिनमैं किया है ऐसै जे पंचदशी आदिक वेदांतके प्रकरणग्रंथ हैं तिनके कर्ता जे आचार्य वे इहां एकदेशी कहिये हैं। भर्तृप्रपञ्चके अनुसारी नहीं ॥ — *HV* 1, *ṭippaṇī* 42

45 वाक्यमप्रतिबद्धं सत्प्राक्परोक्षावभासिते ।
करामलकवद्बोधमपरोक्षं प्रसूयते ॥ — *PD* 1.62

ब्रह्मसाक्षात्कृतिस्त्वेवं विचारेण विना नृणाम् ।
आप्तोपदेशमात्रेण न सम्भवति कुत्रचित् ॥ — *PD* 9.30

46 *HV* 1, *ṭīkā* 22-23.

47 सकृत्प्रवृत्त्या मृद्नाति क्रियाकारकरूपभृत् ।
अज्ञानमागमज्ञानं साङ्गत्यं नास्त्यतोऽनयोः ॥ — *NS* 1.67

48 *SV*, p. 265.

49 अविद्यानाशमात्रं तु फलमित्युपचर्यते ।
नाज्ञातज्ञापनं न्याय्यमवगत्येकरूपतः ॥ — *NS* 2.105.

In the second *taraṅga*, he presents what is called as Prauḍhivāda on the concept of erroneous cognition. He enumerates five conditions resulting in an erroneous cognition as the view of the opponent and refutes them by stating that even without any of these five factors an error can occur.[50] This he discusses at length and in the course presents the Prauḍhivāda of Sarvajñātman, who shows the possibility of similarlity between Self (*ātmā*) and non-self (*anātmā*) as the cause of error. Niścaladāsa refutes the view of Sarvajñātman and establishes that error is possible even without the factor called similarity.[51] Here too, Niścaladāsa does not resort to any supportive source but we find the same established by Śaṅkara in his *Aparokṣānubhūti*,[52] where Śaṅkara expresses his wonder as to how the mutually opposed *ātmā* and *anātmā* can ever be mistaken, but, still one commits the error.

In the third *taraṅga*, while describing the characteristic features of a teacher and a disciple, Niścaladāsa presents his view on the worship or service to a *guru* as superior to the worship of God, which is generally not mentioned in the traditional literature. We do find tradition eulogizing *guru* as equal to or superior to God but here Niścaladāsa shows that the worship of *guru* rather than God yields dual benefit which is absent in the worship of God. He says, in the service to God one gains merit (*adr̥ṣṭa phala*) alone but in service to *guru*, not only one gains merit but also knowledge which is a direct result (*dr̥ṣṭa phala*).[53]

In the context of analysing the ontology of the substratum in which error takes place, Niścaladāsa in the fourth *taraṅga* agrees with the division of substratum as *ādhāra* and *adhiṣṭhāna* of Sarvajñātman. In an erroneous cognition, for instance, seeing a rope as "snake", one expresses "this is snake". The "this" general

---

[50] *HV* 2, *ṭīkā* 83-84.

[51] *HV* 2, *ṭīkā* 84(4).

[52] *AB* 17-40.

[53] जो ईश्वरकी सेवा है सो अदृष्टफलका हेतु है।
औ जो आचार्यकी सेवा है सो अदृष्टफल औ दृष्टफल दोनूंका हेतु है॥ — *HV* 3, *ṭīkā* 11.

aspect, Niścaladāsa says, is known as *ādhāra* of the "snake" and the "rope", the specific part is the *adhiṣṭhāna* of the "snake". Extending this, he says that the false world has the general aspect *sat' ātmā* as its *ādhāra* and the specific aspect of "unassociation" (*asaṅgatva*) as the *adhiṣṭhāna* of the world.[54] He presents a synthetic outlook of a technical differentiation while defining *jivātmā* as the reflected consciousness of *kūṭastha caitanya* or as the reflected consciousness of *brahma caitanya*.[55] In his epistemological elucidation of valid apprehension (*pramā*), Niścaladāsa takes up the discussion on the role of memory.[56] He mentions two views, one that considers memory-knowledge as *pramā* since it is in the form of thought-mode in the internal organ and the second view is memory-knowledge in the form of ignorance as not *pramā*. Niścaladāsa holds the view that memory cannot be included in the definition of *pramā*. His view resonates with the idea as in *Vedānta Paribhāṣā* of Dharmarāja.

In the fifth *taraṅga*, while describing the quintiplication process in the context of creation theory of Advaita, as a rare occasion, Niścaladāsa presents two theories, of which the second theory seems to be preferred by him in order to reconcile the experience of five elements in the gross universe.[57]

In the sixth *taraṅga*, a teaching to the *kaniṣṭha adhikārī*, we get a lengthy argument on the ontology of dream world. Analysis of the states of experience is not only an important method used in the Upaniṣads and *Brahmasūtras*, but also purposeful in establishing one of the key features of Advaita, namely, the falsity of the empirical world. The dream world is proved false and the same arguments are extended to show that the empirical world is also false. In this discussion, Niścaladāsa refutes the idea that the dream world is real. The opponent (in the words of the *kaniṣṭha adhikārī*)

---

[54] *HV* 4, *ṭīkā* 52.

[55] *HV* 4, *ṭīkā* 85.

[56] *HV* 4, 198-99.

[57] *HV* 5, *ṭīkā* 258.

considers that the dream objects are real since the sense-organs leave the physical body during dream and experiences the empirical world. We find the same argument taken up and refuted in *Brahmasūtras* 3.2.1-6, where Śaṅkara in his commentary on these *sūtras* gives counter-arguments and shows that the mind does not leave the physical body during dream. Niścaladāsa echoes those arguments and adds an additional point that the sense-organs cannot leave the physical body during dream because *prāṇa* remains in the body and does not travel during dream, in that case, there is no propeller for the movement of the sense-organs. The sense-organs gain energy from *prāṇa* and hence they cannot independently move away from the body to experience the empirical world during dream.[58] While dealing with the nature of realities, Niścaladāsa strongly favours the view of *dṛṣṭi-sṛṣṭi-vāda*, so much so that VB writes that this teaching is meant for the *uttama adhikārī*[59] (but in *Vicārasāgara* this teaching is imparted to the *kaniṣṭha adhikārī*). In the description of the nature of *Īśvara*, Niścaladāsa takes a new approach to validate the all-pervasive and eternal nature of *Īśvara* by showing its contrary through the well-known fourfold fallacies, viz. the fallacy of self-dependency, mutual-dependency, cyclical defect and infinite regress.[60]

Again in the sixth *taraṅga*,[61] while describing the nature of an enlightened person, Niścaladāsa seems to take to a complicated argument. He wants to show that the combination of knowledge and action (*jñāna-karma-samuccaya*) is not possible in an enlightened person.[62] He explains this by citing the position of a Self-ignorant person (*karmī*) in whom (another kind of) *samuccaya* can be found. Niścaladāsa states that a *karmī* is one who performs *karma* as prescribed in the Vedas in order to obtain results either in this birth or after death. Thus, the *karmī* has the knowledge of Self as

---

58 *HV* 6, 304-08.

59 *SV*, p, 210.

60 *HV* 6, *ṭīkā* 373.

61 *HV* 6, *ṭīkā* 385.

62 See *BS* 3.4.8.

different from the body and that Self is the doer and reaper of results here and in the other world. This knowledge of Self as *kartrātmā* is gained from the scriptures and hence it is indirect knowledge (*parokṣa jñāna*) of Self. The scriptures enjoin actions based on *jāti, varṇa, āśrama,* etc. It is known that *jāti, varṇa,* etc. are the attributes of the body. Since the *karmī* performs the enjoined action it presupposes not only the identification of these attributes with the body but also the identification of oneself with the body. This knowledge of *dehātmā,* i.e. self as body identified with a particular *jāti, varṇa* is direct (*aparokṣa jñāna*) in the case of a *karmī.* Niścaladāsa argues that in a *karmī* there is the possibility of the combination of indirect knowledge of Self (*kartrātmā*) and direct knowledge of body (*dehātmā*) since this indirect and direct knowledge are not opposed to each other. On the other hand, an enlightened person is one who has obtained the direct knowledge of Self as non-doer, non-reaper, etc. Thereby the existence of *kartrātmā* is dismissed by an enlightened person. There is also no direct knowledge of body (*dehātmā*) with attributes like *jāti* and *varṇa* since they are falsified by Self-knowledge. The action performed by an enlightened person is unlike that of the *karmī* and thus Niścaladāsa argues that the combination of knowledge and action is not possible in an enlightened person. Lastly, in the seventh *taraṅga*[63] Niścaladāsa presents a synthetic view on the concept of *videhamukti.*

So far, we had engaged in the extraction of the triple concept of "pedagogy", "language" and "interpretation" from *Vicārasāgara.* The unique feature of *Vicārasāgara* as pointed out earlier is the Advaitic knowledge imparted to different kinds of aspirants by adopting a "suitable" pedagogy. The present study is to derive the "pedagogical concern" exhibited towards the *adhikārīs* and this study is going to be based on the Sanskrit *Vicārasāgara.* Hence, we shall now examine briefly the contribution of VB through his translation and also provide reasons for basing the present study on the Sanskrit *Vicārasāgara.*

---

[63] *HV 7, ṭīkā* 525.

1.5 The Sanskrit Vicārasāgara[64]

First, it is important to mention here that the Sanskrit version of the *Vicārasāgara* cannot be brushed aside as a work of translation bereft of originality. Though the main content of the translation is the same as the Hindi work yet the Sanskrit text manifests its own grandeur. The very format of the original text is customized. The original work consists of verses (*dohās*) and explanations in prose lines (*ṭīkā*). VB combines the idea of *dohā* and *ṭīkā* into prose form. Hence by all means it can be referred to as a "trans-creation".

Second, we find that there are additions, alterations, deletions and modifications carried out in various places. We do not claim here that the Sanskrit translation is an "improvement" over the original Hindi work but the idea is that the changes made by VB are to suit the readers of his region and time. For instance, in the third *taraṅga*, we find a thoughtful deletion by VB of a *ṭīkā* given in the original text. While dealing with the qualities of a *guru*, the Hindi text with an intention to eulogize the Advaitic approach taken by a teacher, reprimands the teacher of Rāmānuja as not being a *guru*, since a *guru* is defined as one who teaches the identity of *jīva* and *Īśvara*. VB retains the definition of a *guru* as given in the original but does not translate the censuring of Rāmānuja and his *guru*. Likewise, many such examples can be seen in the Sanskrit *Vicārasāgara*.

Third, the Sanskrit version includes numerous quotations from the primary and secondary scriptures. VB also profusely quotes from many other works thus adding clarity through cross references. Lastly, *Vicārasāgara* in Sanskrit language lends crispness and brevity to various definitions of Advaitic concepts (see Appendix 1).

The trans-created text retains the name *Vicārasāgara* with the analogical significance of the pursuit of knowledge as crossing over an ocean through the method of enquiry. The poetry and the *ṭīkā* portions of the Hindi text that has been combined into

---

64 A comparative study of *HV* and *SV* is not attempted here.

prose passages are named as *āvarta* in accordance with the imagery of an ocean. Each *āvarta* is titled as in the Hindi text but the numbers do not tally since some of the topics are combined or some deleted and so on. The number of topics in Hindi *Vicārasāgara* is 527 whereas it is 538 in the Sanskrit *Vicārasāgara* (see Appendices 2 and 3).

Pītāmbar's *ṭippaṇī* (also in Hindi) has also been translated by VB to a large extent and again it is not an exact translation. While there are (45 + 553) 598 *ṭippaṇī*s of Pītāmbar in the Hindi *Vicārasāgara*, there are 454[65] *ṭippaṇī*s in the Sanskrit *Vicārasāgara* of VB. *Ṭippaṇī*s in the edition of the Hindi *Vicārasāgara* are numbered continuously throughout the seven chapters whereas in the edition of Sanskrit *Vicārasāgara* it is not in continuous numbering. Hence a comparative study of the *ṭippaṇī*s as in the original and trans-creation is a tedious task. However, by a general survey of the *ṭippaṇī*s we find that VB completely avoids references made to Hindi works in the *ṭippaṇī*. The cross references to *Vṛttiprabhākara* of Niścaladāsa and other Vedāntic works in Hindi mentioned in Pītāmbar's *ṭippaṇī* that are not popular in south India are also not mentioned. VB profusely quotes from *Prasthānatraya*, Purāṇas and other Sanskrit *prakaraṇa*s that seem to be popular in the southern region of India all of which are not found in the original *ṭippaṇī*s. The modified *ṭippaṇī*s of Pītāmbar seems to suit the Sanskrit version but at times the contribution of Pītāmbar to Advaita literature goes unnoticed. In fact, at no place in the Sanskrit version, we find a mention of Pītāmbar as the *ṭippaṇīkāra*.[66]

In many places, we find more details furnished in the Sanskrit *ṭippaṇī*s when compared to that of Pītāmbar's *ṭippaṇī*s. For example, in the context of defining the six indicators to arrive at the purport of a text, Pītāmbar just mentions the six indicators

---

[65] Numbers of *ṭippaṇī*s from *taraṅga*s 1-7 in *SV* are 1-66, 67-117, 118-27, 128-87, 188-250, 251-367 and 368-454 respectively.

[66] Also, if not for the editor's preface to *SV*, the name of the author Niścaladāsa (found at least twice in *HV* 2, *dohā* 15, and 7, *dohā* 112) will not be known to the readers of *SV*, since it is not mentioned anywhere in the Sanskrit text proper.

and refers to his Sanskrit work *Śrutiṣaṭliṅgasaṁgraha*, while the Sanskrit *ṭippaṇī*s demonstrate the application of the six indicators to *Chāndogya Upaniṣad*.[67] While defining *nididhyāsana*, the Hindi text says that "the contrary notion that *jīva* and *Brahman* are different is true", and removal of such an idea is *nididhyāsana*. We find Pītāmbar does not add a *ṭippaṇī* here, but in the Sanskrit version, VB raises a question and answers it. The question raised is "how can the knowledge of duality continue in *nididhyāsana* since in *śravaṇa* and *manana* the non-dual nature of Self is already gained?" The answer given is that even though two kinds of doubts, namely, relating to the means to knowledge (*pramāṇagata*) and the object of knowledge (*prameyagata*), are removed in *śravaṇa* and *manana*, there is the problem of habitual return to the notion of self as limited which is expressed as "duality is real", etc. that rises again and again and this can be removed only by the process of *nididhyāsana*.[68] The Hindi text defines *sakāma karma* and *niṣkāma karma* without mentioning the reason or citing relevant texts. That is, it says, *sakāma karma* is the cause of perpetuation of *saṁsāra*, while *niṣkāma karma* is the cause of refinement of the mind.[69] In the Sanskrit version, we find the mention of Vedic statement for reinforcement to show that *sakāma karma* is the continuation of *saṁsāra* and the role of *niṣkāma karma* is presented with relevant reasons.[70]

Thus, we find that the Sanskrit version is a kind of recreation of the Hindi *Vicārasāgara* with Hindi *ṭippaṇī*s. Based on the number of the topics taken for discussion in each chapter it can be said that the Sanskrit version is an abridged form of the original text. Based on the layout of each chapter it can be said to be a modified version of the original text. Based on the *ṭippaṇī*s, it can be said to be catering to the readers of south India.

---

67 *HV*, p. 9 and *SV*, p. 15.

68 *HV*, p. 12 and *SV*, pp. 17-18.

69 *HV*, pp. 8-9.

70 *SV*, p. 14.

We shall now cite some examples of the additions, deletions and alterations carried out by VB as observed by Pañcāpageśa Śāstrī in his preface to the Sanskrit *Vicārasāgara*.

(a) The very benediction is modified in accordance with the Advaitic concept. The benedictory verse in the original text reads as:

जो सुख नित्य प्रकास विभु नाम रूप आधार ।
मति न लखै जिहिं मति लखै सो मैं सुद्ध अपार ॥

In the Sanskrit version we find the above one couplet presented in two verses:

सुखं नित्यं स्वप्रकाशं व्यापकं नाम रूपयोः ।
अधिष्ठानं बुद्ध्यबोद्ध्यं बुद्धेर्दृग्यत्तु निर्मलम् ॥
अपारं सर्ववेदान्तवेद्यं प्रत्यक् परं महः ।
तदेवाहं न मत्तोऽन्यत् इति मे निश्चिता मतिः ॥

The words *nāma rūpa ādhāra* in Hindi has been modified as *nāma rūpayoḥ adhiṣṭhānaṁ* in the Sanskrit version. This significant change is explained by analysing the words *ādhāra* and *adhiṣṭhāna*. In ordinary parlance, the word *ādhāra* is employed to indicate the ground of an object, say a "pot". In the case of a superimposed entity, like "snake" on rope, the rope is referred to as *adhiṣṭhāna,* meaning substratum of snake. Thus, the employment of the words *ādhāra* and *adhiṣṭhāna* is contextually differentiated with regard to the empirically (*vyāvahārika*) real objects and the apparently (*prātibhāsika*) real objects. In the couplet in Hindi, *Brahman* is introduced as the substratum of the superimposition of the world of name and form. In this regard, the use of the word *adhiṣṭhāna* by VB is justified as more appropriate than the word *ādhāra*.

(b) The words *mati na lakhai jihiṅ mati lakhai* juxtaposes mutually contradictory adjectives, i.e., "not comprehended by the mind" and "cognized by the mind". In Sanskrit, the words *mati na lakhai* is translated as *buddhyabodhyam* by citing the relevant Upaniṣadic text, viz. *yato vāco nivartante.*[71] The literal translation of the Hindi words *mati lakhai* is *buddhi bodhyam* but VB modifies it as *buddherdṛk. Mati lakhai* primarily means that the self-evident *Brahman* is known by the mental modification produced by the valid source, that is, the *mahāvākya*. The mental-mode produced by the valid source, destroys the veiling power of ignorance in *Brahman*. This meaning is unsuitable since the context is description of *Brahman* and not ignorance. Moreover, even if *mati lakhai* is taken to be the description of *Brahman* in the form of destruction of the concealing power of ignorance by the mental-mode produced through the valid source, it is not the direct definition of *Brahman*. Whereas, in the Sanskrit text, we find the word *buddherdṛk* which reveals *Brahman* as the "witness of the mind" and it includes the sense-organs. This modification is based on the Vedic statements.[72] Thus, here the word *buddhyabodhyam* means self-evident *Brahman*, independently shines and *buddherdṛk* means other than *Brahman*, the witness principle, everything else dependently shines. Such a meaning cannot be arrived at from *mati lakhai.*[73]

(c) VB adds two words — *sarvavedāntavedyam* that reveal the cause of conviction with regard to the existence of *Brahman* and the word *pratyak* refers to the immediate knowledge of *ānanda* nature of *Brahman*. This indicates that the inner Self is ever-immediate.

(d) The Hindi *ṭippaṇī* for the word *apāra* is also modified in order to get the meaning that space, time and a second entity are superimpositions that cannot limit *Brahman.*[74]

---

[71] *TU* 3.1.

[72] मनसो मनः । *KeU* 1.2. यन्मनसा न मनुते येनाहुर्मनो मतम् । — *KeU* 1.6

[73] See also Pītāmbar's gloss.

[74] *SV* p. 2.

(e) Further some instances of modifications by VB different from the Hindi text is presented in the following tabulation:

Topic	*Hindi Text*[75]	*Sanskrit Text*[76]
Śama	मन विषयनतै रोकनों	प्राचीनविषयवासनात्यागपूर्वकं विषयेभ्यो मनसः प्रतिनिवर्तनम्।
Śraddhā	सत्य वेद् गुरु वाक्य हैं श्रद्धा अस विस्वास।	गुरुवेदान्तवाक्येषु दृढतरविश्वासः; आस्तिक्यम्।
Uparama	साधनसहित कर्म सब त्यागै।	ससाधनानां ऐहिकामुष्मिक-भोगहेतूनां लौकिकवैदिककर्मणां परित्यागः।
Mumukṣā	ब्रह्मप्राप्ति अरु बंधकी हानि मोक्षको रूप।	स्वरूपभूतब्रह्मावाप्तिः अनर्थ निवृत्तिः च।

(f) We shall now present some of the deletions and alterations carried out in the Sanskrit version. The original text defines *manana* as a process of establishing non-difference between *jīva* and *Brahman* logically.[77] For this, Pītāmbar in his *ṭippaṇī* cites two reasons based on comparison (*upamāna*),[78] of which VB gives only one of them.[79] The second reason is not cited in this context since the discussion is on the means to non-dual knowledge and the same is cited in the fourth *taraṅga* of the text in the context of the nature of *jīva* as identical with *Brahman*.

(g) In the context of describing the "tenth man" story in the *tippaṇī*, Pītāmbar says, "on the way they came across a 'mirage-water' river and crossed it".[80] VB modifies as, "they crossed a deep river and reached the other shore".[81]

[75] *HV*, pp. 5-7.

[76] *SV*, pp. 10-13.

[77] *HV*, p. 10.

[78] *HV*, 1, *ṭippaṇī* 30.

[79] *SV*, p. 16.

[80] *HV*, 1, *ṭippaṇī* 47.

[81] *SV*, p. 20.

The phenomenal experience is modified as an empirical experience. This is done because, according to experience, on seeing mirage-water as even the person approaches it, it disappears, and there is no scope for crossing over a mirage-water. Since this goes against experience, the Sanskrit version modifies and presents it differently. These are some of the observations that highlights the contribution of VB as a trans-creator.

Thus, we find that the Sanskrit version is also significant and VB's Sanskrit translation of Hindi *Vicārasāgara* is important that brings out the originality of this Advaitic preceptor. Having seen the contribution of VB, we shall now present the reasons to consider Sanskrit *Vicārasāgara* as the base for the present study.

1. The Sanskrit *Vicārasāgara* in a modified prose form facilitates better understanding of the presentation of various concepts.
2. The language is lucid and simple that assists in recapturing the earlier works of Advaita in Sanskrit. VB has defined various Advaitic concepts that can be memorized, which facilitates a better understanding of *Prasthānatraya* and other works in Sanskrit.
3. The Sanskrit "translation" is justified as a "trans-creation" since VB interpretatively trans-creates the text *Vicārasāgara*. This brings out the originality of the trans-creator.
4. The present study attempts to record the contribution of VB to the teaching tradition of Advaita Vedānta.
5. More importantly, VB's presentation of the nature of *adhikārī*s provides a basis for a deeper analysis of the role of pedagogy catering to the *adhikārī*s.

The *adhikārī*s presented by Niścaladāsa possess the fourfold qualities as required in full measure. But still they are classified as *uttama*, *madhyama* and *kaniṣṭha adhikārī*s. The basis for such a classification is unclear from the Hindi text, from Pītāmbar's *ṭippaṇī* and also in the Sanskrit version. However, we find there an attempt made by VB in redefining the nature of *adhikārī*s. Thus, the Sanskrit *Vicārasāgara* as the base for the present study is amply justified.

1.6 An Outline of the Present Study

Now, the approach of the present study that is based on the Sanskrit text is briefly explained. In this course of discussion, the Sanskrit text is restructured by way of rearranging the concepts of Advaita in the form of a dialogue between a Vedānta *guru* and the two sets of aspirants. The focus is to bring out the nature of pedagogy adopted in this dialogue. One set of aspirant is the *uttama* and the *kaniṣṭha adhikārī*s of *Vicārasāgara* who attain *jīvanmukti* and the other set is the *madhyama* and the *manda-madhyama adhikārī* who take to *upāsanā mārga*. The former (*manda*) attains *kramamukti* and the latter (*manda-madhyama*) is said to have gained *brahmaloka*. The names of the aspirants based on the story developed by the author is not used in the present study but they are referred to as the "kind" of *adhikārī* (i.e. as *uttama*, *madhyama*, etc.), the manner in which they have been classified in *Vicārasāgara*. This is to facilitate tracing the pedagogical methods as developed based on the *adhikārī* by which we shall attempt to arrive at what is termed here as the "*adhikārī*-based pedagogy". The attempt here is only to highlight the "pedagogical concern" as the central force of the text *Vicārasāgara*.

It is to be noted here that I have not dwelled upon the reasons as to why the author employs certain methods of teaching for a particular *adhikārī* when the same method is not employed for another *adhikārī* while revealing the same concept. In order to study this aspect indepth we need to get a clear picture of the mode of classification of *adhikārī*s in *Vicārasāgara* and the difficulty in understanding this classification is pointed out in the second chapter. Only when the mode of classification of *adhikārī*s are determined, can one take to the study of the reason behind the particular method of teaching to a particular *adhikārī*. This, in fact, is completely another dimension of the text *Vicārasāgara* which is beyond the scope of the present study.

The unique approach, deviations, and some comments of the author and the contributions of the *ṭippaṇīkāra* (Pītāmbar) as found in the Sanskrit *Vicārasāgara* are recorded in relevant places in the name of the trans-creator, VB. Some of the important concepts and other aspects that are not highlighted by the author, commentator or the trans-creator have been specified in relevant portions. Certain remarks, additional arguments and other textual references are provided in the respective footnotes. Chapters 2 to 6 of the present study mark a progressive development of Advaitic concepts, beginning from the nature of *adhikārī* to the nature of liberation. In this varied pedagogical approach adopted to illustrate the Advaitic teaching, we find a non-deviation from the central crux of Advaita, viz. *brahma satyam jagan mithyā jīvobrahmaiva nāparaḥ*. Thus, we place not only Niścaladāsa and Pītāmbar but also VB in the gamut of preceptors who have penned many works for the literary growth of Advaitic thought and also served as teachers catering to different kind of aspirants in their own region and time.

The text *Vicārasāgara* is unique that has allowed itself to be adapted into various languages making it regionally relevant. There is a wider scope to analyse the nature of social, regional, linguistic and other philosophical impacts, which of course is again beyond the scope of the present study. However, the present study single-pointedly focuses on the concern of the text in adopting suitable pedagogical skills in imparting the absolute knowledge to the seekers of Truth. Since the text *Vicārasāgara* is evidently based on the *adhikārī* for whom different modes of teaching are adopted, it is imperative to first define an *adhikārī* and explicate the factors based on which an *adhikārī* is categorized in the earlier texts generally and in *Vicārasāgara* specifically. Hence, we shall now proceed to analyse the nature and classification of *adhikārī* in the tradition of Advaita and also see the manner in which the *adhikārī* is viewed by Niścaladāsa and Pītāmbar (in *HV*) and VB (in *SV*) in the following chapter.

2

On the Nature of Aspirant (Adhikārisvarūpaprakaraṇa)

2.1 Traditional Views on Adhikārī

A SCHOOL of thought primarily declares the preamble or the fourfold factors (*anubandhacatuṣṭaya*) that facilitates in a comprehensive understanding of a text. The *anubandha-catuṣṭaya* consists of the subject matter (*viṣaya*), nature of aspirant (*adhikārī*), benefit (*prayojana*) and relation (*sambandha*). Of these, we shall deal extensively with the nature of the *adhikārī* in the context of Advaita Vedānta. The understanding of *adhikārī* as depicted in *Vicārasāgara* presupposes the study of *adhikārī* as found in *Prasthānatraya* and certain other Advaita *prakaraṇas*. Thus, we begin with a brief analysis of the nature of *adhikārī*, classification of *adhikārī* and *adhikārī*-based pedagogy in the early literature of Advaita. This is followed by the study of the position of Niścaladāsa, Pītāmbar and VB in describing the nature and classification of an aspirant and the subsequent development of pedagogy in different circumstances as found in the text *Vicārasāgara*.

The nature of an aspirant for Vedāntic enquiry is primarily established as one who has gained the fourfold qualities (*sādhanacatuṣṭayasampatti*). A qualified seeker then renounces *karma* (*karmatyāga*) that is prescribed in the Vedapūrva. Such a one is an *adhikārī* for Vedānta. Thus, the word *adhikārī* suggests a twin quality of *sādhanacatuṣṭayasampatti* and its natural consequence of *karmatyāga*, including the course of approaching a *guru* to gain Self-knowledge. These two inseparable qualities are implied in the Upaniṣads, *Gītā* and *Brahmasūtra*.

UPANIṢADS

Upaniṣads through their teachings, in the form of a dialogue, reveal the quality of an aspirant which can be drawn from the discourse between a *guru* and a seeker. The dialogue between Yama and Naciketas in *Kaṭhopaniṣad* reveals the prerequisites of a seeker by the acclamation of the qualities of Naciketas, the disciple. Naciketas requests for Self-knowledge as the third boon revealing the quality of intense desire for liberation (*mumukṣutva*).[1] The Upaniṣad suggests the quality of discrimination (*viveka*) between the path of "superior" (*śreyas* — knowledge) and path of "inferior" (*preyas* — action) by discriminating the seeker of *śreyas* as a spiritualist (*dhīra*) and the seeker of *preyas* as materialist (*manda*).[2] The second quality emphasized is dispassion (*vairāgya*) wherein the material accomplishment is denounced. *Kaṭhopaniṣad* reveals the intense dispassion displayed by Naciketas as one who is detached from the highest material welfare (*atyasrākṣīḥ*).[3] In *Muṇḍakopaniṣad*, the quality of dispassion is revealed through the word *nirveda*.[4] Through the well-known "chariot-imagery", *Kaṭhopaniṣad* conveys the idea that the result of *viveka* is a refined mind. The two important qualities revealed in this context are purity of mind (*śama*) and control of sense-organs (*dama*) and the result of possessing these qualities are declared as attainment of liberation.[5] A direct mention of the qualities of the mind of an *adhikārī* is found in *Bṛhadāraṇyakopaniṣad*. It recommends sixfold disciplines of the mind (*śamādi-ṣaṭkasampatti*) as instrumental in gaining the direct knowledge of Self. The Kāṇva *śākhā* of

---

1 येयं प्रेते विचिकित्सा मनुष्ये अस्तीत्येके नायमस्तीति चैके ।
एतद्विद्यामनुशिष्टस्त्वयाहं वराणामेष वरस्तृतीयः ॥ — *KU* 1.1.20

2 श्रेयश्च प्रेयश्च मनुष्यमेतस्तौ संपरीत्य विविनक्ति धीरः ।
श्रेयो हि धीरोऽभि प्रेयसो वृणीते प्रेयो मन्दो योगक्षेमाद्वृणीते ॥ — *KU* 1.2.2

3 कामस्याप्तिं जगतः प्रतिष्ठां क्रतोरनन्त्यमभयस्य पारम् ।
स्तोममहदुरुगायं प्रतिष्ठां दृष्ट्वा धृत्या धीरो नचिकेतोऽत्यस्राक्षी ॥ — *KU* 1.2.11

4 परीक्ष्य लोकान् कर्मचितान् ब्राह्मणो निर्वेदमायात् । — *MU* 1.2.12

5 यस्तु विज्ञानवान्भवति समनस्कः सदा शुचिः ।
स तु तत्पदमाप्नोति यस्माद्भूयो न जायते ॥ — *KU* 1.3.8

Bṛhadāraṇyaka enumerates five disciplines[6] and the sixth discipline is found in its Mādhyandina *śākhā*.[7] Thus, the sixfold disciplines are the mastery of the mind (*śama*), mastery of the sense-organs (*dama*), renouncing *karma* (*uparama*), perseverance (*titikṣā*), concentration (*samādhāna*) and faith (*śraddhā*). The qualities of *dama* and *śama* are found mentioned in the *Muṇḍaka* also.[8] The prerequisite of renouncing *karma* is declared in *Bṛhadāraṇyaka* that recommends a mendicant life as the means for liberation.[9] The ephemeral nature of *karma* is declared in *Muṇḍaka* and thereby it suggests abandoning *karma* for attaining the absolute *ānanda*.[10] Thus, having renounced *karma* and gaining the fourfold qualities, as an *adhikārī* for Self-knowledge, *Muṇḍaka* says, such a one should approach a *guru*, revealing that the knowledge of the Self can be attained only from a teacher of Vedānta.[11] In the definition of an *adhikārī*, the qualities alone do not suffice, the Upaniṣad expounds that an *adhikārī* is one who approaches a *guru* with reverence displaying the intense desire for liberation. Thus, it calls for a dialogue between an enlightened teacher and a disciple yearning for enlightenment.

Upaniṣads are set in this background of bringing together a "qualified" disciple and a "qualified" teacher (*śrotriya, brahmaniṣṭha*) leading to a dialogue to understand the nature of the Self. While disseminating the knowledge of Self to the aspirants, the Upaniṣads also record the different responses of the aspirants to the same teaching. Thus, invariably there commences a classification of the

---

[6] तस्मादेवंविच्छान्तो दान्त उपरतस्तितिक्षुः समाहितो भूत्वाऽऽत्मन्येवात्मानं पश्यति ।
— *BU* 4.4.23

[7] तस्मादेवंविच्छान्तो दान्त उपरतस्तितिक्षुः श्रद्धावित्तो भूत्वाऽऽत्मन्येवात्मानं पश्येत् । — *BU* 4.2.28

[8] तस्मै स विद्वानुपसन्नाय सम्यक् प्रशान्तचित्ताय शमान्विताय । — *MU* 1.2.13

[9] एतं वै तमात्मानं विदित्वा ब्राह्मणाः पुत्रैषणायाश्च वित्तैषणायाश्च लोकैषणायाश्च भिक्षाचर्यं चरन्ति ।
— *BU* 3.5.1

[10] प्लवा ह्येते अदृढा यज्ञरूपा अष्टादशोक्तमवरं येषु कर्म ।
एतच्छ्रेयो येऽभिनन्दन्ति मूढा जरामृत्युं ते पुनरेवापि यन्ति ॥ — *MU* 1.2.7

[11] परीक्ष्य लोकान् कर्मचितान् ब्राह्मणो निर्वेदमायान्नास्त्यकृतः कृतेन ।
तद्विज्ञानार्थं स गुरुमेवाभिगच्छेत् समित्पाणिः श्रोत्रियं ब्रह्मनिष्ठम् ॥ — *MU* 1.2.12

aspirant in terms of understanding, retaining or assimilating the teaching. In *Kenopaniṣad*, when the nature of the Self is revealed as *Brahman*, Śaṅkara says that the disciple having heard the truth took to seclusion and with a concentrated mind analysed the teaching with the application of reasoning and having realized the truth he approached the *guru* and revealed his enlightenment.[12] The Upaniṣad further elucidates the concepts through a parable to those disciples who had not revealed their understanding of the teaching. Śaṅkara writes that the delusion of a mediocre intellect is removed by the Upaniṣad by presenting the *same* teaching through an anecdote.[13] Thus, the Upaniṣad takes to different methods of presenting the knowledge. Here, begins the pedagogy based on the nature of the aspirant. One of the key pedagogical methods is shown in *Chāndogyopaniṣad*. On the request of Indra, Prajāpati agrees to repeat the entire teaching.[14] Śaṅkara says that if due to some defect the reception of the teaching is obstructed it can be warded off by repeated listening to the same teaching.[15] Thus, the effort to impart the knowledge adopting various methods addressing different aspirants is in-built in the Upaniṣads. If we try to extract the basis of classification of an *adhikārī* in Upaniṣads by a general study of the various disciples presented in different Upaniṣads we find that the categorization of an *adhikārī* to Self-knowledge is based on the stage of life (*āśrama*). Upaniṣads seems to consider a monk desirous for liberation (*vividiṣā saṁnyāsī*) as an ideal *adhikārī* (*mukhyādhikārī*) for Self-knowledge.

---

[12] एवमाचार्योक्तः शिष्यः एकान्तेन उपविष्टः समाहितः सन् यथोक्तमाचार्येण आगममर्थतो विचार्य तर्कतश्च निर्धार्य स्वानुभवं कृत्वा आचार्यसकाशमुपगम्य उवाच मन्येऽहमथेदानीं विदितं ब्रह्मेति। — *KeUŚB* 1.2.1

[13] तथेदं ब्रह्माविज्ञातत्वादसदेवेति मन्दबुद्धीनां व्यामोहो मा भूदिति तदर्थैयमाख्यायिका आरभ्यते। — *KeUŚB* 1.3.1

[14] एवमेवैष मघवन्निति होवाचैतं त्वेव ते भूयोऽनुव्याख्यास्यामि। — *CU* 8.9.3

[15] यस्मात्सकृद्व्याख्यातं दोषरहितानामवधारणविषयं प्राप्तमपि नाग्रहीः अतः केनचिद्दोषेण प्रतिबद्धग्रहणसामर्थ्यस्त्वम्। अतस्तत्क्षपणाय वस अपराणि द्वात्रिंशतं वर्षाणि इत्युक्त्वा तथोषितवते क्षपितदोषाय तस्मै ह उवाच। — *CUŚB* 8.9.3

BHAGAVAD-GĪTĀ

Bhagavad-Gītā also presents an *adhikārī* as one who is endowed with fourfold qualities[16] and such a one should approach a *guru* for knowledge.[17] The consequence of an unrefined mind is presented in stages to reiterate the importance of the fourfold qualities as a means to gain knowledge of the Self.[18] *Bhagavad-Gītā* is emphatic with regard to the role of a refined mind that is instrumental in receiving the absolute truth. While commenting on the 12th verse of chapter II of *Gītā*, Śaṅkara states that a refined mind through *śama*, *dama*, etc. instructed by the *guru* and scriptures is instrumental in direct apprehension of the Self.[19] Śaṅkara emphasizes that one who has renounced action alone is eligible for the knowledge of the Absolute.[20] *Gītā* seems to classify an *adhikārī* based on the quality (*guṇa*) of mind and the lifestyle (*niṣṭhā*).[21] Thus, it suggests, the classification of the seekers based on the qualitative mind.

BRAHMASŪTRA

Brahmasūtra in its opening aphorism indicates the nature of an aspirant through the word *atha* and according to Śaṅkara it refers to one who has acquired the fourfold qualities, thereafter which

---

16 एतज्ज्ञानमिति प्रोक्तमज्ञानं यदतोऽन्यथा। — *BG* XIII.11
श्रद्धावान् लभते ज्ञानम्। — *BG* IV.39
ये हि संस्पर्शजा भोगा दुःखयोनय एव ते। — *BG* V.22
आगमापायिनोऽनित्याः तांस्तितिक्षस्व भारत। — *BG* II.14

17 तद्विद्धि प्रणिपातेन परिप्रश्नेन सेवया।
उपदेक्ष्यन्ति ते ज्ञानं ज्ञानिनस्तत्त्वदर्शिनः॥ — *BG* IV.34

18 *BG* II.62-67.

19 शास्त्राचार्योपदेशशमदमादिसंस्कृतं मनः आत्मदर्शने करणम्। — *BGŚB* 2.21

20 तस्मात् विशेषितस्य अविक्रियात्मदर्शिनः विदुषः मुमुक्षोश्च सर्वकर्मसन्यासे एव अधिकारः। — *BGŚB* 2.21

21 सत्त्वात्संजायते ज्ञानं। — *BG* XIV.17
लोकेऽस्मिन्द्विविधा निष्ठा पुरा प्रोक्ता मयानघ।
ज्ञानयोगेन साङ्ख्यानां कर्मयोगेन योगिनाम्॥ — *BG* III.3

one takes to an enquiry of *Brahman*.[22] In Ubhayaliṅgādhikaraṇa, the aphorism (3.2.11) hints at the teaching of the nature of *Brahman* as *saguṇa* or *nirguṇa* as based on the quality of the seeker. Further analysis on the nature and qualities of a seeker are not found in the aphorisms but we get discussions related to the qualification required to undertake the study of Vedānta.

In Pramitādhikaraṇa, Bādarāyaṇa states that a human being is qualified for Vedāntic study.[23] Śaṅkara gives the reason that a human alone has the ability to acquire the prerequisites for the study of Vedānta.[24] Further, in Devatādhikaraṇa, there is a discussion as to whether a *devatā* is eligible for enquiry into the knowledge of *Brahman*. Śaṅkara ascertains that the *devatā*s have a form and are eligible to pursue the knowledge of the Self.[25] Apaśūdrādhikaraṇa[26] denies the accessibility of performance of Vedic rituals for the fourth class of the Vedic society (*śūdra*),[27] but the study of Vedānta to gain Self-knowledge is not denied for any section of people.[28] It is accessible to anyone with the fourfold qualities.

Thus, in the context of the nature of an aspirant, *Prasthānatraya* uniformly reveals the prerequisites of an *adhikārī* as the fourfold

---

22 नित्यानित्यवस्तुविवेकः इहामुत्रार्थफलभोगविरागः शमादिषट्कसंपत् मुमुक्षुत्वञ्च। तेषु हि सत्सु धर्मजिज्ञासा ऊर्ध्वं च शक्यते ब्रह्म जिज्ञासितुं ज्ञातुं च न विपर्यय। तस्माद् अथ शब्देन यथोक्तसाधन-संपत्यानन्तर्यमुपदिश्यते। — *BSŚB* 1.1.1

23 हृद्यपेक्षया तु मनुष्याधिकारत्वात्। — *BS* 1.3.25

24 मनुष्याधिकारत्वादिति शास्त्रं ह्यविशेषप्रवृत्तमपि मनुष्यानेवाधिकरोति शक्तत्वात् अर्थित्वात् अपर्युदस्तत्वात् उपनयनादिशास्त्राच्च इति वर्णितमेतदधिकारलक्षणे। — *BSŚB* 1.3.25

25 ततश्चार्थित्वादिसंभवादुपपन्नो देवादीनामपि ब्रह्मविद्यायामधिकारः। — *BSŚB* 1.3.33

26 क्षत्रियत्वगतेश्चोत्तरत्र चैत्ररथेन लिङ्गात्।

संस्कारपरामर्शात् तदभावाभिलापाच्च।

तदभावनिर्धारणे च प्रवृत्तेः।

श्रवणाध्ययनार्थप्रतिषेधात् स्मृतेश्च। — *BS* 1.3.35-38

27 वेदपूर्वकस्तु नास्त्यधिकारः शूद्राणामिति स्थितम्। — *BSŚB* 1.3.38.

See also, *TUŚB* 1.11 — सर्वेषां चाधिकारो विद्यायाम् ।

28 श्रावयेच्चतुरो वर्णान् इति चेतिहासपुराणाधिगमे चातुर्वर्ण्यस्याधिकारस्मरणात्। — *BSŚB* 1.3.38

qualities. The response of an *adhikārī*, in every stage of learning gives rise to the employment of pedagogical tools to impart the knowledge. *Prasthānatraya* succeeds in reaching out to different aspirants by the use of such pedagogical instruments. In the course, the *adhikārī* is also classified based on various factors, primarily based on the response of the *adhikārī* to the teaching. Thus, *Prasthānatraya* exhibits the qualities of a seeker, the classification of a seeker, the pedagogy based on the nature of the seeker, and the nature of a seeker for whom the pedagogy is designed. Here, we are concerned with the pedagogy and the classification of the aspirant.

2.2 Adhikārī-based Pedagogy

In the growth of Advaitic literature, we find an attempt to describe the pedagogical devices in keeping with the ability of an aspirant, even when that aspirant is declared to be one endowed with the fourfold qualities. The varied pedagogical measures for a particular aspirant do not deviate from the underlying principle of Advaita, that knowledge is the means to liberation. The *adhikārī*-based pedagogy, that includes the classification of an *adhikārī*, has taken shape to such an extent that we find a mention of the method to be adopted in imparting the knowledge to a particular aspirant.

For instance, in the Sanskrit introduction to *SSLTS*, Pūrṇānandendra Sarasvatī classifies an *adhikārī* as *manda, madhyama* and *uttama* (this classification is not the same as in *Vicārasāgara*) and also presents the pedagogy to be employed with respect to each one of them. He says that the kind of teaching (*upadeśa*) for the *manda adhikārī* is to expatiate the plurality of self, the five elemental nature of the world, *māyā* as the transformative material cause, the gradual process of creation, differentiating dream from the waker's world, perception as generation of knowledge due to sense object contact, the identity of *jīva* and *Brahman* through secondary signification and the nature of *jīvanmukti*. The method of teaching for *madhyama adhikārī*, he says, is revelation that everything other than the Self is a reflection as in dream through the *dṛṣṭi-sṛṣṭi-vāda*. For the *uttama adhikārī*, the instruction is to be the revelation of the self-effulgent nature of Self, the impossibility of duality and thereafter the instructor to remain silent. However, Pūrṇānandendra does not provide the basis on which the *adhikārī*s are classified and the reason for adopting the above said methods for a particular *adhikārī*.

In a recent work titled *Viśuddhavedāntasāra* of Saccidānandendra Sarasvatī the teaching is presented differentiating a *sādhanacatuṣṭayasampanna adhikārī* based on three stages of understanding.[29] He classifies the same *adhikārī* into three categories, viz. *anubhava-dṛṣṭi, mano-dṛṣṭi* and *indriya-dṛṣṭi* based on different perspectives. Here too, he employs an *adhikārī*-based pedagogy in revealing the Advaitic truth.[30]

2.3 Niścaladāsa and Pītāmbar on Adhikārī

Now, we shall take up the study of the nature of an aspirant as dealt with in the Hindi *Vicārasāgara*. The text deals with the nature of an aspirant in various contexts and agreeing with the conventional idea, defines *adhikārī* as a *sādhanacatuṣṭayasampannāḥ*. But, the text is silent or rather vague about the ground on which it classifies an *adhikārī* into *uttama, madhyama* and *kaniṣṭha* (not *adhama*). We shall analyse the various circumstances in which Niścaladāsa speaks about the nature of a seeker. Further, based on the pedagogy employed with regard to each *adhikārī*, we shall attempt to draw a line of division of *adhikārī*s in the text *Vicārasāgara*. The stages of defining an *adhikārī* can be traced as:

ADHIKĀRĪ TO HINDI VICĀRASĀGARA

In the first *taraṅga*, Niścaladāsa extols his text *Vicārasāgara* written in the regional language. He states in his couplet that even though there are many works in Sanskrit, this *Vicārasāgara* in the regional language caters to those who are of dull intellect (*matimanda*) and

---

29 एकस्यैवाधिकारिणः क्रमेण दोषक्षयापेक्षया भूयोभूयः प्रकारान्तरेणोपदेशदर्शनात्। — *VVS* pp. 6-7

30 अनुभवदृष्टिमनोदृष्टीन्द्रियदृष्टिभेदेन प्रकरणं खण्डशो विभज्य वेदान्तोपदेशसारः संगृह्यते। — *VVS* p. 7

(Self) ignorant (*ajāni*).[31] In his *ṭīkā*[32] to the above couplet, Niścaladāsa says that his work in Hindi caters to the dull intellect (*mandabuddhi*) who cannot gain knowledge from the Sanskrit works. They do not have the ability to inquire into the works in Sanskrit, for such a one, this text in regional language is composed. In this context, Pītāmbar in his *ṭippaṇī*[33] differentiates the words *matimanda* and *ajāni* that occurs in the couplet.[34] He says that the word *matimanda* refers to those who cannot analyse the works in Sanskrit and *ajāni* refers to those who are ignorant of the nature of Self. The Hindi *Vicārasāgara* caters to both the *matimanda* and *ajāni*. Thus, the *adhikārī* for the Hindi *Vicārasāgara* is one who is not conversant with Sanskrit language and who is ignorant of the nature of Self. Here, the word *adhikārī* refers to a seeker with the ability to undertake the study of Hindi *Vicārasāgara*.

ADHIKĀRĪ TO THE KNOWLEDGE OF ADVAITA

In defining an *adhikārī* as part of the *anubandhacatuṣṭaya* in the first *taraṅga*, Niścaladāsa states that one who has eliminated the defects in the form of impurity (*mala*) and disturbance (*vikṣepa*) by the practice of action without being anxious of the result (*niṣkāma karma*) and practises meditation (*upāsanā*), and in whom there is the operation of ignorance's power of concealment and one who is endowed with the fourfold qualities is a qualified one, an *adhikārī*.[35] Niścaladāsa here agrees with the conventional idea of an *adhikārī* and establishes that an *adhikārī* is one with fourfold qualities.

In the description of the remote and proximate means to knowledge, Niścaladāsa specifies that an *adhikārī* seeking knowledge is one who has renounced *karma* and the means to

---

[31] सूत्र भाष्य वार्तिकं प्रभृति ग्रंथ बहुत सुरबानि।
मैं भाषा करूं लखि मतिमंद अजानि॥ — *HV*, *dohā* 1.7

[32] *HV*, *ṭīkā* 1.7.

[33] *HV* 1, *ṭippaṇī* 8.

[34] *HV*, *dohā* 1.7.

[35] *HV*, *ṭīkā* 1.11.

karma.[36] While concluding the discussion on the *adhikārī* as part of *anubandhacatuṣṭaya*, Niścaladāsa restates that an *adhikārī* is one who is endowed with the fourfold qualities like discrimination (*viveka*), dispassion (*vairāgya*) etc.[37] Pītāmbar remarks in his *ṭippaṇī* that the word *viveka* includes the other three qualities, thus making it to fourfold qualities.[38] So far, in defining an *adhikārī*, Niścaladāsa has not made an attempt to classify the *adhikārī*.

In the second *taraṅga*, while dealing with specific questions related to the nature of *adhikārī*, Niścaladāsa counters an objection that states that the text *Vicārasāgara* cannot find an *adhikārī* who is defined as possessing the fourfold qualities. Niścaladāsa raises a question as to whether there is absence of many *adhikārī*s or are there no *adhikārī*s at all? and he answers that the first is acceptable, while the second option is to be rejected. That no one is eligible to gain knowledge is untenable. He says that the mind is afflicted with threefold impurities — impurity (*mala*), disturbance (*vikṣepa*) and concealment (*āvaraṇa*). One whose mind is overpowered by *mala* and *vikṣepa* is not an *adhikārī*. Whereas, one who has overcome *mala* by the performance of good actions and removed *vikṣepa* through the practice of meditation is an *adhikārī* qualified for gaining knowledge.[39]

In this context, Pītāmbar classifies an *adhikārī* into two kinds as *kr̥topāsanā* and *akr̥topāsanā*. *Kr̥topāsanā adhikārī* is one who has practised meditation on *Brahman* with attributes (*saguṇa brahmopāsanā*) till he has attained a focused mind (*citta ekāgratā*) and such a one accepts the means to liberation as mentioned in the scriptures. The *akr̥topāsanā adhikārī* is one who is not committed to *saguṇa brahmopāsanā* and therefore lacks *citta ekāgratā*. He is unable to appreciate the means to liberation declared by the scriptures and has to put forth effort to remove contrary notions

36 *HV* 1.16.

37 *HV* 1.23.

38 *HV* 1, *ṭippaṇī* 51.

39 *HV*, *ṭīkā* 2.68.

(*viparīta bhāvanā*) even after the rise of knowledge. For such a one, deliberate contemplation of the teaching (*nididhyāsana*) becomes a compulsory means to liberation.[40] This classification taken up by Pītāmbar, which he had indicated in his *ṭippaṇī* 51 earlier, is based on the quality of the mind of a seeker.

Further, in response to the objection that there cannot be a seeker yearning for absolute *ānanda* since everyone is satisfied with the pleasure obtained from the sense objects, Niścaladāsa offers an answer by classifying people into four, namely, *pāmara, viṣayī, jijñāsu* and *mukta.*[41] The *pāmara* and *viṣayī* categories of people seek happiness through the material world, they do not entertain a philosophical quest. A *mukta*, on the other hand, is a liberated one, who does not seek anything. Of these, the *jijñāsu* kind of person is considered to be an ideal one for gaining absolute *ānanda*, which is the subject matter (*viṣaya*) of *Vicārasāgara*.

Here, Pītāmbar in his *ṭippaṇī*s,[42] further classifies *pāmara, viṣayī* and *jijñāsu* into three varieties as *uttama, madhyama* and *kaniṣṭha* in each group. The classification of *pāmara* and *viṣayī* is not relevant in understanding the nature of an aspirant in this context but the *jijñāsu* categorized into three types gives us a cue to the classification of an *adhikārī* by Niścaladāsa, later (fourth *taraṅga*) in his work. Pītāmbar describes an *uttama jijñāsu* as one who possesses fourfold qualities with an intense desire for knowledge, the *madhyama jijñāsu* as one who desires (*manda jijñāsā*) for hearing the scriptures (*śravaṇa*) and the *kaniṣṭha jijñāsu* is attracted more towards performance of *niṣkāma karma* and *upāsanā*.

In the fifth *taraṅga*, Pītāmbar suggests classification of *adhikārī* based on pedagogy, wherein he states in his *ṭippaṇī*[43] that the *dṛṣṭi-sṛṣṭi-vāda* is meant for *uttama jijñāsu*. In the preface to his work *Vicāracandrodaya*, Pītāmbar adopts the method of classifying

---

[40] *HV* 2, *ṭippaṇī* 96.

[41] *HV*, *ṭīkā* 2.69.

[42] *HV*, *ṭippaṇī*s 97-98 and 101.

[43] *HV* 5, *ṭippaṇī* 289.

an *adhikārī* and he says that his text *Vicāracandrodaya* is meant for mediocre intellect (*matimanda*) but with a refined mind, whom he terms as an *uttama adhikārī*.[44]

Niścaladāsa's classification of the chapters in *Vicārasāgara* as the fourth, fifth and sixth *taraṅgas*, record the dialogue between the *guru* and the *uttama, madhyama* and *kaniṣṭha adhikārīs* respectively who are presented as the three sons of the King Śubhasantati in the parable. Here, the *uttama* and *madhyama adhikārīs* are not explicitly defined. The *kaniṣṭha adhikārī* is defined in the sixth *taraṅga* as one who has a sharp intellect but riddled with doubts.[45] Niścaladāsa states that this chapter (sixth *taraṅga*) primarily employs reasoning (*yukti*) and caters to those who are desirous of reasoning out (*kutarka*) the Self-knowledge gained from a *guru*. Niścaladāsa says that one with a *kutarka* intellect is said to be *kaniṣṭha adhikārī*. From the definition of *kaniṣṭha adhikārī* it can be inferred that the *uttama* and *madhyama adhikārīs* are not obsessed with *kutarka*. But we do not get any further indicators to arrive at the classification of the *adhikārīs* as *uttama*, etc. in the text.

Further in the seventh *taraṅga* the dialogue between *kaniṣṭha adhikārī* and Śubhasantati identified in the present study as *manda-madhyama adhikārī* is described. Though Śubhasantati was introduced in the fourth *taraṅga* as one endowed with dispassion and desirous of seeking salvation, Niścaladāsa does not identify him as an *adhikārī* nor does he classify him as a "kind" of *adhikārī* and hence the dialogue between the king and the *kaniṣṭha adhikārī* in the seventh *taraṅga* is not presented exclusively as found in the case of *uttama* and others. But while reintroducing the king in the seventh *taraṅga*, Niścaladāsa states that the king lacked intense dispassion and hence could not abandon the kingdom and due to moderate dispassion he could not enjoy the sense-pleasures and was desirous of taking to meditation.[46] The elements of qualities

---

[44] Preface to *VCD*.

[45] *HV* 6.304.

[46] *HV* 7.499.

required to be an *adhikārī* are found to be possessed by the king but in lesser degree. Thus, in the Hindi *Vicārasāgara* we find the conventional method of defining the qualities of an *adhikārī* with slight variations but the mode of classifiying the aspirants remain unsolved.

2.4 Vāsudeva Brahmendra on Adhikārī

Here too, the discussion on the nature of an *adhikārī* can be seen from two standpoints.

ADHIKĀRĪ TO SANSKRIT VICĀRASĀGARA

In this translated work, VB does not specify the quality required for the study of a text in regional language (here Hindi) as the text is in Sanskrit. VB's translated work is to cater to those who engage in the study of Advaita in Sanskrit language as part of the traditional learning course. Thus, here VB addresses those seekers of his region with the knowledge of Sanskrit but without any exposure to Hindi. It is imperative to note here that the dedicated teachers in the tradition of Advaita Vedānta always strive to employ language (as a tool) in such a way that the central teaching of the scriptures is conveyed to the seekers. VB is an exemplary himself, who though from south India, had a good knowledge of Hindi that he set to translate it into Sanskrit for the benefit of others who did not know Hindi. This does not in any way suggest that *traditionalists* prefer that the work should be written only in Sanskrit. We do find many instances, especially in parts of Tamil Nadu, where seekers are known to have mastered the concepts of Advaita by studying *Vicārasāgara* (and other such Advaitic works) in Tamil (only). In fact, Ponnambala Swāmigaḷ, a commentator (in Tamil) to the celebrated work *Kaivalyanavanītam* (Tamil Advaitic treatise) of Tāṇḍavarāya Swāmigaḷ, profusely refers to Niścaladāsa's *Vicārasāgara* and *Vṛttiprabhākara* (in Tamil). Thus, the teachers and seekers of Advaita freely utilized the available works in any vernacular or in Sanskrit, in order to gain firm knowledge.

ADHIKĀRĪ TO THE KNOWLEDGE OF ADVAITA

Now, coming back to our topic, we find in Sanskrit *Vicārasāgara* the *adhikārī* is described in order to show the eligibility criteria to gain the knowledge of Advaita. There are also instances where VB seems to throw some light on the nature of aspirants based on the pedagogical tool.

In the first *taraṅga*, while describing the glory of the text, VB says that a *dhīraḥ* obtains the absolute *ānanda*. He explains that a *dhīra* is one who protects his mind from sensory indulgences.[47] The employment of the word *dhīraḥ* is in keeping with the Upaniṣadic idea of an *adhikārī*. While Niścaladāsa had said that an *adhikārī* is one who renounces *karma* and the means to *karma*, VB adds that such a one is an *uttama adhikārī*.[48] Later VB shows the stages of development of an *adhikārī* as one who gains Self-knowledge by enquiring into the contents of Vedānta, and thereby attains liberation by Self-knowledge.[49]

At the end of the fourth *taraṅga*, VB defines the *uttama*, *madhyama* and *kaniṣṭha adhikārī*s.[50] He says that one whose mind is pure because of past merits (*puṇya*), who gains firm-knowledge on the instruction of the *mahāvākya* as instructed by a *guru*, who after the gain of this firm-knowledge does not require further analysis of the scriptures for the sake of removal of doubt, such a one is said to be an *uttama adhikārī*. VB says that one whose mind is not completely pure but affected by *mala* and *vikṣepa* is *madhyama adhikārī* or *kaniṣṭha adhikārī*. Here, VB does not clarify on the line of division between *madhyama* and *kaniṣṭha adhikārī*s. Also, he seems to differ from Niścaladāsa for whom a person with defects of *mala* and *vikṣepa* is not an *adhikārī*, whereas, VB accommodates such a one as an *adhikārī* and also classifies that seeker as either *madhyama* or *kaniṣṭha adhikārī*.

---

47 *SV*, p. 7.

48 *SV*, p. 14.

49 *SV*, p. 20.

50 *SV*, p. 130.

Again, in the fifth *taraṅga*, VB specifies that one who is convinced of *dṛṣṭi-sṛṣṭi-vāda, eka-sattā-vāda, eka-jīva-vāda* is said to be *uttama adhikārī*. In the sixth *taraṅga*, where Niścaladāsa defines a *kaniṣṭha adhikārī*, VB quotes the words of *Gītā* as "one who doubts, perishes" (IV.40) and the teachings of the sixth *taraṅga* is to eliminate the doubts of *kaniṣṭha adhikārī*. In these references we find that an attempt is made to distinguish an *adhikārī* with the method of knowledge presented to each one of them. With regard to the nature of an *adhikārī*, VB also agrees with the conventional view that an *adhikārī* is a *sādhanacatuṣṭayasaṁpannaḥ*.

VB recognizes the classification of *adhikārī*s as *uttama, madhyama* and *kaniṣṭha*. Mention has been made earlier about *uttama adhikārī* as one who is free from *mala* and *vikṣepa* but affected by *āvaraṇa*. VB explains *mala* as impurity in the form of subtle impressions indicated by one taking to prohibited action, with sense object attraction, and rise of impure thoughts. He says that *mala* is removed by the performance of *niṣkāma karma*, developing values like compassion. The second defect, namely *vikṣepa*, gets expressed in the form of an unsteady mind. A mind that does not have the capacity to dwell on the Vedāntic subject matter is said to be afflicted with *vikṣepa*. The means like *japa* and *upāsanā* help to remove the impurity, viz., *vikṣepa*. Repeated listening to the scriptural statements is also prescribed as a means for removal of *vikṣepa*. VB justifies the requirement of qualities for an *adhikārī* to knowledge. He says that just as a brāhmaṇa is entitled to perform Bṛhaspati sacrifice, a kṣatriya, Rājasūya sacrifice, a *vaiśya*, Stoma sacrifice, so also one who is endowed with the fourfold qualifications is entitled to pursue inquiry into the Vedāntic texts.[51] In this analysis too, we find that the principles of classification of *adhikārī* are vague.

2.5 The Fourfold Qualities of Adhikārī

The fourfold qualities required for the study of Vedānta are based on the conventional norm and we shall briefly see each one of

[51] *SV*, pp. 8-9.

them based on *SV*.[52] The fourfold qualities are *viveka* (discrimination) between eternal and non-eternal entity, *vairāgya* (dispassion) with regard to results in this world and in the hereafter, *śamādiṣaṭkasampatti* (sixfold disciplines) and *mumukṣutva* (desire for knowledge).

VIVEKA

Viveka (discrimination) is in the form of knowing the Self as real and of the nature of Consciousness. Self is to be known as that which does not become the counterpositive of its destruction, which means the Self is never subject to destruction (*nāśa-apratiyogī*) and is free from actions (*kriyāśūnya*). On the other hand, non-self is to be realized as the unreal perceived world, of the nature of counterpositive of destruction (*nāśa-pratiyogī*) and associated with action. This discrimination is known as *viveka*.

VB further explains that discrimination is the distinctive knowledge of Self as different from non-self, like the swan filtering milk from water. By *viveka*, he says that one gains the indirect knowledge of the falsity of the world but there is absence of direct knowledge. Thus, other three disciplines are required for a seeker and *viveka* serves as the cause for rise of dispassion, etc. It might be objected that a scholar, who has the mediate knowledge of the difference between the Self and the non-self, is capable of refuting the viewpoints of other schools, and thereby he is said to possess the knowledge of discrimination (*viveka*). But it is not known to give rise to the other disciplines, namely, dispassion, etc. VB answers this objection by stating that it is true that those who have the mediate knowledge of the difference between the Self and the non-self would acquire knowledge of discrimination, however, their mind is not refined as they do not perform *niṣkāma karma* and take to meditative worship. VB likens this to a plantain tree which does not grow on a dry land, but grows abundantly on a fertile land. The relevant point is that the presence of *viveka* in a refined mind, free from *mala* and *vikṣepa*, gives rise to

[52] *SV*, pp. 8-13.

dispassion, and not otherwise. Thus, *viveka* is the cause for the rise of other three disciplines.

VAIRĀGYA

Vairāgya is developed by envisaging the defect of the fleeting nature of sense-pleasures. It is the capacity to abandon anything at anytime effortlessly. VB expounds the quality of *vairāgya* in four stages based on Patañjali's *Yogasūtra*.[53]

1. *Yatamāna* — dispassion entertained at the mental level.
2. *Vyatireka* — abandoning the undesirable qualities through association with noble ones and putting forth effort to implement the acquired desired qualities.
3. *Ekendriya* — dispassion coupled with sense control — is the third stage.
4. *Vaśīkaraṇa* — dispassion coupled with mind control — is further divided into three stages:
   a. *Manda* — dispassion exhibited in dire circumstances.
   b. *Tīvra* — dispassion shown with regard to sensory pleasures of this world.
   c. *Tīvratara* — dispassion towards the sensory enjoyment in the other worlds.

For the development of intense dispassion, one should progress to acquire the sixfold mental disciplines.

ŚAMĀDIṢAṬKASAMPATTI

Śamādiṣaṭkasampatti (sixfold mental discipline) is important in the order presented and each one plays a vital role in the refinement of mind to receive the absolute knowledge.

Śama is the mind control developed after giving up the impressions (*vāsanā*) caused by the experience of objects in the past. The mind is to be turned inwards withdrawing from the sense objects.[54]

[53] *Yogasūtra* 1.15.

[54] यतो यतो निश्चरति मनश्चञ्चलमस्थिरम् ।
ततस्ततो नियम्यैतदात्मन्येव वशं नयेत् ॥ — *BG* VI.26

→

This is developed by observing the defects in the sense objects.

Dama is sense control, wherein the external sense-organs are to be withdrawn from the sense objects. The sense-organs likened to the horses are to be whipped when indulging in the path of sensory pleasures.[55]

Śraddhā is the third discipline, which develops intense faith in the words of the teacher and Vedānta. VB adds that *śraddhā* presupposes *bhakti* (devotion) to God, words of the teacher and Vedic scriptures.

Samādhāna is a single-pointed concentration to attain the goal, i.e. *Brahman*. Further, VB clarifies that rise of concentration is attained by *upāsanā* that removes the defect of *vikṣepa*. He points out the difference between the development of concentration as a result of *saguṇa upāsanā* and *samādhāna*. The first nature of concentration is developed by *upāsanā* and the second kind of concentration is *samādhāna*, i.e. constant remembrance of *Nirguṇa-Brahman*.

Uparati is described here as abandoning the pleasures obtained in this world and the other worlds as one would avoid poison. VB differentiates *uparati* from *vairāgya*. *Uparati* is dispassion shown towards the rise of desire due to the prior experience of sense objects that is aroused when the abandoned sense objects are experienced again. In case of the quality of *vairāgya*, it is the dispassion shown towards the desire that is put off by viewing the defect of the sense objects.

Titikṣā is the endurance of pairs of opposites in the form of heat, cold, hunger, thirst, etc. VB remarks that during the course of *śravaṇa*, one may experience obstacles in the form of heat, cold, hunger, thirst or other kinds of pairs of opposites and these are to be tolerated. Or else, necessary steps should be taken in order to remove hunger, thirst, etc. so that the mind does not wander and *śravaṇa* will be fruitful.

← दुःखं सर्वमनुस्मृत्य कामभोगान्निवर्तयेत्।
अजं सर्वमनुस्मृत्य जातं नैव तु पश्यति ॥ — *MaK* 3.43

55 इन्द्रियाणि हयानाहुर्विषयाꣳस्तेषु गोचरान्।
आत्मेन्द्रियमनोयुक्तं भोक्तेत्याहुर्मनीषिणः ॥ — *KU* 1.3.4

This sixfold discipline, put together, makes one *sādhanā* and hence is enumerated as one of the disciplines in the fourfold qualifications. They are not to be segregated as individual disciplines and counted as nine qualifications. This aspect is elucidated further by VB resorting to the famous chariot-imagery of *Kaṭhopaniṣad*.[56] He shows the mutual dependence of the sixfold discipline by pointing out to their interdependence.

1. Without the control of the mind one cannot master the sense-organs. Thus, *dama* presupposes *śama*.
2. Mind that is extrovert attached to ephemeral things cannot have complete faith in Vedānta, scriptures and *guru*. Thus, *śraddhā* presupposes *śama*.
3. Without the control of the mind, concentration in *Brahman* is not possible, thus, *samādhāna* presupposes *śama*.
4. Though senses are withdrawn, if mind is not under control, then on seeing a sense object, the prior impressions make one get attracted towards the sense objects. Hence, *uparati* presupposes *śama*.
5. A mind under control can endure different experiences like heat or cold and this is not possible by an extrovert mind; hence *titikṣā* presupposes *śama*. Thus, *śama* enhances the other five disciplines.
6. Without the control of the senses, mind cannot be controlled. Hence *dama* presupposes *śama*.
7. Faith in Vedānta, scripture and *guru* is not possible without restraining attachment towards sense objects like form and taste. So, *śraddhā* presupposes *dama*.
8. Without sense control, concentration of mind cannot be developed; so, *samādhāna* presupposes *dama*.
9. Without the control of the sense-organs, due to the impressions of the past experienced sense objects, again

[56] *KU* 1.3.3-9

desire is developed on seeing the sense object. Thus, *uparati* presupposes *dama*.

10. Without the control of sense-organs, due to the proximity of sense-organs, a wavery mind does not endure pairs of opposites like heat and cold. So, *titikṣā* presupposes *dama*. Thus, *dama* enhances the other five disciplines.
11. In the absence of intense faith in the words of *guru*, one cannot take to *śravaṇa*. *Śravaṇa* is possible by faith; hence, *sādhanā*s like *śama* presuppose *śraddhā*.
12. Without concentration, *śama* and other *sādhanā*s cannot be attained. Hence, *śama* and other *sādhanā*s presuppose *samādhāna*.
13. A mind not withdrawn dwells in sense objects and it does not develop *sādhanā*s like *śama*. Thus, such *sādhanā*s presuppose *uparati*.
14. Varied experience such as heat, cold, hunger, thirst, gain and loss give rise to three kinds of pangs and if one cannot endure them, other five disciplines cannot be developed. Hence *śama* and other *sādhanā*s presuppose *titikṣā*.

Thus, all the six disciplines are mutually dependent and together form one discipline of the fourfold qualifications.

MUMUKṢUTVA

Mumukṣutva or intense desire to gain the knowledge of *Brahman*; for removal of sorrow and attainment of liberation is said to be the fourth quality. Just as a hungry person desires for food, and water is sought to put down the fire, in the same way, for one scorched with intense pain (*saṁsāra*), liberation alone is the solution. This intense desire for liberation is *mumukṣutva*. One with a feeble desire for liberation is a *manda mumukṣu* who will not engage in the performance of *niṣkāma karma* in the initial stages. Gradually one develops intense desire and turns to be a *mumukṣu*. In other words, by the performance of *karma* and *upāsanā*, *manda* becomes *tīvra mumukṣu* which means desire for liberation in this case becomes intense. This intense desire alone facilitates one in listening to the scriptures.[57]

2.6 Role of Sādhanās[58]

These fourfold qualifications are presented as the remote means to liberation (*bahiraṅga sādhanā*). The fourfold qualities in turn are said to lead to the triple means (*śravaṇa, manana* and *nididhyāsana*) that are categorized as the proximate means to liberation (*antaraṅga sādhanā*). Both the *bahiraṅga* and the *antaraṅga sādhanā* together contribute to the liberating knowledge. But when compared to the means like sacrifice (*yajña*), charity (*dāna*) and austerity (*tapas*) — (*yajñādi*) — they serve as the *bahiraṅga sādhanā,* then the fourfold qualities and the triple means are said to be the *antaraṅga sādhanā.* Here too, in the rise of knowledge, the proximate means necessarily includes the analysis of the words *tat* and *tvam* in the *mahāvākya.* Thus, the eight means, viz., the fourfold qualities, the triple means and the analysis of the word-meaning of *tat–tvam* constitute the *antaraṅga sādhanā.*[59] VB again compares the *tat–tvam* analysis to a swan that separates water from milk. As butter is churned out of buttermilk, he says that one should take to the analysis, as prescribed in the scriptures, in the form of the cause–effect relation seen in consciousness and matter, matter as the superimposition on the substratum, seer–seen discrimination, witness–witnessed discrimination, etc.

REMOTE AND PROXIMATE MEANS

The words "remote" and "proximate" in connection with the *sādhanā*s are indicated in a relative sense. In different stages, the meaning of the word "proximate" preceding the word "means"

---

[57] *SV*, p. 13.

[58] *SV*, pp. 13-17.

[59] Generally *śravaṇa* includes analysis of the word-meaning of the *mahāvākya.* The analysis of the words *tat* and *tvam* is distinctly mentioned as one of the *sādhanās* in *Vicārasāgara.* The reason for the same can be found in section 2.6 under the sub-title "Śravaṇa" and in Section 2.7 of this chapter and in Section 4.5 under the sub-title "Otaprota Bhāva" of Chapter 4. See also *SV*, p. 35 fn. 1.

designate a completely different set of *sādhanās*. VB cites an example to differentiate the proximate means from the remote means. He says that the fourfold qualities and the triple means are said to be proximate since they are like fixing the arrow in a bow and releasing it towards the target. The released arrow is directly connected to the desired target. Whereas, the bow serves only as an instrument to reach the target but itself remains away from the target. Thus, the bow is said to be the remote means instrumental in reaching the target. In the same way, the performance of prescribed duties is helpful in the removal of defects like *mala* and *vikṣepa*, thus developing concentration which results in the desire for knowledge. Here, the actions serve as the indirect means to knowledge and hence it is known as the remote means and the eight means mentioned above are the proximate instruments to knowledge (see *fig*. 2.1).

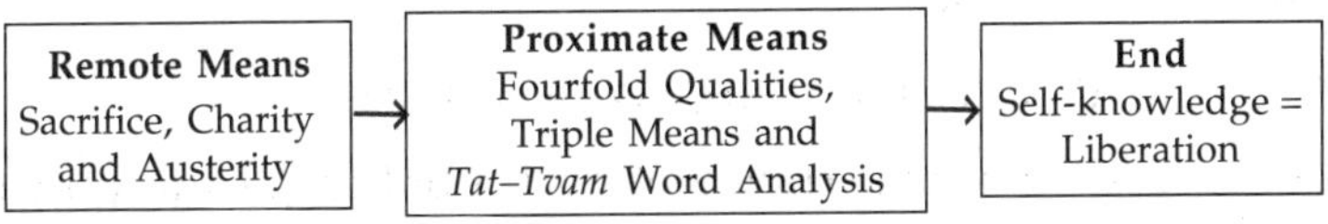

fig. 2.1: The means to knowledge

It is further said that only on gaining the proximate means should one give up the remote means,[60] else prior to attaining the proximate means if the remote means are given up then there will be a twofold loss. One is the loss of heaven (after death) and the other is the loss of gaining the fourfold qualities (while living). VB says, it is like a person who accidentally falls into an uncovered well and holds on to a grass, but he should not leave the grass unless he gets hold of a rope, in the same way, one should not give up the remote means without accomplishing the proximate means to liberation.[61]

The fourfold qualities make one competent to gain Self-knowledge hence they are figuratively said to be the proximate

60 योगारूढस्य पुनः तस्यैव शमः उपशमः सर्वकर्मभ्यो निवृत्तिः कारणं योगारूढस्य साधनम् उच्यते इत्यर्थः ।
— *BGŚB* 6.3

61 *SV*, p. 14.

means to knowledge. Further, the fourfold qualities serve as the means to *śravaṇa, manana* and *nididhyāsana* (the triple means) which in turn serve as the means to knowledge. Thus, when compared to the fourfold qualities, the triple means are proximate means to the rise of direct knowledge. From this standpoint, the fourfold qualities are said to be the remote means. Even though from the standpoint of *śravaṇa,* etc. the fourfold qualities are classified as the remote means, they are still considered as proximate means to knowledge. Since, even after its function of giving rise to *śravaṇa* is complete, the fourfold qualities are not given up unlike *karma* (action). *Karma,* according to Advaita, is utilized to promote the fourfold qualities, but as *viveka,* etc. are acquired, *karma* is dropped. Whereas, even after the rise of *śravaṇa,* the fourfold qualities are not given up.[62] Due to this reason, the fourfold qualities being remote when compared to *śravaṇa,* etc. are said to be the proximate means to knowledge.

IMPORTANCE OF THE FOURFOLD QUALITIES

VB observes[63] the importance of each quality (of the fourfold qualities) as an instrument in giving rise to knowledge. He says that one should commit oneself to *śravaṇa* of Vedānta for a long time. Mere *śravaṇa* without the fourfold qualifications obstructs the rise of direct knowledge. One cannot take to *manana* or *nididhyāsana* without the process of *śravaṇa*. Thus, *śravaṇa,* in order to yield its result, presupposes the fourfold qualities. VB reminds that even one who is an expert in dealing with the scriptures, possessing only the quality of *viveka* and extremely attached to sense objects, performs action for material benefit only. So, through the second means, i.e. *vairāgya,* one should renounce the desire for results of this and the other world. Even though the first and

---

[62] When it is said that the fourfold qualities are not given up after *śravaṇa* it indicates the continuity of *mumukṣutva.* After *śravaṇa, mumukṣutva* dissolves in an enlightened one. But such a one strives to bring about *mumukṣutva* in the minds of the ignorant ones. Hence, the mention of the continuity of the fourfold qualities even after the rise of *śravaṇa* is valid.

[63] *SV,* p. 15.

the second qualities are attained, one may suffer from anger, etc. and in order to monitor them the sixfold mental disciplines are to be developed. The presence of the first three qualities without the desire for liberation also does not lead to *śravaṇa,* etc. hence the fourth quality, *mumukṣutva,* is also important.

ŚRAVAṆA

VB shows that the fourfold qualities give rise to *śravaṇa*. *Śravaṇa* is defined in two ways in two different stages. Initially, *śravaṇa* is described as the contact of the sense of hearing and the statements of Vedānta. Subsequently, *śravaṇa* is described as the analysis of the scriptural statements by the application of the sixfold indicators (*ṣaṭliṅgatātparyanirṇaya*) to establish the consistent subject matter of Upaniṣads (see *fig*. 2.2).

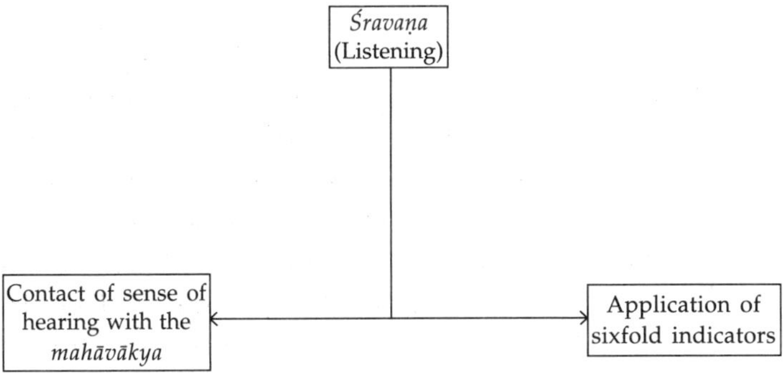

fig. 2.2: Two ways of defining *śravaṇa*

Of these two, the first kind of *śravaṇa* is said to be the primary means (*mukhya sādhanā*) because of which there is the rise of direct knowledge (*aparokṣa jñāna*) of Self. If due to *asambhāvanā* (doubts) and *viparīta bhāvanā* (contrary notions) the benefit of Self-knowledge gets obstructed then it is shown that one should take to the second form of *śravaṇa* which is to be followed by *manana* and *nididhyāsana*.[64] The second type of *śravaṇa* (also called as *vicāritarūpa-śravaṇa*) is defined as the application of the sixfold indicators that proves the non-dual inner Self as the revelation of

---

[64] *SV*, p. 30.

the Vedāntic statements. VB points out that as the knowledge of smoke gives rise to the knowledge of fire, wherein the smoke is the indicator of fire, in the same way, the non-dual nature of the inner-self as the content of Vedānta is known by the sixfold indicators.[65] This second kind of process of *śravaṇa* is evaluated by VB[66] based on *Chāndogya Upaniṣad* as follows:

1. *Introduction–Conclusion* (*upakrama–upasaṁhāra*): The subject matter introduced in the sixth section as *sadeva somya idamagra āsīt ekamevādvitīyam* (CU 6.2.1) as *Ātman* alone is concluded as *aitadātmyam idam sarvaṁ tat satyaṁ sa ātmā* (CU 6.16.3).
2. *Repetition* (*abhyāsa*): The identity of *Brahman* and the inner-self is repeated nine times in the form of the *mahāvākya "tattvamasi"* (CU 6.8.7).
3. *Uniqueness* (*apūrvatā*): The non-dual Self is non-different from *Brahman*, which is not known by other sources of knowledge other than Vedānta. *Brahman*, being self-evident, is eternally immediate and the concealment is removed by the Vedāntic statement alone. This uniqueness is pointed out through the statement *śraddhatsva somya* (CU 6.12.2) and *ācāryavān puruṣo veda* (CU 6.14.2). Faith in the words of the *guru* and Vedānta that the non-dual knowledge is gained from the scriptures is the third indicator.
4. *Result* (*phalam*): *Tasya tāvadeva ciraṁ yāvanna vimokṣye atha sampatsye* (CU 6.14.2) by this statement the result in the form of attainment of *Brahman* is revealed.
5. *Censure-Eulogy* (*arthavāda*): The process of creation is described in the statement *tadaikṣata bahusyāṁ prajāyeya tattejo 'sr̥jata* (CU 6.2.3); thereafter non-difference is established.

---

65 *SV*, p. 15.

66 Ibid.

6. *Logical Presentation* (*upapatti*): It is examining the revelation of non-duality as the central import of the Upaniṣads with appropriate examples. This is revealed in *CU* 6.1.4-6 and 6.8.4, through the examples of clay, etc. wherein *Brahman* is presented as the substratum of the false world. Thus, by the employment of the six indicators one arrives at the non-dual nature of the inner Self which is the essential teaching of the Vedas. This is *śravaṇa*.

MANANA

Manana consists in the negation of duality employing logic and arriving at the identity of *Brahman* and *Ātman*. The process of *manana* is presented in two stages: first, establishing non-duality (*aikyasādhakayukti*) by way of showing that no means to knowledge can prove duality and second, by the analysis of the logic that eliminates duality (*bhedabādhakayukti*), the knowledge of non-difference is emphasized.

Aikyasādhakayukti

1. *Perception*: Is duality proved by perception? There is an apparent notion that perception proves duality since one perceives the "many". But, here the very sense of perception as a reliable source of knowledge is questionable since perceptual experiences like the blue-sky, flat-earth and rising-sun, actually do not exist. The duality revealed by perception cannot obstruct the knowledge of non-duality.
2. *Inference*: By the application of the inferential cognition too, the duality cannot be arrived at. The process of inference begins based on the scriptural statement that, that which is of the nature of Existence, Consciousness, Absolute Happiness is non-different from *Brahman,* and that which is not of the nature of Existence, Consciousness, Absolute Happiness is different from *Brahman*. The scriptures describe *Īśvara* as of the nature of Existence, Consciousness and Absolute Happiness and hence it is derived that *Īśvara*

is non-different from *Brahman*. From our experience, it is known that empirical objects like pot, are not of the nature of Existence, and hence they are different from *Brahman*. In this background, the syllogism drawn is as follows:

Jīva is non-different from *Brahman*

Being of the nature of Existence, Consciousness, Absolute Happiness

Like *Īśvara* (unlike a pot).

3. *Comparison*: The space cannot be differentiated as "pot-space" and "room-space" without the limiting adjunct like the "pot" and the "room" in this case, in the same way, the mind and the primal ignorance serve as the limiting adjuncts, without which there cannot be the difference in the form of *jīvātmā* and *Brahman*. Hence, the experienced duality due to adjuncts being unreal does not dismiss non-duality, the real. This is derived by the application of comparison.

4. *Postulation*: If non-duality is not understood as the central teaching of the scriptures then the Upaniṣadic statements[67] that reproach duality cannot be accounted for. To ward off the fallacy of invalidity of the scriptures, "identity" as the teaching is to be accepted. Just as the knowledge of fatness of Devadatta dismisses the knowledge of the absence of food, in the same manner, the knowledge of duality is dismissed by the statements of the Upaniṣads (*neti neti* — *BU* 2.3.6). Postulation helps to understand the falsity of duality that presupposes reality of non-duality.

Bhedabādhakayukti

The negation of duality is taken up here.[68]

---

[67] नेह नानास्ति किञ्चन। — *BU* 4.4.19 and *KU* 2.1.11.

न तु तद् द्वितीयमस्ति। — *BU* 4.3.23. अतोऽन्यदार्तं। — *BU* 3.7.23.

[68] *MaK* 2.3-10.

1. *Inference* shows that the experience of duality is false. The syllogism drawn is as follows:

   The difference between inner Self and Consciousness is false,
   since the difference is based on the adjunct (*upādhi*)
   as in the case of pot-space and room-space.[69]

2. *Comparison* — Just as the difference between the original Consciousness and the reflected consciousness is false, the difference between *jīvātmā* and *Brahman* is false.

3. *Postulation* — The *mahāvākyas* of Upaniṣads reveal only non-duality. If duality is the truth then the *mahāvākyas* cannot reveal non-duality. But *mahāvākyas* reveal non-duality. Therefore, even by postulation the difference between *jīvātmā* and *Brahman* is false.

4. *Non-apprehension* — The presence of the adjuncts, namely, the gross body and the subtle body in the waking and dream states differentiates the Self from *Brahman*. In the absence of the adjuncts in the deep-sleep state, difference is not experienced. This shows that a "real" difference is not experienced which is proved by non-apprehension. This process of ascertainment is known as *manana*.

NIDIDHYĀSANA

Nididhyāsana means the undisturbed flow of thoughts centring on the knowledge of *Brahman*, which arises subsequent to the cessation of the knowledge of duality. The result of *nididhyāsana* is *samādhi* and such a *samādhi* is a part of *nididhyāsana* and need not be attained by distinct means. VB differentiates *samādhi* from *nididhyāsana*.[70] He says that a branch of a tree that is bent naturally lies low without any effort. In the same manner, the process of being established in the "thought mode" of *Brahman* generated by the *mahāvākya* is known as *samādhi*. On the other hand, if the branch of a tree shoots up, it has to be pulled down with effort.

---

69 यदौपाधिकं न भवति तन्मिथ्या न भवति । — *SV*, p. 17

70 *SV*, p. 17.

Similarly, remaining in the incessant thought of *Brahman* with effort is known as *nididhyāsana*.

Thus, the role of the fourfold qualities is demonstrated in two levels. First, it serves as the cause for *śravaṇa*, etc. Second, along with the triple means, it serves as the cause for the rise of direct knowledge of *Brahman* along with the result of Self-knowledge.[71]

2.7 Sādhanās and the Nature of Adhikārīs

In the case of an *adhikārī*, the *sādhanā*s are performed accordingly and as even the benefit is attained, the remote means are dropped and the proximate means are strengthened. Thus, the *adhikārī* is triumphant in the line of connecting the means (*sādhanā*) and the end (*sādhya*) in each stage of one's spiritual growth. Sureśvara in his *Naiṣkarmyasiddhi*,[72] presenting the role and function of each *sadhānā* leading to liberation, says:

> From the performance of daily obligatory duties merit arises. From the origination of merit comes destruction of sin; and from this arises purification of the mind, and from this comes the understanding of the real nature of bondage; and therefrom dispassion arises; and from this comes a longing for liberation; and this leads to a search for the means thereto; and from this comes the renunciation of all actions and their means; then there is the practice of *yoga*; and from this comes the inclination in the mind towards the inward Self, and then there arises the knowledge of the meaning of the texts such as *tat tvam asi*, and from this results the destruction of ignorance; and thereafter comes the state of remaining as the Self alone, as shown by the texts, "Being but *Brahman*, he is merged in *Brahman*", "Being liberated, one becomes free".[73]

---

[71] अहं ब्रह्मेतिवाक्यार्थबोधो यावद्दृढीभवेत् ।
शमादिसहितस्तावदभ्यसेच्छ्रवणादिकम् ॥ — *VV* 49

[72] नित्यकर्मानुष्ठानाद्धर्मोत्पत्तिः धर्मोत्त्पत्तेः पापहानिः ततश्चित्तशुद्धिः ततः संसारयाथात्म्यावबोधः ततो वैराग्यं ततो मुमुक्षुत्वं ततस्तदुपायपर्येषणं ततः सर्वकर्मतत्साधनसन्न्यासः ततो योगाभ्यासः ततश्चित्तस्य प्रत्यक्प्रवणता ततस्तत्त्वमस्यादिवाक्यार्थपरिज्ञानं ततोऽविद्योच्छेदः ततश्च स्वात्मन्येवावस्थानं ब्रह्मैव सन् ब्रह्माप्येति विमुक्तश्च विमुच्यते इति ।
— *NS*, Introduction to 1.52

[73] Tr. R. Balasubramanian, *NS*, p. 53.

A similar pattern is seen observed by VB while dealing with the *sādhanās* and the final result. VB describes[74] the stages of development of an enlightened person, who is referred to as a *kr̥takr̥tya*. Initially one who is in the state of ignorance, for enjoying the result in this world, engages oneself in activities like farming. Then one progresses to perform *kāmya karma, upāsanā,* etc. for reaping the results in the other worlds. Such a one elevates to perform *niṣkāma karma* for cleansing the mind and developing concentration. Then one acquires the fourfold qualifications to enquire into the scriptural statements. Subsequently, such a one approaches a teacher for instruction on the non-dual *Brahman* to gain direct knowledge. The triple means are employed to eliminate doubts, etc. and the delusion of "remoteness" is eliminated by the analysis of *tat padārtha*, and the delusion of "limitation" is removed through the analysis of *tvam padārtha*,[75] thereby arriving at the essential mutual oneness of *tat* and *tvam*. For liberation, the firm knowledge of non-dual Consciousness and following the above said set of *sādhanās* and means to acquire those *sādhanās* are called as *kartavya*. One who has completed these forms of enjoined *sādhanās* and gained the non-dual knowledge is termed as *kr̥takr̥tya*, i.e. a *jīvanmukta*.

2.8 Obstacles in the Path of Knowledge

The *madhyama adhikārī* (in *taraṅga* 5) seeks clarification related to the "defects" in a seeker that obstructs the rise of direct knowledge. In this context, the *guru* classifies the obstacles (*pratibandha*) into three kinds, as belonging to the present (*vartamāna*), past (*bhūta*) and future (*bhāvī*).[76] The obstacles of the present are explicated by

---

[74] *SV*, p. 35.

[75] The process of elimination of the delusion in the form of "remoteness" and "limitation" through the analysis of the *tat* and *tvam* in the *mahāvākya* is discussed in Section 4.5 of chapter 4 under the sub-title "Otaprota Bhāva". This is presented in *Vicārasāgara* as a distinct proximate means to liberating knowledge in addition to the first type of *śravaṇa* (hearing the *mahāvākya*) mentioned above which is said to be the primary means for the rise of direct knowledge.

[76] *SV*, p. 182.

showing the four defects faced by a seeker. Developing intense attachment formed as impressions in the mind, directed towards a desired object that is expressed as "I" and "mine" is the defect of attachment. The second defect is the incapacity to grasp the teaching as instructed by the teacher. This is inadequacy of intellectual sharpness. Such a seeker, resorts to other means of knowledge since the seeker disbelieves the words of the *guru*. This is the third defect and the fourth defect is clinging to the identification of body, mind and intellect. These four defects are the obstacles of the present (*vartamānapratibandha*). Constant remembrance of wealth, son, wife, etc. and other objects of attachment, even after giving them up, is the obstacle related to the past (*bhūtapratibandha*). Obstacle related to the future is like the concern to reach higher worlds like *brahmaloka* or the anxiety over the nature of residual *prārabdha* subject to future birth (*bhāvipratibandha*).[77] It is hinted that the adherence to enquiry with the prerequisites wards off such obstacles and one gains direct knowledge of *Brahman* on hearing the scriptural statement.

In describing the upward movement of a spiritual seeker, VB is concerned of those who are unable to overcome such obstacles as mentioned above and who struggle to climb up the path to spiritual knowledge. In such case, VB prescribes a "downward" movement,[78] as it were, so as to encourage any kind of aspirant. He says that if one is unable to assimilate the non-dual nature of Self, one can take to meditation of the attributeless *Brahman*. One who is unable to meditate on the attributeless *Brahman* can take to meditation of God with forms. If one cannot dwell on any form of the Lord, then one should perform *niṣkāma karma* and *nitya-naimittika karma*. One who cannot perform *niṣkāma karma* should perform *sakāma karma* as enjoined in the scriptures.[79] If one is not able to perform *sakāma*, then VB warns such a one is deluded and is trapped in the cycle of births and deaths. Thus, we find

---

[77] *PD* 9.38-53.

[78] *SV*, p. 198.

[79] See also *BG* XII.9-11.

alternatives with regard to the *sādhanas* provided to seekers at different levels.

VB cautions[80] that one is said to be a seeker who takes to *śravaṇa, manana* and *nididhyāsana,* and one who does not take to these triple means and resort to any other means is known as *ārūḍhapatita* (slipping away).[81] It ensues from this that a seeker should never give up enquiry till a firm conviction arises.

So far we have arrived at the nature of *adhikārī,* qualities and the role of qualities in different aspirants by surveying the Sanskrit *Vicārasāgara.* Now, based on the nature of *adhikārī* described in the foregoing pages, let us proceed to examine the line of division drawn in the text *Vicārasāgara,* as *uttama, madhyama* and *kaniṣṭha adhikārī*s.

2.9 Classification of Adhikārīs in Vicārasāgara

We shall now enquire into the nature of division of the *adhikārī*s. In the first place, it is to be borne in mind that the *adhikārī*s presented in *Vicārasāgara* are *sādhanacatuṣṭayasaṁpannāḥ.* The difference between them cannot be exactly traced back to their intellectual calibre. Second, it is to be noted that the classification of the *adhikārī* does not pertain to their superior or inferior nature. Third, the use of the words to classify the *adhikārī*s, viz. *uttama, madhyama* and *kaniṣṭha,* impresses us upon the fact that all the three are equally devoted to the knowledge of Vedānta. Fourth, the result of knowledge, i.e. liberation (directly or indirectly), is gained by all the *adhikārī*s. Hence, the differentiation is not wholly based on the result of knowledge. Fifth, all the *adhikārī*s are exposed to Vedāntic knowledge and get enough time for a dialogue with the *guru.* Thus, they do not lack association with the *guru* and the scriptures. Sixth, the *adhikārī*s equally display the stages of development to be adhered to for the rise of knowledge, in the form of approaching a *guru,* expressing the desire for liberation

---

80 *SV,* p. 198.

81 In accordance with the maxim *karasthaṁ madhu santyajya kūrparaṁ leḍhi mūḍhadhīḥ.*

and taking to the means of *śravaṇa, manana* etc. In spite of all these uniform treatments, the *adhikārī*s of *Vicārasāgara* are classified and the only feature that is available to demarcate the *adhikārī*s into three kinds is the pedagogy employed in this work.

The text *Vicārasāgara,* in accordance with the traditional view, accepts an *adhikārī* as one who is endowed with the fourfold qualities. But the classification of *adhikārī* in *Vicārasāgara* poses the difficulty in defining an *adhikārī* in this work. As *Vicārasāgara* adheres to pedagogy suiting different *adhikārī*s, it is essential to study the classification of the *adhikārī*s. Hence, we attempt to justify the classification of *adhikārī*s based on the study of pedagogy employed in the text. Here again it is to be noted that the present study does not focus on the reason as to why a particular pedagogy is employed for a particular aspirant. The idea is to determine the *adhikārī*-based pedagogical classification for which it becomes imperative for us to examine the dialogue between the *adhikārī*s and the *guru* as presented in *Vicārasāgara*.

UTTAMA ADHIKĀRĪ

The fourth *taraṅga,* titled "the instruction to the *uttama adhikārī*", is a dialogue between the *uttama adhikārī* and the *guru*. The question relating to the means for liberation is raised by the *uttama adhikārī,* the first son Tattvadr̥ṣṭi who also represents the desire of his other two brothers, Adr̥ṣṭi and Tarkadr̥ṣṭi. Tattvadr̥ṣṭi's questions can be summarized as:

- the means to attain happiness and remove sorrow,
- the locus of bondage,
- the solution for removal of erroneous sorrow,
- questions relating to the object of knowledge, i.e. the doubt pertaining to the possibility of identity of *jīvātmā* and *paramātmā,*
- questions relating to the means of knowledge, i.e. ascertainment of duality by the enjoinment of *karma* and *upāsanā,*

- the locus of rise of *Brahman*-knowledge,
- the illuminator of *brahmavr̥tti*, and
- the non-perceptual mechanism of rise of *Brahman*-knowledge.

Tattvadr̥ṣṭi is classified as the *uttama adhikārī* in *Vicārasāgara*. He is said to have attained *jīvanmukti*.

MADHYAMA ADHIKĀRĪ

Adr̥ṣṭi, who hears the same teaching, expresses his inability to determine the ontology of scriptures and the *guru* who reveals the false nature of bondage. He questions the validity of scriptures in ascertaining non-dualism. The *guru* imparts the knowledge of identity of *jīvātmā* and *paramātmā* through various methods of discrimination. Adr̥ṣṭi further expresses his difficulty in understanding the identity knowledge and hence the *guru* enunciates different methods of meditation for mental refinement. Adr̥ṣṭi takes to *nirguṇa praṇava upāsanā* with a desire to reach *brahmaloka* and it is said that he attained *kramamukti* in the fifth *taraṅga*, titled "the instruction to the *madhyama adhikārī*".

KANIṢṬHA ADHIKĀRĪ

Tarkadr̥ṣṭi, who remains silent all throughout the discourse, now conveys his difficulty in dismissing empirical reality as false by citing the example of dream world, for according to Tarkadr̥ṣṭi, the dream experience is real. The *dr̥ṣṭi-sr̥ṣṭi-vāda* is taught to Tarkadr̥ṣṭi through the story of Agr̥dhadeva's dream experience. The *mahāvākya* is elaborately analysed and the teaching to Tarkadr̥ṣṭi in the sixth *taraṅga* is titled "Description of *Guru*, Vedānta and Other Means as False". The independent mode of *manana* undertaken by Tarkadr̥ṣṭi is presented in the seventh *taraṅga* where he goes in search of other preceptors and gains conviction that non-dual *Brahman* alone is the content of all branches of knowledge. Tarkadr̥ṣṭi is characterized as the *kaniṣṭha adhikārī*. The *kaniṣṭha adhikārī* is not presented as an *adhama* but the word *kaniṣṭha* signifies his immatured level of grasping the knowledge, unlike that of the *uttama adhikārī*. He yearns for logical reasoning in understanding the same teaching. Tarkadṛṣṭi is said to have attained *jīvanmukti*.

ŚUBHASANTATI AS MANDA-MADHYAMA ADHIKĀRĪ

The seventh *taraṅga* describes both *jīvanmukti* and *videhamukti*. Tarkadṛṣṭi now a *jīvanmukta* meets his father Śubhasantati. The father is perplexed regarding the means to liberation. Śubhasantati identified as *manda-madhyama adhikārī* (in this present study) is described as lacking intense dispassion (*tīvra vairāgya*) and thereby afflicted by sorrow. But there is a moderate dispassion (*manda vairāgya*) and he is not attached to sensory pleasures. Śubhasantati gains the knowledge of *kāraṇa brahmopāsanā* from Tarkadṛṣṭi and is said to have attained *brahmaloka*. It is to be noted here that Tarkadṛṣṭi, the *kaniṣṭha adhikārī,* has learnt the pedagogical measures to suit a particular aspirant. He does not instruct Śubhasantati the same method through which he gained the knowledge of the truth, but judging the ability of his father, he imparts accordingly. Thus, the four kinds of seeker are pedagogically differentiated in the text. The *uttama*[82] and *kaniṣṭha*[83] *adhikārī*s are said to have attained *jīvanmukti* and later *videhamukti,* the *madhyama*[84] is said to have attained *kramamukti* and the *manda-madhyama* is known to have attained *brahmaloka.*[85]

The prominent pedagogical instruments employed with regard to the *uttama adhikārī* are the theory of error revealing the epistemological position of Advaita and the revelation of the metaphysical oneness through *citcāturvidyāprakriyā*. For the *madhyama adhikārī* the pedagogical devices are the discriminative processes to reveal the Self and optional methods of meditation for refinement of mind. The pedagogy adopted for the *kaniṣṭha adhikārī* is the analysis of the nature of Self through the concepts

---

[82] *SV, āvarta* 489.

[83] *SV, āvarta*s 507 and 535.

[84] *SV, āvartas* 315 and 491.

[85] *SV, āvarta* 534.

of Existence, Consciousness and Absolute Happiness, the ontological disposition by *dṛṣṭi-sṛṣṭi- vāda*, and an analysis of the *mahāvākya*. The *manda-madhyama adhikārī* who has not elevated himself to an ideal *adhikārī* is taught the difference between *kāraṇa brahmopāsanā* and *kārya brahmopāsanā*.

2.10 Difficulty in Defining Adhikārīs in Vicārasāgara

Based on the description of an *adhikārī* by Niścaladāsa, Pītāmbar and VB, as explained above and by scrutinizing the pedagogical measures, it becomes complicated to envisage the precise nature of an aspirant in this work. For instance, while it is mentioned that *dṛṣṭi-sṛṣṭi-vāda* is meant for an *uttama adhikārī*, we find that this theory is taught to the *kaniṣṭha adhikārī* and so on. If the text devotes separate chapters for each kind of *adhikārī* (the basis of such a division is the fundamental question raised in the present study), Śubhasantati, who is taught the process of meditation, is neither classified as an *adhikārī* nor his adherence to the means and the result of knowledge presented in a separate chapter. Thus, the kinds of *adhikārīs* are vaguely presented and the basis of classification is unclear. Moreover, the line of division between each aspirant is very thin and often overlapping.

2.11 Modified Presentation of Adhikārī-based Pedagogy

The approach of the present study, therefore, is to bring forth the Advaitic teaching by a *guru* to a seeker in the form of question and answer, where the seekers display broadly two kinds of attitude. One understanding the scriptures and reasoning it out, thereby gains *jīvanmukti* and the other, who prolongs the understanding of identity of Self with *Brahman* takes to intermediary process of meditation and thereby acquires *kramamukti*. In either case, liberation is attained only by the means of knowledge. (Perhaps the result of *brahmaloka* attained by Śubhasantati which is not the goal of Advaita could be the reason for not classifying him as an *adhikārī*.)

The present study is thus a gradual shift from *adhikārī* centric to pedagogy centric. It dissolves the issue of the nature and classification of *adhikārī* and thereby the study of the purpose of employing a particular pedagogy to an *adhikārī* is also dissolved. After this dissolution, the pedagogy employed for each *adhikārī* based on the result of knowledge is highlighted. Against this background, the third and fourth chapters of the present study combines the pedagogy employed for the *uttama* and *kaniṣṭha adhikārī*s, and the fifth chapter is devoted to the analysis of the pedagogy adopted for the *madhyama* and *manda-madhyama adhikārī*s. The final chapter takes up the argument on the nature of a liberated person according to the school of Advaita and also clarifies the doubts related to liberation raised by the *uttama* and *kaniṣṭha adhikārī*s. It concludes with the "kind" of liberation attained by the *adhikārī*s of *Vicārasāgara.* Thus, we attempt to arrive at a comprehensive study of the "pedagogical concern" that is derived from the text *Vicārasāgara.*

3

On the Nature of Knowledge (Jñānasvarūpaprakaraṇa)

Knowledge alone is the direct means to liberation and the *guru* tries to convey the same to the three *adhikārīs* (*uttama, madhyama* and *kaniṣṭha*) who have approached him seeking absolute happiness. The dialogue pertaining to the nature of knowledge occurring in *taraṅgas* 4, 6 and 7 is pooled in along with related discussions as found in *taraṅgas* 1-2 of the Sanskrit *Vicarāsāgara*. Thus, the restructured dialogue in the present chapter is as follows:

1. The purpose of varied branches of knowledge (*taraṅga* 7)
2. On the direct means to liberation (*taraṅgas* 6, 2 and 1)
3. Nature of bondage (*taraṅgas* 2 and 4)
4. Locus and perceiver of falsity (*taraṅga* 4)
5. On the non-dual nature of the Self and the Witness Consciousness (*taraṅga* 2).

As the focus of our study is to derive the pedagogy based on the *adhikārīs*, we proceed to treat the *uttama* and *kaniṣṭha adhikārīs* as one set of aspirants, who through a series of questions and arguments arrive at the identity knowledge, dismiss the experienced world as *mithyā* and attain liberation while living. The *uttama adhikārī* is said to have attained *jīvanmukti* through the teaching received from the *guru,* whereas, the *kaniṣṭha adhikārī* after *śravaṇa* conducts his independent mode of *manana* and meets many other preceptors seeking clarification. Thus, by repeated independent analysis and through debates with other preceptors, the *kaniṣṭha adhikārī* is said to have attained *jīvanmukti* much later. Based on the result of the teaching, viz. *jīvanmukti,* the dialogue related to the nature of knowledge as carried out with the *guru* by the *uttama* and *kaniṣṭha adhikārī*s are plugged together along with the related discussions that occur while establishing the *anubandhacatuṣṭaya* of the text *Vicārasāgara* and they are presented here in a particular sequence.

3.1 Purpose of Varied Branches of Knowledge[1]

The *kaniṣṭha adhikārī* (in *taraṅga* 7) through an independent method of *manana* (after *śravaṇa*) arrives at non-duality as the central teaching of all branches of knowledge and philosophical systems. He not only supplements his conclusion with reasons but also gets it validated through other preceptors who conform that the purport of all branches of knowledge, directly or indirectly, is to reveal the non-dual *Brahman*. We find this idea explicated in *Sūta Saṁhitā,*[2] wherein the same Truth revealed by varied scriptures is interpreted to be the non-dual absolute *Brahman*. The Advaitic preceptors on various occasions employ this technique of converging the numerous discussions to a single focused unit of arriving at the Advaitic thought. We see this approach used by Śaṅkara in his commentary on *Bṛhadāraṇyaka Upaniṣad* 1.4.7,[3] that is further reiterated by Sureśvara.[4] Thus, the primary intention of

---

[1] *SV*, pp. 343-56.

[2] वेदाः सर्वे पुराणानि स्मृतयो भारतं तथा ॥

अन्यान्यपि च शास्त्राणि तथा तर्काश्च सर्वशः।
शैवागमाश्च विविधा आगमा वैष्णवा अपि ॥

अन्यागमाश्च विदुषामनुभूतिस्तथैव च।
अस्मिन्नर्थे स्वसंवेद्ये पर्यवस्यन्ति नान्यथा ॥

बाध्यबाधकतां यान्ति व्यवहारे परस्परम् ।
समुद्र इव कल्लोला इति वेदार्थसङ्ग्रहः ॥ — *SS* 8.22-25

[3] यदर्थः सर्वशास्त्रारम्भः यस्मिन्नविद्यया स्वाभाविक्या कर्तृक्रियाफलाध्यारोपणा कृता यः कारणं सर्वस्य जगतः यदात्मके नामरूपे सलिलादिव स्वच्छान्मलमिव फेनमव्याकृते व्याक्रियेते यश्च ताभ्यां नामरूपाभ्यां विलक्षणः स्वतो नित्यशुद्धबुद्धमुक्तस्वभावः स एषः अव्याकृते आत्मभूते नामरूपे व्याकुर्वन् ब्रह्मादिस्तम्बपर्यन्तेषु देहेष्विह कर्मफलाश्रयेष्वशनायादिमत्सु प्रविष्टः ॥ — *BUŚB* 1.4.7

[4] यदर्थं सर्वशास्त्राणां प्रवृत्तिरतिविस्तरा। आत्मज्ञानावतारार्थः सर्वशास्त्रसमुद्यमः ॥

→

the varied scriptures is said to be the knowledge of the Self. All branches of knowledge culminate in the revelation of *Brahman*, the Absolute Reality. In this light, the *kaniṣṭha adhikārī* classifies the varied scriptures and enumerates their branches mentioning that they have an Advaitic import. In *taraṅga* 7 of *Vicārasāgara*, we do not find any kind of examination or justification with regard to this claim that Advaita is the import of all branches of knowledge. However, here we shall justify the same by not only classifying the scriptures but also by providing corroborative statements.

PURPORT OF PRIMARY SCRIPTURES

Agni Purāṇa[5] classifies the literature (*prasthāna* or *vidyā*) into eighteen kinds consisting of four Vedas, four Upavedas, six Vedāṅgas and four Upāṅgas. Of these, the four Vedas are segregated as the primary scriptures and the other branches are referred to as the auxiliary scriptures. The four Vedas, namely, *Ṛg* (21 branches), *Yajur* (109 branches), *Sāma* (1,000 branches) and *Atharvaṇa* (50 branches) being *apauruṣeya* are the primary scriptures.[6] Of the 1,180 branches of Vedas, 840 constitute *karmakāṇḍa*, 232 branches belong to *upāsanakāṇḍa* dealing with *Saguṇa-Brahman* and 108 branches of Vedas reveal *Nirguṇa-Brahman* which forms part of the Upaniṣadic portion.[7]

The primary tenet of the Vedic scripture is to bequeath the doctrine of Advaita. For instance, we find the basic concepts of Advaita, like the doctrine of *māyā*, the cause of sorrow as the

---

विरोधः सर्वशास्त्राणां स्वाभिधेयव्यपेक्षया। निवृत्त्यर्थेऽविरोधित्वादत एतत्समीरितम्॥
स्वत एव यतः पुंसां प्रवृत्तिः स्वार्थसिद्धये। तत्रानुवादि शास्त्रं स्यान्निवृत्तावेव तन्मितिः॥
— *BUŚBV* 1.4.405-07

5 ऋग्यजुःसामाथर्वाख्या वेदाङ्गानि च षट् द्विजा।
शिक्षा कल्पो व्याकरणं निरुक्तं ज्योतिषां गतिः॥
छन्दोऽभिधानं मीमांसा धर्मशास्त्रं पुराणकम्।
न्यायवैद्यकगान्धर्वं धनुर्वेदोऽर्थशास्त्रकम्॥ — *Agni Purāṇa* 1.15-17

6 *SV*, p. 345.

7 Ibid.

concealment of the nature of *Brahman*, etc. in *R̥gveda*.[8] *Yajurveda* reveals the knowledge of the non-dual Self as the means to freedom from sorrow.[9] *Sāmaveda* describes the secret meaning of the word "I".[10] The Absolute Reality as *Brahman* is declared in *Atharvaveda*.[11] The *kaniṣṭha adhikārī* ponders over the exorcizing actions (*abhicāra karma*) as found in *Atharvaveda* and arrives at such Vedic statements that do not intend action (*pravr̥tti*). The *abhicāra karma* found in *Atharvaveda* is meant to restrain one from performance of instinctive negative actions. A person out of hatred may want to kill his enemy either by poison or by burning his house, to turn him away from such a heinous act; actions in the form of *abhicāra* like *śyena-yāga* is prescribed. The purport of the *karmakāṇḍa* of *Atharvaveda* is for withdrawal from the negative actions. The *karmakāṇḍa* of the other three Vedas through injunctions instigate the seekers to perform action for the sake of refinement of the mind.

Here, VB adds that certain Vedic statements[12] are to be understood by the application of *parisaṁkhyā vidhi* (statement of permission) and not by *apūrva vidhi* (statement of injunction) or *niyama vidhi* (statement of restriction).[13] He quotes *Bhāgavata*

---

8 समाने वृक्षे निमग्नोऽनीशया शोचति मुह्यमानः।
जुष्टं यदा पश्यत्यन्यमीशं अस्य महिमानमिति वीतशोकः॥
— Quoted in *Advaitākṣaramālikā, R̥gveda* VIII.1.20.1

9 यस्तु सर्वाणि भूतान्यात्मन्येवानुपश्यति। सर्वभूतेषु चात्मानं ततो न विजिगुप्सते॥ — Quoted in *Advaitākṣaramālikā, Yajurveda (Śukla) — Saṁhitopaniṣad* 40.6

10 माङ् माने शब्दे च अहमिति शब्द्यते सर्वैर्मनुष्यैरित्यहमः परमेश्वरः अहंशब्दवाच्य इत्यर्थः। सर्वे जनाः कस्त्वमिति पृष्टाः अहमिति स्वात्मानं कथयन्ति। तादृशाय नमः। इति भाष्यम्। — Quoted in *Advaitākṣaramālikā, Sāyana Bhāṣya* on the word "अहमाय" occurring in *Sāmaveda, Samavidhāna Brāhmaṇa* 1.2

11 ब्रह्म होता ब्रह्म यज्या ब्रह्मणा स्वरे वोमिताः।
अध्वर्युर्ब्रह्मणो जातो ब्रह्मणोऽन्तर्हितं हविः॥

ब्रह्म स्रुचो घृतवतीर्ब्रह्मणा वेदिरुद्धिता।
ब्रह्म यज्ञस्य तत्त्वं च ऋत्विजो ये हविष्कृतः॥ संहिताय स्वाहा।
— Quoted in *Advaitākṣaramālikā, Atharvaveda* 19.42.1.2

12 परिणीतामुपगच्छेत्। ऋतौ भार्यामुपेयात्। हुतशेषं भक्षयेत्। सौत्रामण्यां सुराग्रहं गृह्णाति।
— *SV*, p. 346 fn.1.

13 For a brief explanation on the three kinds of *vidhis* see *Mīmāṁsāparibhāṣā* of Kr̥ṣṇa Yajvan.

Purāṇa[14] that reinforces the idea that such statements are not injunctions but a means to overcome the desire to perform such actions. Thus, the conclusion arrived at by the *kaniṣṭha adhikārī,* that the content of *karmakāṇḍa* of the Veda helps to enhance the purity of mind and leads a seeker into the enquiry of non-dual Self, is corroborated by other preceptors.

PURPORT OF AUXILIARY SCRIPTURES

Now the *kaniṣṭha adhikārī* dwells on the essence of the Upavedas that is indirectly instrumental in the rise of *Brahman*-knowledge. Upaveda consists of *Āyurveda, Dhanurveda, Gāndharvaveda* and *Arthaveda* (or *Sthāpatyaveda*). Here again, the relevant portions are not cited in the text *Vicārasāgara* to substantiate the idea that Self-knowledge is the import of all branches of scriptures. We shall extract the relevant portions to justify the same.[15] The role of *Āyurveda* (the science of medicine), according to Advaita Vedānta, is to help in developing dispassion as one experiences recurrence of disease and pain in spite of treatment. The ultimate human goal finds a mention in *Caraka Saṁhitā*.[16] Vātsyāyana's *Kāmasūtra* also intends to develop dispassion by indicating the ephemeral nature of worldly enjoyment. The quality of dispassion purifies the mind which is beneficial in gaining *Brahman*-knowledge. Earlier Advaitic literature have tried to reconcile the content of *Kāmasūtra* and we find Sureśvara stating in his *BUŚBV* that:

> There cannot be any contradiction for the validity of the treatises of Vātsyāyana and others on the ground that they inculcate the knowledge of the Self.[17]

---

[14] लोके व्यवायामिषमद्यसेवा नित्यास्तु जन्तोर्न हि तत्र चोदना ।
व्यवस्थितिस्तेषु विवाहयज्ञसुराग्रहैरासु निवृत्तिरिष्टा ॥ — *BP* 11.5.11.

[15] See *Advaitic Import of All Darśanas.*

[16] आत्मानमेव मन्येत कर्तारं सुखदुःखयोः । तस्माच्छ्रेयस्करं मार्गं प्रतिपद्येत नो त्रसेत् ॥
— *Caraka Saṁhitā,* Nidānasthāna 7.22

[17] अपि वात्स्यामनादीनां शास्त्राणामुक्तहेतुतः ।
प्रामाण्यमविरुद्धं स्यादैकात्म्यज्ञानजन्मने ॥ — *BUŚBV* 1.4.408

Vātsyāyana states:

> The practice of *kāma* is to be in accordance with *dharma* and *artha*, fulfilling which one naturally inclines to *mokṣa puruṣārtha*.[18]

Vātsyāyana also mentions the need to describe certain acts based on the context but has himself forbidden such acts in the following chapters of his work.[19]

Dhanurveda discusses about the employment of weapons in warfare. It is a science to protect law and order by punishing those who violate *dharma*. Thus, it is pointed out that the practice of *dharma* helps in developing a refined mind. *Gāndharvaveda* helps in the purity of mind and developing concentration, which serves as an indirect means to knowledge. *Arthaveda* study results in developing dispassion. This science shows that without the skill to earn wealth one cannot amass wealth, which itself gives rise to dispassion. Thus, the Upavedas play a prominent role in developing purity of mind, concentration and dispassion which is an essential prerequisite for Advaitic enquiry.

The other auxiliary scriptures include the Vedāṅgas consisting of Science of Phonetics (Śikṣā), Science of performance of sacrifices (Kalpa), Grammar (Vyākaraṇa), Etymology (Nirukta), Astronomy and Astrology (Jyotiṣa) and Prosody (Chandas). These scriptures are essential in bringing about a clarity in understanding. We find, the essence of Advaitic teaching, especially, in the Vyākaraṇa of Pāṇini as commented by various grammarians. Nandikeśvara while explaining *Māheśvarasūtra* brings out the core Advaitic tenet

---

18 धर्मार्थं च कामं च प्रत्ययं लोकमेव च।
पश्यत्येतस्य तत्त्वज्ञो न च रागात् प्रवर्तते ॥ — *KS* 7.2.53

एवमर्थं च कामं च धर्मं चोपाचरन्नरः।
इहामुत्र च निःशल्यमत्यन्तं सुखमश्नुते ॥ — *KS* 1.2.39

तदेतत्कुशलो विद्वान् धर्मार्थाववलोकयन्।
नातिरागात्मकः कामी प्रयुञ्जानः प्रसिध्यति ॥ — *KS* 7.2.59

19 अधिकारवशादुक्ता ये चित्रा रागवर्द्धनाः।
तदनन्तरमत्रैव ते यत्नाद्विनिवारिताः ॥ — *KS*, 7.2.54.

of attributeless *Brahman*.[20]

The Upāṅgas namely Mīmāṁsā (Science of Interpretation), Nyāya (Science of Logic), Dharmaśāstras (Ethical Literature)[21] and Purāṇas (Historical accounts) also contain the content of the Vedas. It is observed that the Upāṅgas serve as an aid for an authentic interpretation of the Vedas and the underlying essence of these texts is also essentially Advaita. According to Advaita Vedānta, while the Mīmāṁsā and Nyāya ultimately establish the non-dual nature of the Self, the Dharmaśāstras and Purāṇas also reveal the absolute. The Dharmaśāstras includes texts like *Āpastambasūtra*, *Baudhāyanasūtra* and *Manu-Smṛti*. These texts unanimously declare non-dual *Brahman*. Haradattācārya, while commenting on an aphorism of *Āpastambasūtra*, cites an illustration of a prince who was brought up by the hunters and who identified himself not as a prince but as a hunter. The same illustration is found employed by Śaṅkara in his commentary on *Bṛhadāraṇyaka Upaniṣad*[22] to reveal the cause of sorrow as ignorance of the Self. The introductory and concluding passages of Manu set the cardinal principle of Advaita.[23] The non-difference between *jīva* and *Īśvara*

---

20 अकारो ब्रह्मरूपस्स्यान्निर्गुणस्सर्ववस्तुषु ।
चित्कलामिमं समाश्रित्य जगद्रूप उणीश्वरः ॥

अकारः सर्ववर्णाग्र्यः प्रकाशः परमेश्वरः ।
आद्यमन्त्येन संयोगादहमित्येव जायते ॥

सर्व परात्मकं पूर्णं ज्ञप्तिमात्रमिदं जगत् ।
ज्ञप्तेर्बभूव पश्यन्ती मध्यमा वाक् ततस्स्मृता ।

अकारो ज्ञप्तिमात्रं स्यादिकारः चित्कला स्मृता ।
उकारो विष्णुरित्याहुः व्यापकत्वान्महेश्वरः ॥
— *Advaitākṣaramālikā*, pp. 107-08

21 Yājñavalkya, Viṣṇu, Vasiṣṭha, Dakṣa, Saṁvarta, Parāśara, Gautama, Hārīta, Āpastamba, Śuka, Bṛhaspati, Vyāsa, Kātyāyana, Devala, Nārada and other great seers composed the Smṛti texts.

22 *BUŚB* 2.1.20.

23 योऽसावतीन्द्रियग्राह्यः सूक्ष्मोऽव्यक्तः सनातनः ।
सर्वभूतमयोऽचिन्त्यः स एव स्वयमुद्बभौ ॥ — *MS* 1.7

सर्वभूतेषु चात्मानं सर्वभूतानि चात्मनि ।
समं पश्यन्नात्मयाजी स्वाराज्यमधिगच्छति ॥ — *MS* 12.91

is expressed by Yājñavalkya in his Dharmaśāstra,[24] which is clearly explained in *Mitākṣarā* as:

> The word *bhūta* indicates the modifications of the body, sense-organs-complex. Expressions like "I am fat", "I am thin", "I am blind", "I am deaf", etc. is because of the identification with the physical body. Such a material (mental) self can be purified by the performance of austerity and meditation. The word *tapas* means taking to the enquiry of the Self by the method of five-sheath discrimination and the word *vidyā* means the knowledge of the meaning of *tvam pada* through the Vedic statements, which leads to purification. The "purification" indicates the rise of knowledge by operating the means of knowledge that removes doubt, contradictory notion, etc. The immediate knowledge arising from the statement of identity that leads to the realization of Self is the feature of liberation.[25]

Purāṇas, including the Mahāpurāṇas and the Upapurāṇas, also contain the teachings of Advaita. We find the essence of Advaita declared in the popular *Bhāgavata Purāṇa*.[26]

OBJECTIVE OF PHILOSOPHICAL SYSTEMS

The *kaniṣṭha adhikārī* now examines different systems of philosophy. According to him, the orthodox schools (Āstika Darśanas) also engage in revealing the non-dual *Brahman*, the Absolute. The text *Vicārasāgara* does not show how the orthodox schools are directed towards Advaitic teaching but we shall examine the same based

24 भूतात्मानस्तपोविद्ये बुद्धेर्ज्ञानं विशोधनं।
क्षेत्रज्ञस्येश्वरज्ञानाद्विशुद्धिः परमा मता ॥ — *Yājñyavalkya Smṛti* 1.34

25 भूतशब्देन तद्विकारभूतो देहेन्द्रियसंघो लक्ष्यते। तत्र स्थूलोऽहं कृशोऽहं काणोऽहं बधिरोऽहमित्येवं तदभिमानित्वेन योऽयमात्मा वर्तते स भूतात्मा तस्य तपोविद्ये शुद्धिनिमित्ते। तपस्शब्देन अनेकजन्मस्वेकस्मिन्नपि वा जन्मनि जाग्रत्स्वप्नसुषुप्त्यवस्थासु आत्मनो योयमन्वयस्शरीरादेश्च यो व्यतिरेकस्सोऽभिधीयते यथा तपसा ब्रह्म विजिज्ञासस्व इति पञ्चकोशव्यतिरेकप्रतिपादनपरे वाक्ये। विद्याशब्देन चौपनिषदं असङ्गोह्यमात्मा इत्यादित्वंपदार्थनिरूपणविषयवाक्यजन्यं ज्ञानमुच्यते एताभ्यामस्य शुद्धिः। शरीरादिव्यतिरिक्तबुद्धेस्संशयविपर्ययरूपत्वेनाशुद्धायाः प्रमाणजन्यं ज्ञानं विशोधनम्। क्षेत्रज्ञस्य तपोविद्याविशुद्धस्व त्वंपदार्थभूतस्य तत्त्वमस्यादिवाक्यजन्यात्साक्षात्कारादीश्वरज्ञानात्परमा विशुद्धिर्मुक्तिलक्षणा इति।

26 सर्ववेदान्तसारं यद्ब्रह्मात्मैकत्वलक्षणम्।
वस्त्वद्वितीयं तन्निष्ठं कैवल्यैकप्रयोजनम् ॥ — *BP* 12.13.11

on some important observations.[27] Sage Kapila in his Sāṁkhya system differentiates between *Puruṣa* and *Prakṛti*, and shows that *Puruṣa* is unassociated. This is beneficial in giving the knowledge of the "unassociated" *Puruṣa*, which is further analysed in the *mahāvākya*. The liberating knowledge is revealed by the application of the secondary signification for the word *tvam*. Sage Patañjali's *Yogasūtra* helps in the practice of *nididhyāsana*. The logical reasoning of Nyāya by Sage Gautama is effective in conducting *mananam*. The first two Nyāya *sūtras*,[28] quoted by Śaṅkara in his *Samanvaya* commentary, explicate the Advaitic essence. The Naiyāyika's example of sense of hearing as space enclosed within the earlobe is explained as one space seemingly distinguished in many people due to the adjunct, in the form of earlobe. This argument is a welcome position to the Advaitin who claims that one all-pervasive Self seems to be many due to the adjunct in the form of body–mind–sense complex. Sage Kaṇāda's *Vaiśeṣikasūtras* also enhances the process of *mananam*. In the Nyāyakāṇḍa of *Vaiśeṣika-bhāṣya Ṭīkā*, the benedictory verse[29] reveals the non-dual absolute Consciousness indicating the validity of Advaita-knowledge. Gaṅgeśa in his benediction[30] in Navya-Nyāya indicates conditioned *Brahman* as the creator of the universe, thereby accepting the existence of attributeless *Brahman*. The Dharma-Mīmāṁsā or Pūrva-Mīmāṁsā by Sage Jaimini is a discussion on actions as prescribed by the Vedas. According to Advaita, performance of action leads to purification of mind. Pūrva-Mīmāṁsā, serving as it were, a prelude to Brahma-Mīmāṁsā, is commented upon by Kumarīla Bhaṭṭa, who describes the all-pervasive nature of the Self.[31] Further, *Saṅkarṣana* or *Devatākāṇḍa*

---

27 See *Advaitic Import of All Darśanas.*

28 तत्त्वज्ञानान्निश्रेयसाधिगमम्। — *Nyāya Sūtra* 1.1.1
दुःखजन्मप्रवृत्तिदोषमिथ्याज्ञानानां उत्तोरोत्तरापाये तदनन्तरापायादपवर्गः। — *Nyāya Sūtra* 1.1.2

29 ध्यानैकतानमनसो विगतप्रचाराः पश्यन्ति यं कमपि निर्मलमद्वितीयम्।
ज्ञानात्मने विघटिताखिलबन्धनाय तस्मै नमो भगवते पुरुषोत्तमाय ॥

30 गुणातीतोपीशस्त्रिगुणसचिवस्त्र्यक्षरमयः त्रिमूर्तिर्यस्सर्गस्थितिविलयकर्माणि तनुते।

31 ज्ञानशक्तिस्वभावोऽतो नित्यः सर्वगतः पुमान् इत्याह नास्तिक्यनिराकरिष्णुः आत्मास्तितां भाष्यकृदेत्र युक्त्या। दृढत्वमेतद्विषयः प्रबोधः प्रयाति वेदान्त निषेवणेन।

of Jaimini dealing with different kinds of meditation helps in the development of concentration. A refined concentrated mind is instrumental in gaining *Brahmán*-knowledge. The *kaniṣṭha adhikārī* knows that Bādarāyaṇa's *Uttara-Mīmāṁsāsūtras* directly deals with Advaita *Brahman*. Here, VB recommends the study of Śaṅkara's commentary to the *sūtra* as sufficient to grasp the Advaitic import, while the role of other forty-two commentaries[32] in the tradition is to help gain a firm knowledge.

The Āgama literature also essentially reveals the Advaitic knowledge. The Āgamic branches of knowledge like Pāñcarātra, Pāśupata and Dakṣiṇamārga are helpful in developing concentration. We add here that the varied devotional literature also reveals the Highest Advaitic Truth. Padmapāda in his *Pañcākṣara-bhāṣya* equates the *namaḥ-śivāya mantra* with the *mahāvākya*, wherein *ma* in *namaḥ* indicates *jīva* and *na* refers to the negation of the superimposed individuality and the word *śivāya* reveals the non-dual *Brahman*. Thus, the *kaniṣṭha adhikārī* gets his conclusion regarding the purport of orthodox systems corroborated from other preceptors.

The *kaniṣṭha adhikārī* surveys the system of Vāmamārga and the heterodox school (Nāstika Darśanas) as well and concludes that the study of these systems should be given up as they are not only mutually contradictory but they also do not agree upon Veda as the primary source of knowledge. Thus, he confines to the literature developed based on the Vedas with its essence as Advaita.

We maintain this fervour of deriving the Advaitic essence in all the branches of knowledge, hence we continue to scrutinize and extend the contention that the Nāstika Darśanas can be considered as a stepping stone leading to Advaita.[33] This approach is adhered to by Śaṅkara in his introductory commentary[34]

---

32 See *SV*, p. 351.

33 See *Advaitic Import of All Darśanas*.

34 पुत्रभार्यादिषु विकलेषु सकलेषु वा अहमेव विकलः सकलो वेति बाह्यधर्मानात्मन्यध्यस्यति ॥

— *Adhyāsa Bhāṣya*

(*Adhyāsa Bhāṣya*) to the *Brahmasūtra*. He states:

> Once it is shown that the sheath of food (*annamayakośa*), which is the first among the five sheaths, is the Self, then the strong attachment of selfhood towards many external selves such as wife, children, friends and relatives gets uprooted.

Annamayakośa is the first door by which one enters into the mansion of emancipation. Thus, in a way great help has been rendered by Cārvākas to those desirous of liberation. Sureśvara shows the acceptance of existence of Self by Bauddhas. He states:

> By declaring the impermanence of the external objects and absence of misery, Buddha strives to put an end to attachment, etc. but not to deny the existence of Self.[35]

Ānandagiri in his *Ṭīkā* to this above statement of *Vārttika* further adds:

> The ultimate import of the words of Buddha is in the highest human end, that is, the cessation of all worldly miseries, through a correct knowledge of the four noble truths.[36]

The Jaina system[37] unfolds from the *annamayakośa* to vital-air-sheath (*prāṇamayakośa*), which is a method validated in the Upaniṣads in arriving at the ultimate Self.

The question remains, if non-dual knowledge is the essence of all scriptures then what is the need for different branches of knowledge. The necessity of varied branches of knowledge seems to be justified in *Sūta Saṁhitā*, according to which:

> Different systems have evolved based on various kinds of aspirants. With regard to the contradictory concepts found in

---

35 अनित्यदुःखशून्यत्वं पदार्थानां ब्रुवन्स्फुटम्।
बुद्धोऽपि रागाद्युच्छित्तौ यतते नाऽऽत्मनिह्नुतौ ॥ — *BUŚBV* 1.4.410

36 पदार्थानामनित्यत्वाद्युक्त्या तद्वैराग्यद्वारा प्रत्यग्ज्ञाने वैनाशिकदर्शनं पर्यवसितम्। यथाऽऽह सर्वज्ञवचनार्थो नाम क्षणिकनैरात्म्यादिचातुरार्थ्यसत्यतत्त्वपरिज्ञानेन सकलसंसारदुःखनिवृत्त्याख्यः परमपुरुषार्थ इति। अतो न तद्दर्शनं नैरात्म्यसाधकं तत्प्रतिपादकाभावेन तदसिद्धेरित्यर्थः ॥

— Ānandagiri *Ṭīkā* on *BUŚBV* 1.4.410

37 See *Advaitic Import of All Darśanas*.

> various systems of philosophy, such concepts must be examined in the light of Vedānta. The distinction seen in different scriptures is not real and is meant for ignorant one's steeped in delusion. Like a man who can direct a cow by offering a bunch of grass, the Lord shows some desired but trivial objects and confers upon him the highest knowledge on maturity.[38]

The same idea of unitary position of various paths is revealed by Puṣpadanta, who says that all waves, low or high, abide in the ocean.[39] Thus, the *kaniṣṭha adhikārī* arrives at non-dual *Brahman* as the consistent content of all the scriptures.

3.2 On the Direct Means to Liberation[40]

The knowledge of non-duality is the content of all branches of knowledge. Liberation, in Advaita Vedānta, is discovery of the Self as of the nature of Existence, Consciousness and Absolute Happiness. The scriptures deal with *karma, upāsanā* and *jñāna* as the means to liberation. The *kaniṣṭha adhikārī* (in *taraṅga* 6) expresses his doubt regarding the direct means to liberation. He questions as to "what is the means to liberation — *jñāna, karma, upāsanā* or both *karma* and *upāsanā*?" The *guru* first reveals the nature of *karma/upāsanā* and shows that *karma* is not the direct means to liberation.

---

[38] अतोऽधिकारिभेदेन मार्गा मानं न संशयः ॥
ईश्वरस्य स्वरूपं च बन्धहेतौ तथैव च ।
जगतः कारणे मुक्तौ ज्ञानादौ च तथैव च ॥
मार्गाणां ये विरुद्धांशा वेदान्तेन विचक्षणाः ॥
तेऽपि मन्दमतीनां च महामोहावृतात्मनाम् ।
वाञ्छामात्रानुगुण्येन प्रवृत्ता न यथार्थतः ॥
दर्शयित्वा तृणं मर्त्यो धावन्तीं गां यथाऽग्रहीत् ॥
दर्शयित्वा तथा क्षुद्रमिष्टं पूर्वं महेश्वरः ।
पश्चात्पाकानुगुण्येन ददाति ज्ञानमुत्तमम् ॥ — *SS* 22.22-26

[39] त्रयी सांख्यं योगः पशुपतिमतं वैष्णवमिति प्रभिन्ने प्रस्थाने परमिदमदः पथ्यमिति च ।
रुचीनां वैचित्र्यादृजुकुटिलनानापथजुषां नृणामेको गम्यस्त्वमसि पयसामर्णव इव ॥
— *Śivamahimnā Stotra* 7

[40] *SV*, pp. 263-67.

KARMA/UPĀSANĀ NOT DIRECT MEANS TO LIBERATION

The *guru* first clarifies that *karma* and *upāsanā* cannot be the direct means to liberation since, bondage is false, like the appearance of "snake" on rope. Just as a "false snake" cannot be destroyed by *karma* or *upāsanā*, the false bondage caused by ignorance cannot be removed by *karma* or *upāsanā*. The following two main reasons are cited by the *guru* to show that *karma* and *upāsanā* cannot serve as the direct means to liberation.

1. The results of *karma* (includes *upāsanā*, a mental action) are non-eternal, and hence incapable of producing an eternal result like liberation. If liberation is a result of action then such liberation will be non-eternal like any other result of action. That the result of actions is ephemeral is known from experience and is also revealed in the scriptures.[41] Thus, liberation that is eternal cannot be the result of *karma*.[42]

2. There are five effects of *karma*[43] and they are origination, attainment, modification, purification and destruction.[44] It is shown here that liberation does not fall under any one of these categories:

---

41 परीक्ष्य लोकान्कर्मचितान्ब्राह्मणो निर्वेदमायान्नास्त्यकृतः कृतेन । — *MU* 1.2.12
तद्यथा कर्मजितो लोकः क्षीयते एवमेवामुत्र पुण्यजितो लोकः क्षीयते । — *CU* 8.1.6

42 भावनाजं फलं यत्स्यात् यच्च स्यात्कर्मणः फलम् ।
न तत् स्थास्न्विति मन्तव्यं द्रविडेषु सङ्गतम् ॥ — *NS* 3.93
अविरोधितया कर्म नाविद्यां विनिवर्तयेत् ।
विद्याऽविद्यां निहन्त्येव तेजस्तिमिरसङ्घवत् ॥ — *Aa* 3

43 चतुर्विधस्यापि कर्मकार्यस्य मुक्तावसम्भवान्न मुक्तेः कर्मकार्यत्वम् ।
अज्ञानहानमात्रत्वान्मुक्तेः कर्म न साधनम् ।
कर्मापमार्ष्टि नाज्ञानं तमसीवोत्थितम् तमः ॥ — *NS* 1.24
उपाद्यमाप्यं संस्कार्यं विकार्यं च क्रियाफलम् ।
नैवं मुक्तिर्यतस्तस्मात् कर्म तस्या न साधनम् ॥ — *NS* 1.53

44 Generally, four results of *karma* are enumerated. Here, VB adds the fifth factor, namely, destruction as a result of *karma*, to avoid the argument that liberation can be the result of destruction of bondage.

(a) *Origination*: That which originates in time is subject to destruction, but liberation (*mokṣa*) as defined by Advaita is eternal (*nitya*). The result of *karma* originates and perishes and hence one is constantly engaged in performance of action whereas, *mokṣa* is that which puts an end to all kinds of actions. The *guru* shows that *mokṣa* does not originate from *śravaṇa* since *śravaṇa* does not produce liberation. He explains that *śravaṇa* is undertaken only to gain the knowledge that "for the eternally free Consciousness Self there is nothing to be attained". By the rise of this knowledge, the delusion "I have to perform" gets removed. Even after the process of *śravaṇa* if one "sees action" such a one is not a seer.[45] Thus, liberation is not a result of action in the form of origination.

(b) *Attainment*: One can reach a destination by the action of movement. Liberation is not in the form of reaching a destination as it happens to be the knowledge of the very Self. Thus, liberation cannot be reached by action.

(c) *Modification*: An object with parts alone is subject to modification. As the Self is eternally liberated and without parts, there is the impossibility of a change like the "bound-self" being modified into the "liberated-self".

(d) *Purification*: Liberation is not attained by the method of purification through performance of *karma*. The process of purification can result in either removal of impurity (*doṣa apanaya*) or enhancement of quality (*guṇa ādhāna*). Liberation is neither the removal of

---

[45] ज्ञानामृतेन तृप्तस्य कृतकृत्यस्य योगिनः ।
न किञ्चिदपि कर्तव्यमस्ति चेन्न स तत्त्ववित् ॥ — Quoted in *SV*, p. 265

विज्ञातब्रह्मतत्वस्य यथापूर्वं न संसृतिः ।
अस्ति चेन्न स विज्ञातब्रह्मभावो बहिर्मुखः ॥ — *VC* 442

impurity nor is it the enhancement of quality. The *guru* shows that the removal of impurity can be known in three ways — i.e. as removal of *mala*, removal of *pāpa* and removal of ignorance. It is shown that in all these three cases of removal of impurity, a purificatory process through performance of action is not expected in the case of a seeker of liberation.

(i) Performance of action, like washing a dirty cloth, is employed in order to remove the impurities from the cloth. It cannot be argued that the purification in the form of removal of impurity in a seeker is the result of *karma* (like washing cloth). A seeker is desirous of the removal of impurity in oneself and not of anything else. On knowing the nature of Self as eternally pure there is no requirement of a purificatory process at all.

(ii) Even though it is known that the elimination of impurity in the form of demerit (*pāpa*) in the mind is the result of *karma*, then also, on enquiry it becomes clear that in the refined mind of a seeker there is no impurity in the form of demerit (since it is falsified). Therefore, purification in the form of removal of impurity like demerit is not a result of action in a seeker.

(iii) Self-ignorance is known to be an impurity which is opposed to Self-knowledge. It cannot be removed by action. For a seeker, purification in the form of removal of ignorance is not the result of *karma* (it is by knowledge).

(iv) Just as a white cloth dipped in a colour dye has its quality enhanced, it can be said that through purification by action, an excellence in the qualities is attained by a seeker. In the knowledge of the nature of Self as attributeless, there is again no need for a purificatory process by action to enhance the quality of Self. Thus, liberation is not a result of any of the above methods of purificatory action.

(e) *Destruction*: Just as striking the pot with a stick or a hammer results in the destruction of a pot, the action of a seeker results in some kind of a destruction of some object. Here, one does not desire to destroy another object but wants to remove bondage. Such a bondage, the *guru* says, is absent in the Self but gets falsely superimposed on the Self. The superimposed bondage cannot be destroyed by action. It can be removed only by knowledge. Therefore, liberation in the form of destruction of an object by means of action is not sought. Thus, it is revealed that *karma/upāsanā* is not the direct means to liberation.

REFUTATION OF AIKABHAVIKAVĀDA

In this connection it is imperative to note that *karma* as the direct means to liberation is a widely prevalent view and the same has been taken up while dealing with the *prayojana* of the text *Vicārasāgara* in the second *taraṅga*. This school of thought is refuted by VB to reinforce the Advaitic position that knowledge is the direct means to liberation. We shall, thus, deal elaborately with the views of one such school known as Aikabhavikavādin,[46] who claims *karma* as the direct means to liberation.

Unlike the Advaitins, the Aikabhavikavādins consider bondage as real and accordingly state that knowledge cannot be the solution for removal of a "real" bondage. So, according to Aikabhavikavādins, one can be free from real bondage only through *karma*. Hence the performance of *karma* is compulsory. *Karma* is classified as obligatory duties (*vihita karma*) and prohibited actions (*pratiṣiddha karma*) in Vedas which are capable of producing

[46] We find the refutation of Aikabhavikavādin by Śaṅkara in his *avatārikā* to *Taittirīya Śīkṣāvallī*.

adr̥ṣṭa phala. *Vihita karma* is further classified as compulsory daily actions (*nitya karma*), compulsory occasional actions (*naimittika karma*), desire-prompted actions (*kāmya karma*) and propitiatory or compensatory actions (*prāyaścitta karma*). *Nitya* and *naimittika karmas* are obligatory duties whose non-performance results in a special sin (*pratyavāya pāpa*). *Kāmya karmas* are desire-prompted action, performed for fulfilment of personal desires. *Prāyaścitta karma* is compensatory action, performed to compensate the non-performance of *nitya–naimittika karmas*. Thus, there are five kinds of *karmas* including *pratiṣiddha karma*.

Aikabhavikavādins propose to establish that *karma* is the direct means to liberation and Advaitins show that *karma* cannot be the direct means to liberation.

(1) *Aikabhavikavādin*

> A seeker should avoid *pratiṣiddha* and *kāmya karmas* in the present birth, since *pratiṣiddha* results in lower births and *kāmya* is instrumental for higher births. By avoiding *pratiṣiddha* and *kāmya*, a seeker should perform only *nitya karma* and *naimittika karma*.[47] In doing so, *pratyavāya pāpa* can be avoided and further merit (*puṇya*) is also not accrued, since the performance of *nitya–naimittika karmas* does not yield *puṇya*. Thus, *puṇya* and *pāpa* are nullified resulting in liberation without knowledge.

Advaitin

> Even if one does not perform *pratiṣiddha* and *kāmya karmas* so as to avoid the future births and continue to perform only *nitya–naimittika karmas* still the cause of future birth is not annihilated. It is improper to say that the performance of obligatory duties do not produce any result since it is contradictory to Vedic statement that

---

[47] अपरे तु ऐकभविकन्यायेन आत्मज्ञानमन्तरेणापि निषिद्धकाम्ययोरननुष्ठानात् च न आगामिकर्मोत्पादः। विद्यमानस्य च उपभोगेन क्षयात् सकलकर्मोच्छेदलक्षणमपवर्गम् आहुः॥

— *Vedāntakalpalatikā*, p. 7

enumerate fruit for performance of any kind of action. This has been clearly established in commentaries by resorting to logical reasoning.[48] If the result like *svarga* is not accepted as the consequence of performance of *nitya-naimittaka karma*s, then an action prescribed by the scripture without result will become redundant. Therefore, performance of *nitya–naimittika karma*s definitely yields results like heaven, which is the cause of future births and not liberation. Again, it cannot be argued that by the performance of obligatory duties one avoids *pratyavāya pāpa* that may be incurred due to the non-performance of obligatory duties, as it is fallacious. It is a logical fallacy since absence (non-performance) cannot produce a positive entity (*pāpa*)[49] and such an argument contradicts scriptural statements.[50] It is illogical to say that from a non-existent entity an existent thing arises.[51]

(2) *Aikabhavikavādin*

The performance of *prāyaścitta karma* which is of two kinds, viz. general compensatory actions (*sādhāraṇa prāyaścitta*) and specific compensatory actions (*asādhāraṇa prāyaścitta*), helps in the destruction of all *pāpa*. *Sādhāraṇa prāyaścitta* helps to remove *pāpa*s accumulated due to the performance of prohibited actions in countless past births and the actions done in the present birth unknowingly that may yield *pāpa*. *Asādhāraṇa prāyaścitta* destroys *pāpa*s acquired by the performance of specific prohibited actions done in the current birth. A seeker should perform *sādhāraṇa prāyaścitta*

---

48 यज्ञ दानं तपः इत्येतत् त्रिविधं कर्म न त्याज्यं न त्यक्तव्यम्।
कार्यं करणीयम् एव तत्। — *BGŚB* 18.5

49 अकुर्वन्विहितं कर्म इति। अन्यथा हि अभावाद्भावोत्पत्तिरिति सर्वप्रमाणव्याकोप इति।
— *TUŚB, Śīkṣāvallī Avatārikā.*

50 कथं असतः सज्जायेतेति। — *CU* 6.2.2.
ना सतो विद्यते भावो न भावो विद्यते सतः। *BG* II.16.

51 पूर्वोपचितदुरितेभ्यः प्राप्यमाणायाः प्रत्यवायक्रियाया नित्याकरणं लक्षणमिति शतृप्रत्ययस्य।
— *TUŚB, Śīkṣāvallī Avatārikā.*

to destroy the *pāpa* of countless past births, i.e. the *sañcita pāpa* and the possible *āgāmī pāpa*. The *asādhāraṇa prāyaścitta* is to be performed for the removal of *pāpa* that one may incur because of specific negative actions performed in the current birth.

The actions in the form of *sādhāraṇa prāyaścitta* enjoined in the scriptures give twofold benefits of being both compensatory action as well as desire-prompted action. When the prescribed compensatory actions are performed to accomplish personal desires it is known as *kāmya karma* and when the prescribed compensatory actions are performed by the seekers with no personal desire then the actions in the form of *prāyaścitta karma* destroy the demerits. Just as the Advaitin states that when the actions are performed with a desire, they become the cause of bondage whereas when the same actions are performed without the expectation of results, they become the cause of mental purity and thus leading to liberation. Likewise, the prescribed compensatory actions too possess the dual benefit of being desire-prompted actions or compensatory actions. Therefore, the seekers should perform *sādhāraṇa prāyaścitta* by which the *sañcita pāpa* is destroyed without the aid of Self-knowledge.

Advaitin

It is not possible to destroy the entire demerit by the performance of *sādhāraṇa* and *asādhāraṇa prāyaścitta* since the varied demerits cannot be destroyed simultaneously by the *prāyaścitta karma*s in one birth. The actions classified as *sādhāraṇa prāyaścitta* in the scriptures help to purify the mind that becomes instrumental for the rise of knowledge later and hence such actions are said to be the remover of demerits secondarily and not primarily.

The dual benefit of actions as held by Advaitins cannot be cited here since the suggestion of performance of compensatory actions to nullify the demerits in the past births mentioned above by the opponent refers to the performed actions in the past that can be removed only by the experience of the result. The Advaitins speak of dual benefit of action that are yet to be performed or the change of mental attitude towards the action at the time of performance. Thus, in the course of performing a desire-prompted action when the performer renounces the desire for its result, the same action after the completion of its performance becomes the cause of mental purity. The demerits accrued in the past births can be destroyed only by experience.

Moreover, the destruction of all demerits simultaneously and directly is only through the knowledge of *Brahman* and not by the performance of compensatory actions in one birth. It is declared in the scriptures thus — "the result of action of this one get dissipated when that One is comprehended as Self" (*MU* 2.2.8), "similarly all results of actions are burnt by the fire of knowledge" (*BG* IV.37). Also, the above argument of the opponent is with regard to the destruction of *sañcita pāpa* alone, there is still the continuation of *sañcita puṇya* that is the cause of future births.

(3) *Aikabhavikavādin*

The results of *sañcita pāpa* (result of *pratiṣiddha karma*s in past births) and *sañcita puṇya* (result of *kāmya karma*s in past births) become fruitless by not desiring for their results. Just as the Advaitin claims that while performing the desire-prompted actions if one gives up the desire for its result then that action does not yield results like *svarga* due to the absence of desire. Similarly, even though in past births *kāmya karma* was performed with a desire for its result, due to the absence of such a desire in the present birth the experience of *sañcita puṇya* can be avoided.

Advaitin

Karma in the form of seed produces two kinds of sprouts, viz. invisible result (*adṛṣṭa*) and latent impressions (*vāsanā*). Result of righteous act (*dharma* or *puṇya*) and result of unrighteous act (*adharma* or *pāpa*) are known as *adṛṣṭa*. Noble actions give rise to noble impressions which in turn produce *puṇya*. Ignoble actions give rise to ignoble impressions which produce *pāpa*. The noble impressions become the cause for the performance of righteous actions resulting in *puṇya* that in turn yields pleasurable experience. In the same manner, the ignoble impressions are the cause for the performance of unrighteous actions which result in *pāpa*, giving painful experiences. Thus, *adṛṣṭa* and *vāsanā* are the two sprouts of *karma,* the seed.

Here, the sprout in the form of *vāsanā* gets destroyed by *prāyaścitta,* as suggested by the opponent earlier. The unrighteous actions resulting in ignoble impressions can be destroyed by means of noble association. The righteous actions resulting in noble impressions gets destroyed by ignoble association. The impressions that propel the instinctive tendencies get destroyed by the *puruṣārtha* prescribed in the scriptures.

But, the sprout in the form of *adṛṣṭa* does not get destroyed without yielding its result since it is well known that "without yielding its result an action does not get exhausted" (*sva phalam adatvā naiva karma kṣīyate*). Thus, while an ignorant person has to exhaust *karma* only through experience, an enlightened person completely uproots the *karmaphala* to be experienced since for such a one, the doership, action and its result are absolutely non-existent. Like a dream, these are imagined due to ignorance and ignorance is contradictory to knowledge. Hence, the imagined *karma* due to ignorance is destroyed by knowledge. Just as the dream objects are not obtained on waking up, *tripuṭī* manifesting due to ignorance will be absent on rise of knowledge. Such a destruction is not possible without knowledge.

Moreover, if just by the absence of desire the past accumulated result of actions does not fructify, then *saṅkalpa* of *Īśvara* in the form, "without the experience of the result, action caused by ignorance cannot be destroyed" (*phalabhogamantarā ajñānāṁ karma na naśyati*) would be false.[52] Also if the result of action can be avoided by mere desire then painful results due to performance of prohibited actions can also be avoided by desire which is illogical. Thus, the fruit of actions performed has to be reaped.

The Advaitin's position of the possibility of modification of *kāmya karma* to *nitya karma*[53] by mere desire cannot be cited by the Aikabhavikavādin. This transformation of action held by the Advaitin is during the performance of *kāmya karma*, whereas, the Aikabhavikavādin suggests the avoidance of result of *kāmya karma* by desire that has already been performed in the past births. Such an argument is unsound. By the application of *saṁyoga-pṛthaktva-nyāya*, Advaitin states that an action can yield twofold results. When a performer does not seek *puṇya* such an action produces mental purity (*citta-śuddhi*). At the time of performance of the action if one does not desire for its specific result it does not produce *puṇya*. This is the contention of the Advaitin. But Aikabhavikavādin states that posterior to the action performed, if one desires to avoid its results, the performed action does not yield result. This view is illogical. Since, whether one desires for the result or not, a performed action will certainly yield its result based on the law of *karma*. Also, the *niṣkāma*

---

52 सत्यकामः सत्यसङ्कल्पः । — *CU* 8.1.5 and 8.7.1. This statement would also be falsified.

53 यथा च स्वर्गादिकामार्थिनः अग्निहोत्रादिकर्मलक्षणधर्मानुष्ठानाय आहिताग्नेः काम्ये एव अग्निहोत्रादि प्रवृत्तस्य सामि कृते विनष्टेऽपि कामे तदेव अग्निहोत्राद्यनुतिष्ठतोऽपि न तत्काम्याग्निहोत्रादि भवति ।

— *BGŚB, Avatārikā to BG.*

karma can even be instrumental in rise of *Brahman*-knowledge, only if it is followed by the practice of direct means to knowledge in the form of *śravaṇa,* etc.

(4) *Aikabhavikavādin (Sub-school 1)*

Mere desire cannot annihilate *sañcita pāpa* and *sañcita puṇya*. The entire *sañcita karma* collectively results in one more birth wherein all the *sañcita* is exhausted and one gains liberation thereafter.

Aikabhavikavādin (Sub-school 2)

There is difficulty in the above view, since the entire *sañcita* cannot be destroyed in one birth, the varied *karma*s have to be exhausted in varied bodies and in different conditions. A seeker can exhaust the *sañcita* in one future birth simultaneously assuming many bodies like a *yogī.*

Aikabhavikavādin (Sub-school 3)

The *sañcita karma* cannot result in one future birth as mentioned above. The *sañcita puṇya* alone results in one future birth which is exhausted by simultaneous assumption of varied bodies. In such a future birth, the seeker does not experience even a bit of pain. In the current birth, the seeker exhausts *sañcita pāpa* by the experience of pain caused by the performance of *nitya-naimittika karma.* Thus, without the performance of *prāyaścitta, nitya-naimittika karma* by itself can lead the seeker to liberation. Therefore, *nitya-naimittika karma* has to be performed compulsorily.

Advaitin

One cannot say that *sañcita pāpa* can be annihilated through the pain experienced during the performance of obligatory duties as argued above. The past accumulated negative actions are varied and their results ought to be exhausted in different ways which cannot be destroyed by difficulties involved in mere performance of prescribed duties.

Moreover, the *sañcita karma* is varied and cannot be exhausted in one or two births. It is also impossible to assume varied bodies simultaneously to exhaust varied *karmas* like a *yogī*. Even a *yogī* with *siddhis* cannot attain liberation without knowledge. Thus, the sub-schools of Aikabhavikavādin are also negated who provide options for exhaustion of *sañcita karma*.

ROLE OF NITYA KARMA

It may not be out of place here to refer to the role of prescribed duties (*nitya karma*) that is considered as the means to liberation by the Mīmāṁsā School. In his commentary on the *Bhujyu-Brāhmaṇa* of *Bṛhadāraṇyaka Upaniṣad* (3.3), Śaṅkara dismisses the Mīmāṁsaka's argument who state that liberation is the result of *nitya karma*. The Mīmāṁsakas argue that *mokṣa* is the result (*phala*) of *nitya karma* and it is validated by the scriptural statements. According to the Mīmāṁsakas, if *phala* is not mentioned while enjoining certain obligatory duties in *karmakāṇḍa*, then *phala* should be supplemented based on certain norms. The two norms presented by the Mīmāṁsaka are as follows:

1. There is a general statement in Veda, viz. *karmaṇā pitṛlokaḥ*. Based on this general statement, when *karma* is described without *phala*, *phala* should be understood as *pitṛlokaḥ*. This is known as *karmaṇā pitṛloka-nyāya*.
2. When there are certain *karmas* prescribed without the mention of *phala*, then one should presume *svargaloka* as *phala* as it is desired by all. This law is applied in the case of a ritual called *viśvajit yāga* so it gets the name *viśvajit nyāya*.

Vedas do not mention about *phala* for the *nitya karma*. In such cases, the Mīmāṁsakas argue that either of these above two laws should be applied. The first law, *karmaṇā pitṛloka-nyāya* can be applied only to those rituals that occur in the Vedic portion mentioning *karmaṇā pitṛlokaḥ*. *Nitya karma* does not fall within this domain and hence the first law is inapplicable. So, the second law is to be applied. Here, *svarga* as the *phala* is added in order to attract *adhikārīs* to perform the ritual, since, in the absence of the mention of *phala* one does not act. The *viśvajit nyāya* applies to those who are desirous of attaining heaven. But in the case of *nitya karma, phala* cannot be based on the above two laws and hence the Mīmāṁsakas conclude that the result of *nitya karma* must be liberation.

Śaṅkara dismisses the above argument of the Mīmāṁsakas stating that once *phala* is visualized then such statements should fall under either the first law or the second law as suggested by the Mīmāṁsakas. Either of these laws does not prove eternal liberation as a result of *karma*. The Mīmāṁsakas counter argue that just as the Advaitins claim liberation as a result of knowledge, it can be said that liberation is a result of *nitya karma* that produces invisible result (*adr̥ṣṭa phala*), which has the capacity to destroy ignorance. Śaṅkara reminds that, that which can be explained through visible result (*dr̥ṣṭa phala*), in such cases, visualization of *adr̥ṣṭa phala* is futile. As in the case of *vrīhīn āvahanti*, the separation of grain from the husk is a *dr̥ṣṭa phala* and visualizing an *adr̥ṣṭa phala* in this case is redundant. Likewise, ignorance is removed by knowledge, which is *a dr̥ṣṭa phala*, and it is improper to explain it as an *adr̥ṣṭa phala* of *nitya karma*. Thus, *nitya karma* resulting in liberation remains unproved. Hence, a seeker has to give up action and take to *śravaṇa*, which is the means for knowledge and knowledge alone is the direct means to liberation.

DOCTRINE OF JÑĀNA-KARMA SAMUCCAYAVĀDIN

Having shown the *kaniṣṭha adhikārī* that neither *karma* nor *upāsanā* results in liberation, now the *guru* (in *taraṅga* 6) puts forth the argument of the Samuccayavādin.[54] He then dismisses such a view and establishes the Advaitic standpoint of knowledge as the sole means to liberation. The doctrine of combination of knowledge and action is primarily held by the Mīmāṁsakas and

[54] *SV*, pp. 267-74.

Ekaśāstravādins. They advocate the combinations in the form of *karma* as either subordinate to knowledge (*jñāna-pradhāna samuccaya*), or as principal to knowledge (*karma-pradhāna samuccaya*) or *karma* and *jñāna* in the same footing (*sama-pradhāna samuccaya*). Here knowledge is accepted as the means to liberation but not as the *only* means to liberation. Knowledge combined with *karma* alone is said to be the means to liberation. The Samuccayavādin holds that by any one of these three possibilities, *samuccaya* has to be maintained. It is concluded that since *jñāna* by itself cannot result in liberation, performance of action as enjoined in the scriptures is compulsory for the purpose of liberation. The impossibility of combining *karma* with *jñāna* has been refuted in various ways and in different contexts by Śaṅkara and other preceptors. Sureśvara in his *Naiṣkarmyasiddhi*[55] states that *karma* is not competent to remove ignorance, since it originates from ignorance. Knowledge alone is inimical to ignorance, like light to darkness.

ARGUMENTS OF JÑĀNA-KARMA SAMUCCAYAVĀDIN

Here, the *guru* first presents the view of the Samuccayavādin.

1. Just as a bird requires both the wings to fly and reach a destination, a seeker requires both *karma* (includes *upāsanā*) and *jñāna* to attain liberation.[56]

2. It is said that "real" *pāpa* gets destroyed by seeing the "bridge" (*setu darśana* at Rāmeśvaram). A person who desires to remove *pāpa* should visit the place with devotion and faith. Such a one seeing the bridge with devotion and faith succeeds in the destruction of *pāpa*. In the same manner, for the knowledge of *Brahman* to result in liberation both *karma* and *upāsanā* are mandatory.

3. Some consider *karma* and *upāsanā* as successive means to liberation. Just as by watering the plant grows into a tree

---

55 कर्माज्ञानसमुत्थत्वान्नालं मोहापनुत्तये। सम्यग्ज्ञानं विरोध्यस्य तामिस्रस्यांशुमानिव॥ — *NS* 1.35

56 उभाभ्यामेव पक्षाभ्यां यथा खे पक्षिणो गतिः।
तथा वै ज्ञानकर्माभ्यां नराणां मुक्तिरिष्यते॥ — *Mīmāṁsā Mañjarī*, p. 179

and also yields fruits, *karma* and *upāsanā* not only are the means to give rise to knowledge but also are the means for liberation, which is the result of knowledge.

4. The performance of *karma* and *upāsanā* should continue even after the attainment of liberation in order to protect the risen knowledge. If an enlightened person gives up *karma* and *upāsanā*, then just as even a strong tree dries up due to absence of water, an enlightened person will also lose the knowledge gained. By the non-performance of prescribed actions one may incur *pāpa* and by the non-performance of *upāsanā*, the mind of an enlightened person may be subject to distractions. In such a mind, the knowledge will be unstable and hence performance of *karma* and *upāsanā* should be continued. Thus, *karma* and *upāsanā* become the causes of protection of risen knowledge. The Samuccayavādin thus concludes that *karma*, *upāsanā* and *jñāna* together are the means to liberation and *karma* and *upāsanā* are to be continued even after the rise of knowledge in order to protect it.

REFUTATION OF JÑĀNA-KARMA SAMUCCAYAVĀDIN

The *guru* then proceeds to refute the above views of Samuccayavādin in the following manner:

1. The analogy of a bird in this context is inappropriate. No doubt a bird requires both the wings to reach a destination but they are not mutually opposed to each other. But in this context, knowledge is opposed to *karma*/*upāsanā* and hence they are not to be followed simultaneously.

2. The example of *setu-darśana* also is not apt. *Setu-darśana* is not the cause of direct result (*dṛṣṭa phala*) since the result of removal of *pāpa* is not perceived directly. The knowledge of the destruction of *pāpa* resulting from *setu-darśana* is gained from the scriptures. Therefore, just as the performance of sacrifice is the cause for gaining heaven i.e. *adṛṣṭa phala*, similarly, *setu-darśana* is the cause of

removal of *pāpa* which is also *adr̥ṣṭa phala*. That which gives rise to *adr̥ṣṭa phala* has to be performed along with the prescribed rules and regulations; in this case, *setu-darśana* is to be adhered to with faith and devotion. *Brahman*-knowledge is not an *adr̥ṣṭa phala* but a *dr̥ṣṭa phala*, and hence it does not require the performance of other means to yield its result. Just as, by the mere knowledge of "rope" the erroneous cognition of "snake" is removed which is a direct result, so also, by the knowledge of the substratum there is the direct result in the form of removal of error. If the result of knowledge, i.e. liberation, is also claimed to be an *adr̥ṣṭa phala* like gaining heaven then it contradicts Vedic statements like *na tasya prāṇā utkrāmanti brahmaiva san brahmāpyeti* (*BU* 4.4.6) and *atra brahma samaśnute* (*BU* 4.4.7). Moreover, if it is accepted that liberation is attaining a special place like heaven, then liberation will be non-eternal. By the application of *tuṣyatu-durjana-nyāya*, even if liberation consists in attaining a special place, then also, the means is knowledge alone and not *karma* or *upāsanā*. That which is revealed by the scriptures has to be accepted in keeping with the scriptures. Scripture reveals that liberation is a result of mere knowledge.[57]

3. The example of a "tree" cited by the opponent is also inappropriate. Even if watering is the cause of the tree's growth and sustenance, it cannot be the cause of production of fruits. That is, an old tree is watered for the sake of protection and not for yielding fruits. Water as

---

[57] भिद्यते हृदयग्रन्थिः छिद्यन्ते सर्वसंशयाः । क्षीयन्ते चास्य कर्माणि तस्मिन् दृष्टे परावरे ॥ — *MU* 2.2.8
यदा चर्मवदाकाशं वेष्टयिष्यन्ति मानवाः । तदा देवमविज्ञाय दुःखस्यान्तो भविष्यति ॥ — *SU* 6.20
तमेव विदित्वाऽतिमृत्युमेति । — *SU* 3.8
तरति शोकमात्मवित् । — *CU* 7.1.3
तमेवं विदित्वानमृत इह भवति । — *Puruṣa Sūkta*
ज्ञात्वा देवं मुच्यते सर्वपाशैः । — *SU* 2.15
ज्ञात्वा देवं सर्वपाशापहानिः । — *SU* 1.11

such is not the cause of production of fruits but only nourishes the tree that yields fruits. In the same manner, *karma* and *upāsanā* are the causes for rise of knowledge; but not liberation. Therefore, prior to the rise of knowledge, *karma* and *upāsanā* are practised for gaining purity and concentration of mind.[58] These *sādhanā*s need not be practised after the rise of knowledge or for the sake of liberation.

4. *Karma* and *upāsanā* are not required for the protection of risen knowledge as claimed by the opponent. In the consciousness conditioned by the mind, the result is in the form of rise of thought-mode (*vṛtti*) that "I am unassociated *Brahman*" which destroys ignorance. Having destroyed the ignorance, this thought-mode subsides like the herbs (*kathakareṇu*) without the aid of *karma* or *upāsanā* as the purpose of *Brahman*-knowledge is accomplished. It is absurd to suggest that *karma* and *upāsanā* are required for the protection of knowledge, since for their very performance one need to gain knowledge relating to *karma* or *upāsanā* and not *Brahman*-knowledge. By the application of the maxim that on rise of the second thought the first thought gets destroyed, similarly, on the rise of *Brahman*-knowledge, the knowledge of *karma* or *upāsanā* gets destroyed since they are opposed to *Brahman*-knowledge. Thus, the practice of *karma* or *upāsanā* for protection of knowledge is illogical.

Karma and *upāsanā* cannot coexist along with knowledge. *Karma* can be performed by a person who has the knowledge that self is different from the body. *Karma* is also performed to enjoy the result after the fall of the body. Therefore, the cause of *karma* is based on the knowledge of self as different from the body, and also it gives rise to the expressions like "I am the doer, enjoyer".

---

[58] चित्तस्य शान्तये कर्म न तु वस्तूपलब्धये ।
वस्तुसिद्धिर्विचारेण नान्यथा कर्मकोटिभिः ॥ — *VC* 11

An enlightened person gains the knowledge of the unassociated Self free from merits and demerits. This Self-knowledge does not instigate one to perform *karma*. Thus, *karma* or *upāsanā* being opposed to knowledge cannot be simultaneously practised as claimed by the Samuccayavādin. This combination is also impossible due to the fact that while *karma* results in non-eternal fruit, knowledge results in the discovery of eternal liberation.

There are instances of Janaka, Kr̥ṣṇa and others who are known to be enlightened *gr̥hastha*s in whose case there seems to be a combination of knowledge and action. It has to be understood that activities performed by such enlightened ones, only bear the semblance of action (*karmābhāsa*). Since they perform action without the notion of agency as "I am the doer" they do not yield any result. Thus in the case of the enlightened ones there is no combination of action and knowledge.[59]

ROLE OF KARMA AND UPĀSANĀ ACCORDING TO ADVAITA

If *karma* and *upāsanā* are not the direct means to liberation then the question remains as to its functional utility and role in the pursuit of liberation. In the course of the dialogue the *guru* reveals the role of *sādhanā*s to the *kaniṣṭha adhikārī* (in *taraṅga* 6). First, the *guru* states that one with a desire to attain liberation should give up intense attachment, greed, hatred, desire for sensual enjoyment, etc. since they are the thought-mode (*vr̥tti*) of *rājasa* and *tāmasa* kinds. The *rājasa–tāmasa vr̥tti*s are opposed to knowledge and hence they need to be uprooted in the initial stages of one's spiritual pursuit. The *guru* highlights its importance by saying that without the elimination of *rājasa–tāmasa vr̥tti*s, even if one takes up to Self-enquiry, it will not result in the rise of knowledge. The *guru* then points out that *viveka, vairāgya, śamādiṣaṭkasampatti* and *mumukṣutva* are the fourfold means to knowledge, of which *viveka* is the primary means because of which alone one gains the other three means. The fourfold disciplines here are said to be the remote means (*bahiraṅga sādhanā*) to knowledge. The devotion

---

[59] See also Section 6.3 of Chapter 6.

towards the teacher and *Īśvara* is also said to be the intermediary means (*avāntara sādhanā*) to attain knowledge. The proximate means (*antaraṅga sādhanā*) to knowledge is said to be *śravaṇa*, etc.[60]

In the first *taraṅga*, while establishing the *anubandha-catuṣṭaya* of the text *Vicārasāgara*, VB differentiates *antaraṅga sādhanā* or proximate means from *bahiraṅga sādhanā* or remote means.[61] The *sādhanacatuṣṭayasampatti* is classified as proximate means to knowledge. Whereas, *karma* and *upāsanā* are said to be the remote means to knowledge. Remote means is defined as that which contributes to the refinement of the mind but does not serve as the (direct) means either to *śravaṇa* or to *Brahman*-knowledge. Thus, actions like sacrifices, charity and austerity are the remote means. If the same actions are performed to gain material benefits alone, then, they become the causes for bondage and do not result in mental purity. On the other hand, if the same actions are performed without being anxious of the results, they refine the mind. Thus, *niṣkāma karma* gives rise to the desire for knowledge, and thereby serves as a means to the rise of *Brahman*-knowledge. Further, Śaṅkara in his commentary on *Chāndogya Upaniṣad* mentions that various forms of meditation and worship result in purity of mind.[62] Hence, *upāsanā* also falls under the remote means to knowledge.[63]

So far, it is has been said that the knowledge alone is the direct means to liberation, as a response to the doubt raised by the *kaniṣṭha adhikārī* with regard to the direct means to liberation.

3.3 Nature of Bondage

To understand the position that knowledge is the direct means to liberation, it is important to examine the nature of bondage

60 See sub-heading "Remote and Proximate Means" under Section 2.6 of Chapter 2. Here, the *guru* presents the *sādhanā*s differently to the *kaniṣṭha adhikārī*.

61 See also Section 2.6 of Chapter 2.

62 तान्येतान्युपासनानि सत्त्वशुद्धिकरत्वेन वस्तुतत्त्वावभासकत्वात् अद्वैतज्ञानोपकारकाणि ।
— *CUŚB, Avatārikā.*

63 See Section 6.3 of Chapter 6.

according to Advaita. Hence, we shall proceed to analyse the nature of bondage as discussed while establishing the *prayojana* of the text *Vicārasāgara* in the second *taraṅga.* It is shown that bondage is an error, which is caused by ignorance of the nature of the Self. Thus, Self-ignorance which is the cause of erroneous bondage can be removed only by Self-knowledge. Hence, the Advaitin claims that knowledge alone is the means to liberation.

Knowledge has twofold benefits: the direct benefit is the destruction of ignorance and the indirect benefit is the removal of errors generated by ignorance. The ignorance and error have a cause–effect relation and by the maxim "removal of cause results in removal of effect" (*nimittāpāye naimittikāpāyaḥ*), Advaita contends that the unreal bondage caused by unreal ignorance is destroyed on the rise of knowledge. Thus, the nature of knowledge is defined in contradistinction to the nature of error.[64] According to Advaita, ignorance is the cause of error that leads to bondage. So, we shall now deal with the nature of error to understand the nature of bondage.

NATURE OF ERROR

Error is defined as *atasmin tadbuddhiḥ,* where *atasmin* refers to the absence of "snake" in the rope in the three periods of time and *tadbuddhi* means the apparent experience of "snake" (in rope). The "snake-object" which is external and the "snake-knowledge" that arises in the mind internally are both known as *adhyāsa*. So, error is of two kinds — object-error (*arthādhyāsa*) and object-knowledge-error (*jñānādhyāsa*). The false object seen outside, like the "snake", which is the content of the false knowledge expressed as "there is snake" is known as *arthādhyāsa* and the false knowledge related to the false-object that arises in the mind is *jñānādhyāsa*. This *jñānādhyāsa* is also known as false-knowledge (*mithyā jñāna*) or delusion (*bhrānti*). *Arthādhyāsa* is of two kinds, viz. substance-superimposition (*svarūpādhyāsa*) and property (relation or

---

[64] यत् स्वविषयीभूतवस्तुनिष्ठा अज्ञानतत्कार्याध्यासनिवर्तकत्वमिति। भ्रमज्ञानविषयीभूतमिथ्यावस्तु तद्विषयकभ्रान्तिज्ञानं चाध्यास इत्युच्यते।
— *SV*, p. 44.

association)-superimposition (*saṁsargādhyāsa*). The superimposition of the nature of an entity on another is substance-superimposition like the superimposition of ignorance and its effects on the Self. The superimposition of property or a relation is property-superimposition like the relation of identity (*tādātmya sambandha*) between the Self and the body. In the example of rope-snake, the substance-superimposition is expressed as "snake is" and property-superimposition is expressed as "snake is poisonous" (see *fig.* 3.1).

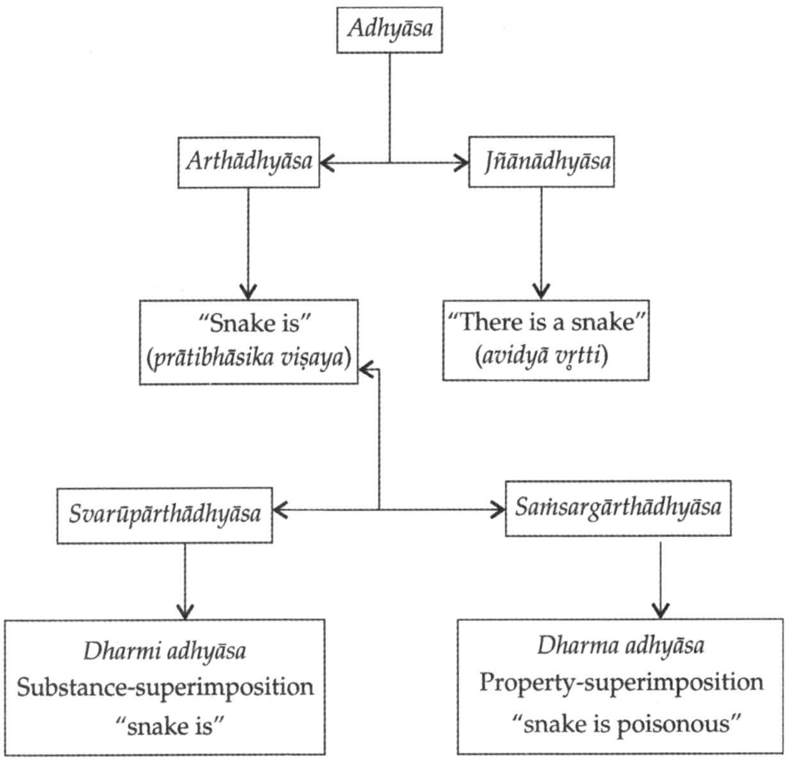

fig. 3.1: Expression of substance-superimposition and property-superimposition

Thus, *adhyāsa* (error) is said to be an effect of ignorance which is said to be the cause of bondage. Since bondage is an error, the solution for its removal is knowledge alone.

PAÑCA ADHYĀSA SĀMAGRĪ

An opponent states that an error is possible only when the following five conditions (either one or all of them) are fulfilled (three defects and two conditions) and shows that bondage claimed as error does not fulfil any of these conditions and, therefore, the opponent concludes that bondage is real and knowledge is not the solution for removal of bondage. The five conditions are described:

1. ***Pramātṛdoṣa*** — Defect in the perceiver in the form of greed, fear, etc. is instrumental for an erroneous perception.

2. ***Pramāṇadoṣa*** — Defect in the instrument of perception like an eye affected by cataract, jaundice, etc. may be the cause of erroneous perception.

   But for the Advaitin, the very perceiver (*pramātā*) and the instruments of perception (*pramāṇa*) are superimposed (erroneous) entities due to ignorance; the posterior effect cannot serve as a cause of its prior phenomenon.

3. ***Prameyadoṣa*** — Error involves similarity in the object perceived along with past impressions. A "snake" is not superimposed on a "shell" and "silver" is not superimposed on "rope". The "shell" is seen as "silver" because of similar feature like brilliance and "rope" is seen as "snake" because of similar features like curve, length and thickness. This defect cannot be accounted for in the case of Self and non-self as they are known to be opposed like light and darkness by the Advaitin.

4. ***Saṁskāra*** — There is a possibility of seeing "silver" in shell or "snake" in rope, due to the impressions or *saṁskāra* caused by the past experience of real silver and real snake. Thus, empirical experience is a presupposition for an apparent (erroneous) cognition. But according to Advaita, *Brahman* alone is the only reality and hence there is no possibility of prior experience of a real bondage to be superimposed later.

5. ***Adhiṣṭhānaviśeṣājñānaṁ tatsāmānyajñānaṁ ca*** — In an erroneous perception of "silver" in "shell", one says "this is silver"; the general aspect "this is" is known but the specific aspect "shell" is not known. Therefore, the general knowledge of the substratum and ignorance of the specific feature are the causes of error. According to Advaita, *Brahman* is devoid of features — general or specific. Thus, knowledge of the general feature and ignorance of specific feature does not arise. Moreover, *Brahman* is self-evident Consciousness opposed to ignorance, and hence there can be no ignorance of the specific feature of *Brahman*. Therefore, bondage as an error in *Brahman*-substratum is untenable and knowledge of *Brahman* as liberation is illogical.

ERROR: ITS MECHANISM

VB dismisses these arguments by showing the possibility of error even in the absence of the above-mentioned three defects and also points out to the existence of the above dismissed two conditions.

1. ***Pramātṛdoṣa refuted*** — According to the opponent, the cause of error is the defect in the perceiver in the form of greed or fear. But an error can take place even when the perceiver is not subject to greed or fear. A dispassionate person who is not greedy may also mistake shell as "silver". Hence defect in the perceiver is not a necessary condition for erroneous cognition.

2. ***Pramāṇadoṣa refuted*** — Error is possible even in the absence of defect in instruments of perception. For instance, in the case of perception of a "dome-shaped blue-sky" there is the universal experience of dome-shape even by the defect-free eyes. In fact, this example of "dome-shaped blue sky" can also be cited to show that none of the defects mentioned by the opponent is a condition for error. The blue sky is perceived in the absence of defect in the perceiver,

instrument of perception and absence of similarity.

3. ***Prameyadoṣa refuted*** — Similarity need not be a definite condition for erroneous cognition, which was mentioned above as *prameyadoṣa*. If similarity is considered as a necessary condition for error then superimpositions like "yellow conch", "bitter jaggery" cannot be explained.

   Objection: Yellowness is not a superimposition on conch, but it is because of jaundice or of the anointment of yellow substance in the eyes.

   Advaitin: The workmanship of embedded gems in a pot by a goldsmith is not only experienced by the goldsmith but by everyone. In the case of yellow conch, the yellowness in the conch is not experienced by all but one with defective instrument of perception. The yellow substance in one's eyes cannot pervade and anoint the conch.

   Objection: If one observes a bird flying initially close-by and then farther, the direction of the flying bird can be known even from a distance. The direction of the bird farther away cannot be easily traced by one who has not observed its movements initially. In the same way, the yellow substance in a person's eye anoints the conch and that yellowness is experienced by that person easily and not by others.

   Advaitin: The movement of the bird in the distance can be indicated to another by pointing out with finger but this cannot happen in the case of a conch. The conch which is not in yellow colour cannot be indicated to another person with the help of a finger that "the conch is yellow in colour". Therefore, the yellowish tinge of the conch is not real but it is an erroneous cognition. The yellowish conch is a superimposition which is experienced even without any similarity. This instance is enough to show that error is possible without the defect of similarity in the object of cognition. To avoid any further problem in the case of yellow conch example, the experience of bitterness in jaggery is cited to show that error is possible without the defect of similarity in the object of cognition.

Śaṅkara in his *Aparokṣānubhūti*[65] brings out the dissimilarity between *ātmā* and *anātmā*, and wonders at the possibility of error even in the case of dissimilarity. Sarvajñātman in his *Saṅkṣepa-śārīraka*[66] describes "error"; wherein he mentions the possibility of the three defects other than ignorance resulting in erroneous bondage.

a. Defect in perceiver (*pramātṛdoṣa*) — due to ignorance with its power of projection (*vikṣepa śakti*) there are imperceptible impressions born of good and bad actions in the mind, which are the causes of defect in a perceiver.

b. Defect in instrument of perception (*pramāṇadoṣa*) — Consciousness being self-evident cannot be revealed by any instrument of knowledge. Ignorance is the defect in the instrument of perception.

c. Defect in object of perception (*prameyadoṣa*) — There is the possibility of similarity in the form of "innerness" (*āntaratva*) and "reality" (*vastutva*) between the Self and the non-self. Self as Consciousness is internal (*āntara*) and the non-self in the form of five sheaths is also internal (*āntara*). Self is the absolute entity (*vastu*) and non-self in the form of world is an indescribable entity (*vastu*). Thus, the similarity in the form of "innerness" and "reality" is said to be the defect in the object of knowledge.

---

65 *AB* 17-21.

66 सदृशसांशपराग्विषयेषु चेद्भवति दोषवशाज्जगति भ्रमः ।
भवतु तत्सकलं वदितुं वयं तदुपचारवशाद् दृशि शक्नुमः ॥ — *SKS* 1.39

This is Prauḍhivāda adopted by Sarvajñātman. VB has differed from Sarvajñātman in this regard and has established above that there is the possibility of error even in the absence of these three defects, viz. defect in the perceiver, instrument of perception and object of perception.

4. ***Saṁskāra is explained*** — Presupposition of a past real experience for a superimposition is not a necessary condition. The criterion for the superimposition lies merely on the prior knowledge of an entity, real or unreal. If past real experience alone is the cause of error as claimed by the opponent then the following will not be possible. A person is ignorant of a real mango tree but has seen a mango tree in a magic show. By hearing the words "this is a mango tree" (pointing to the magical mango tree) this knowledge creates an impression in the mind. That same person who does not know a *madhūka* tree (a tree with leaves similar to a mango tree) sees this tree and recollects the knowledge regarding mango tree and says on seeing the *madhūka* tree, "this is a mango tree". This is an error, as mango tree is superimposed on *madhūka* tree. This instance of an error is not possible based on the view of the opponent since an unreal mango tree was experienced in the past. But there is the possibility of such an error. Hence according to Advaita, even though the mango tree experienced in the past is unreal since there is the impression of the unreal mango tree, this knowledge triggered by the impression is capable of resulting in an erroneous cognition on a *madhūka* tree. The impressions produced by the prior experience of a similar entity serves as the cause for subsequent superimposition. This has to be understood as the first cause of error. With regard to the ontological status of the past entity it can be the experience of either a real or an unreal entity.

   In this context, the statement "*saṁskāra* is the cause of

error" is analysed and two perspectives regarding the cause of error are explained.

(i) *saṁskāra dvārā jñānameva hetuḥ* — knowledge (of an entity) through the impressions is the cause of error, and

(ii) *jñānajanya saṁskāraḥ hetuḥ* — which can also be stated as impression created by the knowledge of an entity is the cause of error.

It is shown that in either case, *saṁskāra* or the impression is the cause of error. Knowledge of an entity is the cause of impression in the mind. The impression caused by knowledge is the cause of error. Thus, by stating that knowledge, through impressions is the cause of error, it amounts to say, that the impression, caused by knowledge, is the cause of error. So, the above two positions mean the same, that is, impression generated by knowledge of an entity is the cause of error.

Knowledge of an entity by itself cannot be the cause of error because a cause should immediately precede its effect. In the case of rope-snake erroneous cognition, a real snake which is cognized in the remote past is superimposed on a rope in the present. Thus, here the cause (real snake cognition) is not immediately preceding the effect (false snake experience). Even though the knowledge of a real snake in the form of thought-mode (*vr̥tti*) is lost over a period of time, the impression of the past experienced real snake in the mind is triggered on seeing a rope. Therefore, the cause of error is impression generated by cognition (*saṁskāra dvārā jñāna* or *jñānajanya saṁskāraḥ*) and it is not mere cognition or knowledge (*jñāna*) of an entity. Now, a series of objection with regard to *saṁskāra* as the cause of error is answered here.

Objection: The cause should, but need not, immediately precede its effect. The condition for prior existence of cause may be immediate or not immediate. If the immediacy of the cause is to be accepted then certain Vedic statements will become futile. The injunctions that by performance of prescribed actions one attains heaven and by performance of prohibited actions one reaps hell will become invalid. *Karma* is performed physically, verbally or mentally. After the performance of *karma*, it gets exhausted immediately. But the respective result of relevant *karma* like heaven or hell is reaped only after a period of time. Therefore, the results like heaven or hell are not the effect of an immediately preceding cause. The cause existed long before its result but still the prescribed and prohibited actions are said to be the causes for attaining the results, viz. heaven or hell. In the same manner, the knowledge of snake attained long before is the cause of superimposition on the rope and thus snake-knowledge is the cause of error.

Advaitin: The above objection that knowledge of an entity alone is the cause of error is untenable since the impression caused by the knowledge of an entity alone is the cause of error. If knowledge attained long before is said to be the cause of error (and not the impressions) and if past action is said to be the cause of heaven or hell (not merit or demerit) then a dead potter or a destroyed stick, wheel, etc. could serve as the cause of pot. But one does not experience the production of pot by a dead potter. Hence, it is said that an immediately preceding cause alone produces an effect.

By accepting this maxim, the Vedic injunctions do not become futile as pointed out by the above objectionist. The performance of prescribed or prohibited actions is not the cause of heaven or hell directly but immediately after the completion of the performance of actions they produce *apūrva* or unseen merit, namely, *dharma* and *adharma*. Both *dharma* and *adharma* remain in the subtle body of the individual that serves as the immediately preceding causes resulting in heaven or hell respectively long after the performance of action. Hence by citing the case of *karma* it cannot be argued that knowledge of an entity, though not immediately preceding an error is the cause of error.

As mentioned earlier, impression caused by the knowledge of an entity, either real or false, alone is the cause of error. Bondage is said to be an error as it is caused by impressions resulting in *arthādhyāsa* — superimposition of world and *jñānādhyāsa* — experience of *ahaṁkāra*. The prior false experience of *ahaṁkāra* creates impression which is the cause of the rise of successive superimposition of *ahaṁkāra* and its knowledge.

Objection: What is the cause of the first error? It is agreed upon that prior impressions are the causes of successive errors. But in the case of the first error both *arthādhyāsa* and *jñānādhyāsa* are absent. If there had been a first *ahaṁkāra* then it can be said that by the experience of the first *ahaṁkāra*, error takes place. The rise of first *ahaṁkāra* cannot be established. Thus, for any object, the first error cannot be accounted for due to the absence of its prior experience.

Advaitin: According to Advaita the following six categories are without a beginning:[67]

(1) *Jīva*

(2) *Īśvara*

(3) *Brahman*

(4) Mutual difference between *jīva* and *Īśvara*

(5) *Avidyā*

(6) Relation between (*adhyāsa sambandha*) *avidyā* and *Brahman*.[68]

---

[67] जीव ईशो विशुद्धा चित् तथा जीवेशयोर्भिदा। अविद्या तच्चितोर्योगः षडस्माकमनादयः॥

[68] अविद्याचित्संयोगः कालः अपि अनादिः।

These six categories are by nature without a beginning (*svarūptaḥ anādi*) as they are not subject to origination. Since the origination of *ahaṁkāra* is mentioned in Śruti[69] and Smṛti,[70] it is said that *ahaṁkāra* is not naturally beginningless, like the above six categories, but is perennially continuing and hence is said to be without a beginning (*pravāhataḥ anādi*). By this it gets proved that the entire world and its objects are also without a beginning, in the sense, there is a perennial continuity of the world in the form of unmanifest and manifest conditions. The concept of *pravāhataḥ anādi* is not known to the opponent and hence the doubt was raised with regard to the cause of the "first error". According to Advaita, no error can be pointed out to be the "first" error but every subsequent error is an effect of its previous error. Therefore, the above question posed as an objection is illogical. Thus, the possibility of erroneous bondage is proved.

Objection: Since world is without a beginning then one has to admit that the world is real based on the inference

World is real,
since it is without a beginning
like *Brahman*.

Advaitin: Such an inference is invalid. It is known that "rope-snake" and "dream" are apparent. This apparent experience may last for a second or extend to hours. Though they are without a beginning, on the rise of "rope-knowledge" and on "waking up", "snake" and "dream" are destroyed respectively. This proves the absence of "snake" and "dream" at three periods of time.[71] The inference thus is:

---

69 तन्मनोऽकुरुत — *BU* 1.2.1.

70 अहंकार इतीयं । — *BG* VII.4 and महाभूतान्यहंकारो । — *BG* XIII.6.

71 त्रैकालिकनिषेधप्रतियोगित्वनिश्चयः ।

World is unreal,
since it is sublated
like snake (and dream).

In the example, "snake" and "dream", whose beginning cannot be determined, are subject to sublation. Similarly, the superimposed world is projected as beginningless at the time of error but on the rise of knowledge of the substratum it is known that the world does not exist in three periods of time. Therefore, the world is unreal.

Thus, the Advaitin's contention is that the condition of *saṁskāra* as the cause of error exists which proves the possibility of an erroneous bondage and the solution for the removal of erroneous bondage is knowledge.

5. ***Viśeṣājñānam and sāmānyajñānam are examined*** — It was pointed out that there is no possibility of the cause of error in the form of general knowledge of the substratum and ignorance of specific features since *Brahman* is an attributeless, partless and self-evident reality. This objection is also untenable because one's own experience proves the possibility of the above-mentioned condition as the cause of error. The expression "I" used by every individual proves the Existence (*sat*) nature of the Self to be omnipresent. No one experiences the absence of oneself to express as "I do not exist". Thus, the *sat* nature of the Self is universally known to all which is a part of the general knowledge (*sāmānyajñānam*). On the other hand, the nature of the Self as Consciousness (*cit*),[72] Absolute Happiness (*ānanda*), divisionless, all-pervasive, eternally pure, eternally free, etc. is not known to all. There is the ignorance of these specific features of the Self in an individual. The self that is known to the ignorant ones shines in the form of *sat* alone. The nature of the Self in

72 The *sat*, *cit* and *ānanda* natures of the Self manifest in *upādhis* — gross, subtle and causal bodies respectively. The *sat* and *cit* natures are known to all. Here, VB takes to the view that the nature of *sat* alone is known to all.

the form of *cit* and *ānanda* is known to the enlightened one (*viśeṣājñānam*) and this is the specific nature of the Self.

An entity that is more pervasive in space and time is known as *sāmānya* and an entity that is less pervasive in space and time is said as *viśeṣa* in the worldly parlance. The *cit* and *ānanda* aspects of the Self also are omnipresent like the *sat* aspect.[73] The difference in the form of *sāmānya* and *viśeṣa* pervasiveness cannot be applied to *sat, cit, ānanda* nature of the Self. The general feature as *sat* and specific features as *cit* and *ānanda* of the Self as mentioned above are only from the standpoint of an ignorant[74] and enlightened one. From the transcendental standpoint, the Self is free from such divisions. However, since in the state of ignorance, the "specific" features of the Self are not known, the condition of *viśeṣājñānam* and *sāmānyajñānam* as the cause of error is to be accepted that can be eliminated only by knowledge.

The opponent also argued that since *Brahman* is self-evident Consciousness opposed to ignorance like light and darkness, there can be no ignorance of the specific feature of *Brahman*. That is, the self-luminous *Brahman* cannot be the locus of ignorance. This is also untenable because self-evident Consciousness is not opposed to ignorance but is the illuminator of the very ignorance. The experience of an individual on waking up from deep sleep proves the coexistence of Consciousness and ignorance. On waking up from deep sleep one says "I slept very well; I did not know anything". This experience of happiness and ignorance in the deep-sleep state does not belong to the waker's world and is not subject to direct perception through sense-organs or mind. It is a recollection of the

73 सत्त्वभासिका चित्क्ववेतरा। सत्तया हि चिच्चित्तया ह्ययम्॥ — *Upadeśasāra* 23

74 In *KU* 2.1.1 *parāṅ paśyati* is shown as an obstacle to Self-knowledge but this is under the presumption that one is ignorant of the non-difference between *cit* and *sat*.

> experience in deep sleep, on waking up. During the state of deep sleep both happiness and ignorance are directly known that is illumined by the self-luminous Consciousness. Therefore, there is the possibility of ignorance of "specific" features of the Self which is the cause of erroneous bondage and knowledge of the nature of the Self alone is the solution.

Thus, the possibility of an erroneous bondage is shown by expounding the *pañca adhyāsa sāmagrī* as pointed out by the opponent. So far, the nature of error due to ignorance of the Self was analysed so as to reveal that Self-knowledge alone is the means to liberation.

3.4 Ontology of Bondage

The *uttama adhikārī* (in *taraṅga* 4) seeks clarification with regard to the experience of bondage by an individual. If the Self is eternally free then the question remains as to who experiences bondage? The *guru* explains that the experienced world or sorrow does not exist in three periods of time either in oneself, or in another self, or in *Īśvara* or any other locus.[75] Just as in the empirical "rope", the "snake" is absolutely non-existent similarly the world/bondage is absolutely non-existent in transcendental *Brahman*.[76]

The *uttama adhikārī* argues that an absolutely non-existent entity can never be experienced; whereas sorrow/bondage is experienced and hence the question related to the one who experiences bondage remains unanswered. The *guru* reveals that one who is ignorant of the Self experiences this world just as one experiences the non-existent dream world, "rope-snake", etc.[77] and further the locus

---

75 अणुमात्रेपि वैधर्म्ये जायमानोऽविपश्चितः ।
असङ्गता सदा नास्ति किमुतावरणच्युतिः ॥ — *MaK* 4.97

76 कार्ये हि कारणं पश्येत् पश्चात् कार्यं विसर्जयेत् ।
कारणत्वं ततो गच्छेदवशिष्टं भवेन्मुनिः ॥ — *AB* 139

77 अर्थे ह्यविद्यमानेऽपि संसृतिर्न निवर्तते ।
ध्यायतो विषयानस्य स्वप्नेऽनर्थागमो यथा ॥ — *BP* 3.27.4

अविद्यमानोऽप्यवभासते द्वयो ध्यातुर्धिया स्वप्नमनोरथौ यथा ।
तत्कर्मसङ्कल्पविकल्पकं मनो बुधो निरुन्ध्यादभयं ततः स्यात् ॥ — *BP* 11.2.38

→

of bondage is explained. Just as the locus of the non-existent dream-world is the "waker" and the locus of the non-existent "snake" is the "rope", similarly the locus of the non-existent world/bondage is *Brahman*. Thus, world/bondage is a superimposition on *Brahman*. By stating bondage is a superimposition on *Brahman*, it is indicated that the experienced bondage is unreal. Thus, the ontology of bondage is said to be false. The unreal nature of bondage is revealed to indicate that one need not strive for freedom. In order to ascertain that experience or sorrow does not prove its reality, the *guru* takes up the discussion on the phenomenon of experience of unreality. Initially, the *uttama adhikārī* tries to examine the four theories of error but is unable to arrive at a conclusion. The *guru*, then, examines the *anirvacanīya khyāti* of Advaita to reveal the false nature of bondage and the subsequent sublation of bondage by the knowledge of the substratum.

THEORIES OF ERROR

We shall examine the theories of error as analysed by the *uttama adhikārī*.

1. According to the Mādhyamika Buddhism the "snake" in rope is absolutely non-existent (*asat*) as it is non-existent in any other place. There is the cognition of an absolutely non-existent "snake" in the rope. This view is known as Asatkhyātivāda.
2. According to the Vijñānavādins there is no "snake" externally either in the rope or elsewhere but only in the mind. Similarly, all objects do not exist external to the mind. The mind alone assumes the form of all objects and that mind is of the nature of momentary consciousness (*kṣaṇika vijñāna*). The consciousness which is subject to origination and destruction every moment illumines the

← नास्ति प्रतीत्यवसरे न पुरा न पश्चात् आश्चर्यमेतदवभाति तथापि विश्वम्।
यद्वा किमद्भुतमिवेह महेन्द्रजालं मायाविकल्पितमपि प्रतिभासते हि॥
— Quoted in *SV*, p. 80

"snake". This is known as *ātmakhyāti*.

3. According to the Old School of Nyāya (Prācīna Nyāya), in an erroneous cognition, one perceives the real snake that exists elsewhere even though it does not fall within the range of perception. The real snake is obstructed from the vision by distance, wall, etc. Due to defects in the eye, the real snake that is visually obstructed (*vyavahita sarpa*) is seen in the rope in front. One may argue that a defective eye cannot perceive a snake present elsewhere that is now visually obstructed. But the Naiyāyikas state that a defect at times gives more power like in the case of a person suffering from imbalance *pitta* consumes more due to increase in digestive power. Similarly, one with a defect in the eye gains more power and perceives the visually obstructed "snake" in the rope. It is said to be an erroneous cognition since an object present elsewhere is seen in front and hence is called as *anyathākhyāti* (of Prācīna Nyāya).

4. The New School of Nyāya (Navya Nyāya) spearheaded by Gaṅgeśa in his polemical work *Tattvacintāmaṇi* differs from the Old School of Nyāya in explaining the phenomenon of erroneous cognition. If a defective eye perceives a visually obstructed real snake then it should also have the power to perceive other objects in between or proximate to the real snake. But it is not so. Therefore, a visually obstructed entity is not perceived by the eyes. On the other hand, the rope does not manifest to the defective eye in its own form but appears in the form of a "snake". An object is seen in another form (*anyathā*) and hence this theory is called *anyathākhyāti* (of Navya Nyāya).

5. The Sāṁkhya and the Prābhākaras hold on to the theory of Akhyātivāda. First, the above theories of error are refuted. The theory of error according to Mādhyamikas is *asatkhyāti* and that is dismissed by stating that if *asat* is perceived then hare's horn also should be perceptible. This

is not so. Due to the impossibility of the perception of a non-existent entity, the *asatkhyāti* is unacceptable.

The Vijñānavādins's theory of *ātmakhyāti* is untenable because, if a thought that lasts for a moment appears as an object externally, then this external object should also last only for that moment. But, in the case of error, there is the perception of a continuously existing (erroneous) object and thus the theory of momentary consciousness cannot explain the phenomenon of erroneous cognition.

The Prācīna Nyāya is dismissed by the Navya Nyāya. Now, the theory of the Navya Nyāya is dismissed as fallacious since it violates the maxim *jñeyādhīnaṁ jñānam* (cognition is dependent on the object of knowledge). Any cognition must have a content (*artha*) which is not examined by the New School of Nyāya. According to them, the object of knowledge is a rope but the knowledge gained is that of a "snake". This is the partial application of erroneous cognitive phenomenon which is contradictory and hence the *anyathākhyāti* as propounded by Gaṅgeśa is also untenable.

The theory of *akhyāti* according to Sāṁkhya and the Prābhākaras is now explained. According to Akhyātivāda, at the time of erroneous perception the eyes contact the rope and that generates the general knowledge expressed as "this is". Due to similarity, the past experience of a snake in the memory gets triggered, which is expressed as "this is a snake". Thus there are two different forms of knowledge, one in the form of knowledge that is grasped as "this is" (*grahaṇajñānam*) and the other in the form of knowledge that is remembered as "snake" (*smaraṇajñānam*). Both the general (this is) and the specific knowledges (snake) are real but one is perceptually real and the other is the real knowledge in the memory. This division of twofold forms of knowledge is unknown to the perceiver. The perceiver does not discriminate that due to defect in the perceiver and the instrument of knowledge, "my knowledge is twofold, one is *grahaṇajñānam* and the other is *smaraṇajñānam*". The cause of error is the non-discrimination between these two forms of knowledge.

Thus, the *uttama adhikārī* concludes his analysis of the theories of error and requests the *guru* for further instruction on the nature of error. The *guru* refutes the above theory of Akhyātivādin also as untenable because the reaction of the perceiver in the form of fear, perspiration, seeking protection by fleeing, etc. on seeing the "snake" remains unexplained. Also, the expression "this is snake" as two forms of knowledge simultaneously occurring in the mind is illogical as mind can entertain only one form of knowledge in a given time. Moreover, none of the schools mentioned above examines the process of negation of "snake" on the rise of "rope-knowledge". Hence, the theories of erroneous cognition known to the *uttama adhikārī* are dismissed as untenable.

ANIRVACANĪYAKHYĀTI

Now, the *guru* explains the theory of error according to Advaita Vedānta. In the case of an erroneous cognition like "rope-snake" or "shell-silver", the Advaitins state that this can neither be categorized as *sat* nor as *asat* and hence is indescribable (*anirvacanīya*). Even though it is different from *sat* and *asat*, there is a false projection of "snake" on rope which "destroys" the knowledge of the real nature of the substratum, rope. This theory is known as *anirvacanīyakhyāti*.[78] In order to reveal the mechanism of erroneous perception, the *guru* examines the mechanism of perceptual cognition and thereafter explains the theory of error according to Advaita.

MECHANISM OF PERCEPTION

While describing the perceptual cognition, the *guru* explains the Advaitic claim that the external inert object is non-luminous since it is said to be concealed by *avidyā*. So, for the knowledge of an external object, a process for removal of *avidyā* is required.

---

78 औपनिषदाः इदं रजतमित्यादिभ्रमे सत्वेनासत्वेन च निर्वचनानर्हं अनिर्वचनीयं सद्विलक्षणत्वे सति असद्विलक्षणं मायिकं तत्कालोत्पन्नं अधिष्ठानतत्त्वज्ञाननाश्यं च मिथ्याभूतं रजतादिकमेव भासते इति अनिर्वचनीयख्यातिं व्यवस्थापयन्ति ।

— *Khyātitattvasamīkṣā*, p. 155

According to Advaita,[79] inert *avidyā* cannot and need not conceal an inert object. *Avidyā* having its locus as the Consciousness conceals Consciousness. For instance, we say the "pot" is not known because *avidyā* conceals consciousness conditioned by the pot (*viṣaya caitanyam*). The criterion of the perceptuality of knowledge is therefore said to be oneness of consciousness reflected in the means of knowledge (*pramāṇa caitanyam*) with the consciousness conditioned by the object (*viṣaya caitanyam*).[80] Therefore, the mechanism of perception is explained by the Advaitin in this manner:

> just as the water of a lake, enters through the openings, flows into the fields and assumes the shape of the field, so also the sentient mind goes out through the sense-organ ("eyes" in the case of visual perception),[81] reaches the place of the object and

---

[79] By the maxim *jaḍe āvaraṇavr̥ttyabhāva nyāya.*

[80] तथा च अयं घटः इति घटप्रत्यक्षस्थले घटाकारवृत्तेर्घटसंयोगितया घटावच्छिन्नचैतन्यस्य तद्वृत्त्यवच्छिन्नचैतन्यस्य चाभिन्नतया तत्र घटज्ञानस्य घटांशे प्रत्यक्षम्। — *VP*, pp. 14-15

[81] (a) Perceiving sound through sense of hearing: Mind with reflected consciousness goes out through the ears, grasps the sound close by or far away and the mental-mode assumes the form of the sound perceived. By the mental-mode the veil of sound is removed. The reflected consciousness illumines the sound.

(b) By the sense of touch, the quality of touch in objects is known. Here the mental-mode through the skin does not go out. But the body comes in contact with the object or object comes in contact with the body. With the help of the body (skin), which is the physical organ, the sense of touch comes in contact with the object by which the qualities of the object like softness and hardness are known. The sense of touch remaining in the skin with reflected consciousness assumes mental-mode in the mind. The mental-mode removes the veil of touch in the object-contacted. The reflected consciousness illumines the sense of touch of the object.

(c) While tastes like sweet and salt are known by the sense of taste the mental-mode does not go out leaving the tongue. But either in the form of tongue contacting the object or objects contacting the tongue, the sense of taste, with reflected consciousness, gains the knowledge. By the mental mode, the veil of taste is removed and the reflected consciousness illumines the tastes.

(d) The sense of smell located in the nostril comes in contact with smell, say fragrance of a flower, or by the contact of the minute particles of flower — by this contact, the sense of smell in tip of nose with the reflected consciousness knows the smell of the object. By the mental mode, the veil of smell is removed. →

modifies into the form of the object. This modification is known as *vṛtti*[82] and the knowledge "this is a pot" (in this case) is known as *vṛtti-jñānam*.

TWOFOLD FUNCTIONS OF PERVASION

There are twofold pervasions (*vyāpti*) in the process of perceptual cognition for an object to be known. First, there is the pervasion of the thought-mode (*vṛtti*) over the object, known as *vṛtti-vyāpti*, which destroys the concealment of *avidyā* (*ajñāna āvaraṇa nivṛtti*). In all the cases of object knowledge, destruction of concealment of *avidyā* alone does not suffice, the second function, namely *phala-vyāpti* is necessitated. That is, the object should be pervaded by "sentiency" or "light". The *vṛtti* along with the reflected consciousness (*pratibimba caitanyam* or *cidābhāsa*) illumines the object (*viṣaya-sphūrti*) and this process is known as *phala-vyāpti*. The word *phala* here refers to the reflected consciousness. The perceptual process remains the same in the case of knowing either the *pramā* or *apramā*. The cause of an erroneous perception is due to the element of "defect".[83]

MECHANISM OF ERRONEOUS PERCEPTION

In the case of an erroneous perception also, like seeing "snake" in "rope", it is said that the internal organ goes out through the sense-organ, reaches the place of object and assumes the form of the external object as in the case of valid cognition. The error takes place due to certain other factors like semi-darkness. It is to be noted here that ignorance is a necessary condition for superimposition. In bright light there is knowledge of both the general (*sāmānya*) (this is) and the specific (*viśeṣa*) (rope). In total darkness, both the *sāmānya* and *viśeṣa* are unknown. In an erroneous

---

← By the reflected consciousness the smell is illumined. Thus, this is the mechanism of perception according to Advaita. — *SV*, p. 114 fn.1.

82 तत्र यथा तडागोदकं छिद्रान्निर्गत्य कुल्यात्मना केदारान् प्रविश्य तद्वदेव चतुष्कोणाद्याकारं भवति तथा तैजसमन्तःकरणमपि चक्षुरादिद्वारा निर्गत्य घटादिविषयदेशं गत्वा घटादिविषयाकारेण परिणमते। स एव परिणामो वृत्तिरित्युच्यते। — *VP*, p. 14.

83 See Section 3.3 of this Chapter.

cognition, the defect can be in the seer, seen or instruments of knowledge, etc. The error occurs due to the defect in any one of these aspects. In the present case, due to semi-darkness there is the knowledge of the general aspect and one is ignorant of the specific aspect of the rope. The *vṛtti* is distorted due to this defect and assumes the form of the object incorrectly. If the *vṛtti* along with the reflected consciousness does not pervade the rope, it does not remove rope-ignorance.

LOCUS OF ROPE-IGNORANCE

According to Advaita the substratum of ignorance is always consciousness. Rope-ignorance rests on consciousness. It may be argued that in such a case, there must be consciousness-ignorance and not rope-ignorance. This is not so, because rope-ignorance rests on consciousness conditioned by rope. This rope-ignorance is called *tūla-avidyā*. The unconditioned consciousness is the substratum of *mūla-avidyā*. The ignorance of rope, in this case, rests on consciousness conditioned by rope.[84] The rope-ignorance is not destroyed even after the pervasion of *vṛtti*. Here, the rope-ignorance conceals the rope and also projects something else, for instance, a "snake". This projected snake is said to be of indescribable nature or *anirvacanīya*. Thus, the erroneous cognition of "snake" in rope is explained as *anirvacanīya khyāti* by the Advaitin. By extending this example, it is said that world is an erroneous cognition in *Brahman*.

ONTOLOGY OF "SNAKE"

The projected snake is said to be *anirvacanīya* or *sadasadvilakṣaṇa*. The "snake" cannot be categorized as *sat* since it is negated on the rise of rope-knowledge. The "snake" cannot be categorized as *asat* since it is perceived at a given time. Thus, the "snake" is neither *sat* nor *asat*. One may object that, a thing should fall under either *sat* category or *asat* category, *sadasat* is illogical. The Advaitin explains that *sadasat* implies a temporary existence of an experienced

---

84 सर्वस्यापि कार्यस्य अस्मन्मते स्वोपादानाविद्याधिष्ठानाश्रितत्वनियमात्। — *VP*, p. 49

thing which is subject to sublation subsequently. This is also known as *mithyā* which is defined as *traikālikaniṣedha pratiyogitvaṁ mithyātvam.* It is *anirvacanīya* as it is negated later and at the same time has a seeming existence. In this manner, in the "shell-silver" (and other similar examples), "silver", exists temporarily, mysteriously produced by *tūla-avidyā* that serves as the material cause. The *tūla-avidyā* gets destroyed when there is the valid knowledge of the empirical object.

ARTHĀDHYĀSA AND JÑĀNĀDHYĀSA

It is further explained that just as the "snake" is a modification of *avidyā*, the "snake" knowledge that arises is also a modification of *avidyā* and is not the modification of the thought-mode (*vṛtti*). If it were a mental modification then it would have been an empirical cognition. In an erroneous perception, *avidyā* modifies itself projecting another object. On the rise of rope-knowledge, both the projected "snake" and "snake-knowledge" vanish. Hence not only the projected "snake" (*arthādhyāsa*) is *anirvacanīya*, the "snake-knowledge" (*jñānādhyāsa*) is also *anirvacanīya*. Thus, both "snake" and "snake-knowledge" are modifications of *avidyā*, they are superimposed and are negated by the rise of rope-knowledge. The uncommon feature is that while the superimposed "snake" is a result of the *tamas* aspect of ignorance located in the consciousness conditioned by rope, the "snake-knowledge" is a result of the modification of *sattva* aspect of ignorance resting on the witness consciousness (*sākṣīcaitanyam*). It is known as *avidyāvṛtti*, being an effect of *avidyā*.

Thus, every *prātibhāsika* creation has two components, *arthādhyāsa* and *jñānādhyāsa*. The material cause for both *arthādhyāsa* and *jñānādhyāsa* is *tūla-avidyā*. The *tūla-avidyā* again has two components, "snake" that is superimposed externally, and the "snake-knowledge" that arises internally in the mind. The ignorance (*tūla-avidyā*) present in the consciousness conditioned by rope conceals the true nature of rope and falsely projects it as "snake", due to its *tamas* aspect. The same ignorance in its *sattva* aspect, being located in the consciousness conditioned by the mind, conceals the knowledge of rope and gives rise to the knowledge of "snake". According to Advaita, a valid or an erroneous cognition has an objective reference. The "snake-cognition" has "snake" for its content. So, *arthādhyāsa* and *jñānādhyāsa* arise simultaneously. The *tamas* aspect of ignorance resting on consciousness conditioned by the rope, due to Vikṣepaśakti, projects the "snake". The *sattva* aspect of ignorance resting on the consciousness conditioned by the mind gives rise to "snake-knowledge". Thus, *avidyā,* the material cause gives rise to two effects, viz. superimposed object externally and superimposed object-knowledge internally. Both are modifications of ignorance. Therefore, in the case of erroneous perception, the superimpositions and their knowledge arise simultaneously and by the direct knowledge of the object both get sublated simultaneously (see *fig.* 3.2).

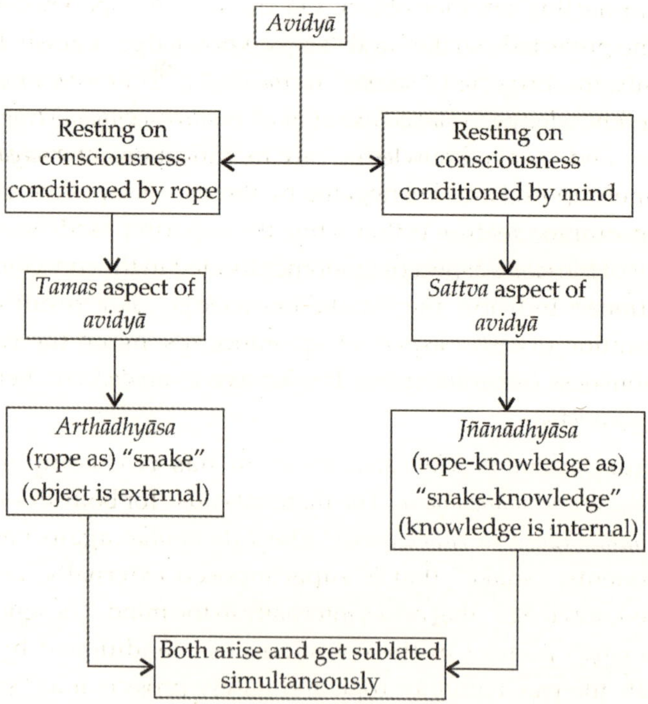

fig. 3.2: The occurrence and sublation of *arthādhyāsa* and *jñānādhyāsa*

"SNAKE" IS ILLUMINED BY WITNESS-CONSCIOUSNESS

It is well known that dream experience is also *prātibhāsika* like the "rope-snake". But in dream, both the projected object and object-knowledge rest internally. The *tamas* aspect of ignorance produces dream objects and the *sattva* aspect of ignorance gives rise to dream object-knowledge, and this ignorance rests on witness consciousness. So the material cause of *arthādhyāsa* and *jñānādhyāsa* in dream is ignorance resting on witness consciousness. The "snake" seen externally in the case of "rope-snake" and the dream objects experienced internally are *arthādhyāsa*s which are manifested by the witness consciousness and hence both are said to be *sākṣībhāsya,* i.e. illumined by the witness consciousness. The knowledge of "snake" or dream object is not the result of *antaḥkaraṇavr̥tti* but is due to the modification of *tūla-avidyā* and hence it is also said to be *sākṣībhāsya.*

Thus, in the case of apparent cognition (*prātibhāsika-jñānam*) either external like "rope-snake" or internal like the dream-world, the mental state in the form of "snake" or "dream" is the product of *tūla-avidyā* and is known through the process of *avidyāvr̥tti* that is illumined by the witness consciousness (*sākṣībhāsya*). On the other hand, in the case of empirical cognition (*vyāvahārika jñāna*) of rope, the mental state in the form of rope is the product of *mūla-avidyā* and this mental modification is said to be known through the process of *antaḥkaraṇavr̥tti* and is manifested by the consciousness conditioned by the mind and hence it is said to be *pramātr̥bhāsya.*

THE MODIFYING CAUSE

Thus, *tūla-avidyā* is the modifying material cause of both *arthādhyāsa* and *jñānādhyāsa* borrowing existence from Consciousness. The *anirvacanīya* "snake" gives rise to "snake-knowledge" that is known as *bhrama, adhyāsa* or error. The material cause of this error is ignorance and Consciousness. Here, ignorance serves as the transformative material cause (*pariṇāmi upādānakāraṇa*), while the Consciousness is the transfigurative material cause (*vivartta upādānakāraṇa*).[85] The material cause, *avidyā*, is *anirvacanīya*. Hence, the "snake" and the "snake-knowledge" are also *anirvacanīya*. As both, "snake" and "snake-knowledge" are of the nature of *avidyā*, i.e. in the form of *avidyā* (as its effects), they are said to be the "transformation" of *avidyā*. The substratal-consciousness conditioned by rope is of the nature of *sat*. The "snake" and "snake-knowledge" are different from *sat*. Therefore, as "snake" and "snake-knowledge" are contrary to the nature of its substratum (Consciousness) and being different from the substratum, they are said to be the "transfiguration" of Consciousness.

LOCUS OF ARTHĀDHYĀSA AND JÑĀNĀDHYĀSA: PṚTHAK ADHIṢṬHĀNA PAKṢA

The *guru* presents two views of Advaita, with regard to the locus of *arthādhyāsa* (snake) and *jñānādhyāsa* (snake-knowledge). Let us differentiate these two views as the *pṛthak adhiṣṭhāna pakṣa* and *eka adhiṣṭhāna pakṣa*. The *pṛthak adhiṣṭhāna pakṣa* advocates that the locus of the "snake" is the consciousness conditioned by rope (not the inert rope but *rajju upahita caitanyam*) and the locus of the "snake-knowledge" is the consciousness conditioned by the mind (*antaḥkaraṇa upahita caitanyam*). Consciousness is the locus of both "snake" and "snake-knowledge" generated by *avidyā*.

The *guru* gives the reason as to why rope by itself cannot serve as the locus of "snake". According to Advaita, the very rope (empirical object) itself has its existence borrowed from the Consciousness and thus the rope by itself is *mithyā*. A *mithyā* entity cannot be the substratum of another *mithyā* entity. So, the substratum of a *prātibhāsika vastu* is also a *pāramārthika vastu* (*vyāvahārika avachinna pāramārthika*).[86]

---

85 परिणामो नाम उपादानसमसत्ताककार्यापत्तिः ।
विवर्तो नाम उपादानविषमसत्ताककार्यापत्तिः । — *VP*, p. 49

86 माधुर्यद्रवशैत्यानि नीरधर्मास्तरङ्गके ।
अनुगम्याथ तन्निष्ठे फेनेऽप्यनुगता यथा ॥

साक्षिस्थास्सच्चिदानन्दास्संबन्धाद्व्यावहारिके ।
तद्द्वारेणानुगच्छन्ति तथैव प्रातिभासिके ॥ — *DDV* 43-44

It may be argued here that the substratum should be rope-attributed consciousness (*rajju viśiṣṭa caitanyam*) and not rope-conditioned consciousness. But, if this is so, then both rope and Consciousness should be taken as the substratum. This leads to the fallacy of dualistic reality and like Consciousness, the rope will remain unnegated on the rise of knowledge. But we find that rope (world) gets negated on the rise of *Brahman*-knowledge. That which remains unnegated alone is the substratum. The error is removed by the knowledge of the substratum. The substratum of "snake" is consciousness conditioned by rope. The corresponding knowledge that arises in the mind (snake-knowledge) has consciousness conditioned by the mind as its locus. Consciousness is the substratum of both *arthādhyāsa* and *jñānādhyāsa*. In all cases of error, the substratum of *arthādhyāsa* is "external" consciousness (*viṣaya avachinna caitanyam*) and substratum of *jñānādhyāsa* is "internal" consciousness (*antaḥkaraṇa avachinna caitanyam*). The non-dual Consciousness is seen differently due to the *upādhi* or conditioning factors like rope and mind.

Removal of Arthādhyāsa

According to Advaita, by the knowledge of the substratum alone error is removed. One may argue that, since it was mentioned earlier that rope by itself is not the substratum of "snake" but only the consciousness conditioned by rope, then it would mean that rope-knowledge cannot be the cause of removal of snake-error. The Advaitins explain this by saying that on the rise of rope-knowledge, two phenomena take place. By *vṛtti-vyāpti*, *avidyā* concealing the rope-conditioned consciousness is eliminated, and by *phala-vyāpti*, the rope is illumined. Rope-knowledge reveals the rope-conditioned consciousness and the rope. Thus, the substratum, which is rope or rope-conditioned consciousness, is illumined. Whether one considers rope as the substratum or rope-conditioned consciousness as the substratum, either way, by the rise of rope-knowledge, snake-error is removed, i.e. knowledge of the true nature of the substratum removes error.

Removal of Jñānādhyāsa

Now, the *pṛthak adhiṣṭhāna pakṣa* explains the mechanism of removal of "snake-knowledge" that has for its locus the consciousness conditioned by the mind or that which is illumined by the witness consciousness. It is argued here that since the loci of "snake" and "snake-knowledge" are different, one requires two different processes for the removal of "snake" and "snake-knowledge". It is already mentioned that "snake" is removed by the knowledge of the substratum, i.e. rope or rope-conditioned consciousness. But rope-knowledge cannot eliminate the "snake-knowledge" since its substratum is different. To resolve this, the *pṛthak adhiṣṭhāna pakṣa* resorts to two approaches:

1. First, it is said that when the object is sublated its corresponding object-knowledge is also eliminated. By the rise of rope-knowledge, the "snake" is sublated and simultaneously the "snake-knowledge" is also sublated or falsified. The elimination of "snake" (outside) is the cause for the removal of "snake-knowledge" (inside).

   Objection: The contention of Advaita is that knowledge of the substratum alone removes error. Here, the removal of "snake-knowledge" is explained by overlooking the above contention. The witness consciousness was said to be the substratum of "snake-knowledge". For the removal of "snake-knowledge" it must be admitted that the "snake-knowledge" gets eliminated by the rise of the knowledge of the witness consciousness. If not, then one may have to say that the "snake-knowledge" is an imagination.

   Advaitin: Even without the knowledge of the witness consciousness the "snake-knowledge" is removed. The process of removal is of two kinds: *ātyantika-nivṛtti* (absolute cessation) and *kāraṇātmanā-avasthitirūpā* (resolution into its potential condition). The absolute cessation is the destruction of material cause. Like in the case of a cloth, destruction of thread, its material cause, is the destruction of the cloth. On the other hand, in the case of a pot, the destruction of pot is its resolution into its material cause, clay. Based on *ātyantika-nivṛtti*, by the direct knowledge of consciousness, the substratum (i.e. rope-conditioned consciousness), "snake" and "snake-knowledge" are removed. In the case of the *kāraṇātmanā-avasthitirūpā*, it is shown that even without the knowledge of the substratum removal of "snake-knowledge" is possible. Like during the deep sleep (*pralaya*), without the knowledge of the substratum, all objects resolve into its cause — the primordial ignorance or *kāraṇaśarīra* and the cause of resolution of all errors is because of the temporary cessation of *karma*. In the same manner, "snake-knowledge" is removed even without the knowledge of the substratum which is the witness consciousness. Thus, by the rise of rope-knowledge, "snake" is sublated and simultaneously "snake-knowledge" is resolved.

2. Second, it is shown that by the rise of rope-knowledge, both "snake" and "snake-knowledge" are removed. This is explained thus: at the time of direct knowledge of rope, the mind goes out through the eyes and assumes the form of the rope. In this process, the difference between consciousness conditioned by mind and consciousness conditioned by rope is resolved into one locus (see *fig.* 3.3).

According to Advaita, the non-dual Consciousness is seen differently due to the limiting adjuncts and the difference is continued when the adjuncts are in different places. When the conditioning factors are in the same locus, the seeming difference between consciousnesses is resolved.[87] The rope-conditioned consciousness is illumined by rope-knowledge and during perception the mind-conditioned consciousness is located in rope-conditioned consciousness, which is also illumined by rope-knowledge.

---

87 अयं घटः इत्यादिप्रत्यक्षस्थले घटादेस्तदाकारवृत्तेश्च बहिरेकत्र देशे समवधानात् तदुभयावच्छिन्नं चैतन्यमेकमेव विभाजकयोरप्यन्तःकरणवृत्तिघटादिविषययोः एकदेशस्थत्वेन भेदाजनकत्वात्। — *VP*, p. 14

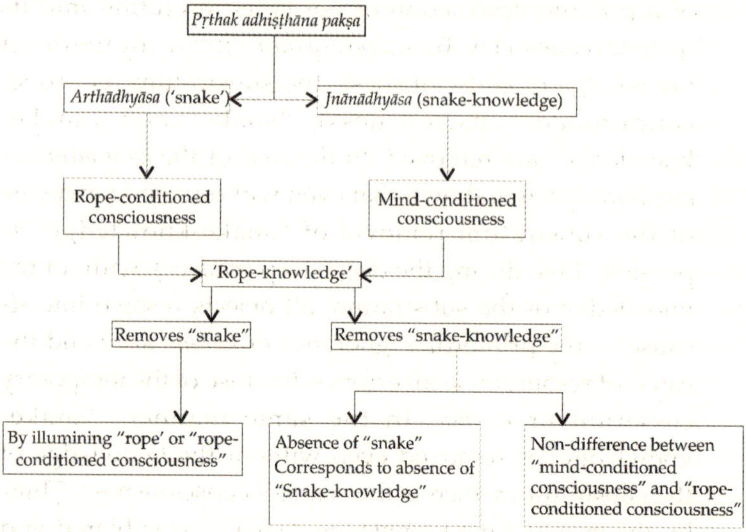

fig. 3.3: Distinct loci of *arthādhyāsa* and *jñānādhyāsa*

LOCUS OF ARTHĀDHYĀSA AND JÑĀNĀDHYĀSA: EKA ADHIṢṬHĀNA PAKṢA

The *ekādhiṣṭhāna pakṣa* advocates that the locus of both "snake" and "snake-knowledge" is one and the same. Based on this view, the substratum of both "snake" and "snake-knowledge" should be either the rope-conditioned consciousness or the mind-conditioned consciousness. By the former, the error occurs outside in the rope but it cannot be the locus of "snake-knowledge" and by the latter view, though it can be the locus of "snake-knowledge", the error is internal leading to *ātmakhyāti*. In an erroneous cognition, according to Advaita, the locus of error is the object seen outside. So, rope-conditioned consciousness cannot be the substratum of "snake-knowledge" and mind-conditioned consciousness cannot be the substratum of "snake". Thus, the view of *ekādhiṣṭhāna pakṣa* seems to pose some difficulty.

The *guru* resolves this by stating that the mind-conditioned consciousness is the locus of both "snake" and "snake-knowledge". That is, the mind goes out through the eyes and reaches the place where the rope is, the ignorance located in the consciousness conditioned by the thought-mode "this" (*idamākāra vṛtti*) modifies into "snake" and "snake-knowledge". The material cause of the "snake" is the *tamas* aspect and of the "snake-knowledge" is the *sattva* aspect of ignorance located in the consciousness conditioned by the mind. Thus, the locus of "snake" and "snake-knowledge" is the consciousness conditioned by the mind. The mind-conditioned consciousness is outside in the place of rope and the rope-conditioned consciousness is also external. Therefore, the "external" consciousness alone is the locus of the "snake". The witness principle is there where the mind is. The mind located in the body alone modifies into a thought. Therefore, mind-conditioned consciousness in the form of thought alone is the witness principle. Thus, the mind-conditioned consciousness is the locus of "snake-knowledge". On the rise of rope-knowledge, there is non-difference between consciousness conditioned by the rope and consciousness conditioned by the mind and, therefore, both the "snake" and the "snake-knowledge" are destroyed (see *fig.* 3.4).

In explaining the mechanism of erroneous perception, the Advaitin states that the indescribable ignorance, that cannot be categorized as *sat* or *asat* modifies into indescribable error (snake) and hence this is popularly known as *anirvacanīya khyāti*.

LOCUS OF THE FALSE WORLD

So far, the world/bondage has been revealed as false to the *uttama adhikārī* through the examination of the theories of error, locus of error and the removal of error by the knowledge of substratum. Now, the *uttama adhikārī* raises the question with regard to the locus of the false world/bondage. He asks as to "what is the *ādhāra* of the false world that is experienced and what is its *adhiṣṭhāna*?"

The *guru* replies that the false world manifests because of the ignorance of the Self. Just as the experienced false "snake" is due to rope-ignorance wherein the rope is both the *ādhāra* and *adhiṣṭhāna* of the false "snake", the experienced false world is because of Self-ignorance and the Self alone is both the *ādhāra* and

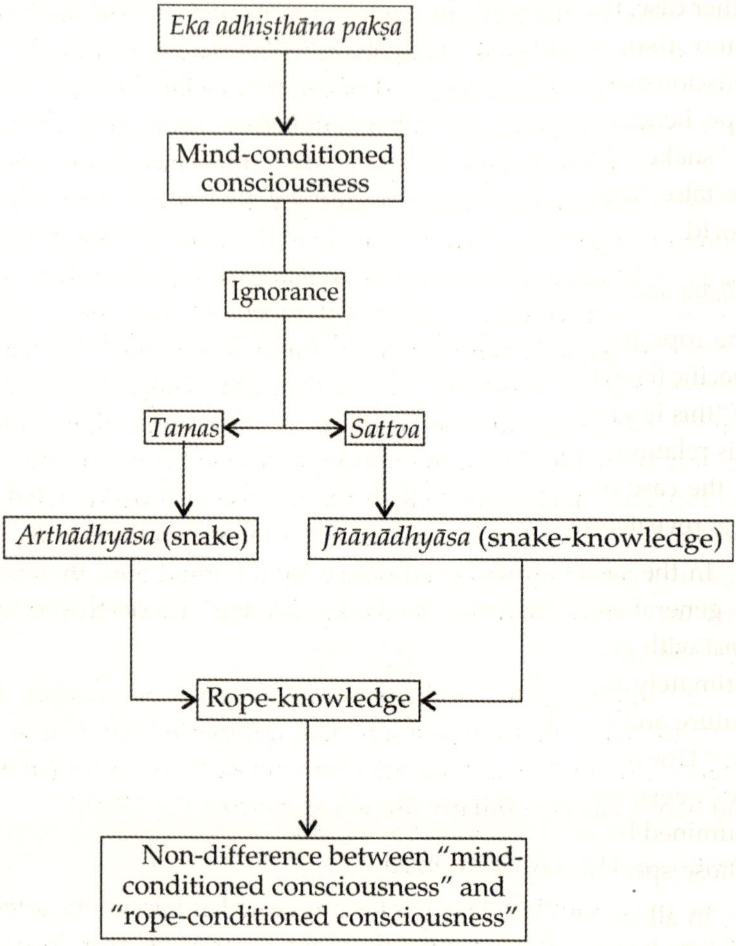

fig. 3.4: One locus of *arthādhyāsa* and *jñānādhyāsa*

adhiṣṭhāna[88] of the false world. According to the *ekādhiṣṭhāna pakṣa* the *adhiṣṭhāna* of "snake" is consciousness conditioned by the thought-mode (*vṛtti*) and according to the *pṛthak adhiṣṭhāna pakṣa* the *adhiṣṭhāna* of "snake" is rope-conditioned consciousness; in

[88] *Saṅkṣepaśārīraka* 1.31-32.

either case, the inert rope by itself is not said to be the substratum. Then also, since according to the *pṛthak adhiṣṭhāna pakṣa*, consciousness is the *adhiṣṭhāna* that is conditioned by the adjunct rope, hence superficially it is said that rope alone is the *adhiṣṭhāna* of "snake". Thus, just as the rope is the *ādhāra* and *adhiṣṭhāna* of the false "snake", the Self is the *ādhāra* and *adhiṣṭhāna* of the false world.

Ādhāra and Adhiṣṭhāna

The rope has two features — general (*sāmānya*) as "this is" and specific (*viśeṣa*) as "rope". In an erroneous cognition, it is expressed as "this is a snake" — the false "snake" coexists with "this is" and this relation is known as relation of identity (*tādātmya sambandha*). In the case of an error, the specific feature is not evident which gets revealed by the rise of direct knowledge of the substratum.

In the same manner, the Self or the *ātmā* has "two features" — general as "I am" and specific as "eternal". (This division of *ātmā* with general and specific features is only a temporary view, ultimately there are no such features.) Here, *sat* is the general feature and the specific features are *asaṅgatva, nityatva, śuddhatva,* etc.[89] Due to Self-ignorance, one says, "there is gross, subtle bodies, etc."; even in this state of delusion, the false gross body, etc. is illumined by *sat*. Therefore it is said that *sat* is the general feature whose specific features are unknown.

In all cases of error, the general feature is the *ādhāra* and the specific feature is the *adhiṣṭhāna*. In the case of "this is a snake" error, the *ādhāra* is "this is" and the *adhiṣṭhāna* is "rope". Similarly, *ātmā* as *sat* is the *ādhāra* of the false world and features like *asaṅgatva,* etc. is the *adhiṣṭhāna*.

Perceiver of the false world

In the case of "rope-snake", there is a perceiver different from the "rope-snake"; based on this the *uttama adhikārī* questions with

---

89 न हि भानादृते सत्त्वं नर्ते भानं चितोऽचितः ।
चित्संभेदोऽपि नाध्यासादृते तेनाहमद्वयः ॥ — *AM* 7

regard to the perceiver of the false world. The *uttama adhikārī* infers that *ātmā* cannot be the perceiver of the world on the following ground:

> The perceiver of the false world cannot be the Self; Since Self is the substratum of the false world; Like the rope that is the substratum of the false "snake".

The *guru* initially clarifies the importance of understanding the examples that are cited. The "rope-snake" example is given to reveal the action of withdrawal, *nivṛtti* and the "shell-silver" example is mentioned to show the action of pursuit, *pravṛtti*. In both these examples, the substratum is an inert entity (actually conditioned consciousness is the substratum but for all practical reasons inert entity is said to be the substratum). The substratum itself is of two kinds — Consciousness and matter. When it is said that the substratum (rope) is an inert entity then there is a perceiver different from the substratum (rope) since an inert entity cannot perceive itself. When Consciousness is said to be the substratum then it is to be known that the objects are superimposed on the Self and the Self itself is the perceiver of the superimposed objects.

In order to understand the perceiver of the false world, the *guru* resorts to the dream-experience. The substratum of the dream-world is the witness consciousness that experiences the dream-world. Similarly, the substratum of the waker's world is the Consciousness that is the perceiver of the waker's world.[90] In the initial stages it is said that the inert entity like a rope is the substratum of the superimposed "snake", but in reality, the contention of Advaita is that the substratum of all superimpositions is the witness consciousness and that itself is the perceiver. Thus, the perceiver and the substratum of the entire creation is one witness consciousness. Just as a magician who creates an enemy

---

[90] उभयोरपि वैतथ्यं भेदानां स्थानयोर्यदि । क एतान्बुध्यते भेदान्को वै तेषां विकल्पकः ॥
कल्पयत्यात्मनात्मानमात्मा देवः स्वमायया । स एव बुध्यते भेदानिति वेदान्तनिश्चयः ॥
— *MaK*, 2.11 and 12.

through his magical powers does not put forth any effort to destroy that projected enemy, the *guru* states that one need not strive to end this false world.[91]

3.5 Knowledge of Self

The world/bondage has been revealed as false like the dream-world, but since the false bondage is experienced, the *uttama adhikārī* seeks the means for the removal of sorrow. He states that though it is known that when the cause of misery is false the means to remove such a cause is also to be false. But it is known that in the case of false dream experience which turns into a nightmare one resorts to prayers; in the waking world, in the same way, *uttama adhikārī* argues that the false sorrow is sought to be removed and therefore the question related to the means of happiness (liberation) is raised.[92]

The *guru* reminds the *uttama adhikārī* that the means related to absolute cessation of "false" sorrow has been already explained in detail through the examination of the ontology of bondage. So, he asks the *uttama adhikārī* to ascertain this knowledge firmly by developing faith (*śraddhā*) and devotion (*bhakti*). However, the *guru* repeats the essence of the entire teaching for the benefit of his disciple — "due to the ignorance of non-dual, unrelated, Pure Consciousness nature of the Self, the sorrow in the form of world appears in you and it can be eliminated only by the knowledge of the true nature of yourself. Just as the appearance of "snake", caused by rope-ignorance, is removed by rope-knowledge alone, the appearance of the world/bondage, because of Self-ignorance, can be removed only by the direct knowledge (*aparokṣa jñāna*) of

---

91 प्रपञ्चो यदि विद्येत निवर्तेत न संशयः। मायामात्रमिदं द्वैतमद्वैतं परमार्थतः॥ — *MaK*, 1.17.
अज्ञानमेव न कुतो जगतः प्रसङ्गो जीवेशदेशिकविकल्पकथाऽतिदूरे।
एकान्तनिर्मलचिदेकरसस्वरूपं ब्रह्मैव केवलमहं परिपूर्णमस्मि॥ — Quoted in *SV*, p. 92

92 सत्यं मृषा वा चिदिदं जडं वा दुःखं सुखं वेति मुधा विवादः।
अदृष्टलोका निरहंप्रतीतिर्निष्ठाऽविकल्पा परमाखिलेष्टा॥ — *SD*, 5.

दुर्वारसंसारदवाग्नितप्तं दोधूयमानं दुरदृष्टवातैः।
भीतं प्रपन्नं परिपाहि मृत्योः शरण्यमन्यद्यदहं न जाने॥ — *VC* 36

the Self.[93] The world/bondage is absent in the Self in three periods of time and hence is false like the dream-world. A false entity cannot affect its substratum. The desert land cannot be dampened by mirage water. In the same way, the false world cannot affect the Self. Thus, the knowledge that "I am Existence, Consciousness, Absolute Happiness, Non-dual, Unassociated *Brahman*" is to be ascertained and this knowledge alone is the means to "liberation". Thus, in this dialogue between the *uttama adhikārī* and the *guru*, the nature of bondage and the nature of the Self have been thoroughly analysed.

PLURALITY OF SELF

While dealing with the *viṣaya* of the text *Vicārasāgara*, in the second *taraṅga* an opponent raises a question on the identity of *jīva* and *Brahman*. According to this opponent, the identity of *jīva* and *Brahman* is impossible since *jīva*s are many and *Brahman* is one, non-dual reality. The plurality of the self is proved by the opponent in the following manner:

1. *Perception* — Every person differentiates the body from the self through subjective references implying the cause for the difference in the selves. The self cannot be said to be one, non-dual entity in all the bodies since the expressions like "you", "I" and "this", indicating differences, are employed. Therefore, the plurality of self is well known.

2. *Inference* — The self is different in each body, since through each body there are interactions expressed in the form of "I" and "you", and this proves the individual subject to be different in each body. Thus, inference also proves the plurality of self.

3. *Postulation* — In the absence of plurality of selves, expressions like "you", "I" and "this" cannot be employed.

[93] *Brahman* or the Self as not an object of sense-organs of knowledge and sense-organs of action are discussed in *SV*, pp. 124-27.

Without postulating the difference in selves, the usage of different expressions cannot be proved. Hence, postulation also proves the plurality of self.

4. *Testimony* — The plurality of self is revealed in the scriptures in the form of description of beings like *deva, dānava, yakṣa, rākṣasa, gandharva, kinnara* and *mānava.*
5. *Logic* — If self is said to be one in all bodies, then the pleasure or pain experienced in one body will be experienced in all bodies. Also, the rise of knowledge in one mind will enlighten all or if one is bound then all the others will also be bound. This leads to the redundancy of scriptural statements dealing with liberation and action. Thus, the plurality of self is to be accepted.

PLURALITY OF SELF: ITS REFUTATION

The above reasons revealing the plurality of self are dismissed by the Advaitin on the following grounds:

1. The expressions like "I" and "you", do not reveal the plurality of self. In expressions like "I am a child; I am young, I am old"; different stages of life are indicated referring to the same self. Moreover, if the self is different in different stages of life, then the incidents of childhood cannot be remembered in youth and so on. Thus perception does not prove the plurality of self.
2. The inferential statement is refuted by citing two defects in the middle term. The first defect is *vyabhicāra hetvābhāsa,* wherein an exception to the given reason is shown. The difference in self cannot be said because of the difference in bodies expressed as "I", since an individual constituting of three bodies (gross, subtle and causal) refers to all the three bodies with the same expression "I". The second defect is *bādhita doṣa,* wherein it is shown that the dream body and waker's body are different but the dream experience is recollected on waking up by the same person. This proves the absence of difference in the self and hence

inference does not prove the plurality of self.

3. The postulation of distinction in the selves due to different expressions does not hold good because the body with different parts is collectively addressed as "I". In the same manner, the varied bodies are addressed as "I", "you", etc. but the self is one. Thus, postulation does not prove the plurality of self.

4. The different beings like *deva* and *dānava* described in the scriptures refer to the physical bodies and not the Self. The nature of Self is Consciousness which is one, non-dual and its difference can never be proved. The Vedic statements[94] reveal the non-dual *Brahman*.

5. Different experiences also do not prove plurality of Self because this difference is based on the *upādhi* or internal organ. The varied experience of happiness or sorrow is based on *prārabdha karma*. One experiences both pleasure and pain in the same body due to difference in *karma*. Moreover, there is no danger of universal enlightenment or bondage (thereby scriptures being futile) or experience, since the differences such as ignorance, knowledge, experience belong to the limiting adjunct. The Self is one Consciousness principle and knowledge arises in that mind-conditioned consciousness through a mental modification due to an object contact and not otherwise. Thus the knowledge in the form of mind's mental mode is limited and hence the rise of knowledge or experience

---

[94] एको देवः सर्वभूतेषु गूढः सर्वव्यापी सर्वभूतान्तरात्मा ।
कर्माध्यक्षः सर्वभूताधिवासः साक्षी चेता केवलो निर्गुणश्च ॥ — *SU* 6.11

एकस्तथा सर्वभूतान्तरात्मा — *KU*, 2.2.9

यस्मिन्सर्वाणि भूतान्यात्मैवाभूद्विजानतः ।
तत्र को मोहः कः शोक एकत्वमनुपश्यतः ॥ — *IU* 7

सलिल एको द्रष्टाद्वैतो भवति — *BU* 4.3.32

मृत्योः स मृत्युमाप्नोति य इह नानेव पश्यति । — *BU* 4.4.19

एकधैवानुद्रष्टव्यमेतदप्रेमयं ध्रुवम् । — *BU* 4.4.20

of bondage in one does not result in the rise of knowledge or experience of bondage in everyone.

WITNESS CONSCIOUSNESS DIFFERENT FROM BRAHMAN : TWO VIEWS

1. The opponent disagrees with the above-mentioned Advaitin's view that pleasure and pain are the characteristics of the mind and these experiences are limited to the individual due to the limiting adjunct and that the witness consciousness is one, unassociated illumining the diverse experiences. This is inadmissible because, according to the opponent, the presence of a witness consciousness different from doer and enjoyer is not known through any means of knowledge. Even if one admits a witness principle, it cannot be one but should necessarily be many.

   According to Advaita Vedānta, the characteristics like pleasure and pain that occur in the mind is known by the witness consciousness. If the witness consciousness is one, then it should know the experiences of all the minds. This is not so. In order to overcome this problem, the Advaitin has to admit the plurality of witness consciousness. If it is so, then the varied witness principles cannot be identical with one *Brahman*. In this view, the existence of a witness principle is not accepted.

2. The above view is dismissed by another opponent, who accepts the existence of a witness principle. It is said here that the sense-organs can objectify the external world but not the internal organ. The internal organ, in turn, being the substratum of the thought-mode (*vr̥tti*), cannot objectify its thought-mode. The thought-mode, on the other hand, cannot objectify its substratum (the mind) and its characteristics (attachment, aversion, etc.). Thus, the mind and its characteristics are not known by the sense-organs or thought-modes, but only by the witness principle.

This is the contention of the Advaitin also. But the objection here is with regard to the non-dual nature of the witness consciousness. The plurality of witness consciousness is to be accepted because of the reason cited by the first opponent, and hence the difference between many witness principles and one *Brahman* remains unsolved.

WITNESS CONSCIOUSNESS NON-DIFFERENT FROM BRAHMAN

The nature of witness consciousness is explained through the epistemological dimension by distinguishing *upādhi* from *viśiṣṭa.*[95] The distinguishing factor is twofold: one is *upādhi* that distinguishes an object from another without being an integral part of the substance, and the other is *viśiṣṭa* that which distinctly reveals an object being an integral part of that object[96] (see *fig.* 3.5).

Based on this division, according to the Advaitin, the mind as a qualifier or conditioning factor distinguishing Consciousness is from two different standpoints. For the one who is ignorant of the true nature of the Self, the "I" includes the mind (mind is

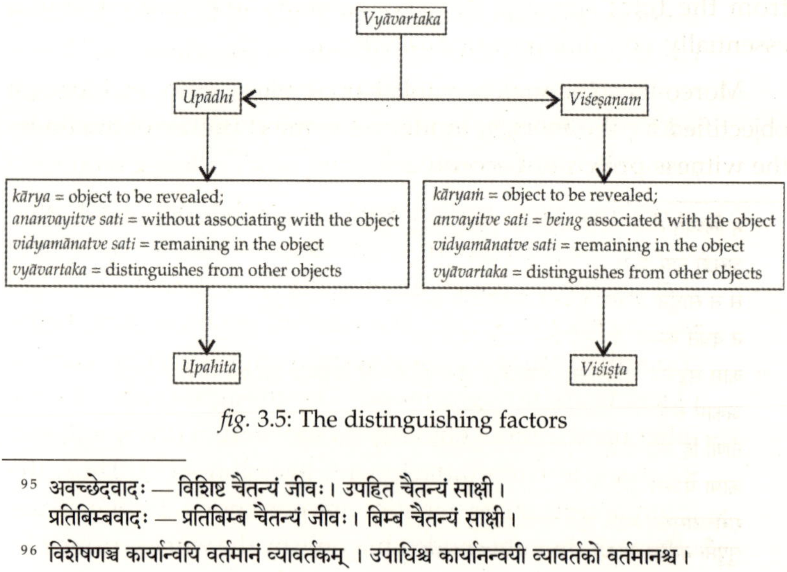

fig. 3.5: The distinguishing factors

95 अवच्छेदवादः — विशिष्ट चैतन्यं जीवः। उपहित चैतन्यं साक्षी।
प्रतिबिम्बवादः — प्रतिबिम्ब चैतन्यं जीवः। बिम्ब चैतन्यं साक्षी।

96 विशेषणञ्च कार्यान्वयि वर्तमानं व्यावर्तकम् । उपाधिश्च कार्यानन्वयी व्यावर्तको वर्तमानश्च।
— *VP*, p. 37

viśeṣaṇa), and for an enlightened one, "I" does not include mind (mind is *upādhi*). The one, non-dual Consciousness is said to be the witness principle considering mind as *upādhi*. The same Consciousness is said to be *jīva* as doer, enjoyer, etc. considering mind as *viśeṣaṇa*. The mind unassociated with Consciousness reveals the conditioned Consciousness through the witness principle. Thus, the mind is the *upādhi* of the witness principle and the Consciousness conditioned by the mind is known witness consciousness (*sākṣī*). And, the mind is *viśeṣaṇa* through which the conditioned Consciousness is revealed as the doer, enjoyer, etc. This conditioned Consciousness is *jīva*. While the Consciousness the *viśeṣya*, is unassociated,[97] the mind as *viśeṣaṇa* experiences sorrow, etc.[98] Thus, essentially *jīva* is non-different from the *sākṣī*.

The Advaitin claims that one *Brahman* cannot be identical with many witness principles. According to Advaita, the witness consciousness is of two kinds — *Īśvarasākṣī* and *jīvasākṣī*.[99] *Īśvarasākṣī* is one and *jīvasākṣī*s are many and limited. But the essential nature of *jīvasākṣī* is being non-different from the all-pervasive *Brahman*. As even the pot-spaces are many and limited but is non-different from the total space, *jīvasākṣī*s are many and limited, but is essentially non-different from *Brahman*.

Moreover, it cannot be said that pleasure, pain, etc. are not objectified by the thought-mode in the mind but is illumined by the witness principle, because, any kind of knowledge requires a

---

97 न लिप्यते लोक दुःखेन बाह्यः — *KU* 2.2.11
असङ्गो ह्ययं पुरुषः — *BU*, 4.3.15 and 16.
स न साधुना कर्मणा भूयान्नो एवासाधुना कनीयान् — *BU* 4.4.22
न वर्धते कर्मणा नो कनीयान् — *BU* 4.4.23

98 काम सङ्कल्पो विचिकित्सा श्रद्धाश्रद्धा धृतिरधृतिर्ह्रीर्धीर्भीरित्येतत्सर्वं मन एव — *BU* 1.5.3
अकामं रूपं शोकान्तरम्। — *BU* 4.3.21
तीर्णो हि तदा सर्वाञ्छोकान्हृदयस्य भवति। — *BU* 4.3.22
कामा येऽस्य हृदि श्रिताः — *BU* 4.4.7 and *KU* 2.3.14
रागेच्छासुखदुःखादि बुद्धौ सत्यां प्रवर्तते।
सुषुप्तौ नास्ति तन्नाशे तस्माद् बुद्धेस्तु नात्मनः॥ — *Aa* 23

99 तत्र प्रत्यक्षं पुनर्द्विविधम् जीवसाक्षि ईश्वरसाक्षि चेति। — *VP*, p. 37.

mental modification. In this case, the modification in the form of pleasure or pain in the mind is known through the modification of the mind in the form of pleasure or pain object-knowledge. Thus, there are two kinds of modifications — *pramāṇa pariṇāma* and *prameya pariṇāma*. The mental modification in the form of knowledge conditioned in the witness principle illumines pleasure or pain in the mind. In other words, the pleasure is the content of *sākṣī*, and without the mental mode, mere witness principle cannot objectify the characteristics of the mind.[100]

The space contained within the pot has a purpose, i.e. to hold water, and the purpose of pot-space cannot be determined without *upādhi*, namely, the pot. In the absence of *upādhi*, there is only one space. The pot-space is non-different from the total-space, and the pot-space being a product, with a name and form, is false. In the same way, the Pure Consciousness with the name "witness" is false that is said to illumine the mind supporting the characteristics like pleasure and pain. In the absence of the mind as *upādhi*, the "witness" consciousness cannot illumine and, in fact, there is one Consciousness alone. Thus, the witness consciousness is essentially non-different from *Brahman*.[101] The mind as *upādhi* generates differences, without which the name *sākṣī* is not possible, there is only Pure Consciousness. Based on this, it is said that *sākṣī* is one and without the *upādhi*-difference, the plurality and limitation of *sākṣī* are not revealed by itself.

Thus in the *mahāvākya "tattvamasi"*, the *tvam pada* secondarily refers to *jīvasākṣī* and the *tat pada* in its secondary sense means *Īśvarasākṣī*. The essential nature of the witness consciousness is the same and there is a seeming difference as *jīva* and *Īśvara*. Just as the space enclosed within a pot and the space enclosed within a room are non-different, and the difference is due to the limiting adjunct, the difference between *Brahman* and *Ātman* is but because of the limiting factor. *Brahman-Ātman* are non-dual in nature. Thus,

---

100 न चान्तःकरणतद्धर्मादीनां वृत्तिविषयत्वाभ्युपगमे केवलसाक्षिविषयत्वाभ्युपगमविरोध इति वाच्यम्। न हि वृत्तिं विना साक्षिविषयत्वं केवलसाक्षिवेद्यत्वम्। — *VP*, p. 29

101 In this connection, VB cites a novel example. *SV*, p. 43.

the knowledge of the non-dual nature of the Self alone is the means to liberation.

Let us recapitulate the pedagogical tools found in the above analysis centring on the nature of knowledge in Advaita Vedānta.

1. Advaita as the purport of varied branches of knowledge was arrived at with ample examples as examined by the *kaniṣṭha adhikārī* in the seventh *taraṅga.*
2. Knowledge of Identity (*aikya-jñāna*) as the direct means to liberation was explained to the *kaniṣṭha adhikārī* after refuting the views that *karma* or combination of *karma* and *jñāna* as the means to liberation as found in the sixth *taraṅga.*
3. While dealing with the role of *karma,* the arguments of Aikabhavikavādin as presented in the second *taraṅga* were examined. Later, the difference between the remote and proximate means to knowledge was indicated as in the first *taraṅga.*
4. Nature of bondage was discussed by analysing the nature of error and by refuting the fivefold factors as the cause of error based on the second *taraṅga.*
5. The erroneous nature of bondage was explained to the *uttama adhikārī* as in fourth *taraṅga* through the analysis of theories of error and the mechanism of erroneous perception. The mode of removal of false bondage was explained by the analysis of nature of erroneous object and its corresponding object-knowledge.
6. The locus and perceiver of falsity were revealed as the witness consciousness and the knowledge of identity was declared as the means to absolute happiness to the *uttama adhikārī* as in the fourth *taraṅga.*
7. The nature of non-dual Self was arrived at by refuting the views on plurality of self. The non-difference between witness consciousness and *Brahman* (the Self) was established as discussed in the second *taraṅga.*

4

On Impediments to Knowledge and Their Remedies (Jñānapratibandhanivṛttiśca)

THE *guru* had revealed the core content of Advaita, viz. *Brahman* is real, world is false and *jīva* is non-different from *Brahman* (*brahma satyam, jagan mithyā, jīvobrahmaiva nāparaḥ*). The reality of *Brahman*, the Self, was revealed by analysing the nature of the substratum; the falsity of the world was shown through the analysis of the ontology of bondage and the non-dual knowledge was pointed out by the examination of the nature of the Self. Thus, in the dialogue between the *guru* and the *uttama adhikārī* (in *taraṅga* 4) and *kaniṣṭha adhikārī* (in *taraṅga* 6) presented in the third chapter of the present study, the nature of the non-dual knowledge has been elaborately analysed.

In the course of this teaching, one may encounter with several impediments to knowledge in the form of doubt or misconception in connection with the reality of the Self, or falsity of the world or identity-knowledge. In the present chapter, we shall examine the pedagogical measures adopted by the *guru* in eliminating the specific problems raised by the *uttama adhikārī* (in *taraṅga* 4) and *kaniṣṭha adhikārī* (in *taraṅga* 6) related to the identity-knowledge and the falsity of the world.

The *uttama adhikārī* raises his doubt with regard to the identity-knowledge from two perspectives, viz.:

(a) the object of knowledge (*prameyagata saṁśaya*), and

(b) the means of knowledge (*pramāṇagata saṁśaya*).[1]

Such doubts[2] are an obstacle in understanding the core content of Advaita. The identity-knowledge is ascertained by the *guru* by addressing the object of knowledge through the method of *citcāturvidyā* and the means of knowledge by analysing the scriptural statement.

The second part of the doubt, for the *uttama adhikārī* is with regard to the locus of identity-knowledge. The *guru* had already revealed the locus of ignorance that implies the locus of knowledge too. But, the *uttama adhikārī* specifically questions the locus of identity-knowledge which is revealed by the *guru* through the analysis of the seven states of *ābhāsa.*

The *kaniṣṭha adhikārī* expresses his non-acceptance of the falsity of the world and the same is proved through a series of argument by the *guru* highlighting the *dṛṣṭi–sṛṣṭi prakriyā.* The identity-knowledge is explained to the *kaniṣṭha adhikārī* through the analysis of the *mahāvākya.* Thus, we shall see the restructured dialogue in this chapter as follows:

1. Identity-knowledge through *citcāturvidyā prakriyā* (*taraṅga* 4)
2. Revelation of non-dual Self in scriptures (*taraṅga* 4)
3. Locus of identity-knowledge (*taraṅga* 4)
4. Ontological displacement (*taraṅga* 6)
5. Identity-knowledge through *mahāvākya vicāra* (*taraṅga* 6)
6. and the role of *mahāvākya* (*taraṅga* 1).

4.1 Nature of Identity-knowledge

The *uttama adhikārī* (in *taraṅga* 4) poses his question: "The nature of *jīva* and *Brahman* is different and hence the solution of identity-

---

[1] प्रतिबन्धचतुष्टयं च विषयभोगवासना प्रमाणगतासंभावना प्रमेयगतासंभावना विपरीतभावना च इति। तत्र विषयासक्तेः श्रवणाङ्गभूताः शमदमादयो निवर्तकाः प्रमाणगतासंभावनायाः श्रवणं निवर्तकम् प्रमेयगतासंभावनाया मननं विपरीतभावनायाश्च निदिध्यासनं निवर्तकम् इति ॥

— *Vedāntakalpalatikā,* pp. 11-12

[2] *SV,* p. 30 fn.1.

knowledge mentioned by the *guru* is not tenable. *Jīva* is the performer of actions and reaper of its results and for whom there is the appearance of the world. In order to cease the cycle of transmigration, *jīva* yearns to uproot the prime cause of the world, viz. ignorance and thereby desires to attain *Brahman*-knowledge. The afflictions caused by repeated births and deaths do not affect *Brahman*. Hence, *Brahman* does not desire to attain knowledge. Therefore, since the nature of *jīva* and *Brahman* is different, their identity is not possible. Even when the bondage is really not in me, then also, the false bondage appears to me, like dream, due to delusion. There is the absence of such an appearance in *Brahman*. Thus, *jīva* and *Brahman* being different in these respects, the Advaitic stand of oneness of *jīva* and *Brahman* as the liberating knowledge is impossible." This doubt related to the object of knowledge is known as *prameyagata saṁśaya*.

CITCĀTURVIDYĀ PRAKRIYĀ

The *guru* presents the method of *citcāturvidyā*[3] to the *uttama adhikārī* in which the nature of *jīva, Īśvara* and Consciousness as *kūṭastha* and *Brahman* are analysed so as to arrive at the essential oneness of *jīva* and *Brahman* that is revealed through the *mahāvākya*s. Through the analogy, the appearance of one undivided space as many due to the adjuncts and the falsity of the reflection of space are revealed. In the same manner, the appearance of one undivided Consciousness as many due to adjuncts[4] and the falsity of reflection of consciousness are revealed. The "division" of space and Consciousness due to adjuncts is described in Table 4.1.

---

[3] कूटस्थो ब्रह्म जीवेशावित्येवं चिच्चतुर्विधा।
घटाकाशमाहाकाशौ जलाकाशाभ्रखे यथा॥ — *PD* 6.18

[4] आकाशस्य यथा भेदस्त्रिविधो दृश्यते महान्। जलाशये महाकाशस्तदवच्छिन्न एव हि। प्रतिबिम्बाख्यमपरं दृश्यते त्रिविधं नमः॥

बुद्ध्यवच्छिन्नचैतन्यमेकं पूर्णमथापरम्। आभासस्त्वपरं बिम्बभूतमेवं त्रिविधा चितिः॥

साभासबुद्धेः कर्तृत्वमवच्छिन्नेऽविकारिणि। साक्षिण्यारोप्यते भ्रान्त्या जीवत्वं च तथाबुधैः॥

आभासस्तु मृषा बुद्धिरविद्याकार्यमुच्यते। अवच्छिन्नं तु तद्ब्रह्म विच्छेदस्तु विकल्पतः॥

— *Adhyātma Rāmāyaṇa* 1.1.45-48

Table 4.1: The Division of Space and Consciousness due to Adjuncts

Fourfold "Division" of Space	Fourfold "Division" of Consciousness
Ghaṭākāśa (space contained within a pot)	*Kūṭastha* (Consciousness obtained within the bodies)
Jalākāśa (space reflected in the waters contained in the pot)	*Jīva* (Consciousness reflected in the subtle body)
Meghākāśa (space reflected in the waters contained in the rain-bearing clouds)	*Īśvara* (Consciousness reflected in the subtle universe)
Mahākāśa (total space)	*Brahman* (total Consciousness)

FOURFOLD DIVISION OF SPACE

The pot-space or *ghaṭākāśa* refers to the space contained within a pot that holds water. There is the reflection of space along with stars, etc. in the waters within the pot. This reflection of space and the pot-space together is known as *jalākāśa*. It may be argued here that there can be the reflection of stars, etc. but not of space since space is formless. There can be a reflection of an entity with form alone. Hence, formless space cannot get reflected. This argument is dismissed by the Advaitin by citing the example of the difference in the dimension of the reflection of space in the water contained in the footprints of a cow and an elephant. An example of "reflection" of sound is also cited to prove the same, wherein the formless sound "reflects" in the form of echo. Thus, the possibility of reflection of a formless entity is tenable.

The space occupied by the cloud and the reflection of space in the waters contained within the cloud together is known as *meghākāśa*. If it is argued here that the presence of waters in the cloud and the reflection of space in it cannot be proved since it is not perceptible, the Advaitin dismisses this idea by employing the means of postulation and inference. If the presence of waters in the cloud is not accepted then one cannot explain the phenomenon of rains. Thus, by postulation, the presence of waters in the cloud is proved. By the following syllogism, viz.:

the water contained in the cloud reflects the space,
since it is a pure substance,
like a mirror

If there is water in the clouds then it cannot be bereft of reflection of space. Thus, the waters in the cloud and the reflection of space in it are known through inference. The space that pervades everything is known as total-space (*mahākāśa*).

The space contained within the pot (*ghaṭākāśa*) and the all-pervading space (*mahākāśa*) are non-different. The reflection of space in the waters contained within the pot-space (*jalākāśa*) and the reflection of space in the waters contained in the cloud-space (*meghākāśa*) are false. Now, the example of the fourfold division of space is applied to the fourfold division of Consciousness so as to arrive at the identity-knowledge.

FOURFOLD DIVISION OF CONSCIOUSNESS

In the analogy, the *ghaṭākāśa* refers to the space conditioned within a pot and in the analogue, the pot-space is compared to *kūṭastha,* wherein *kūṭastha* is the Consciousness conditioned by an adjunct like mind. The *jalākāśa* is compared with *jīva* who is the reflection of Consciousness in the adjunct, mind. The reflection of Consciousness in the adjunct *māyā* is *Īśvara,* comparable to the *meghākāśa* in the analogy. The *mahākāśa* (total-space) is unconditioned and hence unlimited, and it is compared to *Brahman.* As in the example, so also in the analogue we arrive at the oneness of *kūṭastha* and *Brahman,* and falsity of *jīva* and *Īśvara.* The *guru* analyses the nature of each "division" of Consciousness to impart the non-dual knowledge to the *uttama adhikārī.*

NATURE OF KŪṬASTHA

The consciousness as the substratum that is conditioned by the mind (*sūkṣma śarīra*) or conditioned by ignorance (*vyaṣṭi ajñāna* or *kāraṇa śarīra*) is known as *kūṭastha.* If it is said that *jīva* is consciousness conditioned by the mind or subtle body, in such a case, *kūṭastha* is the Consciousness that is the substratum of the subtle body. If it is held that *jīva* is consciousness conditioned by micro-ignorance or causal body, then, *kūṭastha* is Consciousness that is the substratum of causal body. Thus, *kūṭastha* is the substratal consciousness of the factor (i.e. subtle or causal body) which defines *jīva*.

This *kūṭastha* is free from origination, destruction, etc.[5] That is, *kūṭastha* is not different from *Brahman* like the reflected consciousness that is different from *Brahman*. *Kūṭastha* is of the nature of *Brahman*. Just as the pot-space is non-different from total-space, *kūṭastha* is non-different from *Brahman*. The secondary signification of the word *ātmā* is *kūṭastha* which is also known as *pratyak, nijasvarūpa, jīvasākṣī*, etc. and is compared to *ghaṭākāśa* in the example.

NATURE OF JĪVA

Jīva is defined here as the consciousness reflecting in the subtle body which is the locus of countless impressions (*vāsanā*s) of desire, action, etc. In the example, *jalākāśa* was defined as the reflection of space in the water contained within pot-space, similarly here *jīva* is said to be the reflected consciousness along with *kūṭastha-caitanyam*. Therefore, the reflected consciousness in the mind and the substratal Consciousness of the mind put together is said to be *jīva*. Thus, primarily *jīva* is said to be endowed with three components:

(a) mind (i.e. subtle body with reflected consciousness and modifying *vr̥tti*) or ignorance (i.e. causal body with *avidyā vr̥tti*),

(b) reflected consciousness, and

(c) the Consciousness principle that is the substratum of both the mind and its reflection.

These three — mind, reflected consciousness and substratal Consciousness — constitute *jīva* and this is established by examining six alternatives.

---

[5] निर्विकारेण येनासौ कूटस्थ इति चोच्यते ॥ — *PD* 8.21

1. *Mind alone is jīva* — If *jīva* is said to be only the inert mind, then an inert pot can also be called as *jīva*. In order to distinguish the mind from a pot, one may argue that the mind like a mirror has the ability to reflect unlike a pot. In such a case, a mirror itself can be said to be *jīva*. This is dismissed by stating that a mirror, though with the capacity to reflect, cannot be *jīva* because it is an external entity, whereas, the mind is an internal organ (*antaḥkaraṇa*). If this is the argument, then the *jīvatva* can be attributed to the sense-organs that are also internal. It cannot be so, as the mind is more interior when compared to the sense-organs. So, the sense-organs cannot be *jīva*. Now, it is argued that if interiority proves *jīva* then the *ānandamaya kośa* or the ignorance which is the interior-most should be *jīva*. This argument does not hold good because *jīva* is sentient and an insentient ignorance cannot be *jīva*.
2. *Reflected consciousness alone is jīva* — Since reflection cannot be formed without a reflecting medium, reflected consciousness alone cannot be *jīva*.
3. *Consciousness alone is jīva* — Since *jīva* is subject to modifications, the unchanging Consciousness which is the substratum cannot be *jīva*.
4. *Mind with reflected consciousness is jīva* — Both mind and the reflected consciousness are superimpositions that presuppose a substratum and the eternity of *jīva* also cannot be proved with this combination.
5. *Consciousness and the reflected consciousness is jīva* — Consciousness is free from modifications and its reflection by itself cannot modify in the form of doer, enjoyer *jīva*. Modification of reflection is possible only due to a reflecting medium. If *jīva* does not modify there cannot be doership or enjoyership.
6. *Consciousness and mind together is jīva* — If this is so, then a mirror and the Consciousness which is the substratum of

the mirror can also be said to be *jīva,* which is illogical. Therefore, mind, the consciousness reflecting in the mind and the substratum of both which is the *kūṭastha* Consciousness, all these three together is *jīva.*[6] Here, *kūṭastha* cannot be bound and *jīva* alone is bound.

The *guru* also indicates that *prājña* is also included in the definition of *jīva.* In deep-sleep state, the mind is resolved and hence the reflection in the mind is also absent and here *jīva* is said to be the reflection in the microcosmic ignorance (*kāraṇa śarīra* or *ānandamaya kośa*) along with the *kūṭastha caitanya,* which is the substratum of the microcosmic ignorance.

Nature of "reflection"

Through the analogy of *ghaṭākāśa* and *jalākāśa,* the nature of *jīva* as the *kūṭastha caitanya* along with the reflected consciousness has been revealed. Now, the question is with regard to the source of reflection. There are two *prakriyā*s in the school of Advaita with regard to the explanation of the source of reflection in the definition of *jīva.* They are:

1. *Jīva as kūṭastha pratibimba caitanya* — According to this sub-school, the source of reflection in the mind is *kūṭastha caitanya* and not the "external" *brahma-caitanya* (all-pervasive Consciousness). It is like the redness of a flower that gets reflected in a crystal. The crystal placed on a red flower reflects the redness of the flower; similarly, the *kūṭastha caitanya* behind the mind gets reflected in the mind which is known as *cidābhāsa.* Since the mind has *kūṭastha* Consciousness as its substratum, the reflection of *kūṭastha* alone is said to be *jīva.*

2. *Jīva as brahma pratibimba caitanya* — According to another sub-school of Advaita, the reflection in the mind is that of *brahma caitanya.* For instance, the external total-space gets

---

6 चैतन्यं यदधिष्ठानं लिङ्गदेहश्च यः पुनः। चिच्छाया लिङ्गदेहस्था तत्सङ्घो जीव उच्यते ॥
— *PD* 4.11

reflected in a pot filled with water, the water here does not reflect the space conditioned by the pot. Thus, the reflection formed in the mind is that of the all-pervasive *Brahman* Consciousness and, therefore, *jīva* is said to be *brahma pratibimba caitanya.*

Both the above views are based on the theory of reflection (Pratibimbavāda).

The Avacchedavāda (theory of delimitation) of Advaita school dismisses the above idea of the possibility of the reflection of the formless *Brahman* Consciousness, since reflection of a thing is possible only when it is tangible, with a form. *Brahman* being formless and all-pervasive cannot get reflected in any medium. The Pratibimbavādin shows the possibility of the reflection of a formless entity by citing two examples as seen while describing *jalākāśa*. One is the reflection of the space in the waters along with the reflection of depth of the formless space and the second example is the echo which is a reflection of the formless sound. Thus, in this definition of *jīva,* three factors are involved — mind, reflected consciousness (reflection of either *kūṭastha* or *brahma caitanya*) and Pure Consciousness.

Attributes of Jīva

An interaction of *jīva* constitutes both *kūṭastha* and *cidābhāsa*. However, the attributes of *jīva* like doership, enjoyership, merits, demerits and bondage rest on the reflected consciousness alone. Due to delusion, these characteristics are falsely superimposed on *kūṭastha caitanya.* The *guru* then points out that, on further analysis, these features like doership and bondage belong to the mind and not to the reflected consciousness. It appears to belong to reflected consciousness due to the total-identity (*tādātmya*) of the mind and the reflected consciousness. But, on further analysis, the *guru* says that, in fact, doership, bondage, etc. do not belong to the mind also. Mind is inert by nature and since it is a superimposition of ignorance, it is false, therefore it cannot be the locus of features like doership and bondage. There is the manifestation of the experience of doership, bondage, etc. like the dream experience, which is an effect of ignorance.[7] The non-existence of doership, bondage, etc. is known to a discriminative person.[8] Thus, actually, doership, bondage, etc. do not belong to the Consciousness, or the reflected consciousness, or the mind. But, in the state of delusion, it is said that attributes like doership and bondage belong to either the mind or the reflected consciousness.

Tvam pada

It follows from the above discussion that the primary meaning of the word *jīva*, indicated by the word *tvam* in the *mahāvākya* (*tat tvam asi*), includes the mind, the reflected consciousness and *kūṭastha caitanya*. The secondary meaning of the word *tvam* is *kūṭastha caitanyam*.

NATURE OF ĪŚVARA

The reflected consciousness in *māyā* and the Consciousness as the substratum of *māyā* put together is known as *Īśvara*. This *Īśvara* is compared with *meghākāśa* in the example. *Īśvara* is also referred to as *antaryāmī* since *Īśvara* dwells within all beings and controls them. Due to the absence of concealment of the nature, *Īśvara* is eternally liberated (*nityamuktaḥ*). Therefore, there is no experience of bondage in the form of repeated cycles of birth or death for *Īśvara*. Moreover, *Īśvara* is also omniscient (*sarvajñaḥ*) being the possessor of *śuddha sattva guṇa* predominant *māyā*[9] as the adjunct. There is the rise of knowledge due to *sattva guṇa* and hence it is of the nature of illumination like the light. For *Īśvara* who is the reflected consciousness in the *sattva* predominant *māyā*, there is no concealment of the content of oneself or of others. Therefore, *Īśvara* is *nityamuktaḥ* and *sarvajñaḥ*. *Īśvara* is the creator, sustainer

---

[7] यत्र वा अन्यदिव स्यात्तत्रान्योऽन्यत्पश्येत् अन्योऽन्यज्जिघ्रेत् अन्योऽन्यद्रसयेत् अन्योऽन्यद्वदेत् अन्योऽन्यच्छृणुयात् अन्योऽन्यन्मन्वीत अन्योऽन्यत्स्पृशेत् अन्योऽन्यद्विजानीयात्॥ —*BU* 4.3.31

[8] यत्र हि द्वैतमिव भवति तदितर इतरं पश्यति। —*BU* 4.5.15

[9] स्वप्रतिबन्धकीभूतरजस्तमसी अभिभूय स्वयं ताभ्यामनभिभूतो यः सत्त्वगुणस्तस्य शुद्धसत्त्वमित्याख्या।
— *SV*, p. 102

and dissolver of the universe. The qualities like showering grace to devotees and overlordship also belong to *Īśvara*.

There are different views with regard to the nature of *Īśvara*,[10] like:

(a) The Virāṭ meditators argue that Virāṭ is *Īśvara* since the physical universe experienced is the physical form of *Īśvara*.

(b) The Prajāpati meditators argue that if the physical body consisting of hands and legs is said to be *Īśvara* then even insects like centipedes can be said to be *Īśvara* and hence the view of Virāṭ meditators is incorrect. The four-faced Brahmā alone is *Īśvara*.

(c) Meditators like Vaiṣṇavas, Śaivas, Gaṇapati meditators, Bhairava and Mairala, dismiss all the views and establish their supreme deity, viz. Viṣṇu, Śiva, Gaṇapati, Bhairava and Mairala respectively as *Īśvara*.

The *guru* defines the nature of *Īśvara* again as, the reflected consciousness in *māyā* with Pure Consciousness as the substratum. The varied forms attributed to one formless *Īśvara* are meant for meditation and other spiritual disciplines.

Further, there are different views with regard to the difference between *Īśvara* and *jīva*:

1. According to the followers of Yoga school, *Īśvara* is the Consciousness in whose presence the *prakṛti* gets activated and this *Īśvara* different from *jīva* is known as the *puruṣa*. *Īśvara* is unaffected by *kleśa*, *karma* and its result,[11] is unassociated and sentient like the *jīvas*. In *jīva* also there is the absence of *kleśa*, etc. but they appear to be in *jīva* due to non-discrimination. This is the difference between *jīva* and *Īśvara*.

2. According to the Nyāya School, the unassociated *Īśvara* cannot be the controller of *prakṛti* and hence the view of

---

10 *SV*, p. 101 fn. 1.

11 क्लेशकर्मविपाकाशयैरपरामृष्टः पुरुषविशेष ईश्वरः ॥ — *Yogasūtra* 1.24

Yoga School is incorrect. *Īśvara* possesses qualities like knowledge, desire and effort that are eternal, and these qualities are non-eternal in *jīva*.[12] Hence, *Īśvara* is different from *jīva*.

3. According to the Hiraṇyagarbha meditators, the view of Nyāya School is incorrect. It is argued here that if the qualities of *Īśvara* are eternal then it will contradict the Vedic statements like "He desired" (*TU* 2.6) that reveal the origin of knowledge in *Īśvara* during the origination of creation. Also, there will be the defect of eternal origination of creation (*sṛṣṭi prasaṅga*). *Īśvara* is Hiraṇyagarbha only. Even though Hiraṇyagarbha possesses a subtle body, due to the absence of ignorance, action, etc. it is different from *jīva*.

Here the *guru* points out that the attributes of *Īśvara* are different from that of *jīva* due to the difference in the adjuncts, viz., *māyā* and *avidyā* respectively and this difference is compared with the difference between *meghākāśa* and *jalākāśa* in the example.

Īśvara as the Cause of the Universe

There is a discussion with regard to the cause of the universe in *taraṅga* 6. Here, a question is raised as to "who is the creator of the world?" It is said that *māyā*, supported by all-pervasive Consciousness, which itself is the object of *māyā*, is beyond *sat* and *asat*, and is the mysterious power known as ignorance. Therefore, it is said that from ignorance the world rises, rests and dissolves. By this the following gets established:

1. Consciousness conditioned by *māyā* is *Īśvara*, and
2. that *Īśvara* is the cause for origination, sustenance and dissolution of the universe.

In other words, the question "is there a creator of the universe or did the universe emerge by itself?" is analysed by replying to

---

[12] बुद्ध्यादयोऽष्टावात्ममात्रविशेषगुणाः। बुद्धीच्छा प्रयत्ना द्विविधाः। नित्या अनित्याश्च। नित्या ईश्वरस्य अनित्या जीवस्य ॥
— *Tarkasaṅgraha*

the question re-framed as "is the creator of the universe *jīva* or *Īśvara*?".

First, some prevalent opinions related to the cause of the universe is presented wherein each of these views is dismissed and it is established that *Īśvara* is the cause of the universe.[13] Second, it is shown that *Īśvara* alone is the cause of the universe and not *jīva*.

1. Asatkāraṇavādin considers that the world is without a cause — If this is so, then any product would be produced without a cause. This is against perceptual experience.
2. Some consider non-existence as the cause of the world. This is also untenable since it is contradictory to experience, as every effect presupposes the existence of its cause.
3. Void is said to be the cause of the world — If this view is accepted then one can say that plant sprouts without seeds.
4. For the Naiyāyikas, atoms are the cause of the world. It is unacceptable, since the partless inert atoms cannot conjoin by itself in a particular order.
5. Time is said to be the cause of the world — it cannot be so because if "time" is taken as the common factor behind all creations, it leads to the fallacy of all things being produced at all times. Also, Time itself is ruled out as a cause since it is inert.
6. Cārvākas consider nature as the cause, it cannot be so. The presence of male seed in a barren woman does not produce a child.
7. For Mīmāṁsakas, *adr̥ṣṭa* is the cause. This is untenable since there will be no certainty that from a particular cause a particular effect will emerge.
8. The Pratyakṣavādin considers the cause of the world as mere chance. "Chance" theory is inapplicable as it cannot

[13] *SV*, p. 260 fn.1.

create elements to form an orderly universe.

9. The Pratyakṣapramāṇavādin posits that from the five elements like earth emerge other five elements. This is not accepted since the inert element like earth itself is an effect presupposing a cause; it cannot serve as the cause of another set of elements.
10. Sāṁkhyas consider *Prakṛti* as the cause of the universe. This is illogical since an inert *prakṛti* by itself cannot produce anything.
11. For Yoga (Hairaṇyagarbhavādins), *asaṅga puruṣa* in the form of Hiraṇyagarbha is the cause of the universe. This is untenable since an unassociated *puruṣa* cannot be the cause.
12. Some say that *jīva* is the cause of the world. *Jīva* cannot be the cause being limited in power and knowledge.
13. The supreme *Brahman* is the cause. *Brahman* is free from modifications and cannot produce a world.[14]

Thus all the thirteen views are defective. The position of Advaita that "*Brahman* with *māyā* is *Īśvara* who is the cause of the universe" is pointed out as tenable.

Now the arguments are put forth to show that *Īśvara* alone is the cause of the universe and not *jīva*. First it is shown here that there is a creator of the universe since the world cannot originate by itself. If the world can originate without a creator then a pot can be produced without a potter. It cannot be so, hence creator of the world is to be accepted. Thereafter it is shown that the creator is *Īśvara* who is omniscient (*sarvajñaḥ*), omnipotent (*sarvaśaktimān*) and independent (*svatantraḥ*).

One who is the creator of an entity produces, knowing the effect and its material cause (*upādāna kāraṇa*). Therefore, the creator of the world also produces the world, knowing the material cause of the universe. Since the creator of the world knows the material

[14] *MaK*, 3.3-30.

cause of the universe, such a one has to be omniscient. The creator of the world is also omnipotent. The *jīva* who possesses limited knowledge cannot even conceive the universe. The creator of the mysterious world possesses mysterious power and therefore the creator is omnipotent. The creator is also independent. One with limited power is dependent and an omnipotent one is not dependent on anything. Therefore, the creator is independent. The creator of the world is, thus, omniscient, omnipotent and independent, and such a one is said to be *Īśvara.*

Jīva, on the other hand, is limited in knowledge, power and is dependent. Even though limitations are not in *jīva,* from the transcendental angle, then also the false limitations produced by *avidyā* is experienced by *jīva.* The delusion in the form of limitations caused by *avidyā* alone is the cause of individuality (*jīvatva*). Such delusion of limitations is not in *Īśvara.* But omniscience, etc. caused by *māyā* is in *Īśvara.* Thus, the creator of the universe is not *jīva* but *Īśvara* alone.

Īśvara Is Both the Material and Intelligent Cause of the Universe

So far, *Īśvara* as the cause of the universe has been revealed. Now, the nature of the cause is analysed as in *taraṅga* 5. There are two kinds of causes, namely, the material cause (*upādāna kāraṇa*) and the intelligent cause (*nimitta kāraṇa*). The cause that is inherent in the nature of its effect, without which the effect cannot exist, is known as the material cause. On the other hand, the intelligent cause is that which is not inherent in the effect, but remaining different from the effect produces the effect. It does not get destroyed on the destruction of its effect.

For instance, the material cause of pot is the clay and the intelligent cause of the pot is the potter (stick, wheel, etc. are the instrumental causes used by the intelligent cause). There is the inherence of clay in the pot and the pot does not have an existence without the clay. Thus, clay is the material cause of the pot. The potter is not inherent in the pot, and the potter remaining different from the pot is the creator of the pot. On the destruction of the pot, the potter does not die. The potter is the intelligent cause of the pot. Thus, the twofold causes are the material cause and the intelligent cause.

Īśvara alone is both the material and intelligent causes of the universe and this is shown by analysing the theories of creation.[15] With regard to the origination of the universe there are three main theories — Ārambhavāda, Pariṇāmavāda and Vivarttavāda.[16]

1. *Ārambhavāda*: According to Vaiśeṣika, a thing originates from something else as cloth from threads. Cloth is a new product that has resulted by the combination of threads, and this cloth was non-existent in the threads prior to its production. It has come into being as a newly-created entity from its prior non-existent state. This doctrine is called Ārambhavāda and is also designated as Asatkāryavāda. On this basis, the Vaiśeṣika School attributes the creation of the world to the conjunction of primal atoms. For Advaita, this view is untenable since there is incompatibility in the conclusion that the production of an object is non-existent prior to its creation.[17]
2. *Pariṇāmavāda*: The creation theory of transformation advocated by the Sāṁkhya[18] School is otherwise known as Satkāryavāda, since it states that the object is existent in an unmanifest form in its cause the *prakṛti*, from which the world evolves due to the disturbance in the equilibrium of the three *guṇa*s. Advaitin argues that since according to Satkāryavāda the existent object originates, it is futile to bring forth the existent object; for, the object is already existent and as such it need not be produced. According to the *upāsaka*s too, *Brahman* modifies to become the

---

15 *SV*, p. 154 fn.1.

16 *SKS*, Introductory notes, pp. 115-17.

17 *BS* 2.1.11-20.

18 *BS* 2.2.1-10.

universe. This view too is untenable since the partless, indivisible *Brahman* is not subject to modification.

3. *Vivarttavāda*: Advaitin advocates the theory of transfiguration or Vivarttavāda. *Brahman* does not modify to become the world but manifests in the form of the world as "silver" in shell.[19] The principle that accounts for the erroneous presentation of *Brahman* as the universe is *māyā*. *Māyā* is the transformative material cause and (*Saguṇa*) *Brahman* is the transfigurative material cause.[20] *Māyā* being the power of *Īśvara* is an inseparable entity. Hence, it is said that *Īśvara* is both the material and intelligent cause of the world.

Further it is shown that as *jīva* is both the material and the intelligent cause of its own dream world, *Īśvara* is both the material and the intelligent cause of the empirical world. Just as a spider[21] produces thread from its own body and spins a web, thereby being both the material and intelligent cause of its web, *Īśvara* is both the material and intelligent cause of this world. The inert body of the spider from which it spins the web is the material cause and the Consciousness conditioned by the mind of the spider is the intelligent cause.[22] In the same manner, the inert *māyā* which is the body of *Īśvara* is the material cause and the Consciousness principle is the intelligent cause of this universe.[23] When *Īśvara* is

---

[19] वस्तुनि अवस्त्वारोपः अध्यारोपः ॥ — *VS* p. 20

[20] That which does not inhere the effect but remaining different from the effect provides existence to the effect, by whose destruction the effect does not get destroyed is known as the Intelligent Cause or the Efficient Cause. A potter does not inhere the pot, remaining different from the pot produces the pot and in the posterior production of the pot, the demise of the potter does not destroy the pot. Thus, there are two kinds of causes: the material and the intelligent cause. Intelligent cause is responsible only for the origination of the product.

[21] यथोर्णनाभिः सृजते गृह्णते च । — *MU* 1.1.7

[22] यथा लूता तन्तुकार्यं प्रति स्वप्रधानतया निमित्तं स्वशरीरप्रधानतया उपादानं च भवति ॥
— *VS*, p. 42

[23] अज्ञानोपहितं चैतन्यं स्वप्रधानतया निमित्तं स्वोपाधिप्रधानतया उपादानं च ॥
— *VS* p. 40

not required (*vimukha*) to bestow result of action of *jīva*s then there is the resolution of the world and when *Īśvara* is required (*abhimukha*) to bestow the result of action of the *jīva*s then there is the creation of the world. Thus, the creation and resolution of the world depends upon the *karma*s (action) of *jīva*s. The nature of creation is further analysed by examining the purpose of creation.[24]

Purpose of Creation

Does *Īśvara* desire to create this world out of sorrow or as a means to overcome sorrow, or out of happiness or as a means of enjoyment? *Īśvara* is free from sorrow and its cause (ignorance) and hence the desire to remove sorrow cannot be the desire of *Īśvara* to create this world. *Īśvara* is ever-fulfilled and hence there can be no desire for happiness or its cause. Hence, *Īśvara* can never have a desire.[25] Moreover, it cannot be claimed that as a child plays without any motive *Īśvara*'s creation also is baseless.[26] Even a child engages in a play for entertainment through which it seeks happiness. *Īśvara* being ever-contented cannot have even such a desire. Then, what is the purpose of this creation?

By nature *kalpavṛkṣa*, etc. fulfil the desires of everyone. *Īśvara* also by nature bestows *karmaphala* for which the cause is the merit and demerit of *jīva*. Thus, there arises the knowledge to create and an effort is put forth to create the world. The desire, knowledge and effort of *Īśvara* get activated with regard to the *karma* of each and every being and continue to exist throughout the activities of creation, sustenance and dissolution. Thus, the desire, effort, etc. of *Īśvara* are said to be eternal. *Īśvara* is the

---

[24] *SV*, p. 155 fn.2.

[25] इच्छामात्रं प्रभोः सृष्टिरिति सृष्टौ विनिश्चिताः ।
कालात्प्रसूतिं भूतानां मन्यन्ते कालचिन्तकाः ॥
भोगार्थं सृष्टिरित्यन्ये क्रीडार्थमिति चापरे ।
देवस्यैष स्वभावोऽयमाप्तकामस्य का स्पृहा ॥ — *MaK* 1.8-9

[26] अकामस्य क्रिया काचिद् दृश्यते नेह कर्हिचित् ।
यद्यद्धि कुरुते किंचित्तत्तत्कामस्य चेष्टितम् ॥ — *MS* 2.4

knower of all three periods of time.[27] The events like rain, heat, drought and famine are not eternal; everything takes place in keeping with the time principle (here the desire of *Īśvara* is the general cause). *Īśvara* manifests and withdraws, thus controls the creation and dissolution in accordance with the fructification of the *karmaphala* of *jīva*s. Thus, *Īśvara* creates the beings based on their merits and demerits and hence there is no defect of partiality or cruelty on the part of *Īśvara*.[28]

If it is argued that prior to the first creation there is no *karma* to determine the kind of birth of *jīva*s and since there is the first creation with variations of superior and inferior births, it reveals the partial and cruel nature of *Īśvara* — such an argument is untenable. It has been mentioned earlier that world is beginningless and therefore every subsequent creation is based on the actions of the beings of the previous creation. As there is the impossibility of determining the "first" creation such defects do not exist in *Īśvara*.

Causeless Īśvara[29]

It was shown that *Īśvara* is both the material and intelligent of the universe and is endowed with all qualities in full measure (without any limitations). If it is argued that *Īśvara* is not omnipresent then such *Īśvara* will be non-eternal since for whom there is limitation by space; there will be limitation by time also. A non-eternal entity that is limited by space and time will be an effect of a cause. That is, if *Īśvara* is said to be non-eternal then it must have a cause and the impossibility of the presence of a cause of *Īśvara* is proved by revealing the fourfold fallacies:

1. If it is said that the creator of *Īśvara* is *Īśvara*, this leads to the defect of self-dependency (*ātmāśraya doṣa*). Self-dependency is that logical defect in which the same entity

---

27 वेदाहं समतीतानि वर्तमानानि चार्जुन।
भविष्याणि च भूतानि मां तु वेद न कश्चन॥ — *BG* 7.26

28 वैषम्यनैर्घृण्यं न सापेक्षत्वात्तथा हि दर्शयति। — *BS* 2.1.34

29 *SV*, pp. 261-62.

is both the doer and object of an action. In the case of production of a pot, the potter is the doer of action and pot is the object, similarly in all cases, the creators of action and object are different. They are not identical. In the same way, if it is said that *Īśvara* is the creator of *Īśvara* in whom both doer and object are identical it is a logical fallacy. Therefore, one may have to accept another creator of *Īśvara*.

2. If a second creator is accepted then it must be created by the first creator alone since the cause of the second creator must be different from itself. If the first creator *Īśvara* is said to be the cause of the second creator, it leads to the fallacy of mutual-dependency (*anyonyāśraya doṣa*) since the second creator is accepted here in order to arrive at the cause of the first creator.

3. Therefore, a third creator is introduced. If the third creator is created by the second creator again there is the defect of mutual-dependency. By accepting the first creator, there is cyclical defect (*cakraka doṣa*) as follows:

   (a) First creator creates second creator,

   (b) the second creator creates the third creator,

   (c) the third creator creates the first creator, and

   (d) the first creator creates the second creator and so on.

   In this cyclic process, since each expects another as its cause, nothing gets established. Thus, along with the defect of mutual dependency there is also the defect of mutual expectancy. Without proving the first, the second cannot be proved.

4. (a) A potter does not create himself, but he is the son of his father, similarly the first creator cannot create itself and hence must have a creator.

   (b) The potter's father is not born of his son, but is the son of his father, similarly the second creator is not born of the first creator, and there must be a different creator.

(c) The grandfather of the potter is not born of the potter, not even by the father of the potter but from a fourth cause, in the same manner, the third creator is not the creator of the first creator or the second creator but itself is an effect of a fourth cause. The cause of the fourth is the fifth and so on. This results in the fallacy of infinite regress (*anavasthā doṣa*).

By accepting the chain of creators (*anavasthā dhārā pravāha*) it cannot be definitely said that "this is the creator of the universe". Such a defect where logic is absent, it results in non-conclusiveness (*vinigamanāviraha*). Some consider that the last creator in the chain of creators is the creator of the universe. In that case, acceptance of the earlier creators are futile leading to the defect known as *prāglopa*. This defect persists even in the case of halting the chain of creators, the prior and the posterior creators become redundant. Thus, by accepting a spatial limitation and thereby leading to non-eternity of *Īśvara*, there will be a necessity to accept *Īśvara*'s origin which in turn results in the above-mentioned fallacies. Therefore, *Īśvara* who is omnipresent and eternal is causeless.

Tat pada

Based on the above discussion regarding the nature of *Īśvara*, it is pointed out that the primary meaning of the word *tat* in the *mahāvākya* (*tat tvam asi*) refers to *Īśvara*, who is defined as Pure Consciousness and reflected consciousness conditioned in *māyā*. *Īśvara* as creator, sustainer and destroyer as revealed in Śruti texts refers to the reflected consciousness. The reflected consciousness conditioned by *māyā* creates world, etc. Qualities like omniscience showering grace to devotees, bestowing prosperity, etc. also belong to the reflected consciousness. The secondary meaning of the word *tat* is *brahma caitanya*, which is unassociated like total-space.

NATURE OF BRAHMAN

The *guru* now reveals the nature of *Brahman* comparable to the total-space. *Brahman* is all-pervasive, non-dual Consciousness. *Brahman* or the "total" Consciousness is to be understood as the true nature of the Self. Self is different from the body, sense-organs, mind, intellect, etc.[30] It is neither a doer nor a reaper. It is of the nature of Existence–Consciousness–Absolute Happiness and is attributeless one witness consciousness.

Sat[31]

Self or *Brahman* is of the nature of *Sat* or Existence. That entity which gets sublated by knowledge is said to be *asat*. That which is not subject to sublation at any period of time is *sat*. Everything gets sublated in *Brahman* the substratum, but *Brahman* remains unsublated. If *Brahman* is subject to sublation then there should be another substratum (*anuyogī*) for the sublation of *Brahman* and then for that *Brahman* to get sublated there must be another substratal *Brahman* and so on, thus giving rise to the fallacy of infinite regress. The ultimate substratum cannot be void due to the impossibility of object of absence (*abhāva pratiyogī*) and locus of absence (*anuyogī*) in void. Moreover, if the sublation of *Brahman* is accepted then the question arises "who experiences the sublation of *Brahman*, the Self?" Self cannot experience its own sublation, being illogical and that which cannot be experienced is *asat*. Hence, Self or *Brahman* is of the nature of *Sat*.

Cit

Self is of the nature of *Cit* or Consciousness (knowledge). Consciousness is indestructible[32] and is knowledge in the form of

---

30 नाहं देहो नेन्द्रियाण्यन्तरङ्गो नाहंकारः प्राणवर्गो न बुद्धिः ।
दारापत्यक्षेत्रवित्तादिदूरः साक्षी नित्यः प्रत्यगात्मा शिवोऽहम् ॥
— *Advaita Pañcakam* 1

सदा सर्वगतोऽप्यात्मा न सर्वत्रावभासते ।
बुद्धावेवावभासेत स्वच्छेषु प्रतिबिम्बवत् ॥ — *Aa* 17

नाहं प्राणो नैव शरीरं न मनोऽहं नाहं बुद्धिर्नाहमहङ्कारधियौ च ।
योऽत्र ज्ञांशः सोऽस्म्यहमेवेति विदुर्यं तं संसारध्वान्तविनाशं हरिमीडे ॥
— *Harimīḍhe Stotra* 36

31 The nature of *Sat, Cit* and *Ānanda* is briefly analysed here based on the dialogue of the *guru* with the *kaniṣṭha adhikārī* as in the sixth *taraṅga*.

32 यद्वै तन्न पश्यति पश्यन्वै तन्न पश्यति न हि द्रष्टुर्दृष्टेर्विपरिलोपो विद्यतेऽविनाशित्वात्। न तु तद्द्वितीयमस्ति ततोऽन्यद्विभक्तं यत्पश्येत् ॥ — *BU* 4.3.23

illumination (*prakāśa rūpa*).

1. If a non-illumined self is accepted, then the non-self inert objects can never be illumined.
2. it cannot be said that the objects are illumined by the mind and sense-organs, i.e.:
   (a) that which is limited is a product like pot,
   (b) that which has an end in time and situated in space is said to be limited, and
   (c) that which is an effect is an inert entity.

The mind and sense-organs are products of the five elements and hence they are inert and limited in nature. Thus, mind or sense-organs cannot illumine an object. Self alone is to be known as the illuminator of all objects and hence it is said to be of the nature of light.

Objection: Self is not of the nature of illumination because it is an inert entity. Self possesses the attribute called consciousness. This quality illumines both the self and the non-self.

Advaitin: Is the consciousness described as a quality of the self, eternal or non-eternal in nature?

1. If it is said that consciousness is eternal, then the nature of Self as consciousness gets established. That is based on the law that everything other than the Self is non-eternal.[33] If consciousness is said to be different from the Self then consciousness would be non-eternal. If the eternity of consciousness is agreed upon then consciousness as different from the Self will be illogical.
2. If consciousness is non-eternal then it would be inert like a pot. That which is non-eternal is known to be inert. It is illogical to say that "consciousness is inert". Therefore, the nature of Self is the eternal Consciousness.

---

[33] *BU* 4.3.23-30.

If the non-eternity of consciousness is accepted then it will be a quality of the self and will be different from the self. By accepting the eternity of consciousness, it is not differentiated from the Self. Consciousness is not a quality but it is the nature of the Self. Moreover, if consciousness is considered to be non-eternal, then one may have to admit that consciousness is a product of either the sense-organs or the mind. This is untenable. The sense-organs are withdrawn during the deep-sleep state but there is the knowledge of happiness which is expressed as "I slept well", on waking up. Hence, sense-organs do not produce knowledge/consciousness. Knowledge or Consciousness is eternal. Just as fire without heat is not possible, similarly Self without knowledge is not possible since "heat" and "knowledge" are not qualities but the very nature of the "fire" and "Self" respectively.

Ānanda

Self is of the nature of *ānanda*. If the Self is not of the nature of *ānanda*, then one cannot experience happiness by the contact of sense object. An object by itself is not a cause of happiness or sorrow, if so, then it must be either the cause of happiness for everyone or cause of sorrow for everyone. Certainly we find that one and the same object gives happiness to one and sorrow to another. According to Advaita, if one derives happiness from object-contact, the mind of such a person is undisturbed in which the *ānanda* nature of Self manifests. The mind of another is disturbed by object-contact in which the *ānanda* nature of Self does not manifest.

Objection: The desire for an object that exists in the form of "desire thought-mode" (*icchā rūpa vr̥tti*) in the mind gets destroyed on obtaining that desired object. Now, there is no cause for another thought-mode or another thought-mode has not yet risen. It is known that in the absence of thought-mode the *ānanda* nature of the Self cannot manifest. Therefore, happiness must be in the sense-object alone.[34]

[34] See Section 6.1 of Chapter 6.

Advaitin: This is untenable:

1. The *ānanda* nature of the Self does not get manifested in the *icchā vṛtti*, since it is of the nature of *rajas guṇa* and the manifestation of happiness is in *sāttvika vṛtti* only. On obtaining a desired object, the mental-mode objectifying the desired object is in the form of knowledge mental-mode (*jñāna rūpa antaḥkaraṇavṛtti*). This *jñāna vṛtti* is of the nature of *sattva guṇa* because it is known that knowledge arises from *sattva guṇa*[35] and happiness gets reflected in that *sāttvika vṛtti* only. But, here that *jñāna vṛtti* is external (*bahirmukha*). That is, the *ānanda* nature in the mind-conditioned consciousness cannot be grasped by this *bahirmukha jñāna vṛtti*. There is the manifestation of the *ānanda* nature in the object-conditioned consciousness and that object-conditioned consciousness is non-different from the Self. This amounts to say that the *ānanda* of the Self (*ātmānanda*) alone manifests in the object.
2. Vidyāraṇya explains this mechanism in another way. He says that other than the external *vṛtti* in the form of knowledge of sense object there is an internal *vṛtti* (*antarmukha*).[36] The rise of such an *antarmukha vṛtti* is during the absence of desire. On obtaining a desired object, the desire thought-mode is destroyed, and on gaining the knowledge of the object, an *antarmukha* thought-mode arises, in which the *ānanda* of the consciousness conditioned by mind gets reflected. The expression "I am happy" expressed on obtaining the object is because of the simultaneous rise of the knowledge of the sense object and the reflection of *ānanda*-nature in the *antarmukha vṛtti*. A non-discriminative person (*avivekī*) thinks that the object

---

35 *BG* XIV.17.

36 काचिदन्तर्मुखा वृत्तिरानन्दप्रतिबिम्बभाक् ।
पुण्यभोगे भोगशान्तौ निद्रारूपेण लीयते ॥ — *PD* 3.9

is the source of happiness. This is due to the false transference of the reflected happiness to the object through the *antarmukha vṛtti* that arises on obtaining the object. This is inferred from the repeated action of obtaining more objects, considering it to be the cause of happiness. On the other hand, a discriminative person, due to the absence of the above-mentioned delusion, understands the unconditioned *ānanda* as the nature of the Self.

Sat, Cit, Ānanda not Attributes

According to Advaita, *Sat*, *Cit* and *Ānanda* are mutually non-different and are not the attributes of *Brahman*.[37] If they are the qualities of Self then it could be said that these are mutually different. Since they are of the nature of the Self, they are non-different. The Self is *Sat* (eternal) since it is free from destruction (*bādhyatva abhāva*). The Self is *Cit* or Knowledge-Consciousness since it transcends the inert world. It is of the nature of "light" (*jāḍyatva abhāva*). The Self is *ānanda* and is the content of the reflected happiness (*duḥkha abhāva*). The world of objects (including body and mind) is differentiated based on names and forms, reflect *sat*, *cit* and *ānanda* nature of the Self. While the names and forms vary, *sat*, *cit* and *ānanda* are unchanging.[38] Thus, *sat*, *cit*, *ānanda* are not attributes of *Brahman*. If *Brahman* or Self is said to be endowed with attributes then it leads to certain logical fallacies.

Vidyāraṇya in his *Pañcadaśī*[39] says that if one wants to prove the existence of an attribute then its existential position is to be determined. An attribute has to exist in a locus, being an attribute. Now, the question arises as to, in which substance does an attribute exist? The *vikalpa* method of argument is employed and the

---

37 *TUŚB* 2.1.

38 अस्ति भाति प्रियं रूपं नाम चेत्यंशपञ्चकम्।
आद्यत्रयं ब्रह्मरूपं जगद्रूपं ततो द्वयम्॥ — *DDV* 20

39 विकल्पो निर्विकल्पस्य सविकल्पस्य वा भवेत्।
आद्ये व्याहतिरन्यत्रानवस्थात्माश्रयादयः॥ — *PD* 1.50

possibility of the locus of existence of an attribute is dismissed. Three options are provided; there is the substance "*s*" and the attributes "*a*1", "*a*2", "*a*3" etc.

1. *a*1 resting on *s* which has no attribute, *a*1 = *s* – *a*
2. *a*1 resting on *s* with the same attribute, *a*1 = *s* + *a*1
3. *a*1 resting on *s* with a different attribute *a*2, *a*1 = *s* + *a*2.

The untenability of each of these options is shown:

1. attribute is resting on attributeless substance is known as contradiction (*vyāhati doṣa*).
2. this implies *a*1 is resting on both *s* and *a*1, *a*1 rests on *s* and *a*1 rests on *a*1. The problem here is of self-dependence (*ātmāśraya doṣa*).
3. *a*1 is resting on *s* + *a*2. Here there is no problem of contradiction or self-dependence. But the defect can be seen in the next stage. *a*2 is an attribute which belongs to *s*. *a*2 is resting on which substance? There can be four options:

3A. *a*2 can rest on *s* – *a*

3B. *a*2 is resting on *s* + *a*1

3C. *a*2 is resting on *s* + *a*2

3D. *a*2 is resting on *s* + *a*3

3A. contradiction

3B. in the first stage *a*1 is resting on *a*2; here we find *a*2 is resting on *a*1. This logical fallacy is called fallacy of mutual dependence (*anyonyāśraya doṣa*).

3C. self-dependence

3D. no immediate problem but a question arises if *a*3 belongs to *s*, on what does *a*3 rests on. Five options are given here:

*a*3 rests on *s* – *a* — fallacy of contradiction

*a*3 rests on *s* + *a*1 — fallacy of cyclicity (*cakraka doṣa*)

*a*3 rests on *s* + *a*2 — fallacy of mutual dependence

*a*3 rests on *s* + *a*3 — fallacy of self-dependence

*a*3 rests on *s* + *a*4 — no fallacy now, but where does *a*4 rests, *a*5 on *a*6 on *a*7 . . . leads to infinite regress (inconclusiveness) (*anavasthā doṣa*).

Thus, the existence of an attribute can never be proved, since the substance on which the attribute exists can never be traced (see *fig.* 4.1). Hence, according to Advaita, *sat, cit* and *ānanda* are not attributes but is the very nature of the Self.

Etymological Derivation of the Word "Brahman"

So far, the nature of *Brahman* has been explicated and now a brief analysis on the word *Brahman* is taken up. Śaṅkara in his *Sūtrabhāṣya* brings out the etymological derivation of the word *Brahman*.[40] It is further explained in *Ratnaprabhā* based on the grammatical derivation. The root *bṛ̥h* means "extremely big", which implies absence of any kind of limitation, declared as *ananta* in the scriptures. By stating, *Brahman* as unconditionally big, the limitation caused by space and time is dismissed, since space and time are superimposed entities, they cannot limit their substratum.[41] The *guru* shows that one can enquire into the meaning of the word *Brahman* and arrive at non-duality. The root *bṛ̥h* with the meaning of "bigness" is referred to here as *pratiyogī-viśeṣa-anupadāna*, i.e. the word *pratiyogiviśeṣa* here refers to a particular noun which determines the dimension of the adjective. The absence of any noun to restrict the dimension of the adjective is indicated by the word *anupadāna*. The adjective here is unrestricted (*niratiśaya*). Thus, the meaning of the word *Brahman* means "unconditionally big".

---

40 ब्रह्मशब्दस्य हि व्युत्पाद्यमानस्य नित्यशुद्धत्वादयोऽर्थाः प्रतीयन्ते बृहतेर्धातोरर्थानुगमात्।

— *BSSB* 1.1.1

41 न व्यापित्वाद्देशतोऽन्तो नित्यत्वान्नापि कालतः।
न वस्तुतोऽपि सार्वात्म्यादानन्त्यं ब्रह्मणि त्रिधा॥
देशकालान्यवस्तूनां कल्पितत्वाच्च मायया।
न देशादिकृतोऽन्तोऽस्ति ब्रह्मानन्त्यं स्फुटं ततः॥ — *PD* 3.35-36

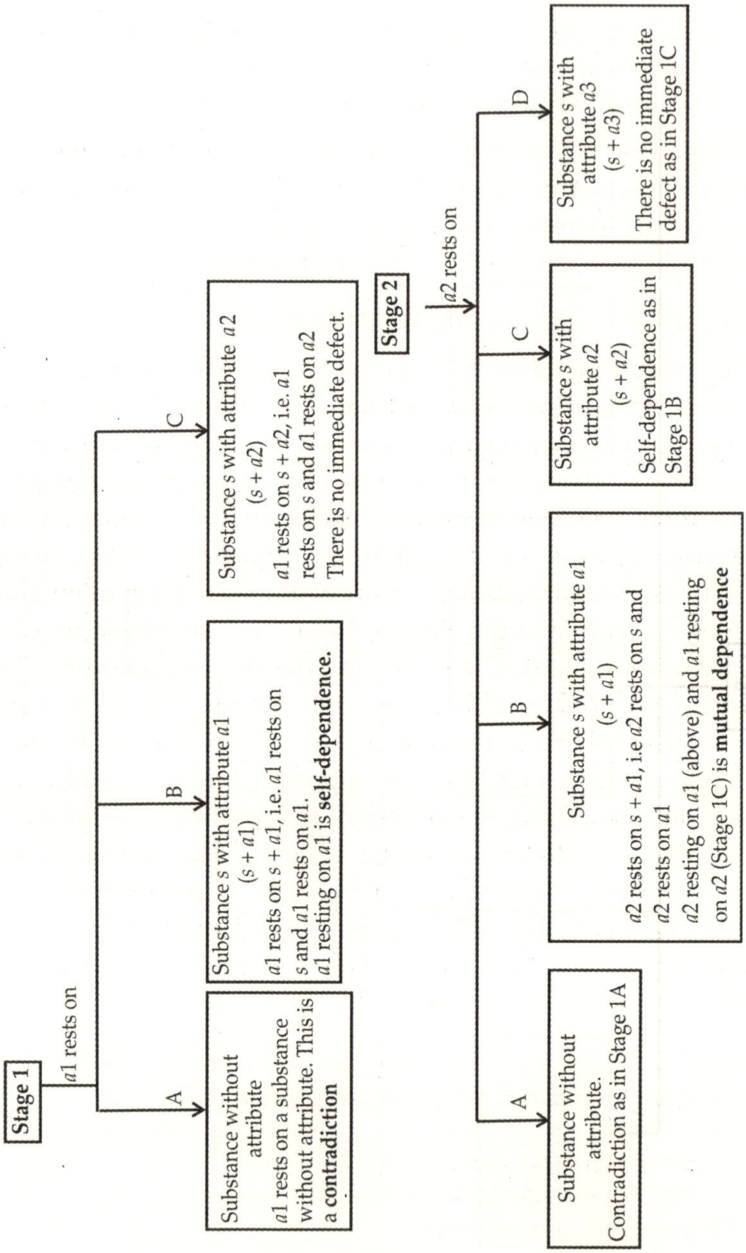
Stage 1
a1 rests on
A
Substance without attribute
a1 rests on a substance without attribute. This is a **contradiction**
B
Substance s with attribute a1
(s + a1)
a1 rests on s + a1, i.e. a1 rests on s and a1 rests on a1.
a1 resting on a1 is **self-dependence.**
C
Substance s with attribute a2
(s + a2)
a1 rests on s + a2, i.e. a1 rests on s and a1 rests on a2
There is no immediate defect.
Stage 2
a2 rests on
A
Substance without attribute.
Contradiction as in Stage 1A
B
Substance s with attribute a1
(s + a1)
a2 rests on s + a1, i.e a2 rests on s and a2 rests on a1
a2 resting on a1 (above) and a1 resting on a2 (Stage 1C) is **mutual dependence**
C
Substance s with attribute a2
(s + a2)
Self-dependence as in Stage 1B
D
Substance s with attribute a3
(s + a3)
There is no immediate defect as in Stage 1C

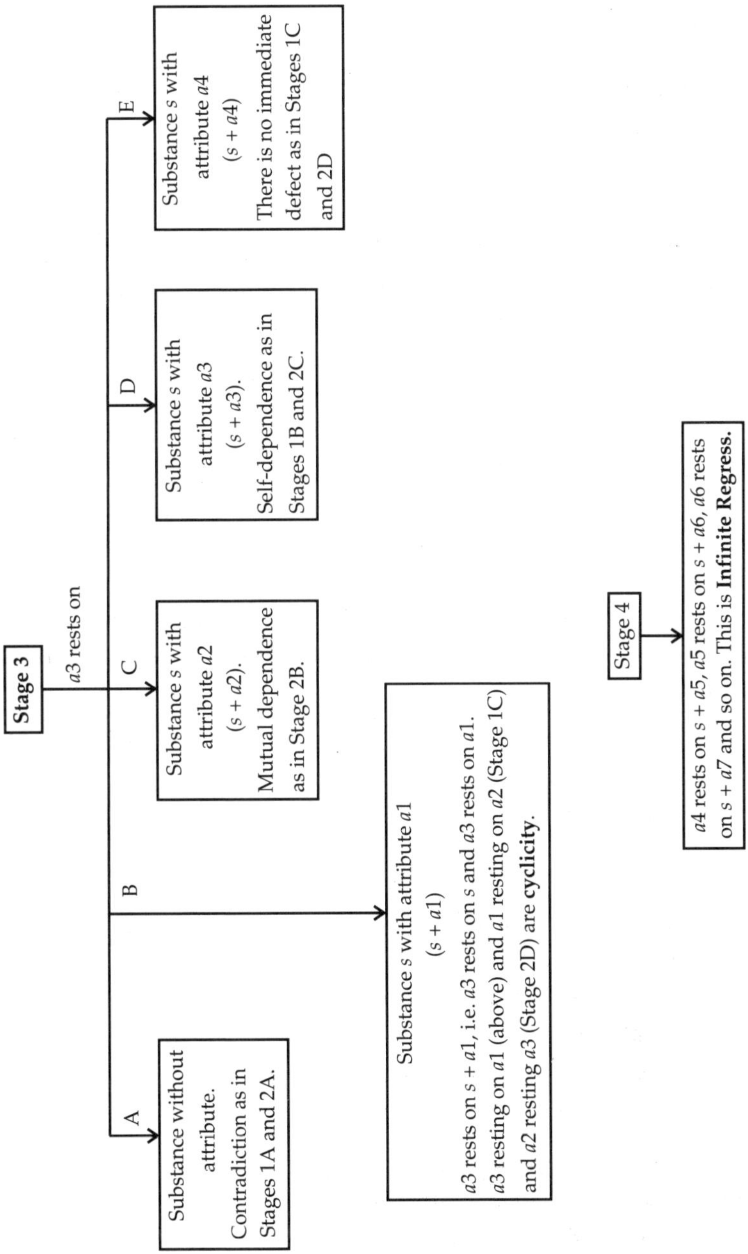

(s = Substance; a = Attribute)

fig. 4.1 Fivefold fallacies

The primary meaning of the word *Brahman* is that which is conditioned by the quality of pervasiveness. The "pervasive" quality is of two kinds — *sāpekṣa* and *nirapekṣa*. From the standpoint of the effects like earth, its material cause *māyā* is more pervasive. But, from the standpoint of *Brahman*, *māyā* is less pervasive. Thus, *māyā* is categorized as *sāpekṣa sarvagata* and *Brahman* is said to be *nirapekṣa sarvagata*.[42] These two kinds of pervasiveness are present in *Brahman* "blemished" with *māyā*.[43] The Pure *Brahman* is more pervasive when compared to *Brahman* with *māyā*. Transcendentally, *Brahman* conditioned with *māyā* is non-different from Pure *Brahman*. Thus, primarily *Brahman* means, the consciousness conditioned by *māyā* and secondarily, *Brahman* refers to the Pure Consciousness. Therefore, the words *Īśvara* and *Brahman* reveal the same meaning. Conventionally the word *Brahman* is known by its secondary meaning and at times in its primary meaning and the word *Īśvara* is conventionally known by its primary meaning and at times in its secondary meaning. In the *mahāvākya, tat tvam asi*, the secondary significance of the words *tat* and *tvam* refers to *brahma caitanya* and *kūṭastha caitanya* which are non-different.

So far, the oneness of *jīva* and *Brahman* is revealed to the *uttama adhikārī* by the method of *citcāturvidyā* and with this the *prameyagata saṁśaya* is answered.

4.2 Revelation of Non-dual Self

(1) Now, the *uttama adhikārī* raises doubt relating to the non-dual nature of Self as seen in the *pramāṇa*, i.e. the Upaniṣads. He quotes the *mantra* that seem to explicitly reveal duality. In such a case, the *uttama adhikārī* says he is unable to assimilate the teaching of non-duality. He explains the *mantra* as follows:

---

[42] न तस्य कार्यं करणं च विद्यते न तत्समश्चाभ्यधिकश्च दृश्यते ।
परास्य शक्तिर्विविधैव श्रूयते स्वाभाविकी ज्ञानबलक्रिया च ॥ — *SU* 6.8

[43] न कृत्स्नब्रह्मवृत्तिः सा शक्तिः किन्त्वेकदेशभाक् ।
घटशक्तिर्यथा भूमौ स्निग्धमृद्येव वर्तते ॥ — *PD* 2.54

द्वा सुपर्णा सयुजा सखाया समानं वृक्षं परिषस्वजाते ।
तयोरन्यः पिप्पलं स्वाद्वत्ति अनश्नन्नन्योऽभिचाकशीति ॥
— *MU* 3.1.1

The above Vedic statement reveals that two birds are perched on the same tree which is compared to the mind. Of these two birds, one is the reaper of result of action and the other is disassociated, pure and free from experiences who illumine the reaper of result of actions. The one who reaps the results of action is said to be *jīva* and the other who illumines the reaper is said to be *Īśvara*. Thus, this Vedic statement obviously reveals duality by differentiating *jīva* from *Īśvara*. This is the first objection with regard to the *pramāṇa* raised by the *uttama adhikārī*.

The *guru* teaches the Advaitic interpretation of the above *mantra*. The Advaitic interpretation is again based on the *citcāturvidyā prakriyā*. When it is said that *jīva* is a doer and reaper, it refers to the reflected consciousness and not to *kūṭastha caitanya*. *Kūṭastha* is unassociated, that illumines everything. In this *mantra*, the "two birds" do not refer to *jīvātmā* and *paramātmā* but, one bird refers to the semblance or reflected consciousness that reaps the results, while the other bird refers to the *kūṭastha caitanya* which is the illuminator of everything. The *mantra* is a description of the nature of *jīvātmā* and does not convey duality.

(2) The *uttama adhikārī* raises a second objection with regard to the identity of *jīva* and *Brahman*. The identity-knowledge is improper because in such an identity resulting in the non-difference between *jīva* and *Brahman*, the individuality is absent leading to absence of a performer of action. Then, the Vedic injunctions to propitiate *Īśvara* in various contexts become redundant. Duality is to be maintained to validate the Vedic statements that instructs on performance of *karma* or *upāsanā*.

The *guru* replies that the reflected consciousness in the

nature of *jīva* is the performer and the reflected consciousness in the nature of *Īśvara* is the bestower of results. Thus, there is a performer and the Vedic injunctions are not redundant. However, the Consciousness which is the substratum of *jīva* has no relation with the doership, enjoyership, etc. and the Consciousness which is the substratum of *Īśvara* also has no relation with the bestowing of results. The "doership" and "bestowership" are falsely attributed to the Consciousness. In the *citcāturvidyā prakriyā* the non-difference between *kūṭastha caitanya* and *brahma caitanya* has been revealed.

(3) Further the nature of identity of *jīva* and *Brahman* is questioned by the *uttama adhikārī*.

(a) Does *jīva* resolve into *Brahman* and *jīvatva* disappears, or

(b) does *Brahman* resolve into *jīva* and *brahmatva* (*Īśvaratva*) disappears?

The *uttama adhikārī* considers that the identity is not possible as said in either of these above two alternatives. In the first alternative, *jīva* resolves into *Brahman* would mean *jīva* being of the nature of *Brahman* is not qualified to perform *karma* or *upāsanā*, thereby again the Vedic statements revealing *karma* and *upāsanā* will be redundant. In the second alternative, *Brahman* resolves into *jīva* and *brahmatva* (*Īśvaratva*) disappears; then the Vedic statements on *upāsanā* will be futile due to the absence of object of meditation. Also, the actions will not yield results due to the absence of bestower of action. The view of the Mīmāṁsaka that "*karma* independently gives result" also cannot be accepted since *karma* is inert and incapable of producing a result of its own. Thus, oneness of *jīva* and *Brahman* is impossible.

According to Advaita, *jīva* and *Brahman* are non-different and hence the *guru* dissolves the above question of the *uttama adhikārī* and shows the possibility of identity-knowledge. The Consciousness which is the substratum of *jīva* and *Īśvara* is non-different like the pot-space and total-space as revealed in the *citcāturvidyā prakriyā*. In the *mahāvākya*, "I am *Brahman*", the word "I" refers to the *kūṭastha caitanya*. The word *Brahman* means the Pure Consciousness compared to the total-space, which is known through the secondary meaning. The identity between "I am" and *Brahman* is not possible in its primary sense but only by employing the secondary meaning. Thus, the *guru* conveys the identity of *jīva* and *Brahman* to the *uttama adhikārī* without referring to the kind of resolution that the *uttama adhikārī* had asked for.

4.3 Locus of Identity-Knowledge

The *uttama adhikārī* (in *taraṅga* 4) seeks clarification on the locus of the rise of identity-knowledge. He questions as to whether the knowledge "I am *Brahman*" arises:

(i) In the reflected consciousness — If the reflected consciousness is the locus of knowledge, then it must be an erroneous knowledge (since reflected consciousness is different from *Brahman*) by which the world cannot be negated. He arrives at the syllogistic statement as follows:

(a) Knowledge of *Brahman* is false,

Since such knowledge arises in the mind which is part of false world (*jñānāśraya mithyā*)

It like quenching thirst by mirage-water

How can such a false knowledge eliminate *saṁsāra*?

or

(b) Knowledge of *Brahman* is false,

Since the content of knowledge is identity of false *jīva* and (real) *Brahman* (*jñāna viṣaya mithyā*)

Like the knowledge of identity of rope–snake. (The content of "rope–snake" knowledge is "rope–snake" which is false.)

How can there be identity of a false and real entity?

(ii) Or (does the knowledge "I am *Brahman*" arise) in the *kūṭastha* — If it is said that knowledge arises in the *kūṭastha*, then one must accept that *kūṭastha* is subject to modification. If it is so then *kūṭastha* cannot be an eternal entity thereby it will be false like the changing world.

REFLECTED CONSCIOUSNESS IS LOCUS OF KNOWLEDGE

The locus of identity-knowledge as the reflected consciousness is revealed by the *guru* through the elucidation of the seven states of *ābhāsa*.[44] According to this *prakriyā*, the seven states of reflected consciousnesses are not associated with the *kūṭastha* and "I am *Brahman*" knowledge falls under the fifth state. The seven states[45] are:

1. Ignorance (*ajñāna*),
2. concealment (*āvaraṇa*),
3. delusion (*bhrānti/vikṣepa*),
4. indirect knowledge (*parokṣa jñāna*),
5. direct knowledge (*aparokṣa jñāna*),
6. destruction of sorrow (*śokanāśa/anarthanivṛtti*), and
7. highest happiness (*atiharṣa/niratiśayānandaprāpti*).

The first two states of reflected consciousnesses are ignorance and concealment. The cause of the verbal expression "I do not know *Brahman*" is ignorance.[46] The cause of the verbal expression

---

[44] *PD* 7.23-34.

[45] अज्ञानमावृतिः सम्यग्विक्षेपश्च परोक्षधीः।
अपरोक्षमतिः शोकहतिस्तृप्तिर्निरङ्कुशा ॥ — *PD* 7.33

[46] Consciousness is the primary locus. The mind with the reflected consciousness cannot serve as the locus since it is a product of ignorance. That which is a product of something cannot be the locus of its cause. Therefore, Pure Consciousness alone is the locus of ignorance.

"*Brahman* is non-existent and non-luminous" is concealment. There are two kinds of expressions in case of concealment because of the two powers of ignorance. The two powers of ignorance are *asattva-āpādaka-āvaraṇa* (that veiling power by which the existence of *Brahman* is covered) and the other is *abhāna-āpādaka-āvaraṇa* (that veiling power by which the evidence of *Brahman* is covered). Both the powers are generally known as "concealment".[47]

The third state of reflected consciousness is delusion. The *saṁsāra* in the form of birth and death experienced in the *kūṭastha* is an error or delusion. This *saṁsāra* is denoted by the word *śoka* in the scriptures.[48] The Śruti statements reveal that sorrow is removed by knowledge, which implies that sorrow is *vikṣepa* (delusion).

The fourth and fifth states of reflected consciousnesses are indirect and direct knowledge. Due to *asattva-āpādaka-āvaraṇa* there is the knowledge of non-existence of *Brahman* and the scriptural statement that "*Brahman* exists" is the indirect knowledge that destroys this kind of veiling. This indirect knowledge revealed as *satyam jñānam anantam brahma* is opposed to the notion "*Brahman* is non-existent". The knowledge "I am *Brahman*" is the direct knowledge that is opposed to ignorance and its effects. Thus, the effects of ignorance in the form "I do not know *Brahman*", the two kinds of concealment, viz. "*Brahman* is non-existent" and "*Brahman* is not evident", the delusion in the form "I am not *Brahman* but am the *jīva* who is subject to results of actions"; are entirely uprooted by the direct knowledge.

In the epistemological process, the oneness of object-consciousness and mental-mode consciousness is known as perceptual cognition or *sākṣātkāra*. This perceptual cognition is of five kinds.

---

[47] अज्ञानी विदुषा पृष्टः कूटस्थं न प्रबुध्यते ।
न भाति नास्ति कूटस्थ इति बुद्ध्वा वदत्यपि ॥ — *PD* 6.27

[48] यस्मिन्सर्वाणि भूतानि आत्मैवाभूद्विजानतः ।
तत्र को मोहः कः शोक एकत्वमनुपश्यतः ॥ — *IU* 7
तरति शोकं आत्मवित् । — *CU* 7.1.3

1. *Antaḥkaraṇavṛtti* — mind through the sense-organ contacts the object outside, the knowledge of which is gained by the knower is known as *pramātṛ bhāsya.*
2. The perception of pleasure, pain, etc. without the sense-organs contacting the external objects is known as *sākṣī bhāsya.*
3. *Avidyāvṛtti* — knowledge of "snake" in the rope is *sākṣī bhāsya.*
4. *Māyāvṛtti* — the knowledge of *Īśvara.*
5. The knowledge of *Brahman* through *mahāvākya* is known as *sākṣātkāra.*

The direct cognition may arise through the mental-mode by object-contact or through words. In the case, "you are the tenth person", the knowledge arises through words that are related to the object "tenth person" by which a mental-mode is formed in the internal organ. Thus, when the words convey an immediate object, the knowledge generated by the words results in perceptual apprehension. In the case of knowledge of *Brahman,* figuratively it is said that *Brahman* is the object of knowledge. Even though *Brahman* is not known by *phala-vyāpti* but *Brahman*-knowledge cannot occur without *phala-vyāpti.* That is, the witness-principle, without the external means, shines in the form of the thought "I am *Brahman*". So, the knowledge of *Brahman* is *sākṣī bhāsya.* The "I" thought illumines both the witness consciousness and the reflected consciousness simultaneously. The internal organ along with the reflected consciousness gets illumined as the object of witness consciousness. The reflected consciousness along with the internal organ cannot objectify the self-luminous witness consciousness.

The sixth state is destruction of sorrow. Sorrow or delusion is destroyed on identifying the true nature of Self as *kūṭastha* that is free from *saṁsāra.* The negation of *saṁsāra* in *kūṭastha* is destruction of sorrow.

The seventh state of reflected consciousness is the attainment of unconditional *ānanda*. On the rise of the direct knowledge "I am non-dual *Brahman*", one experiences the benefit of such knowledge. This is known as *atiharṣa*.[49] These seven states belong to the reflected consciousness. The knowledge that "I am *Brahman*" belongs to the fifth state of the reflected consciousness.

NATURE OF BRAHMAN-KNOWLEDGE

The *guru* now clarifies on the nature of *Brahman*-knowledge that was enunciated by the *uttama adhikārī* through two types of syllogistic statements. In the first inferential argument, it was said that since knowledge of *Brahman* is false, arising in the false mind, it cannot remove sorrow like the mirage-water that cannot quench the thirst. Hence, the question was how can false knowledge remove *saṁsāra*?

The *guru* replies that though the falsity of *Brahman*-knowledge arising from the scriptural statement as a mental modification is accepted, this false knowledge destroys false bondage.[50] It is known that a "true" means is incapable of removing a "false" entity. For instance, the sufferings experienced in dream cannot be removed by the means available in the waker's world. A dreamer roaming about can quench his thirst only by "dream" water. The water available in the waker's world has no purpose in dream. But, it has been already shown that sorrow is false.[51] Thus, the removal of false sorrow does not require a real means. It has to be understood that by the rise of a false knowledge, the false *saṁsāra* is destroyed.

The question then remains, as to how can mirage-water (being false) quench the thirst? The apparent mirage-water cannot quench the thirst experienced in the empirical world. The *guru* states that

---

49 साङ्कुशा विषयैस्तृप्तिरियं तृप्तिर्निरङ्कुशा ।
कृतं कृत्यं प्रापणीयं प्राप्तमित्येव तृप्यति ॥ — *PD* 7.252

50 By the maxim *yakṣānurūpo 'yam bali*.

51 See Section 3.4 of Chapter 3.

this example is not correct because in the case of scriptures the declarations of liberation and bondage are of the same order of reality; whereas, in the example cited, the mirage-water and thirst belong to different orders of reality. So, based on the logic, *samānasattākayoreva padārthayoḥ parasparaṁ sādhakabādhakabhāvaḥ* it is said that the scriptural teaching annihilates sorrow because being of the same order of reality they have supporter–supported relation or *sādhaka–bādhaka sambandha* unlike the mirage-water and thirst that is cited as the example. Thus, the false knowledge is remover of false bondage is revealed to the *uttama adhikārī* by which the first syllogism is answered.

In the second inferential argument, it was said that *Brahman*-knowledge is false since it reveals the identity of false *jīva* and real *Brahman.* Thus, the question was how can there be identity between false *jīva* and real *Brahman*?

The *guru* explains this by reiterating the nature of *jīva* and *Brahman* as explained through the method of *citcāturvidyā,* wherein it was said that the *kūṭastha caitanya* and *brahma caitanya* are non-different and the reflected consciousnesses are false.[52] Here, the *kūṭastha* = *brahma caitanya* is real and hence non-different; whereas the reflected consciousnesses along with their adjuncts are unreal and hence they are not said to be non-different. This is further explained by the *guru* by resorting to two kinds of appositional usages employed to arrive at the oneness of *jīva* and *Brahman.*

The word "I" in the knowledge "I am *Brahman*" refers to *kūṭastha* with reflected consciousness. *Kūṭastha* referred to by the word "I" is always non-different from *Brahman.* Thus, it is said that *kūṭastha* and *Brahman* are always identical by the application of primary appositional condition called *mukhya sāmānādhikaraṇya* (or *aikya sāmānādhikaraṇya*).[53] Just as the word-meaning are in primary apposition, the words (i.e. I = *kūṭastha* and *brahma*) being

---

[52] See Section 4.1 of the present Chapter.

[53] When two entities are non-different always, they are said to be in primary/identical apposition or *mukhya/aikya samānādhikaraṇyam.*

grammatically co-ordinated also are said to be in *mukhya sāmānādhikaraṇya*. In the example, the pot-space and total-space are always non-different, and by the primary apposition it is known that pot-space is the total-space and the words, viz. "pot-space" and "total-space" are also in primary apposition (i.e. grammatical coordination). That is, *mukhya sāmānādhikaraṇya* is applied to the words as well as the object of the words revealed through the word-meaning.

In the word "I", in "I am *Brahman*", there is the reflected consciousness constituent that is sublated as unreal by the application of the second appositional usage called *bādhāyām sāmānādhikaraṇya*,[54] by which the oneness with *Brahman* gets established. Just as the word-meaning, viz. sublated reflected consciousness and *Brahman* are in apposition, the words being grammatically coordinated are identical through *bādhāyām sāmānādhikaraṇyam*. In the example "snake is rope", the delusion of snake in a rope is resolved by rope-knowledge, by which an identical knowledge is arrived at as "the snake is rope". The non-difference between "snake" and "rope" is arrived at after the sublation of "snake" as unreal. Thus, the oneness of "snake" and "rope" entities and the oneness of these words are in *bādhāyām sāmānādhikaraṇyam*.

By this explanation, the *guru* shows that the identity is not between false *jīva* and real *Brahman* but the scriptures reveal the eternal identity of *kūṭastha* and *Brahman*, and sublated reflected consciousness and *Brahman* by the above two methods of appositional application (see *fig*. 4.2).

KŪṬASTHA NOT LOCUS OF KNOWLEDGE

The second alternative posed by the *uttama adhikārī* was that if *kūṭastha* is the locus of knowledge then it will be subject to modification, non-eternal and changing like the world. The *guru*

---

[54] When the identity is established through the method of sublation of one of the entities, then it is said to be in sublative-apposition or *bādhāyām samānādhikaraṇyam*.

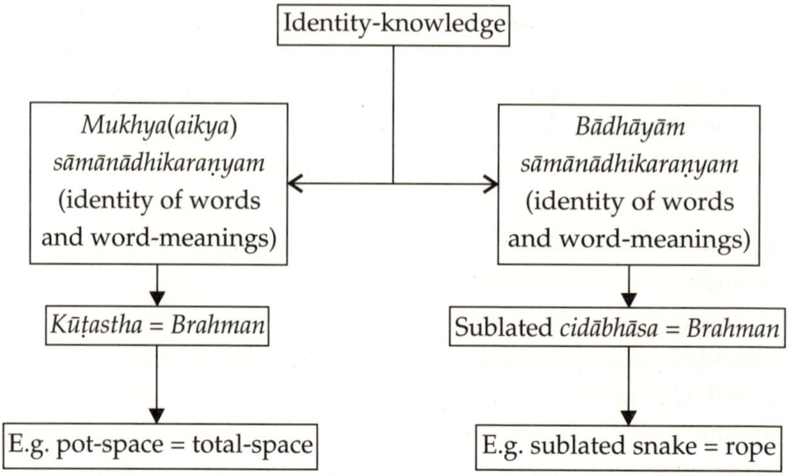

fig. 4.2: The identity-knowledge through appositional usage

dismisses this argument too. It was already mentioned that the knowledge "I am *Brahman*" arises in the mind along with the reflected consciousness and not in *kūṭastha* by the method of seven states of *ābhāsa*. Hence *kūṭastha* is not subject to modification, thereby is eternal and not changing like the word. Thus, the elucidation of locus of identity-knowledge is concluded.

4.4 Ontological Displacement

The *guru* is conveying the central essence of the scriptures, viz., *brahma satyam, jagan mithyā, jīvobrahmaiva nāparaḥ* as the liberating knowledge. The *guru* eliminated the obstacles faced by the *uttama adhikārī* in understanding the oneness of *jīva* and *Brahman*. Now, the impediments in assimilating the central essence of the scriptures as faced by the *kaniṣṭha adhikārī* (in *taraṅga* 6) are analysed that specifically pertains to the non-acceptance of the falsity of the world. The *kaniṣṭha adhikārī* dismisses the earlier statement of the *guru* who had said that the empirical world which is non-self is false like the dream world. For the *kaniṣṭha adhikārī* the very dream-world is not false and thereby the falsity of the empirical world remains unproven. He puts forth his argument in the following manner:

A totally unknown entity does not occur in the dream but that which has been experienced in the waking world alone is remembered during dream. Since the memory contains the real empirical experience, the memory-knowledge of it in the dream is also real. Therefore, by citing the dream example the falsity of the empirical world cannot be ascertained.

This argument is based on the view as held by Nyāya School according to whom the dream experience is memory (*mānasa viparyāsa*) of the empirical experience. Further, the *kaniṣṭha adhikārī* provides an alternative argument to show that dream experience is real. He says that the dream-world is real and not false because during dream the subtle body leaves the physical body and experiences the real empirical world.

The ontological displacement encountered by the *kaniṣṭha adhikārī* is clarified by the *guru* by pointing out the falsity of the dream-world and later by extending the same argument the *guru* reveals the falsity of the empirical world also thereby establishing *jagan mithyā* part of the Advaitic teaching. Later, the identity knowledge is revealed to the *kaniṣṭha adhikārī* by the analysis of the *mahāvākya*.

ONTOLOGY OF DREAM WORLD

First, the *guru* negates the idea of the *kaniṣṭha adhikārī* according to whom dream is memory-knowledge of the empirical experiences. The knowledge of the past experience is called memory (*smṛti*). The experience of an elephant in the past is recollected as "that elephant" and on seeing the elephant in front one says "this elephant" and this knowledge is not memory but perception. In dream, one experience as "this elephant", "this river is flowing", "this mountain is beautiful" and thus dream experience is not recollection of the empirical experiences but there is the direct cognition of dream objects. It cannot be argued that — "what one experiences in the waking world alone appears in the dream, and there is no knowledge of the objects in the dream that are not experienced in the waking world, therefore from the impressions caused by the experience of empirical objects there is the rise of knowledge of the dream-world" — this is untenable. The perceptual knowledge is twofold:

1. Knowledge that arise by sense-organ contact with sense object is called *abhijñā pratyakṣa* as "this is elephant" is the knowledge caused by the contact of sense of sight with the sense object (elephant), and
2. the knowledge that arise by the impressions of past experience and by the contact of sense-organ at present is called as *pratyabhijñā pratyakṣa* as "this is that elephant" is the knowledge caused by the past experience of elephant that is perceived in front now. Here, there is the impression of the past experienced elephant and the contact of the sense of sight with the elephant in front. Thus, there is no such maxim declaring that knowledge born of impressions is memory alone; since *pratyabhijñā pratyakṣa* is also born of impressions, and memory-knowledge is also born of impressions without the sense-organ contact.

The *guru* gives further reasons to show that dream experience is not recollection (*smṛti*).

1. The experience of elephant in dream is not merely born of impressions (*saṁskāra*) but is also born of defect in the form of sleep. Like the superimposition of objects in dream there is the superimposition of sense-organs too. Therefore, in dream the knowledge of elephant (i.e. knowledge of superimposed dream objects) is the result of sense-organ contact (i.e. superimposed dream sense-organs). Even though dream objects are illumined by the Witness Consciousness (*sākṣī bhāsya*) and are not the object of knowledge of sense-organ contact (as in empirical cognition) then also from the standpoint of the dreamer the dream objects are said to be known because of contact of sense-organs (created in dream). Thus, the knowledge of dream-world is not recollection of empirical experience.

2. Moreover a person on waking up from dream says "I saw an elephant in dream" and if the knowledge of elephant were memory then one would have said on waking up that "I remembered an elephant in dream", but no one says in this manner. Thus, dream is not a recollection of empirical experience.
3. It cannot be said that dream experience involves only those experienced in the empirical world because what is not experienced in waker's world or in this birth also appears in dream.[55] Therefore, the knowledge in dream is not memory.
4. Also, the object of memory is not available in front whereas the objects of the dream-world are experienced directly; hence dream is not memory.

The alternative argument of the travel of subtle body during dream given by the *kaniṣṭha adhikārī* is dismissed by the *guru* wherein he argues that since the departure of the subtle body from the gross body is said to be the death of the gross body it cannot be said that during dream the subtle body leaves the gross body to experience the empirical world. The gross body is alive with vital air during dream also and hence it is improper to say that the subtle body goes out of the gross body during dream.

It may be counter-argued here that during dream only the mind and the sense-organs leave the body to experience the empirical world and the vital air remains in the gross body itself because of which the gross body is alive. Also, the travel of vital air during dream is redundant since it is an organ of action and not an organ of knowledge. The mind and sense-organs of knowledge alone are required to travel and perceive the empirical world. Thus, during dream the mind and the sense-organs of knowledge leave the body, experience the empirical world and then return to the gross body with vital air and sense-organs of

---

[55] देशदिगन्तरैश्च प्रत्यनुभूतं पुनः पुनः प्रत्यनुभवति दृष्टं चादृष्टं च श्रुतं चाश्रुतं चानुभूतं चाननुभूतं च ।
— *PU* 4.5

action. Therefore, dream experience is not false.

The *guru* dismisses this argument by providing two answers:

(A) The vital air alone is the predominant entity of both the gross and subtle bodies. In the absence of vital air in the gross body it is considered inauspicious and is disposed off. Hence, the essence of the gross body is the vital air alone. Similarly, vital air alone is the essence of the subtle body too. The predominance of the vital air when compared to all the other sense organs is illustrated in *Chāndogya* and *Bṛhadāraṇyaka Upaniṣad.* Thus, the travel of the mind and the sense-organs of knowledge, abandoning the vital air, during dream are illogical.

(B) The mind and the sense-organs of knowledge are the products of the *sattva* aspect of the five elements and hence they possess the power to gain knowledge (*jñānaśakti*) and not the power to act (*kriyāśakti*). The vital air possesses *kriyāśakti* because of which alone at the time of death the subtle body travels to another world leaving the physical body. Also, because of the *kriyāśakti* of the vital air alone, during an empirical cognition, the mind goes out through the sense-organs and reaches the place of the object outside. The mind cannot travel outside the gross body without the aid of the vital air. Due to this interrelation of mind and the vital air alone, the Yoga system shows that without the control of the vital air, the mind cannot be restrained. In the imbalance of the vital air, the mind becomes unstable. So, one who wishes to practise *rājayoga* in the form of mastery of the mind has to necessarily practise *haṭhayoga* which is the control of the vital air. Thus, due to this reason also the movement of the mind is dependent on the vital air and hence it is said that mind and the sense-organs of knowledge cannot travel independent of the vital air. During dream the vital air is present in the gross body and thus the travel of the mind to experience the empirical world (during dream) is impossible.

The *guru* then provides further reasons to dismiss the idea that the dream experience is real. A person may have been engaged in various activities in the dream-world but such activities are not continued on waking up. If the mind is said to have travelled during dream gaining the empirical experiences then the continuation of such activities on waking up must also be experienced, but it is not so and hence experience in dream is not that of the empirical world. Moreover, there are so many geographical discrepancies in dream which cannot be accounted for if the dream world is a real experience. Also, there is a geographical dislocation, wherein as a dreamer, one would have travelled to a distant land but on waking up one finds oneself in one's own place. Such a dislocation cannot be accounted for if the dream-world is said to be real.[56] Thus, the arguments of the *kaniṣṭha adhikārī* that the dream experience is a recollection of the empirical experience and that the mind travels outside the body to experience the empirical world during dream are shown to be incorrect.

Creation of Tripuṭī in Dream

So far it has been shown that dream experience is neither recollection of the empirical experience nor is it the experience of the empirical world by the mind. Now, the *guru* emphasizes the idea that as in the waker's world, in dream-world too there is the appearance of the triad (*tripuṭī*) in the form of knower (*jñātā*), object of knowledge (*jñeya*) and knowledge (*jñāna*), and this implies that in dream the *tripuṭī* is created which is different from the *tripuṭī* of the waking world.[57] Thus, in dream the objects of the waking world are not experienced. The dream objects like mountain, river, sun and moon are new and created at that moment. The *guru* elucidates that if in dream the objects are not created then one cannot directly perceive the dream objects. But in dream the objects are directly perceived. The relation of objects

---

[56] *BSŚB* 3.2.3.

[57] *MaKSB* 3.1-4. स्वप्नस्थानोऽन्तःप्रज्ञः । — *MaU* I.4; *BU* 4.3.9-10.

with sense-organs and mind with thought-modification is the cause for perceptual cognition. Thus, the objects and its corresponding instruments of knowledge like mind, sense-organs are all created afresh in dream.

The *guru* addresses an objection here. One may argue that the dream objects like shell-silver are illumined by the witness consciousness (*sākṣī-bhāsya*) and hence mind is not required for the cognition of dream objects. Here, the objectionist accepts the origination of dream objects as in the case of shell-silver but denies the origination of (dream) knower and (dream) means of knowing. Thus, in the *tripuṭī,* the origination of *jñeya* is accepted and not that of *jñātā* and *jñāna.* The *guru* gives the following reasons to prove the origination of *tripuṭī* in dream.

1. Just as the objects like mountain and rivers appear in dream, the subtle body with mind, sense-organs and vital air also appears in dream. Hence the origination of *tripuṭī* in dream is to be accepted.
2. Objects belonging to the same order of reality alone can interact mutually. In dream, the objects are perceived with "dream" eyes and not with the empirically available eyes. Even when the empirical eyes are in the physical body, it cannot perceive the objects of the dream-world as it belongs to a different order of reality.
3. There cannot be an experience of an absolutely non-existent entity. In dream, there is the appearance of the experience of happiness and sorrow, its knowledge and its knower as the substratum of that knowledge, and hence the origination of *tripuṭī* in dream as different from that of the waker's world is to be accepted. According to Advaita, in all cases of erroneous knowledge there is the origination of indescribable (*anirvacanīya*) object. Knowledge cannot arise without any corresponding object of knowledge. Therefore, in dream too, since there is the knowledge of dream objects, the origination of corresponding dream

object is to be accepted. Thus, the appearance of *tripuṭī* in dream as different from that of empirical world is proven.

Falsity of Dream World

Based on the above reasons, if the origination of the experienced objects in dream is to be accepted then it may be argued that like the empirical objects that are subject to origination and hence real, the dream-world is also real since it originates. The syllogism may read as follows —

The dream-world is real
Since there is the origination of dream objects
As in the case of empirical world.

The *guru* proves the falsity of dream-world by taking up two main arguments.

1. Absence of appropriate place and time principles (*ucita-deśa-kāla-sāmagrī-abhāva*).
2. Absence of appropriate cause–effect relationship (*ucita-kāraṇa-kārya-sambandha-abhāva*).

The *guru* states that the objects created in dream are false,[58] since they are created without appropriate place (*deśa*) and time (*kāla*) principles (*ucita-deśa-kāla-sāmagrī-abhāva*). For instance, an elephant seen in dream does not appear in "proper" *deśa* or *kāla*. In a flash of a moment, the dream elephant is experienced. Hence the dream elephant is false. Moreover, the dream *deśa* and *kāla* and the dream-objects arise simultaneously. They do not have mutual cause–effect relationship. Thus, the dream objects that arise without appropriate place or time principle is false.

Also, in dream one may experience one's parent. Here the dream father and mother are not the cause of the dream son. Since the mother, father and son originate simultaneously in

[58] नर्मार्थो जक्षतिर्ज्ञेयो हर्षार्थो मोदतिस्तथा। अविद्यया भयं चेह स्वप्ने तद्धेत्वसंभवात्॥
आराममेव मायोत्थं स्वप्ननिर्माणलक्षणम्। मायिनस्तस्य पश्यन्ति न तं पश्यति कश्चन॥
— *BUŚBV* 4.3.943-44

dream they are not related mutually as cause and effect. The cause for the origination of dream objects is ignorance along with the defect of sleep. Hence dream objects are false like the shell-silver that is experienced due to ignorance (of shell) along with defects (in perceiver, instrument of perception, etc.).

Practical Efficiency of Dream Experience

At this juncture, we must note that Advaita School is not totally against the view of the utility and practical efficiency (*arthakriyākāritva*) of the dream experience.[59] The dream experience is shown as indicators of future event in the waker's world.[60] Advaitin accommodates this line of argument to show that an unreal thing can reveal the real.[61]

Non-difference between Dream-world and Empirical World

Now, the arguments put forth to prove the falsity of dream is extended to show that the empirical world is also false. This is done by analysing the material cause and locus of dream-world and the waker's world. According to Sr̥ṣṭi-dr̥ṣṭi-vāda or Trividha-sattā-vāda, the material cause of the dream-world is the internal organ and the substratum of the dream-world is Witness Consciousness. Whereas, according to Dr̥ṣṭi-sr̥ṣṭi-vāda or Eka-sattā-vāda, primal ignorance (*mūla-avidyā*) is the material cause of dream-world and *Brahman*-consciousness is the substratum of the dream-world. Thus, the dream-world is either a modification of the internal organ or primal ignorance. The transfigurative material cause is Consciousness. The *guru* takes up an objection here and replies.

Objection: If the material cause of dream is primal ignorance (according to Dr̥ṣṭi-sr̥ṣṭi-vāda) and the substratum is *Brahman* then

---

59 स्वप्नः शुभाशुभफलागमसूचकः स्यान्मिथ्यापि सन्निति च सूत्रकृदाह यत्नात्।
गुर्वादि सर्वमिदमद्वयबुद्धिहेतुर्मायानिबन्धनमिति प्रतिपादनाय ॥ — *SKS* 1.338
सूचकश्च हि श्रुतेराचक्षते च तद्विदः। — *BS* 3.2.4 and *Ratnaprabhā* 3.2.4.

60 *CU* 5.2.7 and *BSŚB* 3.2.4.

61 *BSŚB* 3.2.4.

the division of waker's world as empirical (*vyāvahārika*) and dreamer's world as phenomenal (*prātibhāsika*) is not proper. The waker's world is said to be empirical being a product of primal ignorance with *Brahman* as the substratum. So, either both the waker's world and dreamer's world must be empirical or both must be phenomenal in nature. The difference in their orders of reality is untenable.

Advaitin: The waker's and dreamer's worlds are not the same. In waker's world, ignorance alone is the cause for the origination of body, sense-organs, etc., whereas, ignorance along with the defect of sleep (that has a beginning, *sādi nidrā*) is the cause for the origination of dream objects. Hence, the division of waker's world as empirical and dreamer's world as phenomenal is tenable. There is a difference between the objects of the waker's world from that of the dream-world. This argument is based on the theory of three orders of reality (Trividha-sattā-vāda).

On analysis, this theory of three orders of reality also is not tenable. The mutual difference between waker's world and dreamer's world does not exist. If it is further argued that Trividha-sattā-vāda is discussed in many Vedāntic works, the *guru* says that one should understand that it is meant for aspirants with dull intellect. For the aspirants of higher cadre the difference between waker's world and dream-world is resolved.

ONTOLOGY OF EMPIRICAL WORLD

Now, the two main arguments, viz. *ucita-deśa-kāla-sāmagrī-abhāva* and *ucita-kāraṇa-kārya-sambandha-abhāva* employed to prove the falsity of the dream-world is extended by the *guru* to reveal the falsity of the empirical world so as to arrive at *jagan mithyātva*. It was mentioned that that which originates without proper *deśa* or *kāla* constituents is known as *mithyā* (false). Based on this argument, the *guru* now says that the (empirical) world was originated from *Brahman* without appropriate *deśa* and *kāla* constituents. *Brahman*, devoid of *deśa* and *kāla*, is the substratum from which *ākāśa*, etc. emerged. Since *ākāśa* originated without *deśa* and *kāla* constituents, the creation is said to be false like the dream-world. Just as, even though there is an appropriate *deśa*, a magician creates elephant, mountain, etc. in less time and hence they are false, in the same manner, the dream-world created in limited *deśa* (in the *nāḍī* located in the neck) and in less time is said to be false. By the strength of this example, it is said that the waker's world is also false.

The *guru* takes up a series of alternative arguments and proves the falsity of the empirical world. The empirical world is experienced in *Brahman* which is devoid of appropriate *deśa* and *kāla* constituents. The cause of the world cannot be said as:

(i) non-different from *deśa* and *kāla*, or

(ii) different from *deśa* and *kāla*.

Brahman is the absolute entity and another entity non-different from *Brahman* is unacceptable. If it is said that *deśa* and *kāla* are different from *Brahman*, the question is whether they are:

(a) real, or

(b) unreal?

They cannot be treated as real as it is against non-dualism. If they are said to be unreal, then like the world, *deśa* and *kāla* should be an effect. If this is so, the cause of *deśa* and *kāla* is to be determined. Here, the *guru* points to the fourfold fallacies if one tries to determine the cause of *deśa* and *kāla*:

1. *Deśa* and *kāla* cannot create itself resting on itself; it leads to the defect of self-dependence (*ātmāśraya doṣa*).
2. If it is argued that the first *deśa-kāla* is the cause of second *deśa-kāla* and the second *deśa-kāla* is the cause of first *deśa-kāla*, i.e. they are mutually created, this leads to the defect of mutual-dependence (*anyonyāśraya doṣa*).
3. The cause of first *deśa-kāla* is the second *deśa-kāla*, which is the cause of third *deśa-kāla* and the third *deśa-kāla* is the cause of first *deśa-kāla*, leads to the defect of cyclicity (*cakraka doṣa*).

4. If the cause of *deśa-kāla* is traced to infinite *deśa-kāla* chain, it leads to the fallacy of infinite regress (*anavasthā doṣa*). Therefore, *Brahman* as the cause of *deśa* or *kāla* cannot be established.

Brahman which is devoid of *deśa*, *kāla* and causality cannot create an empirical world; the experienced empirical world is a superimposition. This view is known as Ajātivāda.[62] The falsity of the empirical world is stated in an inferential statement:

> Waker's world is false
> Because of absence of appropriate deśa and kāla
> Like the dream-world
> Therefore, the waker's world is proved to be false like the dream-world.[63]

Superimposition of Causality

Here, the nature of causality is examined further. The empirical world originates from *Īśvara* with *māyā*. The cause-ness is superimposed on *deśa* and *kāla*, the effect-ness is superimposed on the world. *Māyā* is the cause of *deśa*, *kāla* and *jagat*, and also is the cause of superimposition of cause-ness in *deśa–kāla* and effect-ness on the world. The world of objects cannot be conceived without *deśa* or *kāla*. So, *deśa* and *kāla* are to be preconceived to know an object. Therefore, cause-ness is superimposed on *deśa* and *kāla*.[64] In reality, *deśa* and *kāla* are not the cause of *ākāśa*, etc.

---

62 न तस्य कार्यं करणं च विद्यते न तत्समश्चाभ्यधिकश्च दृश्यते ।
परास्य शक्तिर्विविधैव श्रूयते स्वाभाविकी ज्ञानबलक्रिया च ॥ — *SU* 6.8

कार्यकारणता ह्यत्र न किञ्चिदुपपद्यते । यादृगेव परं ब्रह्म तादृगेव जगत्त्रयम् ॥
— Quoted in *SV*, p. 212

तुच्छाऽनिर्वचनीया च वास्तवी चेत्यसौ त्रिधा ।
ज्ञेया माया त्रिभिर्बोधैः श्रौतयौक्तिकलौकिकैः ॥ — *PD* 6.130

63 स्वप्नेन्द्रजालसदृशमचिन्त्यरचनात्मकम् ।
दृष्टनष्टं जगत्पश्यन् कथं तत्रानुरज्यति ॥ — *PD* 7.171

स्वस्वप्नमापरोक्ष्येण दृष्ट्वा पश्यन् स्वजागरम् ।
चिन्तयेदप्रमत्तः सन्नभावनुदिनं मुहुः ॥ — *PD* 7.172

64 धिया सहोदेति धियाऽस्तमेति लोकस्ततो धीप्रविभास्य एषः । — *SD* 9

The *guru* presents an argument based on the view of Madhusūdana Sarasvatī[65] according to whom the *deśa* and *kāla* are superimposed on *māyā*, prior to the creation of the world. It means time is created prior to the creation of the world, this leads to logical fallacy. The *guru* clarifies the statement of Madhusūdana and states that it means the world and time principles emerge simultaneously. It is *samāna kālika adhyāsa*. There is no chronological creation of the time principle followed by the creation of the world. In fact, the chronology itself is a simultaneous superimposition.

Nature of Superimposed Causality

The *guru* analyses the *kāraṇatva svarūpa* (the nature of cause-ness) attributed to *deśa* and *kāla*. Based on *anyathā khyāti*, it is said that the *kāraṇatva dharma* in *Brahman* is transferred to *deśa* and *kāla* like the transference of redness of hibiscus to pure crystal or like the experience of mountains, etc. as real in dream. In such cases, Advaitin accepts *anyathā khyāti*. According to Advaita, in the case of shell-silver, the transforming material cause is ignorance and Consciousness is the transfigurative material cause. Both the indescribable silver and its knowledge arise. One and the same object (shell) is mistaken as "silver". This is *anirvacanīya khyāti*. In the case of red-crystal, two objects are in proximity, wherein the property of one (red flower) gets transferred to another (colourless crystal) and the internal organ contacts both "red" and "crystal". Thus, the causal state of the substratal Consciousness gets transferred to *deśa* and *kāla* due to *anyathā khyāti*.

One may argue, since *anyathā khyāti* is accepted in certain cases by Advaitin, then, just as it is claimed that the reality of *Brahman* is transferred to the entire world, in the same manner, it can be said that the causal state of *Brahman* is transferred to the entire world. Such an argument is untenable. This is explained — in dream, two bodies are created — father and son. Both are supported by the substratum consciousness, but the cause-ness is transferred to the father's body alone. In the same manner, the

[65] See *Siddhāntabindu* commentary to *Daśaślokī*.

cause-ness of the substratum consciousness supporting the world is transferred to the *deśa* and *kāla* alone. In fact, according to Advaita, the unassociated substratal consciousness is not a cause. The reflection of *māyā* too is not a cause since the nature of reflection is false. When the reflection itself is false it cannot be a cause of something. Here, *anyathā khyāti* also is ruled out. If *Brahman* is said to be the cause of the world then the cause-ness is falsely seen in *deśa* and *kāla*. There is no cause-ness in *Brahman*. Thus, *Brahman* which is devoid of characteristics like cause-ness the transference of cause-ness to *deśa* and *kāla* cannot be said.[66] There is the possibility of creation of indescribable *deśa* and *kāla* by *māyā* (*dharmī adhyāsa*) and indescribable cause-ness (*dharma adhyāsa*). In reality, *deśa* and *kāla* do not possess cause-ness. An unmarried person in dream can see his son and grandson. Here, the body of son and grandson along with cause and effect relation is said to be created indescribably. In the same manner, *deśa* and *kāla* along with their cause and effect relationship appear indescribably. Thus, even without appropriate *deśa* and *kāla sāmagrī*, the waking world is created. So, waking world is false like dream-world.[67]

Now, the *guru* elucidates the second argument, viz. *ucita-kāraṇa-kārya-sambandha-abhāva* in order to arrive at the falsity of empirical world. The *guru* advocating the Dṛṣṭi-sṛṣṭi-vāda[68] to the *kaniṣṭha adhikārī* says that in reality the objects in the waker's world like that of dream-world are also not mutually related as cause and effect. The objects of the waker's world are directly the effects of *avidyā*, like shell-silver and dream. Hence they are

---

66 एतद्ब्रह्मापूर्वमनपरमनन्तरमबाह्यमयमात्मा ब्रह्म। — *BU* 2.5.19

न तत्र चक्षुर्गच्छति न वाग्गच्छति नो मनः।
न विद्मो न विजानीमो यथैतदनुशिष्यात्॥ — *KeU* I.3

67 तस्य त्रय अवस्थास्त्रयः स्वप्ना अयमावसथोऽयमावसथोऽयमावसथ इति।
— *AU* 1.3.12

68 A second kind of Dṛṣṭi-sṛṣṭivāda is discussed in *SV*, fn. 1, p. 208.

सत्ता सर्वपदार्थानां नान्या संवेदनादृते।
ज्ञानस्वरूपमेवाहुर्जगदेतद्विचक्षणः॥
अर्थस्वरूपं भ्राम्यन्तः पश्यन्त्यन्ये कुदृष्टयः। — Quoted in *SV*, p. 220

phenomenal and are illumined by the witness consciousness conditioned by *avidyā vṛtti*. The cognizer and cognition modification of *avidyā* are simultaenous events that arise and are destroyed like the dream.[69] The objects in the waker's world are thus not produced over a period of time. Hence, there is no subject–object relation. As in dream, duration of time is also superimposed in the waking world.[70] There is no waking world different from the dream-world. Everything other than *Brahman* is false. This is known as Dṛṣṭi-sṛṣṭi-vāda (or Eka-jīva-vāda).[71] The Advaitic sub-school of Sṛṣṭi-dṛṣṭi-vāda and Dṛṣṭi-sṛṣṭi-vāda is divided based on the acceptance of the orders of reality and the *guru* here argues in favour of Dṛṣṭi-sṛṣṭi-vāda.

Simultaneous Rise of Object and Object-knowledge

Objection (Sṛṣṭi-Dṛṣṭi-Vāda (SDV)): One returns to the waking state after the dream experience. The previously known waking world experience is known again, that was separated by a dream experience. On waking up, the experience of the waker's world is continuous. But such an experience in dream is not found. The events of the dream-world do not continue in an orderly manner, the next day, like in the waking world. Therefore, dream is different from waking world.

Answer (Dṛṣṭi-Sṛṣṭi-Vāda (DSV)): All objects are the result of transfiguration of consciousness and transformation of primal ignorance. Therefore, if an object appears like shell-silver, then the ignorance supported by the substratal consciousness undergoes two kinds of transformations. The *tamas* aspect of ignorance is the cause of modification of objects like pot, etc. The *sattva* aspect of ignorance modifies in the form of object-knowledge. Consciousness alone is knowledge and primarily the modification

---

[69] कर्तारं च क्रियां तद्व्यावृत्तविषयानपि ।
स्फोरयेदेकयत्नेन योऽसौ साक्ष्यत्र चिद्वपुः ॥ — *PD* 10.9

[70] *PD* 13.86-89.

[71] न बन्धोऽस्ति न मोक्षोऽस्ति कदाचित् कस्यचित् क्वचित् । सर्वमात्ममयं शान्तमित्येवं प्रत्ययं स्फुटम् । स बाह्याभ्यन्तरं राम सर्वत्र दृढतां नय । — Quoted in *SV*, pp. 221-22.

of *sattva vṛtti* should not be expressed as knowledge (*jaḍatvāt*). The difference is explained by stating that the all-pervasive consciousness is not knowledge, but the reflected consciousness in the *vṛtti* is known as knowledge. Consciousness by itself cannot produce knowledge (*jñānasvarūpatvāt*). *Vṛtti* alone gives cognition status to consciousness and hence consciousness is known as knowledge (*vṛttau jñānatva upacāra*). It is well known that there are expressions like, "there is pot-knowledge; there is cloth-knowledge" and so on. Thus, the object-knowledge consists of two factors: *vṛtti* and consciousness. While there is an origination of the *vṛtti*, the consciousness does not originate, it is ever-present. The reflected thought consciousness by itself rises and falls which is conditioned (*upādhi* = transfers its attributes to consciousness) but it is expressed as the rise and fall of knowledge. The word "knowledge" is used for *vṛtti* which is the modification of *sattva* aspect of ignorance. There is the reflection of consciousness since *vṛtti* is *śuddha*. This reflected consciousness is said to be the "knowledge". The *tamas* aspect of ignorance modifies as the object; being *malina* it cannot reflect consciousness. Therefore, reflected consciousness is not formed here. The *upahita caitanya* (unrelated consciousness) is the witness-principle. The object is not capable of reflecting consciousness thus the consciousness obtaining in the object is not known as knowledge or witness-principle.

As the dream-world originates due to primal ignorance; the waker's world also is a product of primal ignorance. Since both are a product of ignorance, they are said to be false. World born out of ignorance has two aspects: *arthādhyāsa* — objects seen outside (cognized object), and simultaneously *jñānādhyāsa* — in the form of *vṛtti* (cognition). In the case of dream, on waking up there is an end of both *arthādhyāsa* and *jñānādhyāsa* of the dream-world. In deep-sleep state, the *arthādhyāsa* and *jñānādhyāsa* of the waker's world ends. The waker's world does not continue in deep sleep. On waking up, both the *adhyāsas* of the waker's world arise simultaneously. Therefore, the waker's world is phenomenal like the dream-world. Thus, the objects of the waking state and its knowledge simultaneously rise and fall. Therefore, the continuity of the experience of waker's world after dream or deep sleep is not possible.

Continuity Does not Prove Reality

Objection (SDV): The recognition of the objects on waking up from dream proves the continuity of the waker's world. The rise of object and object-knowledge in the waking world is untenable. The waker's world (empirical external world) continues even when one is in deep-sleep state (*ajñāta sattā*). Thus, the empirical reality of the waker's world is to be accepted.

Answer (DSV): It is not so. In dream, the objects like mountain, river and ocean are produced at that moment but one does not know (in dream) that these objects were available even before one's birth. The dream objects that are created instantaneously are experienced as being continuous. This is also an error. Therefore, the same ignorance which creates the dream objects also gives rise to the longevity of those objects, and its knowledge is also produced indescribably. In the same manner, the objects of waking world are not permanent, the waker's world and its continuity are produced by ignorance indescribably.

Cause–effect Relationship

Objection (SDV): While the dream objects are a direct modification of ignorance, the waker's world is not a direct modification of ignorance. In dream, products are many but the cause is one that is *mūla-avidyā* which is general (*sādhāraṇa kāraṇa*). But in *jāgrat*, each product has its own cause. There are the specific causes too (*asādhāraṇa kāraṇa*). A pot is created with the help of stick, wheel and the potter. In the same way, the entire waker's world is born out of its own specific cause (*asādhāraṇa kāraṇa*). If the waker's world is said to be born directly from ignorance, then the *sṛṣṭi vākya*[72] of the Veda will be invalid. Hence, the waking world is a

[72] तस्माद्वा एतस्मादात्मन आकाशः संभूतः। — *TU* 2.1

creation of *Īśvara* and is the modification of its own material cause and not a direct modification of ignorance. Instead the dream objects are direct modifications of ignorance and hence knowledge of such objects rises simultaneously from ignorance. On waking up, the waker's objects that originate from their respective causes are experienced. The dream "pot" resolves into the waker-consciousness but the waker's pot resolves into clay. The objects of the empirical world say, pot, etc. remain in the form of clay (the material cause) prior to its origination. Thus, the effects in waking world remain for some time while the causes comparatively remain for a longer period. Thus, we observe that the objects of longer duration and the objects of shorter duration have a cause and effect relation in the waking world. This, however, is not possible in the dream-world. On these grounds, it is not possible to maintain the same order of reality for the objects of the waking world and dream-world.

Answer (DSV): It is not so. Like in the waking world, in the dream-world too, one sees a cause–effect relation. There are experiences in dream like, "My cow gave birth to a calf" "my wife has given birth to a son". These dream objects have risen simultaneously but the cause-ness is superimposed on cow, wife as existing for a longer period. The calf, son, etc. are seen as born later and hence effect-ness is superimposed on them. Actually, they do not have a cause–effect relation. The cow, wife, etc. and calf, son, etc. are directly originated by ignorance which is the material cause. In the same manner, at the waking state, some objects remaining for a long time or the earlier ones are taken to be the cause, and some objects remaining for some time or later ones are taken to be the effect. Both are nothing but a superimposition. At any point of time, an object is neither a cause nor an effect. Due to ignorance, these objects are seen as it is. Therefore, like dream the waking world too is the effect of *avidyā* directly. This is stated in a syllogism:

> That which is a product of ignorance is phenomenal
> The waker's world is phenomenal
> Since it is a product of ignorance, Like the dream-world.

It may be added here that the Vedic statements describing the creation process are not meant for establishing creation but to teach only the non-dual *Brahman*. The world of name and form is non-different from *Brahman*.[73] Veda describes creation only to reveal non-dual *Brahman* and there is no other specific purpose.[74]

The waker's world is phenomenal and is born out of *avidyā*. It is not a product of *Īśvara*. In dream, the mind and its objects are born simultaneously, similarly in the waking world, *vṛtti* and objects are simultaneously created. In the absence of *vṛtti* there is no object. The origination of the five elements is not from *Īśvara* but from *avidyā*. There is no cause–effect relation, nor prior and later time. An order described in the *sṛṣṭi vākya*, the *guru* says, is for those who are unable to grasp the crux of Advaitic teaching. The description of the order of origination, the order of resolution into its cause (*Brahman*), the meditation on the resolution of all effects, etc. are meant to reveal the essence of Advaita knowledge. They are not meant to reveal the order of the creation as from space, etc. nor are they meant to reveal the mutual cause–effect relationship. The intention is to show that the cause of everything is ignorance. The cause–effect relation shown in the *sṛṣṭi vākya* is for *layacintana* (this is dealt with in the following chapter), i.e. it is shown that the effect is non-different from the cause. Therefore, the objects in the waking world also do not have mutual cause–effect relation.

So far, the *guru* elucidated the ontology of dream-world and empirical world to the *kaniṣṭha adhikārī* in order to establish the falsity of the world. Now, the central teaching of Advaita being the knowledge of identity is revealed through the analysis of the *mahāvākya*.

4.5 Mahāvākya Vicāra

The identity-knowledge is revealed to the *kaniṣṭha adhikārī* by

---

73 यत् यत् विवर्तभूतं तत् तत्स्वरूपमेव भवति न ततोऽतिरिच्यते । — *SV*, p. 219

74 *BSŚB* 2.1.14-20.

analysing the *mahāvākya*.[75] The Upaniṣads reveal the oneness of *jīva* and *Brahman* through the *mahāvākyas* and the same was revealed to the *uttama adhikārī* by adopting the method of *citcāturvidyā prakriyā*. Now, through the epistemological and linguistic analysis of the *mahāvākya,* the *guru* reveals the identity-knowledge to the *kaniṣṭha adhikārī*.

RELATION BETWEEN WORD AND ITS MEANING

Now, the explanation to the *kaniṣṭha adhikārī* pertaining to an analysis of the relationship between word and its meaning to facilitate the understanding of the *mahāvākya* is examined. The identity of *jīvātmā* and *paramātmā* is arrived at by the application of *jahadajahallakṣaṇā*. That which is related to the meaning of a word is known as *vṛtti* (*vṛtti* = a method by which word reveals its meaning). A calf identifies its mother from a herd of cows because of a relation and this relation is known as *janya–janaka bhāva sambandha*. In the same way, the words seek their own meaning and this is possible because of some kind of relation. A word and its direct meaning have *vācya–vācaka sambandha*. The relation of a word with its indirect meaning is known as *lakṣya–lakṣaka sambandha*. The relationship of the relation of a word and its direct meaning and indirect meaning, together possess *smarya–smāraka sambandha*. The functional relation gathered by a word is also related to the meaning of the word. Such a functional relation is known as *vṛtti* of a word. This *vṛtti sambandha* differs as *śakti* (*vācaka*) and as *lakṣaṇā*. Thus, *vṛtti* is of two kinds — *śakti* and *lakṣaṇā*. The power possessed by a word to reveal its meaning is known as *śakti* or *abhidhā*. A word is said to be related with its meaning in the form of *śakti*. This relation is like the *saṁyoga sambandha* between pieces of earth, or like the *samavāya sambandha* between the cause and its effect, or like the *tādātmya sambandha* between heat and iron piece. Therefore, *śakti* and *śaktivṛtti* that are in the word along with their meaning are said to have a direct

[75] In the sixth *taraṅga* of *Vicārasāgara* this is revealed through the dream of Agṛdhadeva.

relation. The *śaktivṛtti*, that is directly related, is of three kinds: (1) *yoga*, (2) *rūḍhī*, and (3) *yogarūḍhī*.

1. A word that has the capacity to give rise to knowledge by the combination of words with its own meaning is said to have *yoga–śakti sambandha*. This relation of a word is known as *yogavṛtti*. For instance, in the word *pādarakṣa*, there are two parts, which when combined reveals the meaning as that which protects the feet from thorns, etc. like shoes Thus, the meaning of the word *pādarakṣa* is derived by *yoga–śakti sambandha*.
2. A word, whose meaning cannot be derived from the constituents of a word, but there is a common agreement (*saṅketa* or *paribhāṣā*) that this word has a particular meaning is said to have *rūḍhī–śakti sambandha*. This relation of the word is known as *rūḍhivṛtti*. For instance, the constituents of the word *uṣṇīṣa* do not make sense, but conventionally it refers to a turban worn on the head.
3. That word whose constituents convey the meaning and also is conventionally known by that same meaning is said to have *yogarūḍhī-śakti* (a combination of *yoga* and *rūḍhī*). For example, the word *aṅgarakṣa* has two components, viz., *aṅga* and *rakṣa*, and it conventionally means a *kañcuka* (dress).

The *yoga*, *rūḍhī* and *yogarūḍhī vṛtti*s are also known as *mukhyavṛtti*. If the meaning of a word is directly revealed through the *śaktivṛtti sambandha* then it is known as *śakyārtha*. When the meaning of a word is related to *śakyārtha* and reveals the intended meaning of a speaker then it is known as *lakṣaṇāvṛtti* and the meaning derived is known as *lakṣyārtha*.

ŚAKTI–ŚAKYĀRTHA

According to the Nyāya School, a word has a capacity to convey the meaning because every word has a power (*śakti*). The *śakti* of a word to convey a meaning is the desire of *Īśvara*. According to Advaita, the capacity to reveal the meaning of word lies in a word itself. A word reveals its meaning because of the power not desired by *Īśvara,* but is intrinsic in a word. It is untenable to consider that power lies in *Īśvara,* since the power of the word cannot have the desire of *Īśvara* as its locus. The Vaiyākaraṇas consider that a word is related to its meaning from beginningless time, just like from time immemorial, the sense-organs are meant to reveal the sense objects. As even when the words originate, it has the eligibility (*yogyatā*) to render its meaning. In the word "pot" there is the eligibility in the form of knowledge of pot. This eligibility is known as *śakti.* Advaitin questions the Vaiyākaraṇa: does a word have *sāmarthya* or not? If yes, then Vaiyākaraṇa has to accept *śakti* as defined by Advaitin since *sāmarthya* is another word for *śakti.* If no, then the cause of generation of meaning by word remains unanswered. Thus, a word has the power to reveal its meaning, is the contention of Advaita. The Bhāṭṭas state that *tādātmya sambandha* or *bheda–abheda sambandha,* between a word and its meaning, is known as *śakti.* This is explained — a word and its meaning are not absolutely different, since the word conveys its meaning, and are not absolutely non-different since the effect of the meaning is not experienced by mere utterance of the word. For instance, the word "fire" and its meaning are not absolutely different because the word "fire" does not convey the meaning of water, etc. Similarly, the word "fire" and its meaning are not absolutely non-different because by the utterance of the word "fire" one's mouth does not get burnt. This relation of difference and non-difference between the word and its meaning is known as *tādātmya sambandha.*

This relation of *tādātmya* alone reveals the direct meaning of the word which is known as the *śakti* of a word. The Advaitin refutes the view of Bhāṭṭas, stating that the contradictory features like difference and non-difference cannot have the same locus. Hence, the relation of *tādātmya* between word and its meaning is illogical. The relationship between word and its meaning should either be different or non-different. In this case, the word "fire" is different from its meaning. The Bhāṭṭas resort to the Śruti

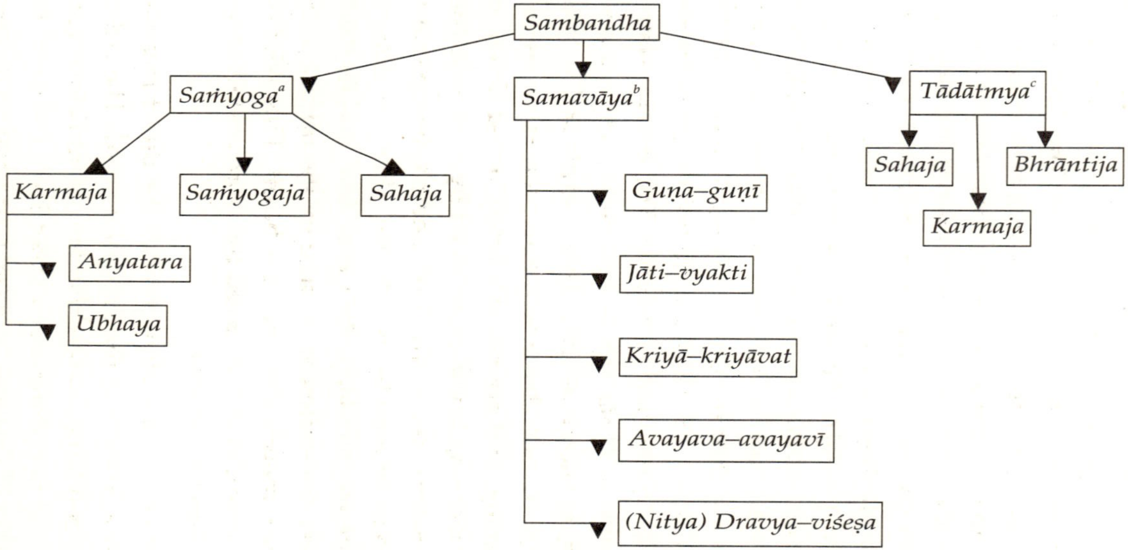

a Accepted both by Advaitins and Naiyāyikas.
b Accepted only by Naiyāyikas.
c Accepted only by Advaitins.

fig. 4.3: The three types of relation

statements *omityetadakṣaraṁ*,[76] *omiti brahma*,[77] and say that, the meaning of the word *oṁ* is *Brahman*. Thus, the word *oṁ* reveals *Brahman* which is non-different from it. The Advaitin shows that the identity of *oṁkāra* and *Brahman* revealed by the scriptures does not intend to reveal the non-difference between word and its meaning. Śruti intends to say that the statements revealing the identity of *oṁkāra* and *Brahman* are to enable a seeker to meditate on *oṁkāra* in the form of *Brahman*.[78] The Bhāṭṭas show the fallacy in Advaitin's view on *śakti*, by stating that, if the direct meaning of the word "pot" is totally different from the word "pot", then being different, the word "pot" cannot reveal the object pot. Advaitin refutes such an idea saying, even though the word "pot" is different from the object pot, the word has the capacity to reveal the object pot and not the object cloth, etc. Thus, maintaining the difference between word and its meaning, the Advaitin concludes that the word has *śakti* to convey its meaning.

The direct meaning of a word has been referred to as *śakyārtha*. One should have the knowledge of *śakyārtha* in order to understand the nature of *lakṣyārtha* since the nature of *lakṣyārtha* is related to *śakyārtha*. Thus, *śakya* is the capacity of the word to reveal the meaning. The primary or direct meaning is *śakyārtha* which is also known as *vācyārtha, abhidheyārtha, mukhyārtha,* etc. The word that reveals the direct meaning is known as *vācaka*. A word primarily conveys its meaning through a genus (*jāti*), attribute (*guṇa*), activity (*kriyā*) or relation (*sambandha*) which exists in the meaning that is conveyed; and this power present in the word is known as the primary significative power.

Lakṣaṇā–Lakṣyārtha

When the primary meaning of a sentence is incongruous, then one of the words constituting the sentence conveys another sense that is invariably connected to the primary meaning; and this

---

[76] *MaU* 1.1.

[77] *TU* 1.8.

[78] See Section 5.4 of Chapter 5.

power is known as the secondary significative power. The secondary or indirect meaning of a word is known as *lakṣyārtha* and this secondary significative power is known as *lakṣaṇā* that is related to the *vācyārtha*. This *lakṣaṇā* is of three kinds and they are explained.

Jahallakṣaṇā

The case where the direct meaning is completely abandoned and the secondary meaning is taken up is known as *jahallakṣaṇā*. For instance, one says "well is walking". Here, the direct meaning of the word "well" is the pit on the ground with water which cannot move hence this meaning is to be given up. The meaning related to "well" (water) is the leather bag with well water tied to two oxes that move. Thus, by giving up the direct meaning of the word "well" completely, its related meaning is taken up and the meaning understood here is "oxes are walking".[79]

Ajahallakṣaṇā

When the direct meaning of a word does not fit completely in a context, another meaning related to the word is taken up; this is known as *ajahallakṣaṇā*. For instance, "brown is running", here the word "brown" is a colour which cannot perform an action. So, the meaning of the sentence is to be understood by relating the word "brown" colour to its substance "horse" (here). Thus, conveying another meaning that is related to the primary meaning without abandoning the primary meaning is known as *ajahallakṣaṇā*.[80]

Jahadajahallakṣaṇā

Application of both *jahad* and *ajahallakṣaṇā* in certain cases is known as *jahadajahallakṣaṇā*, wherein one part of the meaning is retained and another part of the meaning is given up. For instance, in the statement "this is that Devadatta", the meaning is derived by the

[79] गङ्गापदं हि निजमर्थमपास्य तीरे यद्वर्तते भवति सा जहती प्रसिद्धा । — *SKS* 1.155

[80] शोणः स्थितो बहिरितीह तु लक्षणायामादाय शोणिमगुणं तुरगे प्रवृत्तिः । — *SKS* 1.155

application of *jahadajahallakṣaṇā* also known as *bhāgatyāgalakṣaṇā*. The *vācyārtha* of "this" in the sentence refers to Devadatta as relating to the present time and a particular place. The *vācyārtha* of "that" refers to Devadatta as relating to the past time and a different place. But the words, "this" and "that" refer to one Devadatta. This is arrived at by the application of the third kind of secondary meaning, viz. *bhāgatyāgalakṣaṇā*. Here, the primary meanings of the words "this" and "that" are abandoned and the unitary sense of relating to one Devadatta is retained and understood.[81]

Advaita Vedānta constructs the epistemological base to arrive at the identity-knowledge, which is its metaphysical conclusion through the *mahāvākya*. The central purport of the *mahāvākya* as the means to liberation is explained by Śaṅkara[82] and the importance of the analysis of the *mahāvākya* in gaining the non-dual self is pointed out by Sarvajñātman.[83] The *guru* elaborates on the process of arriving at identity-knowledge through the *mahāvākya* to the *kaniṣṭha adhikārī*.

LAKṢAṆĀ IN "TATTVAMASI"

The *mahāvākya* instructed in the *sadvidyā* section of *Chāndogya Upaniṣad* reveals the identity of *jīvātmā* and *paramātmā*. This identity-knowledge is gained through the application of the secondary sense. The mechanism of the operation of the secondary meaning is elaborated here. The word *tat* in the *mahāvākya* refers to *Īśvara* or *Paramātmā*. The primary meaning reveals the omnipotence, omniscience and omnipresence nature of *Īśvara*. *Īśvara* is free and not bound, endowed with powers. Hence the direct meaning refers to *Īśvara caitanya*. The word *tvam* in its primary sense refers to *jīva caitanya*, who is limited in power, knowledge and with spatial limitation.

---

81 सोऽयं पुमानिति वचस्युभयप्रकारा देशादिभागपरिवर्जनतः प्रसिद्धा ।
पुंसश्च केवलमुपात्ततया पदाभ्यामेवं त्रिधा भवति लाक्षणिकी प्रवृत्तिः ॥
— *SKS* 1.156

82 तत्त्वमस्यादिवाक्योत्थं यज्जीवपरमात्मनोः ।
तादात्म्यविषयं ज्ञानं तदिदं मुक्तिसाधनम् ॥ — *VV* 6

83 विना महावाक्यमतो न कश्चित् पुमांसं अद्वैतं अवैति जन्तुः । — *SKS* 3.303

Incompatibility of Śakyārtha

The *śakyārtha* or *vācyārtha* of the *mahāvākya* is:

Tat = creator of the universe, omnipotent, omniscient, *Īśvara*.
Tvam = less powerful, limited knowledge, etc. is *Jīva*.
Asi = are.

Although the words *tat* and *tvam* are in apposition and thereby supposed to convey identity, they refer to two different entities which are opposed to each other in their qualities, making the identity impossible. Thus, the identity cannot be derived with the help of *śakyārtha*, and one has to resort to the secondary sense.

Incompatibility of Jahallakṣaṇā

The witness Consciousness (*tvam pada lakṣyārtha*) and *Brahman* Consciousness (*tat pada lakṣyārtha*) are the objects of knowledge revealed in Vedānta. Both the entities namely, Witness Consciousness and the *Brahman* Consciousness are the integrated part in the *tvam pada vācyārtha* and *tat pada vācyārtha*. In *jahallakṣaṇā*, the *vācyārtha* is to be completely given up and a related meaning is to be taken. In such a case, if *jahallakṣaṇā* is applied to the *mahāvākya*, then the consciousness principle in the *vācyārtha* is to be completely given up and a new entity other than the two consciousness principles is to be taken.[84] Other than the consciousness principle, what remains is the inert principle, which is false and cause of sorrow. By arriving at the false inert sorrowful principle one cannot gain liberation. Therefore, the application of *jahallakṣaṇā* to the *mahāvākya* serves no benefit.

Incompatibility of Ajahallakṣaṇā

In *ajahallakṣaṇā*, the entire *vācyārtha* is not given up, retaining *vācyārtha*, a new related component is added to *vācyārtha* in order to arrive at *lakṣyārtha*. If *ajahallakṣaṇā* is applied in the *mahāvākya*, then the entire *vācyārtha* is to be applied in the sentence meaning.

---

[84] अत्र गङ्गायां घोषः प्रतिवसतीतिवाक्यवत् जहल्लक्षणापि न सङ्गच्छते । — *VS*, p. 92

Retention of *vācyārtha* amounts to retaining the contradictory characteristics of *jīvātmā* and *paramātmā*. In such a case, identity can never be arrived at.[85]

Application of Jahadajahallakṣaṇā

The difficulties faced in the application of *jahallakṣaṇā* and *ajahallakṣaṇā* are overcome by applying the third type of *lakṣaṇā*.[86] *Īśvara*, referred to by the word *tat*, is a mixture of consciousness conditioned by *māyā* and the reflected consciousness. Due to a qualitatively finer medium, viz., *māyā*, the features of *Īśvara* are superior. *Jīva*, referred to by the word *tvam* is a mixture of consciousness conditioned by the mind and the reflected consciousness. Due to a qualitatively inferior adjunct, viz., the mind, the features of *jīva* are inferior. By the application of *jahadajahallakṣaṇā*, the medium and the reflected consciousness, which are the opposing features are given up, and the pure consciousness that is the substratum of the medium and its reflection is retained. This identity of *jīvātmā* and *paramātmā* is arrived at in three stages:[87]

1. *Samānādhikaraṇya sambandha*: Two words, that are grammatically in coordination, referring to the same locus (*adhikaraṇa*), are said to be in *samānādhikaraṇa*. The relationship of the words in the same grammatical coordination, thereby forcing their respective word meanings to refer to a common locus is termed as *samānādhikaraṇya sambandha*. For instance, the words "white lotus" refer to the same locus since the words "white" and "lotus" are in apposition. The words *tat* and *tvam* in the *mahāvākya* are in grammatical coordination and hence refers to the same locus. The identity of *jīvātmā* and *paramātmā* cannot be arrived by mere application of

---

85 अत्र शोणो धावतीतिवाक्यवत् अजहल्लक्षणापि न सम्भवति। — *VS*, p. 95.

86 *PD* 5.1-8.

87 सामानाधिकरण्यमत्र भवति प्राथम्यभागन्वयः पश्चादेष विशेषणेतरतया पश्चाद्विरोधोद्भवः।
उत्पन्ने च विरोध एकरसके वस्तुन्यखण्डात्मके वृत्तिर्लक्षणया भवत्ययमिह ज्ञेयः क्रमः सूरिभिः॥
— *SKS* 1.196

samānādhikaraṇya sambandha because the word-meanings have to be analysed.

2. *Viśeṣya–viśeṣaṇa sambandha*: It is the relationship of being the qualification and the qualified. The relationship of *viśeṣya–viśeṣaṇa sambandha* is between the word-meanings. The word-meanings that mutually delimit each other, is known as *anyonya viśeṣya–viśeṣaṇatā sambandha*. In the case of "white lotus", the word-meaning of white is "white-ness" that qualifies the word meaning of the lotus, "lotus-ness". In this first stage of delimitation, the "white-ness" is the qualifier and the "lotus-ness" is the qualified. In the second stage of delimitation, the "white-ness" is the qualified and the "lotus-ness" is the qualifier. By these dual mutual delimiting processes, the common object is arrived at. Now, in the application of *anyonya viśeṣya–viśeṣaṇatā sambandha* in the word-meanings of *tat* and *tvam*, we do not arrive at the common locus because of the contradictory word-meanings of *tat* and *tvam*.

3. *Lakṣaṇā–lakṣya sambandha*: *Lakṣaṇā* is that which reveals the special quality. The meaning of that sentence is *lakṣya*. In the sentence, "This is that Devadatta", the words "that" and "this" are to be given up as they reveal contradictory qualities, and person Devadatta is to be retained. Thus, "this is that Devadatta" is revealed by *lakṣaṇā–lakṣya*. In the same way, in the *mahāvākya tat-tvam-asi*, the word-meaning of *tat* and *tvam* with contradictory attributes is to be given up and the consciousness is to be retained by *lakṣaṇā–lakṣya* relation. Therefore, by giving up the contradictory parts and retaining consciousness part in *tat tvam asi* is *lakṣaṇā*. The non-dual consciousness is *lakṣya*. This is already explained as the application of *jahadajahallakṣaṇā*. Now, the four main *mahāvākya*s are analysed.

JAHADAJAHALLAKṢAṆĀ IN TATTVAMASI

Vidyāraṇya in his *Pañcadaśī*[88] explains the derivation of the identity meaning through the *tattvamasi mahāvākya*. Here, the pronoun *tat* contextually refers to *jagat kāraṇa brahma,* that is Pure Existence, prior to the creation was free from names, forms and limitations. The word *tat* refers to the remote Existence. Remoteness is of two kinds — spatial remoteness and temporal remoteness. By stating *tat* is prior to the creation, it refers to temporal remoteness of Existence (*bhūtakāla viśiṣṭa sat*). Thus, the *tat pada vācyārtha* is *sat* related to time and *tat pada lakṣyārtha,* arrived at by the application of *jahadajahallakṣaṇā,* is Pure *Sat* unrelated to time. The word *tvam* refers to *jīvātmā,* who exists in the present time (*vartamānakāla viśiṣṭa sat*). Consciousness by itself does not have past, present or future but when it is associated with the body, it is constrained within time. As associated with the body, "I am *kāryātmā*" related to the present time. The *tvam pada vācyārtha* is *Cit* as an effect related to present time and it cannot be equated with timeless *Brahman*. Therefore, *vācyārtha* is given up and by the application of *jahadajahallakṣaṇā,* the effect of present time is dismissed and what remains is *Cit*. The implied meaning of *tat* and *tvam* is timeless *Sat* and timeless *Cit* respectively and they are not different entities but non-dual, timeless *Sat* is timeless *Cit*.

JAHADAJAHALLAKṢAṆĀ IN "PRAJÑĀNAM BRAHMA"

The *mahāvākya prajñānam brahma* that occurs in *Aitareya Upaniṣad* 3.5 is analysed. Here too, for similar reasons, *vācyārtha* is inadmissible and the first two *lakṣaṇā*s are unfitting and hence *jahadajahallakṣaṇā* is applied and the identity meaning is arrived at. Vidyāraṇya describes the process and says that the word *prajñānam* secondarily refers to the consciousness because of which the sense-organs operate and know the world. The primary meaning of the word *prajñānam* is the reflected consciousness or

---

88 एकमेवाद्वितीयं सन्नामरूपविवर्जितम्। सृष्टेः पुराधुनाप्यस्य तादृक्त्वं तदितीर्यते॥
श्रोतुर्देहेन्द्रियातीतं वस्त्वत्र त्वंपदेरितम्। एकता ग्राह्यतेऽसीति तदैक्यमनुभूयताम्॥ — *PD* 5.5-6

the *cidābhāsa* and the secondary meaning is the consciousness or *bimba caitanya* or *Cit*. The word *brahma* secondarily refers to the consciousness that is obtaining in all the beings. The *mahāvākya* reveals the oneness of the consciousness that illumines the world and that is present in all beings.

JAHADAJAHALLAKṢAṆĀ IN "AHAM BRAHMĀSMI"

The *mahāvākya aham brahmāsmi* that occurs in *Bṛhadāraṇyaka Upaniṣad* 1.4.10 is analysed. Since the primary meanings and the first two secondary implications do not fit due to contradictory features revealed by the words *aham* and *brahma* in the *mahāvākya*, the secondary implication of the third kind is applied. The word *aham* secondarily refers to the consciousness known in the body that is the witness of the intellect which is self-luminous. The word *brahma* secondarily refers to the all-pervading consciousness that is immanent in all the bodies. Thus, the *mahāvākya* reveals the non-difference between the witness consciousness obtained within a body and the all-pervading consciousness.

JAHADAJAHALLAKṢAṆĀ IN "AYAMĀTMĀ BRAHMA"

In the *mahāvākya ayamātmā brahma* that occurs in *Māṇḍūkya Upaniṣad* 1.2; the word *ayamātmā* primarily means *jīvātmā* and the word *brahma* in its primary sense refers to *paramātmā*. The primary meanings of *jīvātmā* and *paramātmā* reveal contradictory features and hence identity is impossible. So, the secondary meaning is to be applied. The word *ayam* in the *mahāvākya* secondarily refers to the self-evident consciousness that is intimately obtained. Thus, the innermost consciousness is indicated by the word *ayamātmā*. The secondary sense of the word *brahma* refers to the inner essence of the universe. The inner essence of the universe is available in the form of ever experienced consciousness in an individual. Thus, the identity of the essence of the individual and the essence of the world is revealed.

There are four *mahāvākyas* in the scriptures[89] and these *mahāvākyas* are conventionally well known to represent the four

---

[89] Rāmacandrendra Sarasvatī in his *Mahāvākyaratnāvalī* extracts 1008 *mahāvākyas* from 108 Upaniṣads.

Vedas. They are classified in the following manner: *prajñānam brahma* as *svarūpabodhaka vākya; aham brahmāsmi* as *anubhavabodhaka vākya; tattvamasi* as *upadeśabodhaka vākya* and *ayamātmā brahma* as *aparokṣabodhaka vākya.*

LAKṢAṆĀ FOR BOTH THE WORDS "JĪVA" AND "ĪŚVARA"

Objection: There are two words in the *mahāvākyas* and acceptance of secondary meaning for both the words is futile. The contradictory features of the two words in the *mahāvākya* do not give a unitary meaning and hence secondary meaning is applied to both the words. But, this tedious process can be avoided by the application of secondary meaning to only one of the two words and the contradiction can be removed. There cannot be identity between one who is omniscient and one endowed with limited knowledge. Even then, one word's secondary sense revealing Pure *Brahman* can have identity endowed with the other word-meaning. An instance is cited here: "this brāhmaṇa is a kṣatriya human". The "brāhmaṇa" and "kṣatriya" attributes are contradictory. But in the statement "this brāhmaṇa is a human", the "human" without the quality "kṣatriya" and with the quality "brāhmaṇa" are identical and there is no contradiction. In the same way, Consciousness with limited qualities and Consciousness with limitless qualities cannot be identical since they are contradictory. Even then, in the words *jīva* and *īśvara*, consciousness alone can be retained by secondary sense, one word by secondary sense can mean consciousness alone, that secondary meaning can be identical with the primary sense of one word with limited qualities or limitless qualities without any contradiction. Thus, applying secondary sense to both the words is improper.

Advaitin: Based on the above objection let us consider the options of applying the secondary sense to any one of the two words. If it is considered that, in all the (four) *mahāvākyas*, the first word should be taken in its secondary sense and not the second word, it is untenable. Also, application of the secondary meaning to the second word and not to the first word is untenable, as both the words convey mutually contradictory meaning. In the *mahāvākyas*, *aham brahmasmi, prajñānam brahma, ayamātmā brahma* the first word refers to *jīvātmā*. By applying the secondary meaning to the first word, we arrive at the Consciousness. The primary sense of the second word is *Īśvara*. Here, the identity of the consciousness with that of limitless *Īśvara* is arrived at. In *tattvamasi* the first word refers to *Paramātmā* and the second word refers to *jīvātmā*. By following the above method, we apply the secondary meaning to the first word and arrive at consciousness and retain the primary meaning of the second word, *jīvātmā*. The identity knowledge derived from *tattvamasi* is consciousness of the nature of limited *jīvātmā*. Both the conclusions are illogical. On the other hand, by taking recourse to the second option, *vācyārtha* of the first words of the *mahāvākyas* are retained and the secondary sense is applied to the second word. Then, the sentence-meaning arrived is, the limited *jīvātmā* is identical with pure consciousness. In *tattvamasi mahāvākya*, by this method, the meaning arrived is, limitless *paramātmā* is identical with pure consciousness. Thus, the sentence-meaning arrived through the four *mahāvākyas* are mutually contradictory. So, by either of these options of applying secondary sense partially to the *mahāvākya* is improper. Hence, the Advaitic stand is to apply the secondary meaning to both the words in the *mahāvākya* and arrive at the identity meaning.

LAKṢAṆĀ TO THE WORD "ĪŚVARA" ONLY IS UNTENABLE

Another option is suggested by an opponent. Application of the secondary sense to either the first word or the second word of the *mahāvākya* may be improper. Therefore, apply the secondary sense to the word referring to *Īśvara* in all the *mahāvākyas*. This also is improper because, if the word-meaning *Īśvara* alone is taken in the secondary sense, then all the *mahāvākyas* will reveal the identity of consciousness with *jīvātmā* which is limited in knowledge, dependent, subject to births and deaths, sorrowful, *saṁsārī*, such a *jīvātmā* is to be known. This will result in the defect of *mokṣahāni*.

LAKṢAṆĀ TO THE WORD "JĪVA" ONLY IS UNTENABLE

To avoid the defect of *mokṣahāni*, it may be argued that in all the *mahāvākyas*, the word referring to *jīvātmā* is to be taken in the secondary sense and not the word referring to *paramātmā*. In the secondary sense, *jīvātmā* means consciousness, identical with *paramātmā* with limitless powers. This meaning is to be firmly known by the seekers who will attain the highest *Īśvara*. Thus, the application of secondary sense to the word-meaning *jīvātmā* is proper. This contention of the opponent is also improper. The *tvam padārtha lakṣya* as *Īśvara* is not logical because the question raised here are:

1. Does the secondary sense of the '*tvam*' *pada* refer to the all-pervasive consciousness? or
2. does the secondary sense of the '*tvam*' *pada* refer to the witness consciousness conditioned by the limiting adjunct?

The first possibility is untenable, because that which forms a part of the *vācyārtha* alone can be considered for *bhāgatyāga lakṣanā*. The all-pervasive consciousness is not included in the *vācyārtha* of '*tvam*' *pada* but it includes the witness consciousness conditioned by the limiting adjunct of *jīvātmā*. The secondary sense of the '*tvam*' *pada* refers to the witness consciousness that is part of the '*tvam*' *pada vācyārtha*. The witness consciousness does not have the features of *paramātmā*. Moreover, witness consciousness is always direct (*aparokṣa*). The quality of indirectness (*parokṣatva*) of *paramātmā* is not found here. The *mahāvākya* revealing the identity of witness consciousness with *paramātmā* is untenable.

OTAPROTA BHĀVA[90]

Thus, the above-mentioned defects can be overcome only by the application of the secondary sense to both the words that occur in the *mahāvākya*. The primary meaning of both the words with contradictory attributes cannot be identical. The secondary meaning of both the words is arrived at by giving up all these

---

[90] Refer Section 2.6 of Chapter 2.

qualities and retaining only the self-luminous consciousness, which is free from all attributes. The nature of consciousness is non-dual, pure, free from limitations. The limitations experienced are due to *upādhi* and its attributes. In the example of pot-space, by giving up the pot identity, there cannot be identity with the room-space. The identity is possible only by giving up the "room" notion too. In the same way, *vācyārtha* of both the words is to be given up that includes *upādhi* and its attributes, this alone will lead to identity. Thus, the *guru* says that the *otaprota bhāva* in the *mahāvākya* in the form, *tat tvam* and *tvam tat* is to be known. Literally, *otaprota* means *anyonya miśra* (mutual combination). In the form, *tat tvam*, the *aparokṣatva* of *tvam* displaces the *parokṣatva* of *tat*. In the form, *tvam tat*, the limitlessness of *tat* displaces the limitations in *tvam*. To remove the two delusions, remoteness and limitation, the *mahāvākya* is to be read twice reversing the subject and the predicate. Else, the non-immediacy-delusion in the *'tat' padārtha* and limitation-delusion in the *'tvam' padārtha* will continue.

The *guru* emphasizes here that, in order to remove these two delusions, one should analyse the *otaprota bhāva* after receiving the *mahāvākya* teaching. This *otaprota* is known by the principle of co-presence and co-absence. The meaning of the *mahāvākya* by *otaprota bhāva* removes the "indirect limited" delusion. The *guru* explains the continuation of the twofold delusion even after the *mahāvākya* analysis.[91]

There arises a doubt that even after the teaching of the *mahāvākya*, some seekers find the continuity of the delusion of "remoteness" while understanding the nature of *paramātmā* and "limitation" in the nature of *jīvātmā*. The cause of such a delusion is due to *māyā* (ignorance), "supported" by *Brahman* and *avidyā*, located in *Ātman*. *Māyā* and *avidyā* are destroyed on the analysis of the *tat* and *tvam pada* by the seekers. Just as on analysis of the nature of a pot, the ignorance related to the pot is destroyed, on analysis of *Brahman*, *māyā* and *avidyā* are said to be destroyed.

---

[91] *SV*, p. 318.

Thus, from the standpoint of an *adhikārī jñānī*, *māyā* and *avidyā* are sublated in *Brahman*. The question remains as to the locus of *māyā-avidyā* remaining in which the twofold delusions continue even after the *mahāvākya* analysis. Since *māyā-avidyā* being inert needs Consciousness for its existence and in this case, *māyā-avidyā* is sublated in the only Conscious principle, namely, *Brahman*.

The *guru* clarifies regarding the locus of *māyā-avidyā* that is the cause of the twofold delusion even after the analysis of the *mahāvākya*. On the rise of *Brahman*-knowledge through the *mahāvākya* (*śravaṇa*), the *māyā-avidyā* gets sublated in *Brahman*. But in the case of absence of *manana* and *nididhyāsana* and non-assimilation of the *mahāvākya*, it is said that *māyā-avidyā* is not sublated which generates the twofold delusion of "remoteness" and "limitation". To remove this delusion *otaprota bhāva* method is to be applied. By the *otaprota bhāva*, there is a firm knowledge of oneness and *māyā-avidyā* is completely annihilated. The delusion of remoteness and limitation are destroyed.

The method of *otaprota bhāva* is applied to the *mahāvākya*. *Tat tvam* reveals the identity of *tat padārtha* with *tvam padārtha*. The witness consciousness known through *tvam pada* is eternally direct. The remoteness or indirect delusion is removed. *Tvam tat* reveals the identity of *tvam padārtha* and *tat padārtha*. The *tat padārtha* reveals all-pervasiveness. By this, the limitation-delusion is removed. In the same manner, *aham brahmāsmi*, *prajñānam brahma* and *ayamātmā brahma* also remove the notion of limitation. Moreover, *brahma aham*, *brahma prajñānam* and *brahma ātmā* remove the sense of remoteness. Thus, in all cases of the *mahāvākya* instruction, one should apply *jahadajahallakṣaṇā* to arrive at the identity-knowledge.

ROLE OF MAHĀVĀKYA

The analysis of the nature and role of *mahāvākya* is presented as found in the first *taraṅga* of *Vicārasāgara*. The Vedāntic text employs two kinds of statements, one is known as *avāntara vākya* and the other as *mahāvākya*. *Avāntara vākya*s are those statements which reveal the nature of *jīvātmā* and *paramātmā*. *Mahāvākya*s are those statements which reveal the identity of *jīvātmā* and *paramātmā*. One gains an indirect knowledge from the *avāntara vākya* that is expressed as "*Brahman* exists" and a direct knowledge is gained from the *mahāvākya* expressed as "I am *Brahman*". While discussing the role of *śravaṇa*, VB shows that *mahāvākya* produces direct knowledge based on the Śābdāparokṣavāda. Two other views on the role of *śravaṇa* by post-Śaṅkara Advaitins are presented here.[92]

Vidyāraṇya states in his *Pañcadaśī*,[93] that the *mahāvākya* combined with *śravaṇa*, *manana* and *nididhyāsana* alone gives rise to direct knowledge. That is, *mahāvākya* by itself gives rise to indirect knowledge and only *vicārita mahāvākya* gives rise to direct knowledge. If by mere listening to the *mahāvākya*, direct knowledge is produced then the triple means of *śravaṇa*, etc. will be futile. The role of the triple means is to remove the doubts and errors.

Sarvajñātman in his *Saṁkṣepaśārīraka*[94] says that the general view that words produce indirect knowledge is incorrect. Words produce two kinds of knowledge: direct and indirect. An entity that is obstructed or limited by space and time is known as *vyavahita* or *parokṣa*. An entity that is not obstructed or limited by space or time is *avyavahita* or *aparokṣa*. The words related to indirect object will produce indirect knowledge. Objects like heaven and *deva* revealed by the scriptures are objects of indirect knowledge, and hence they are *nitya-parokṣa*. But, the knowledge with regard to a direct object can be either direct or indirect. In the case of "you are the tenth man",[95] the words reveal the object of knowledge that is direct. But if one understands as "tenth man

---

92 *SV*, p. 19.

93 For Vidyāraṇya's view on the rise of direct knowledge, see *PD* 1.62, 9.30 and thereon.

94 *SKS* 1.14-19.

95 The story of the tenth man — Ten travellers once visited a country. On the way they crossed a deep river. In order to know if all of them had crossed the river, they assembled in a line and one person counted excluding himself. They concluded that the tenth one is missing and were in intense grief. At that moment, another traveller passed by and knowing the cause of their sorrow, he counted and →

exists" it is an indirect knowledge even though the object of knowledge is direct. If it is understood as "I am the tenth man", it is the direct knowledge of the direct "object". Similarly, the *mahāvākya* reveals the direct knowledge of the inner self which is not an object of indirect knowledge. The *mahāvākya* is the direct means to knowledge and the role of the triple means is to remove the defects like doubts and errors that obstruct the knowledge. Since the triple means to knowledge play a vital role in the removal of doubts, etc. they are figuratively referred to as the means to knowledge.

At the end of the (respective) dialogue, VB states that the *uttama adhikārī* and *kaniṣṭha adhikārī* attain *jīvanmukti*. The *madhyama adhikārī* finds it difficult to confront the Advaitic teaching of absolute reality. Hence he raises question relating to the validity of Advaitic teaching. The position of the *madhyama adhikārī* is analysed in the following chapter.

Before proceeding to analyse the dialogue with the *madhyama adhikārī* let us pause to derive the pedagogical approach in the process of *śravaṇa/manana* of the *uttama* and *kaniṣṭha adhikārī*s revolving around the "impediments to knowledge" as found in the above discussion.

1. The nature of identity-knowledge was revealed by the analysis of the division of space and consciousness (*citcāturvidyā prakriyā*). The method of arriving at oneness by analysing the meaning of the word *brahman* was also pointed out to the *uttama adhikārī* as found in fourth *taraṅga.*

← declared "ten are there". One among them asked "where is the tenth man?". The traveller said "that tenth man is you". On hearing these words, there is the direct knowledge of the tenth man. Even though the tenth man is present, and even when the instruments (eyes) are available, without the "instruction" from another person as "you are the tenth man", the tenth man is not known, the tenth man in this case is to be an indirect object. The words, "you are the tenth man" of a trustworthy person is the direct means for the rise of direct knowledge. Mind, free from defects, serves as an aid to give rise to direct knowledge. *Śravaṇa* does not contribute to knowledge but removes obstacle to knowledge.

2. The nature of non-dual self was taught to the *uttama adhikārī* by examining the scriptural contention (*Muṇḍakopaniṣad* 3.1.1) and the further questions related to the role of Vedapūrva and the nature of identity knowledge was examined as in fourth *taraṅga.*
3. The locus of identity-knowledge was explained to the *uttama adhikārī* through the seven states of *ābhāsa* as in fourth *taraṅga.*
4. Ontology of the world (dream and empirical) was elaborated through the theory of *dṛṣṭi-sṛṣṭi prakriyā* to the *kaniṣṭha adhikārī* as in sixth *taraṅga.*
5. The knowledge of identity was taught to the *kaniṣṭha adhikārī* through the analysis of the *mahāvākya* that included an elaboration of the linguistic features. The importance of application of *anyonya miśra/otaprota* (mutual combination) to the words in the *mahāvākya* was highlighted as in the sixth *taraṅga.*
6. The role of *mahāvākya* as the means of direct or indirect knowledge was discussed based on the first *taraṅga* of *Vicārasāgara.*

The *uttama* and *kaniṣṭha adhikārī*s are said to have attained *jīvanmukti* in the text *Vicārasāgara.*

5

On the Nature of Meditation (Upāsanasvarūpaprakaraṇa)

THE attention is now on the *madhyama adhikārī*, who is not convinced with the teaching so far imparted that was assimilated by the *uttama* and *kaniṣṭha adhikārīs* who gained *jīvanmukti*. The *madhyama adhikārī* in the fifth *taraṅga* marks his non-acceptance of identity-knowledge as the direct means to liberation. He presents his difficulty in understanding the experienced duality as false, for which the *guru* teaches the identity-knowledge by various methods of discrimination of self and non-self. The *madhyama adhikārī* is then introduced to a series of optional types of meditation for refinement of mind so as to develop the mind to assimilate the identity-knowledge that has already been reiterated as the only direct means to liberation. The *madhyama adhikārī* still faces difficulty in understanding non-duality and hence the *guru* elaborates on *oṁkāra upāsanā* that is instrumental to understand the *mahāvākya* later. The methods presented so far, if practised and enquired into, would enable one to acquire knowledge and attain *jīvanmukti*. But, the text *Vicārasāgara* tells us that the *madhyama adhikārī* attained *kramamukti*. After listening to various other optional methods to arrive at the identity-knowledge, the *madhyama adhikārī* took to *oṁkāra upāsanā* but did not graduate to take up an enquiry into the *mahāvākya* while living. He remained an *upāsaka* and after death is said to have attained *brahmaloka* wherein he continued the *oṁkāra-mahāvākya vicāra* and through the knowledge of oneness attained liberation.

The various optional methods of discrimination to arrive at identity-knowledge and the various types of meditation leading to an enquiry that would result in *jīvanmukti* and the means taken for *kramamukti* in the dialogue of the *guru* with the *madhyama adhikārī* is presented in the first part of this chapter.

In the final part of this chapter, the position of *manda-madhyama adhikārī*[1] as found in seventh *taraṅga* is presented who is said to have attained *brahmaloka.* The *manda-madhyama adhikārī* has not listened to the teaching of identity-knowledge. He decides to take up meditation but is not clear with the object of meditation. His teacher is the *kaniṣṭha adhikārī* who introduces the *kāraṇabrahma upāsanā,* taking to which the *manda-madhyama adhikārī* attains *brahmaloka.* Thus, here we primarily focus on the pedagogical flexibility with respect to the *adhikārī*s who are not able to ascertain the falsity of the world and its effects as found in the teaching of Advaita Vedānta.

We shall briefly see the pedagogical tools employed for the *madhyama* and *manda-madhyama adhikārī*s as presented in this chapter. The *madhyama adhikārī* is taught at different levels:

1. The notion of duality is said to be an obstacle for the recognition of non-dual knowledge. The *guru* reveals this by pointing out that scriptures not only reveal non-duality as the central teaching but also reproach the idea of duality. An erroneous knowledge caused by extraneous factors as an obstacle for rise of non-dual knowledge is further examined through the story of minister Bharchu. The unreality of bondage and liberation is presented through the dream of a king.

2. To arrive at the identity-knowledge the three main methods of discrimination, viz., (a) pañcakośa viveka, (b) avasthā-traya viveka, and (c) śarīra-traya viveka, are elaborated after dealing with the nature of *māyā* and its effects.

---

[1] For details on (Śubhasantati as) *manda-madhyama adhikārī* see under sub-title "Pedagogy" in Section 1.4 of Chapter 1.

3. The *madhyama adhikārī* is unable to arrive at the identity-knowledge by any of the above-described methods of discrimination. An alternate method of *layacintana* is presented by the *guru* to ascertain the falsity of the world and to arrive at the non-dual self. *Layacintana* is introduced as a form of meditation that can be adopted by a seeker whose obstructed mind is unable to grasp the oneness revealed through the *mahāvākya*.
4. The *guru* then presents the difference between knowledge and meditation followed by different types of meditations like (a) *ahaṁgraha upāsanā*, (b) *ahaṁgraha praṇava upāsanā*, and (c) *nirguṇa praṇava upāsanā* without desiring to reach *brahmaloka*. By the practice of any of these, the *madhyama adhikārī* could take to the enquiry of *mahāvākya* again so as to gain *jīvanmukti*. But he could not arrive at the identity-knowledge nor was he convinced of *mithyātvam*.
5. So the *guru* presents now the *nirguṇa praṇava upāsanā* with a desire for attaining *brahmaloka* which was taken up by the *madhyama adhikārī* who is said to have attained *kramamukti*.
6. For the *manda-madhyama adhikārī* the method of *kāraṇa brahma upāsanā* is taught by which he attains *brahmaloka*.

Let us now elaborately analyse the flexibility of pedagogical measures that is described in the fifth and seventh *taraṅga*s of *Vicārasāgara*.

5.1 Refutation of Duality

In the previous chapter it was established that one gains the knowledge of non-dual *Brahman* through the instruction of the *mahāvākya* (through a *guru*). The *madhyama adhikārī* raises the question relating to the reality of Vedānta (and the *guru*). He states:

(i) If both Vedānta and *guru* are real then duality gets established.

(ii) On the other hand, if both are unreal, then sorrow cannot be removed by an unreal *guru* and Vedānta, just as thirst cannot be quenched by mirage-water, thereby the human goal remains unattained.

Thus, in either of these above cases (i) and (ii), there is the impossibility of the rise of non-dual knowledge. Therefore, *madhyama adhikārī* concludes that the view of Advaita as established by Śaṅkarācārya is invalid since duality cannot be negated.

The *guru* first establishes that since duality is censured in the scriptures, the teaching of non-duality by Śaṅkarācārya and other preceptors is valid. Further, the *guru* points out that the erroneous knowledge is an obstacle for the rise of non-dual knowledge and this he reveals through the story of minister Bharchu. The reply to (i) and (ii) is given by the *guru* through the narration of the dream of a king.

Before examining the teachings to the *madhyama adhikārī*'s question, we shall briefly see the refutation of dualism as found in the third *taraṅga* of *Vicārasāgara* while defining the quality of a *guru*. It is said that a *guru* is one who removes logically, the five kinds of duality experienced. The five kinds of duality are the difference between:

1. *Jīva–Īśvara*
2. *Jīva–Jīva*
3. *Jīva–Jaḍa*
4. *Īśvara–Jaḍa*
5. *Jaḍa–Jaḍa*.

Negation of all these five kinds of duality is possible only by a *guru*. The logic employed in negating the five kinds of duality are:

1. Just as the difference between the pot-space and room-space is caused by the adjuncts, the difference between *Jīva* and *Īśvara* is due to *avidyā*, and so this difference is false.

2. Like the difference in many pot-spaces, the mutual difference between *jīva*s is because of the reflected consciousness along with the conditioning factor and hence it is false.
3. The difference between *jīva* and *jaḍa* is that, while *jīva* is the reflected consciousness with an internal organ, the *jaḍa* principle has *māyā* as its conditioning factor without reflected consciousness and hence this difference is also false.
4. *Īśvara* is the reflected consciousness with *māyā* as its adjunct and is the creator of the insentient world with names and forms. The difference between *Īśvara* and *jaḍa* is also due to the adjuncts and hence false.
5. Like the difference between the rope and its superimposed entities like snake and stick, the difference between the inert objects is born because of their name and form, which is false. Moreover, duality as the cause of fear is proclaimed in the Upaniṣads.[2] A *guru* is one who imparts direct knowledge (*aparokṣa jñāna*) to the disciple, which is expressed as "I am non-dual *Brahman* free from all kinds of impurities like ignorance, etc."

REPROACH OF DUALISM IN SCRIPTURES

Now, the question of the *madhyama adhikārī*, related to the validity of non-duality as the central teaching of the scriptures brought out by Śaṅkarācārya, is explained by the *guru* citing various Purāṇas.[3] Vālmīki, the author of *Yogavāsiṣṭha*, which is in the form

---

[2] यदा ह्येवैष एतस्मिन्नुदरमन्तरं कुरुते। अथ तस्य भयं भवति। — *TU* 2.7
द्वितीयाद्वै भयं भवति। — *BU* 1.4.2

[3] कलौ युगे तु वेदार्थो वर्ण्यते ह्यन्यथाऽन्यथा। शङ्कराचार्यरूपेण शिवः साक्षात्तदा किल॥
अवतीर्यान्यथाभूतं जैनबौद्धादिकं मतम्। निर्मूल्यिष्यत्यखिलं वेदवाक्यैः सयुक्तिभिः॥
उद्धृत्य मूर्तिं गङ्गायाः स्थापयिष्यति वै प्रभोः। सूर्यलोकेन जगतो ह्यन्धकारविनाशने॥
यथावस्थितभानं तु पदार्थानां यथा भवेत्। नाशश्च विपरीताख्यभावनाया यथा भवेत्॥
सर्वसंशयनाशश्च भगवत्पूज्यपादभृत्। शङ्करोऽपि तथैवेह लोकानुग्रहकाङ्क्षया॥

→

of a dialogue between Vasiṣṭha and Rāma, reveals the Advaitic teaching as valid. It establishes repeatedly the views of Dṛṣṭi-sṛṣṭi-vāda or Eka-jīva-vāda or Eka-sattā-vāda through various examples, historical events, anecdotes, etc.[4] The view of dualistic philosophy is contradictory to the teachings of Vyāsa and Vālmīki. The dualistic system contradicts logic and reasoning which, the *guru* states, is established in Śrī Harṣa's *Khaṇḍanakhaṇḍakhādya* and Nṛsiṁhāśramā's *Bhedadhikkāra*, etc. The "philosophy of dualism" is criticized in the scriptures.[5] This proves the validity of non-duality as the central teaching of all scriptures.

NOTION OF DUALITY AS AN OBSTACLE

The *guru* reveals that as long as one remembers duality that brings about an erroneous knowledge, so long the non-dual knowledge will not rise. He narrates the story of Bharchu to convey this idea. Bharchu was a famous minister of a certain king. He was an able minister loved by the king and naturally he earned the wrath of

---

वेदार्थविषयाज्ञानं भ्रान्तिसंशयकारणम्। निश्शेषं नाशयित्वाऽसौ साधयित्वाद्वयं परम्॥
अद्वयब्रह्मविद्यां च स्थापयेदवनीतले। अन्यथा वर्णयेद् यस्तु वेदार्थं स तु मूढधीः॥
शिवे मदंशसंभूतः शङ्करः शङ्करोत्तमः। चतुर्भिः सह शिष्यश्च कलाववतरिष्यति॥
तस्मै चोपनिषद्विद्या मया दत्ता महेश्वरि। भूमौ पाषण्डानां खण्डनं स करिष्यति॥
बिभेत्यल्पश्रुताद्वेदो मामयं प्रतरिष्यति। इतिहासपुराणाभ्यां वेदं समुपबृंहयेत्॥
— Quoted in *SV*, pp. 131-32

4 यत्संकोचविकासाभ्यां जगत्प्रलयसृष्टयः। निष्ठा वेदान्तवाक्यानामथ वाचामगोचरः॥
प्रातीतिकत्वं वेदान्तसिद्धान्ते जगतः स्फुटम्। अतः सुप्तौ जगल्लीनं प्रबोधे जायते पुनः॥
दृष्तिसृष्टिमिमां ब्रह्मानुभवी बहुमन्यते। बद्धो मुक्तो महाविद्वान् अज्ञ इत्यादिभेदतः॥
एक एव सदा भाति नानेव स्वप्नवत्स्वयम्॥
अतः स्वमुक्त्यै वान्येषामाभासानामपि ध्रुवम्। मुक्तिं जानाति हे देवा आत्मना ह्यात्मविद्वरः॥
स्वसंसारदशायां तु स्वभ्रान्त्या सर्वदेहिनाम्। आभासानां च संसारं वेद मुक्तिं तथैव च॥
— Quoted in *SV*, p. 132
तुच्छाऽनिर्वचनीया च वास्तवी चेत्यसौ त्रिधा। ज्ञेया माया त्रिभिर्बोधैः श्रौतयौक्तिकलौकिकैः॥
— *PD* 6.130

5 द्वितीयाद्वै भयं भवति। — *BU* 1.4.2
अथ योऽन्यां देवतामुपास्तेऽन्योऽसावन्योऽहमस्मीति न स वेद यथा पशुरेवꣳस देवानाम्।
— *BU* 1.4.10

other attendants. Once they hatched a plan against Bharchu. They engaged forest-thieves to loot the kingdom. The king appointed Bharchu to tackle this mishap. Bharchu was victorious in driving away the thieves and rendering the kingdom free from troubles. The attendants passed on the wrong message of death of Bharchu in this encounter. The king trusted the words of the attendants and mourned over the death of his minister. He appointed a new minister who saw to it that Bharchu did not enter the kingdom. Meanwhile, Bharchu roamed in the forest and took to mendicant life having discriminated the ephemeral from the absolute truth. He recollected the Purāṇic teaching of a simple life.[6] He contemplated on the defects of sensuous pleasures and concluded that renunciation is extremely blissful. Thus, Bharchu engaged in monastic life. The new minister was frightened that if the king comes to know that Bharchu is alive he may be in danger. So, he along with other attendants spread a rumour that Bharchu is roaming in the forest in the form of a ghost. Once when the king was hunting in the forest, he came across Bharchu. He remembered the words of the new minister and concluded that "this Bharchu is a ghost". Even though the king saw Bharchu with his own eyes, since he trusted the words of the new minister, he considered Bharchu as a ghost.

The purpose of this narrative is to show the mechanism of rise of knowledge. The means or instruments of knowledge generates valid apprehension. Even after the employment of the means of knowledge, if valid knowledge does not arise it implies that there is an obstacle for the rise of valid knowledge. On the removal of the obstacle, the same thought-mode generates valid knowledge. It amounts to say that on the removal of obstacle, a "new" knowledge is not generated. Similarly, at the time of *śravaṇa*, direct knowledge (*aparokṣa jñāna*) is generated and (for

---

6 सत्यां क्षितौ किं कशिपोः प्रयासैर्बाहौ स्वसिद्धे ह्युपबर्हणैः किम्।
सत्यञ्जलौ किं पुरुधाऽन्नपत्र्या दिग्वल्कलादौ सति किं दुकूलैः॥ — *BP* 2.2.4

चीराणि किं पथि न सन्ति विशन्ति भिक्षां नैवाङ्घ्रिपाः परभृतः सरितोऽप्यशुष्यन्।
रुद्धा गुहाः किमजितोऽवति नोपसन्नान् कस्माद्भजन्ति कवयो धनदुर्मदान्धान्॥ — *BP* 2.2.5

some) due to certain obstacles, it is not known to be valid knowledge. But by repeated *śravaṇa* or *manana*, etc. the same thought-mode "transforms" into knowledge.

According to the Bhāmatī School, *śravaṇa* produces indirect knowledge (*parokṣa jñāna*), wherein the thought-mode (*vṛtti*) has to be repeated in *nididhyāsana*, and a "new" *pramāṇa* gives rise to *aparokṣa jñāna*. Thus, mind is the *pramāṇa* for Bhāmatī School.[7] In the view of the Vivaraṇa School the rise of direct knowledge is from the Vedic statement which is the *pramāṇa*.

In the above anecdote, the "Bharchu *vṛtti*" is generated by the *pramāṇa* for the king, but it does not have the capacity to give rise to direct knowledge (*jñānatva*), since it is obstructed by the knowledge that "Bharchu is a ghost". Unless the erroneous knowledge is removed, even the direct perception of Bharchu will never give rise to the knowledge that "this is Bharchu". Based on this story, the *guru* shows that one who trusts the word of a dualistic philosopher will not gain the knowledge of non-dual reality, even when there is the rise of the mental-mode of direct knowledge of *Brahman* as instructed by the *guru* through the *mahāvākya*. The seeker is to understand that duality is false, then alone *mahāvākya* will "produce" direct knowledge of *Brahman* (*brahmasākṣātkāra*).

FALSITY OF BONDAGE AND LIBERATION

The question of the *madhyama adhikārī* that "if both *guru* and Vedānta are false then they cannot remove ignorance (sorrow)" is answered here through another narrative. The *madhyama adhikārī* holds on to the view that sorrow or bondage is real and thereby seeks a "real" solution. The *guru*, once again, shows[8] that the bondage is unreal, which can be removed by the unreal *guru* and Vedānta. He narrates an incident. There was a powerful king. Once he was asleep in his well-guarded palace, on a bed decorated

---

[7] दृश्यते तु अग्रयया बुद्ध्या सूक्ष्मया सूक्ष्मदर्शिभिः ॥ — *KU* 1.3.12
एषोणुरात्मा चेतसा वेदितव्यः । — *MU* 3.1.9

[8] See Section 3.3 Chapter 3.

with flowers. The king dreamt as if he was attacked by a jackal. He could not get rid of the jackal and he yelled for help, but no guards came to his rescue. He hit the jackal's head with a stick and the jackal ran away. There was intense pain in the king's leg and he limped to a doctor for aid. The doctor said he could treat if the king gave him money for treatment. The king did not have any money and he was extremely sad. He thought, "if I were wealthy the doctor would have come to my house and cured". Thus thinking, the king came out of the doctor's house. On the way he meets a mendicant who treated the king without expecting any payment. The king was cured. Suddenly, the king woke up from his dream and found no jackal, doctor or the mendicant. The *guru* points out that, the anecdote is to reveal that a false problem is solved by a false solution. The king, who dreamt that he was suffering was cured by a mendicant in dream. Neither his wealth, nor doctor or guards present in waking state could save him. Here, the problem faced by the king was false and the solution he gained in dream is also false. Similarly, by the means of the "false" *guru* and Vedānta the "false" sorrow gets completely eliminated.

The *guru* reminds[9] that it is not proper to cite mirage-water as an example to show that it cannot quench the thirst of a person because they (thirst and mirage-water) belong to different orders of reality; whereas, bondage and the removal of bondage are revealed as belonging to the same order of reality. The *guru* shows that other than Consciousness, everything else is false and they fall either under empirical reality or phenomenal reality.[10]

THREE ORDERS OF REALITY

The *guru* explains the nature of the three orders of reality to reiterate that the relation between the means (*sādhaka*) and the subsequent sublation (*bādhaka*) is possible only when both belong to the same order of reality. The empirical reality is that wherein without the *Brahman*-knowledge, the empirical world does not

[9] See Section 4.3 Chapter 4.

[10] See Section 4.4 Chapter 4.

get sublated. The creation of *Īśvara* is empirically real. The empirical world along with body, sense-organs, mind, etc. cannot be sublated without the rise of *Brahman*-knowledge. The word "sublation" (*bādha*) means the firm direct knowledge of the falsity of the matter principle.[11] Since the primal ignorance (*mūla-avidyā*) and its effects in the form of the universe are empirically real, the bondage in the form of birth, death, etc. and the means to remove bondage also belong to the empirical world.

The second order of reality is described by the *guru* as the phenomenal reality which is negated by any other knowledge other than *Brahman*-knowledge. He cites instances of rope, shell, dry land, etc. by whose knowledge the error like snake, silver, mirage-water respectively are sublated. The experience of the phenomenal entity is as long as the phenomenon exists, i.e. the modal-ignorance (*tūla-avidyā*) and its effects that are experienced are sublated on the removal of modal-ignorance.

The third order of reality, i.e. the transcendental reality, is the unsublatable consciousness that is unaffected in the three periods of time. Thus, the *guru,* and the Vedānta, who are treated to be unreal from the transcendental angle, could resolve the bondage that again is unreal from the standpoint of transcendental reality. Hence, the *guru* concludes that the empirical world is sublated by the teaching in the empirical world. In order to point out that sublation of unreality is possible only through knowledge; the *guru* first describes the nature of *māyā* and its effects so as to later bring about the knowledge of oneness through the methods of discrimination.

5.2 Nature of Māyā

Based on the law that, "that which is born of ignorance is sublated by knowledge", the *guru* describes the origination of the universe.

---

[11] नाप्रतीतिस्तयोर्बाधः किन्तु मिथ्यात्वनिश्चयः।
नो चेत्सुषुप्तिमूर्छादौ मुच्येतायत्नतो जनः॥
परमात्मावशेषो हि तत्सत्यत्वविनिश्चयः।
न जगद्विस्मृतिर्नो चेज्जीवन्मुक्तिर्न संभवेत्॥ — *PD* 6.13-14

Since ignorance (*māyā*) is said to be its material cause, the nature of *māyā* is discussed first. The fundamental nature of *māyā* in Advaita is presented as that which rests (superimposed) on Pure Consciousness, devoid of plurality like *Īśvara* and *Jīva*. Here, two main features of *māyā* are highlighted:

(i) *Māyā* is beginningless (*anādi*), and

(ii) *Māyā* is neither existent nor non-existent entity (*sadasadvilakṣaṇa*).

The *guru* explains the nature of *māyā* as beginningless. If the origin of *māyā* is accepted then the cause of *māyā* should be assumed to be any of the four — *Brahman, Īśvara, jīva*, or *jagat*. *Jīva, Īśvara* and *jagat* cannot be the cause of *māyā* since their very "existence" is due to *māyā*. *Māyā* should precede these three chronologically. It results in the defect of mutual-dependence. *Māyā* cannot be an effect of *Brahman* since *Brahman* is free from modifications and is unassociated. If *māyā* is said to be an effect of *Brahman* then pure *Brahman* will be subject to modifications and hence will be non-eternal. Moreover, it will lead to *anirmokṣa prasaṅga* if *māyā* is said to continue with *Brahman* in liberation and also the means to liberation will be redundant. Therefore, the origination of *māyā* is not accepted. Hence it is said to be without a beginning; but on the rise of *Brahman*-knowledge *māyā* gets destroyed. The *guru* does not differentiate *māyā* from *avidyā* and accepts the prevalent view that *māyā* is one.

The *guru* then explains the nature of *māyā* as *sadasadvilakṣaṇa*, i.e. it cannot be categorized as either *sat* or *asat*. *Sat* is that which remains unsublated in the three periods of time and since *māyā* gets sublated on the rise of *Brahman*-knowledge it cannot be categorized as *Sat*. That which is not comprehended in the three periods of time like hare's horn, sky-lotus, etc. is said to be *asat*. Prior to *Brahman*-knowledge, *māyā* and its effects are experienced. To explain the experience of *māyā*, the experience of the three states are examined.

In the waking state one expresses as "I am ignorant, I do not know *Brahman*", due to *māyā*. The dream-world has *māyā* as its material cause. The experience of *māyā* in deep-sleep state is known when on waking up one verbally expresses that "I slept happily and I did not know anything" where there is the expression of ignorance. In all the three states of experience, *māyā* is experienced. Hence, *māyā* is not a non-existent entity. The effect of the indescribable *māyā* is the world which is also indescribable. In Advaita, the entity that is beyond existence and non-existence (*sadasadvilakṣaṇa*) is known as *mithyā* also otherwise referred to as the indescribable (*anirvacanīya*). The existence of indeterminable *māyā* and its effects does not affect the non-dual nature of *Brahman*.

MĀYĀ ACCORDING TO BHĀMATĪ AND VIVARAṆA SCHOOLS

According to Vācaspati Miśra, ignorance rests on *jīva* and has *Brahman* as its content. In the experience expressed as "I am ignorant, I do not know *Brahman*"; the word "I am" primarily refers to *jīva* and the word "ignorant" reveals the locus of ignorance. Therefore, *jīva* as the locus of ignorance is evident in this statement. The expression "I do not know *Brahman*" reveals the object of ignorance and that is *Brahman*. Thus, ignorance rests on *jīva* and conceals the nature of *Brahman*. The ignorance or *māyā* is not one but many. If *māyā* is one, then on rise of *Brahman*-knowledge in one *jīva*, there will be destruction of ignorance in all *jīva*s. But this is not so. To avoid this difficulty, if it is argued that *Brahman*-knowledge does not arise in any *jīva*, then there will be the defect of futility of hearing scriptures (*śravaṇa*) and other means to liberation. Therefore, ignorance is many, resting on all *jīva*s. Since *jīva*'s ignorance is many, the superimposed *Īśvara* is also many and the universes are many. When *Brahman*-knowledge arises in one *jīva*, then the superimposed universe and *Īśvara*, by that *jīva*, get destroyed and for other ignorant *jīva*s, the world and *Īśvara* continue. *Jīva*, *Īśvara* and world are superimpositions of ignorance. The plurality of ignorance in every *jīva* will give rise to manifold *Īśvara*s and manifold creations like many *jīva*s. So, Vācaspati Miśra has considered many *jīva*s, many *Īśvara*s and many worlds. *Īśvara* as a superimposition of *jīva*'s ignorance is contradictory to Śruti, Smṛti and Purāṇas. The plurality of *Īśvara* and the world exclusive for each *jīva* contradicts all means of knowledge.

The locus of *māyā* is Pure *Brahman* and not *jīva* since the *jīva*-notion itself is an effect of ignorance. *Māyā* that can never exist independently without a locus cannot give rise to *jīva*-notion. Ignorance primarily has a substratum as its locus and then produces its effect, namely, *jīva*. Like *jīva*, *Īśvara* also is an effect of ignorance.[12] Therefore, *Īśvara* also cannot serve as the locus of *māyā*. By the application of *pāriśeṣa nyāya,* beginningless ignorance rests on Pure *Brahman*. The relation between beginningless *Brahman* and *māyā* is also beginningless. Although the beginningless relation of *Brahman* and *māyā* and the effects, viz., *jīva* and *Īśvara* also are without a beginning yet since *jīva* and *Īśvara* are dependent on ignorance, they are said to be the effects of ignorance.

The followers of the Bhāmatī School contend that if *jīva* is not the locus of *māyā*, then how are we to account for the experience of ignorance of *jīva* and the corresponding expression as "I am ignorant"? The Vivaraṇa School argues that *jīva* being an effect of ignorance cannot be the locus of ignorance. Hence it is the Pure *Brahman* that serves as both the locus and content of ignorance. The expression "I am ignorant" reveals the *jīva*'s identification with ignorance and not the locus of ignorance. It may be added here that according to Vācaspati, "I" primarily refers to consciousness conditioned by internal organ that is *jīva*. Here the substantial part is the witness consciousness, i.e. *Brahman* which serves as the locus of ignorance. Logically stating, the characteristics of a substance are attributed to the conditioning factor and thereby it can be said that *jīva* is the locus of ignorance. Thus, the view of Bhāmatī in this line of argument is admitted. Ignorance is that which is destroyed by knowledge. The knowledge rising in the consciousness conditioned by one mind destroys the ignorance resting on the consciousness conditioned

---

12 उपशान्तजगज्जीव शिष्याचार्येश्वरभ्रमम्। स्वतः सिद्धमनाद्यन्तं परिपूर्णमहं महः॥ — *AM* 27

by that mind and hence the individual *jīva* attains freedom. The ignorance in other minds continues and hence the other *jīva*s remain bound. Just as darkness, although is one, is conditioned in different rooms. On lighting a lamp, darkness in relation to that particular room is removed while it continues to pervade the other rooms. This lamp is not efficacious in removing the darkness in other rooms, due to the presence of walls which serve as the limiting factor. In the same way, the limiting adjunct, mind is many and the rise of thought-mode in a particular mind destroys the ignorance in that mind alone and the ignorance relating to other minds continue to exist. Hence there is no contingency of instantaneous liberation of all, when one's ignorance gets destroyed. It emerges from the above that bondage and liberation could be satisfactorily explained even by admitting ignorance to be one. The *guru*, however, does not dismiss the view of Bhāmatī as incorrect. He says, if one is convinced with the theory of "plurality of ignorance" then also the teaching of Advaita is not affected. He reminds here that a seeker can take to any *prakriyā* and remain established in non-dual knowledge.[13]

Māyā resting on Pure *Brahman* is also referred to as *avidyā* and *ajñāna*. It is known as *māyā* because it is incomprehensible, with infinite power, and that which cannot be logically determined. Since *māyā* is destroyed by knowledge (*vidyā*) it is known as *avidyā*. Since *māyā* conceals the nature (of consciousness) it is known as *ajñāna*. *Brahman*-Consciousness is not opposed to *māyā* but it is the substratum of *māyā*. Consciousness lends existence and illumines *māyā*. Consciousness with *Brahman* thought-mode is said to be opposed to *māyā*. Just like the bright sunlight which illumines cotton but when captured in a lens burns the cotton, in the same way, *māyā* supported by *Brahman* gets sublated on the rise of *Brahman*-knowledge.

---

[13] यया यया भवेत्पुंसां व्युत्पत्तिः प्रत्यगात्मनि ।
सा सैव प्रक्रियेह स्यात्साध्वी सा चानवस्थिता ॥ — *BUŚBV* 1.4.402

PROCESS OF CREATION

The *guru* now describes the creation process which is an effect of *māyā*. The *guru* initially clarifies that the world emerges like a dream-world without any order and the one who is desirous of knowing the order of creation is said to be diving into mirage-water.[14] The scriptures describe the origin of creation in a manifold manner which is subsequently dismissed as unreal. This shows that the purpose of scriptures is not to reveal any order of creation. The scriptural statements related to origination of the universe are examined.

If it is asked that when an orderly creation is not accepted then how does one understand the statement of *Taittirīya Upaniṣad*?[15] This is explained — one sees inconsistency in the description of creation by the scriptures. *Chāndogya Upaniṣad* describes the evolution of three elements from *Brahman*.[16] *Taittirīya Upaniṣad* states that five elements emerged from *Brahman*. It also describes the evolution without mentioning any order from *Brahman*.[17] *Muṇḍaka Upaniṣad* describes creation differently.[18] Thus, the different descriptions of creation by the Upaniṣads indicate the unreality of the world. If the world is real then the Upaniṣads would not have described differently. There cannot be differences in reality. Thus, the creation of the world is not the essential teaching of the Upaniṣads.

The Upaniṣads intend to reveal the absolutely real non-dual *Brahman* by the method of acceptance and negation (*adhyāropa-apavāda*).[19] The experienced world is superimposed on the

---

14 स्वप्नेऽर्थशून्ये सृजति स्वशक्त्या भोक्त्रादिविश्वं मन एव सर्वम्।
तथैव जाग्रत्यपि नो विशेषस्तत्सर्वमेतन्मनसो विजृम्भणम्॥ — *VC* 170

15 तस्माद्वा एतस्मादात्मन आकाशः संभूतः। — *TU* 2.1

16 तदैक्षत बहु स्यां प्रजायेयेति तत्तेजोऽसृजत तत्तेज ऐक्षत बहु स्यां प्रजायेयेति तदपोऽसृजत तस्माद्यत्र क्वच शोचति स्वेदते वा पुरुषस्तेजस एव तदध्यापो जायन्ते॥ — *CU* 6.2.3

17 इदꣳ सर्वमसृजत। — *TU* 2.6

18 एतस्माज्जायते प्राणो मनः सर्वेन्द्रियाणि च। खं वायुर्ज्योतिरापः पृथिवी विश्वस्य धारिणी॥ — *MU* 2.2.3

19 अध्यारोपापवादाभ्यां निष्प्रपञ्चं प्रपञ्च्यते। — *PK* 1

substratum and subsequently negated as false to reveal the reality of the substratum, viz., *Brahman*. To explain this, an instance is cited here: a person makes a doll-elephant for entertainment and with the help of a machine the doll-elephant flies in the sky. While flying in the sky, the ear and the tail of the doll-elephant gets twisted. The person does not try to set it right. Similarly, for attaining the non-dual *Brahman* knowledge the perceived dualistic world is superimposed for subsequent negation.[20] The intention is not in analysing the superimposed world. Therefore, Śruti does not describe the creation in any one particular pattern.[21]

ORDER OF CREATION

There is a discussion regarding the creation of the world in the second chapter of *Brahmasūtra*. It has been established that the description of creation in *Taittirīya Upaniṣad* is to be considered as the import of all the Upaniṣads and the *guru* remarks that this is meant for *manda adhikārī* (this does not refer to the classification of aspirants in *Vicārasāgara*). In this context, the *madhyama adhikārī* is referred to as *manda* only from the standpoint of understanding the nature of the world. The world as a false appearance, the *guru* states, cannot be understood by a *manda adhikārī* and to avoid confusion relating to the apparent contradictory statements on creation in Upaniṣads, *Brahmasūtra* describes the order of creation from space and so on. An orderly creation is accepted to facilitate the process of meditation on the resolution of the world. Thus, the discordance in Śruti is ignored by describing an orderly creation established in *Brahmasūtra* and its *Bhāṣya*. Hence, the *guru* undertakes a brief description of the creation process.

Evolution of Subtle World

Īśvara desires[22] to produce the universe because of which *māyā* turns to be *tamas* predominant. Prior to creation, the *sattva guṇa* is

---

20 लोकप्रसिद्धं त्विदं रूपद्वयं ब्रह्मणि कल्पितं परामृशति प्रतिषेध्यत्वाय शुद्धब्रह्मस्वरूपप्रतिपादनाय चेति निरवद्यम्। — *BSŚB* 3.2.22

21 यत्र यत्र विगानं तत्र न तात्पर्यम्।

22 सोऽकामयत। — *TU* 2.6

predominant in *māyā* which serves as the adjunct of *Īśvara*, holding the seed of the universe in the form of *Brahman*-reflection and then this seed matures into ignorance "adjunct" with countless *jīva*s and the universe in subtle form. At the beginning of creation, *māyā* which is of the nature of pure-*sattva guṇa*, becomes the primordial matter with *tamas* predominance because of the power of concealment, thus matured for origination. From the *tamas* predominant *māyā*, emerges the five elements — space, air, fire, water and earth. But we find the statement in *Taittirīya Upaniṣad* that reveals the origin of elements from *Brahman*. This apparent contradiction is reconciled by stating that *māyā* creates the world but not independently.

The five elements possess the qualities of sound, touch, form, taste, smell respectively. The first element namely space along with sound as its property emerges from *māyā*. The evolution process progresses from space to air, fire, water and earth. In the evolution of each element, they emerge with their respective quality and every effectual element borrows the property of its immediate cause. Thus, finally, the earth element possesses all the five qualities.[23] The primal cause of everything is *Īśvara*. *Īśvara* has two aspects (*aṁśa*s) — Consciousness and Matter.[24] The qualities in the form of name, form and falsity seen in the effects are from its cause, *māyā*. The manifestation of "Existence" in the entities belongs to the Consciousness.

Origin of Internal Organ and Sense-organs of Knowledge

From the total *sattva* aspect of the non-grossified subtle five elements emerges the internal organ, which is also known as *sattva*. The internal organ is the cause of origination of knowledge.[25] Therefore, internal organ is an effect of *sattva guṇa*. This is an

---

23 अस्ति भूस्तत्त्वशून्यास्यां शब्दस्पर्शौ सरूपकौ ।
रसश्च परतो गन्धो नैजः सत्ता विविच्यताम् ॥ — *PD* 2.94

24 एकस्वभावं सत्तत्वमाकाशे द्विस्वभावकः ।
नावकाशः सति व्योम्नि स चैषोऽपि द्वयं स्थितम् ॥ — *PD* 2.61

25 सत्त्वात्संजायते ज्ञानं । — *BG* XIV.17

inferential knowledge based on the result (*phala-bala-kalpanā*); where the *sattva guṇa* is inferred since the mind produces knowledge but *sattva guṇa* is not visible.[26] The modification of mind is known as thought-mode (*vṛtti*). The internal organ has fourfold functions and based on the functions it is known as mind, intellect, memory and ego.[27] The *sattva guṇa* of each element individually gives rise to the sense-organs of knowledge. They are five in number, namely, the sense of hearing, sense of touch, sense of sight, sense of taste and sense of smell.

Origin of Vital Airs and Sense-organs of Action

The five vital airs emerge from the total *rajas* aspect of non-grossified elements. The airs are of five kinds depending on their function and place. *Prāṇa* is in the heart, with the function of bringing about hunger and thirst. *Apāna* is in the excretory organ and its function is to evacuate solid and liquid wastes from the body. *Samāna* remains in the navel, whose function is to digest (cook) the consumed solid and liquid food that is fit for absorption. *Udāna* is in the throat whose function is exhalation. *Vyāna* circulates in the entire body and its function is to transport the nourishment through the nerves and blood vessels. The Sāṁkhyas[28] consider another set of five airs namely *nāga, kūrma, kṛka, devadatta* and *dhanañjaya.* The function of *nāga* is reversal process. *Kūrma* helps in winking of the eye and hiccups. Cause of sneezing is because of *kṛka*. Yawning is the function of *devadatta. Dhanañjaya*'s function is swelling. These are secondary airs which are considered to be the products of *rajas* of each element respectively. Even the five primary vital airs are considered as the product of *rajas* aspect of each element respectively. Some say, vital airs are not products of total *rajas* aspect of all elements.

---

[26] सर्वद्वारेषु देहेऽस्मिन्प्रकाश उपजायते ।
ज्ञानं यदा तदा विद्याद्विवृद्धं सत्त्वमित्युत ॥ — *BG* XIV.11

[27] संशयो निश्चयो गर्वः स्मरणमिति । एवंविधवृत्तिभेदेन एवमप्यन्तःकरणं मन इति बुद्धिरिति अहङ्कार इति चित्तमिति चाख्यायते । — *VP*, p. 32

[28] केचित्तु नागकूर्मकृकदेवदत्तधनञ्जयाख्याः पञ्चान्ये वायवः सन्तीति वदन्ति ।
— *VS*, p. 51

The *guru* shows that these secondary vital airs are not accepted in Advaita.[29] According to Advaita, the vital airs are products of total *rajas* aspect of all the elements. The five airs are part of the subtle body. The vital airs are in the form of energy. The nature of *rajas* is activity. The sense-organs of action are the effect of *rajoguṇa* in each element. They are the sense of speech, grasping, locomotion, excretion and reproduction. The non-grossified elements and its effect, the elementals in the form of internal organ, vital airs, sense-organs of knowledge and action are the subtle creations. The subtle creation is not known through the sense-organs. The orifices like eyes and ears are the objects of senses. The internal organ behind each sense-organ can never be an object of a sense-organ. After the emergence of the subtle universe by the desire of *Īśvara,* the gross universe manifests by undergoing the process of grossification (*pañcīkaraṇa*).

Evolution of Gross World

The *guru* presents two kinds of process of grossification. In the first kind of grossification, the *tamoguṇa* in each subtle element, which is in equilibrium, gets divided into two halves. Each half element gets sub-divided into four. One-eighth of the element gets transferred to other elements other than its own. Thus, the grossification takes place. Thus, each element has one-half of its own and one-eighth of the other elements. Each gross element is a constituent of all the five elements and is said to have undergone the grossification process (see *fig.* 5.1). In this first *prakriyā,* after grossification each element consists of one half of its own and one-eighth of other elements. It is pointed out that there is the problem of other elements overpowering the other half of the element. In gross space, there will be the dominance of other elements. In gross space, space will not be dominant, even though this is not experienced. So, the *guru* introduces a second kind of grossification.

---

29 तन्न श्रुतौ पञ्चानामेव श्रवणात् नागादीनां प्राणाद्यन्तर्भावौचित्यात्।
— Gaṅgādhara's *Candrikā* to *PK*, p. 64

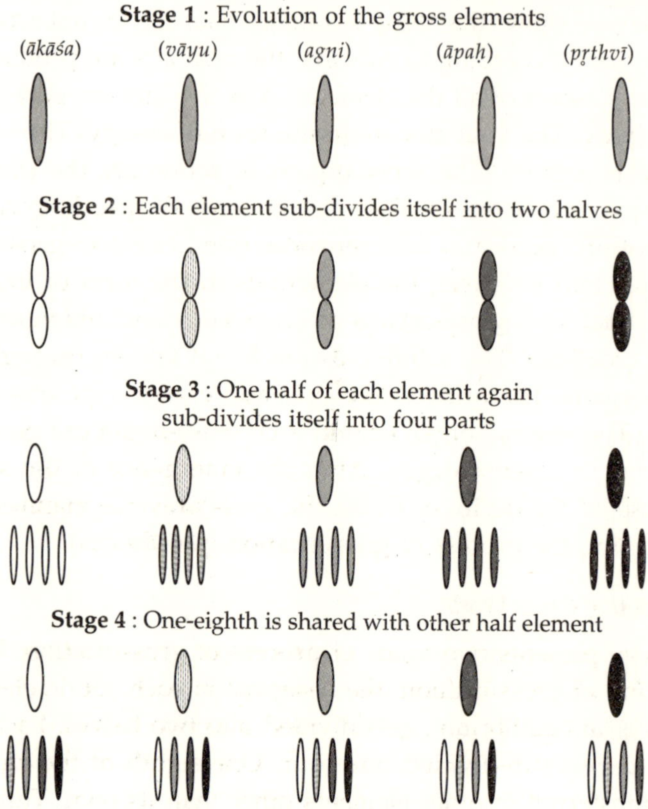

fig. 5.1: *Pañcīkaraṇa Prakriyā* 1

The second kind of grossification process reveals the dominance of the specific element. Each subtle element divides itself into five parts. Then each one-fifth part gets subdivided into five parts again. Totally twenty-five parts are formed in two stages. Of these, four parts are exchanged with other elements. There are remaining twenty-one parts. *Ākāśa* distributes $\frac{1}{25}$th to other elements and receives $\frac{1}{25}$th from other elements. So *ākāśa* now is a composition of $\frac{21}{25}$th *ākāśa*, $\frac{1}{25}$th of *vāyu*, $\frac{1}{25}$th *agni*, $\frac{1}{25}$th *jala* and $\frac{1}{25}$th *pr̥thivī* and so on. Hence in this *prakriyā*, *ākāśa* is dominant and the other elements are insignificant. Therefore, their non-experience or non-visibility gets explained (see *fig.* 5.2).

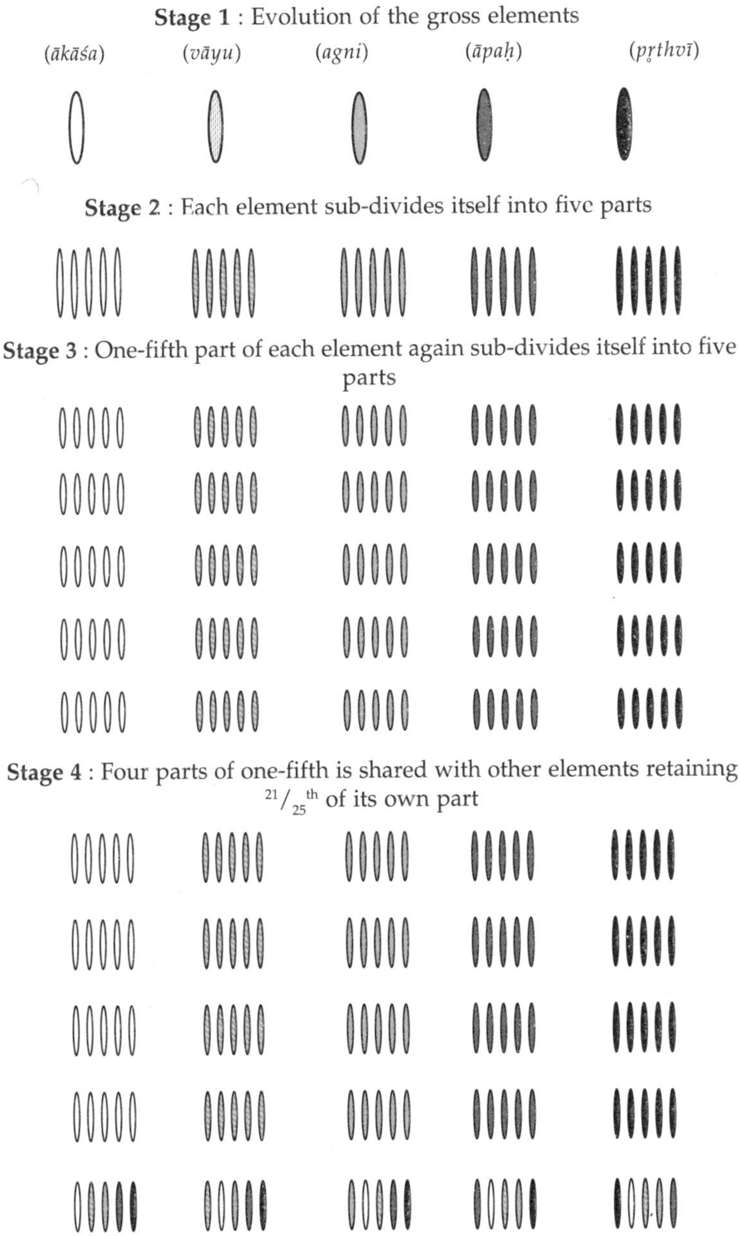

fig. 5.2 *Pañcīkaraṇa Prakriyā* 2

In the first kind of *pañcīkaraṇa*, one-half of the element is its own. The other half of the element is of the other four elements. Like, in the space element, one-half is space element and the other half is $^{1}/_{8}{}^{th}$ of air, fire, water and earth. In the second kind of *pañcīkaraṇa*, one part of the element is $^{21}/_{25}$ part of its own element. It has received only $^{1}/_{25}{}^{th}$ part from the other elements. Just as in the case of space, one part of space is with $^{21}/_{25}$ parts of space element and the other part of the space element is $^{1}/_{25}{}^{th}$ each of air, water, fire and earth. In this second *prakriyā* each element has its own feature dominant and this explains the experience of each distinct element. Thus, the gross universe evolves. Having described the creation process, the *guru* then states that the manifestation of *māyā* is unfathomable. The individual being is a combination of gross, subtle and causal bodies. The gross body has twenty-five factors.[30]

The Five Sheaths

The quality of *māyā* is found in its effect namely the three bodies or the five sheaths. The gross body is known as the food-sheath (*annamayakośa*), the vital air and the sense-organs of action is known as the air-sheath (*prāṇamayakośa*), the mind and the sense-organs of knowledge is known as the mental-sheath (*manomayakośa*), the intellect is known as the intellect-sheath (*vijñānamayakośa*) and the causal body is the bliss-sheath (*ānandamayakośa*). Here, both *Īśvara* and *jīva* are said to possess five sheaths (*kośa*).[31] Just as a sheath covers a knife, the five sheaths cover the nature of Self (*sat* and *cit* are not concealed). The macrocosmic ignorance in the form of *māyā* is the causal body of *Īśvara*, which is the bliss-sheath. The subtle body of all *jīva*s is the subtle body of *Īśvara* known as Hiraṇyagarbha. This includes the intellect-sheath, the mental-sheath and the air-sheath. The intellect-sheath of *Īśvara* is the macro intellect in the form of *mahat* or Brahmā who identifies with macro intellect. The mental-sheath of *Īśvara* includes the presiding deities of organs of knowledge and macro mind-identification. The air-sheath of *Īśvara*

---

30 *SV*, pp. 161-62.

31 कोश इवासेः । — *MUSB* 2.2.10; कोशवत् आच्छादकत्वात् । — *VS*, p. 28

includes the presiding deities of action and the macro air or identification with the macro air. The gross body or the food-sheath of *Īśvara* is the gross universe known as Virāṭ.

5.3 Methods of Discrimination

The *guru* employs the well-known methods of discrimination between Self and non-self to reiterate the reality of Self and falsehood of non-self. Three methods of discrimination, viz., discrimination of the five sheaths, discrimination from the three states of experience and discrimination of the three bodies are presented here elaborately by the *guru*.

PAÑCAKOŚAVIVEKA

From the standpoint of the five sheaths, the *guru* takes up the discussion on the prevalent views on the nature of Self and presents them in the language of Advaita. He reviews the ideas of various schools that holds on to a particular sheath as the Self. The *guru* then reveals the concealment of Self by the sheaths at micro and macro levels. This is presented as the first method of discrimination of Self from non-self.

Annamayakośa as Self : Its Refutation

Some, in keeping with the view of Virocana consider that Self is the food-sheath. The following argument is put forth:

1. Self is that in which the "I" thought arises. That "I" thought refers to the gross body and this is known from the experience that "I am human", etc. "Human-ness", etc. which are the characteristics of the gross body. Therefore, the object of "I" thought is gross body which is the Self.
2. There is an instinctive love for survival of the Self.[32] One loves wife, children, wealth, animals, etc. if they are

---

[32] इयमात्मा परानन्दः परप्रेमास्पदं यतः ।
मा न भूवं हि भूयासं इति प्रेमात्मनीक्ष्यते ॥ — *PD* 1.8
अहमस्मि सदा भामि कदाचिन्नाहमप्रियः । — *AM* 2
तदेतत्प्रेयः पुत्रात् प्रेयो वित्तात् प्रेयोऽन्यस्मात्सर्वस्मात् अन्तरतरम् यदयमात्मा । *BU* 1.4.8

favourable to the body. If they are not the source of happiness then they are rejected. Thus, the gross body alone is the Self. Therefore, decorating the physical body and merriment alone are the ultimate goals according to Virocana's School.[33]

A similar view is held by the Cārvāka school of thought. They consider that the body is a product of four elements and puts forth the following arguments:

1. The object of "I" is the physical body which is the Self. Body conditioned by these characteristics alone is the object of experiences like "I am human" and "I am fat".
2. Self is the object of highest love. The love for others is based on the happiness gained through the physical body.
3. The highest goal of happiness is achieved by decorating the body.
4. Death alone is liberation.
5. Perception alone is the source of knowledge.

That the physical body is not the Self is proved on the following grounds:

1. The object of "I" in the expressions, "I see", "I speak", etc. include the sense-organs also.
2. "My body is fat", etc. such expressions presuppose the identification with the body as "mine". That which is the object of "mine-ness" cannot be the object of "I-ness". Since the notion of "I" varies from the physical body to sense-organs, etc. the physical body cannot be said to be the Self.
3. Though one's own body is loved more than wife, children, etc. there is the experience of intense love with regard to the senses more than the body. In such a case, physical body is not the Self.

---

[33] तस्मादप्यद्येहाददानमश्रद्दधानमयजमानमाहुरासुरो बतेत्यसुराणाꣳ ह्येषोपनिषत्प्रेतस्य शरीरं भिक्षया वसनेनालंकारेणेति सꣳस्कुर्वन्त्येतेन ह्यमुं लोकं जेष्यन्तो मन्यन्ते ॥ — *CU* 8.8.5

4. Self is sentient, body being combination of matter is devoid of consciousness and hence body is not Self.
5. The combination of matter does not result in consciousness; otherwise we must agree that a pot possesses consciousness.
6. Body is also inert in deep-sleep, death, coma, etc. like a pot. Therefore the inert body cannot be the Self.
7. If body is the Self, then there cannot arise the experience "I am that", recognizing the childhood state in old age.
8. The body that undergoes birth, death, etc. does not possess existence prior to birth and posterior to death. If the continuance existence of the Self is not accepted then there will be the defect of destruction of the result of performed action and reaping of result of a non-performed action.
9. Decoration of physical body cannot be considered as the highest *ānanda* since sensual pleasures do not have the capacity to yield liberation.
10. Death as liberation is contradictory to scriptural declaration on liberation.
11. Perception alone cannot be accepted as the source of knowledge because the very acceptance of perception is based on inference. For instance, the knowledge that consumed food will remove hunger in future is based on inference. The words of a relative informing the death of one's father in a distant land are gained through words and not perception. Thus, accepting perception alone as source of knowledge is irrelevant. The views of Virocana and Cārvāka are improper.

Indriya as Self : Its Refutation

Some consider that the sense-organ is the Self because the physical body functions due to the presence of senses and in the absence of senses the physical body does not function. As long as the sense-organs are in the body and engage in their respective actions the body is said to be alive. When one expresses as "I speak", "I hear", the word "I" refers to the senses. This is the view of the Lokāyata School and the same is refuted by the following arguments:

1. Sense-organ cannot be declared as Self based on the co-presence and co-absence reasoning (*anvaya vyatireka*) since in the absence of any one of the senses a person continues to live.
2. In the expression, "I see", "I speak", etc. the object of "I" is not the sense-organs. In the expressions, "my eyes are powerful", "my eyes are weak", the senses are the object of "mine-ness". Since, the senses are the object of "I" and "mine" there is variation and it cannot be declared as the Self.
3. Sense-organs are also the object of perception because the characteristics of sense-organs are known. That which is an object of perception is not the Self.
4. The sense-organs function only when enlivened by mind. When the mind is preoccupied ears do not perceive sound.
5. If sense-organ is said to be the conscious Self then the following questions arise:

   Is one sense-organ the Self, or
   all sense-organs put together is the Self, or
   each sense-organ is the Self?

   The first possibility is ruled out because in the absence of one sense-organ the individual gains knowledge through the other senses. The second possibility is also ruled out because destruction of one sense-organ would amount in destruction of the group, but this is not experienced. The third possibility is ruled out on the ground that plurality of Selves in an individual leads to confusion.
6. In this context, the *guru* shows that the Śruti statement[34]

[34] *CU* 5.1.6-12.

describing the dialogue between the sense-organs is to be understood as dialogue between the presiding deities of the sense-organs. Moreover, this scriptural statement does not serve as the source for indicating the sentiency of the sense-organs.

Prāṇa as Self : Its Refutation

Hiraṇyagarbha meditators consider *prāṇa* as the Self. The following argument is given. When a person does not respond, breath of the person confirms whether the person is alive or dead. The absence of vital air is considered to be the death of a person. In case of the expression like "my eyes", it confirms of a Self other than the sense-organ. In deep sleep, all the sense-organs resolve but the vital air functions. The survival and death of a person are determined by the presence and absence of *prāṇa*. So, *prāṇa* is the Self.[35] This idea is refuted on the following grounds:

1. Like the external air, the *prāṇa* in the body is only another form of air.
2. The absence of *prāṇa* need not indicate death. The *prāṇa* is imperceptible in the plant kingdom, but plants are living organisms. In certain cases, a person in unconscious stage may lose *prāṇa* for a moment or so but is not declared dead.
3. *Prāṇa* is present in deep sleep, but it is not aware of an intruder or a guest entering the room. This shows that *prāṇa* is inert in nature. If *prāṇa* is the Self, it should have stopped the thief or invited the guest.[36]
4. The absence of *prāṇa* alone does not indicate death of a person, the quitting of *jāṭhara agni* also indicates death.
5. The eulogy of *prāṇa* in the Śruti is for the sake of meditation.

---

35 न प्राणेन नापानेन मर्त्यो जीवति कश्चन ।
इतरेण तु जीवन्ति यस्मिन्नेतावुपाश्रितौ ॥ — *KU* 2.2.5

36 *BU* 2.1.

The *Taittirīya Upaniṣad*[37] statement adopts the method of *sthūla-arundhatī-nyāya* to reveal the Self from known to unknown.

6. In Śruti,[38] there is a dialogue between *prāṇa* and the sense-organs and it is mentioned that *prāṇa* re-enters the body. Here, it only means that the presiding deity of *prāṇa* re-enters.
7. Expressions like "my *prāṇa* is weak because of hunger", by consumption of food it is said *prāṇa* is satiated. Such expression reveals that *prāṇa* is an object of mine-ness. Thus, *prāṇa* is not the Self.
8. *Prāṇa* is *sākṣī bhāsya*. The movement of *prāṇa* is known. That which perceives the movement of *prāṇa* is different from *prāṇa*.

Manas as Self : Its Refutation

Some consider that bondage and liberation are dependent on mind. The cause of bondage is attraction of mind towards sense objects and absence of object-impression in the mind is the cause of liberation. The mind alone is the cause of all activities. Therefore, mind is the Self. This is refuted thus:

1. Mind is an instrument like a chisel.
2. Mind is an inert entity that is absent in deep sleep.
3. "My mind is somewhere else; now it is here" this expression reveals that mind is object of mine-ness. The firmness and fickleness of mind are witnessed by the Self that is different from the mind.
4. Mind is an enjoyer only when associated with consciousness. Mind is not independent. Thus, the enjoyer mind is not the Self.

---

[37] *TU* 3.3.

[38] *BU* 6.1.

5. "Mind alone is the cause of bondage and liberation of human beings. Bondage is due to object-attraction and detached mind is liberation."[39] This has to be understood in the following manner. An extrovert mind is an obstacle for self-enquiry and is the cause of error leading to bondage. An introvert mind, free from impression is negated by gaining Self-knowledge, is the cause of liberation. The above statement does not reveal mind as the Self but indicates mind as an instrument of knowledge.
6. The *Taittirīya Upaniṣad* statement, as mentioned earlier, adopts the method of revealing the Self from known to unknown.

Buddhi as Self : Its Refutation

The Yogācāra Buddhist claims that the intellect alone manifests as the mind and this intellect is of the nature of momentary consciousness, which is the Self. All objects are forms of cognition. The cognition is of effulgent form. The successive cognition is similar to the prior cognition. The prior cognition gets destroyed on the arrival of next cognition. There is thus a continuous flow of cognitions like the flow of a river. The flow of cognition is of two kinds. One is the *ālaya* flow of cognition. Another is the *pravṛtti* flow of cognition. The continuous flow of cognition in the form of "I" is the *ālaya* flow of cognition. The *ālaya* flow of cognition is the intellect. Cognition in the form "this is pot", "this is body", etc. is known as the *pravṛtti* flow of cognition. The *ālaya* flow of cognition arises from the *pravṛtti* flow of cognition. The nature of mind is also within the *pravṛtti* flow of cognition. So, mind is an effect of the *ālaya* flow of cognition. By knowing, intellect as the Self, the *pravṛtti* flow of cognition ceases and there is a continuous flow of *ālaya* cognition that attains stability. This firm and steady flow of *ālaya* cognition is known as liberation. Thus, the Yogācāra considers the momentary consciousness, which is the intellect as

---

39 मन एव मनुष्याणां कारणं बन्धमोक्षयोः । बन्धाय विषयासक्तं मुक्त्यै निर्विषयं स्मृतम् ॥
— *Brahmabindūpaniṣad, Mantra* 2

self-luminous. This momentary flow of cognition is taken to be the Self by the Buddhists which is now refuted as follows:

1. Intellect (*buddhi*) cannot be taken to be the Self. The sense-organs serve as the instruments in gaining the knowledge of the external world which is confirmed by the intellect. The knowledge confirmed by the intellect is witnessed by another principle different from the intellect.

2. Self being self-luminous is ever-evident. As sun is self-luminous and is the illuminator of all objects, intellect is illumined by the illuminator Self and hence Self is different from the intellect. The light pervades and illumines the pot but light is different from the pot. The Self, of the nature of knowledge, pervades the thought in intellect. Self assumes the form of thought and illumines it. Self, in reality, is different from the intellect. Self is of the nature of eternal, pure, unassociated consciousness.

3. The internal organ is the product of total *sattva* aspect of non-grossified elements. When the internal organ functions as a rational faculty it is known as the intellect and when it takes the role of indecisiveness, it is known as the mind. Thus, intellect being an integral part of internal organ is not the Self.

4. In the *rathakalpanā* described in *Kaṭhopaniṣad*,[40] Self is compared to a traveller and the intellect to a charioteer. Just as the traveller is different from the charioteer, Self is different from the intellect.

5. The expressions "my intellect is dull now", "my intellect is sharp", etc. indicate intellect as an object of mineness and hence it cannot be the Self.

6. The momentariness of Self is invalid. If this is so, a lender cannot claim his money back from the borrower, since

---

[40] आत्मानं॰ रथिनं विद्धि शरीररथमेव तु। बुद्धिं तु सारथिं विद्धि मनः प्रग्रहमेव च॥ इन्द्रियाणि हयानाहुः विषयां॰स्तेषु गोचरान्।

— *KU* 1.3.3-4

the Self of lender that lent money dies the next moment. Also a person consuming food this moment cannot express contentment the next moment. There must be a continuous Self other than the momentary activities.

7. Moreover, it serves no purpose to pursue any means to liberation by a Self that is momentary.

Ānandamayakośa as Self : Its Refutation

The *guru* presents the views of different schools who claim *ānandamayakośa* as Self by putting forth different arguments. The views of all the four schools — Bhāṭṭa Mīmāṁsā, Śunyavāda Buddhist, Prābhākara Mīmāṁsā and Nyāya — are negated here.

Kumarīla Bhaṭṭa, the *Vārttikakāra*, says in *Pūrva-mīmāṁsāsūtra* that Self is not fleeting like lightning but stable. That Self is inert and luminous. The inertness of the Self is known through the expression "I slept well, not conscious of anything". The experience in deep-sleep state is recollected on waking up and in deep sleep there is no other means of knowledge other than the Self. Thus, the recollected knowledge proves a luminous Self. The knowledge or the conscious entity during deep sleep is said to be the Self. This Self is like a glow-worm, possesses light and non-light. Since the Self is of the nature of knowledge, it is said to be luminous; being inert, it is non-luminous. The bliss-sheath is of luminous and non-luminous nature. Bliss-sheath is ignorance with reflected consciousness (in deep sleep) that reflected consciousness is luminous and ignorance is non-luminous. Thus, according to Bhāṭṭas, the bliss-sheath is the Self.

The Śūnyavāda Buddhists say that the Self is devoid of parts. The same Self cannot be both luminous and non-luminous. In the case of a glow-worm, it consists of parts and therefore one part is luminous and another part is non-luminous. Self being without parts cannot be the locus of two contradictory features. If two features are in the same Self, then Self is to be accepted as consisting of parts like a pot. In such a case, the Self will be subject to origination and destruction. If the Self is said to be subject to origination and destruction, then its non-existence gets proved prior to its origination and posterior to its destruction.[41] Thus, by being an entity subject to origination and destruction, the Self will be a non-existent entity like a pot. Then, all other entities different from this Self, being subject to origination and destruction, are non-existent. In this line of argument, both Self and non-self will be non-existent entities and what remains is only void.

The view of Bhaṭṭa that considers Self as both matter and consciousness is refuted by Śūnyavādins. The knowledge *ayam daṇḍī* arises when one sees the stick held by a man and not merely by seeing the stick. Similarly, by merely seeing the inert part, Self cannot be known as a combination of both matter and consciousness. Or, it should be said that, since there is the experience of sentiency, the inertness of Self is to be imagined. If the reality of consciousness and matter is agreed upon then the relationship between consciousness and matter is to be established.

The question raised is, of what kind is the relation, is it a relation of conjunction, identity, or as object–subject? The first possibility (conjunction), has two conditions. Conjunction is possible between two impermanent entities or two entities with parts. If conjunction relation is accepted it would lead to an impermanent Self. In the second possibility, by the relation of identity, both matter and consciousness will be of the same nature, then the consciousness part will be material in nature and vice versa. Based on the third possibility of subject–object relation, like the inertness of both the "pot-knowledge" and "pot", both consciousness and matter will be non-self. Thus, consciousness and matter cannot have a subject–object relation. Also, the scriptural statements[42] do not support the view that Self is partly

---

41 आदावन्ते च यन्नास्ति वर्तमानोऽपि तत्तथा ।
वितथैः सदृशाः सन्तोऽवितथा इव लक्षिताः ॥ — *MaK* 2.6

42 प्रज्ञानं ब्रह्म । — *AU* 3.1; सत्यं ज्ञानं अनन्तं ब्रह्म । — *TU* 2.1;
विज्ञानं आनन्दं ब्रह्म — *BU* 3.9.28.7

conscious and partly matter. The expression on waking up that "I slept like a log of wood" is the memory in sleep that has ignorance as its object. Thus, the combination of matter and consciousness in the Self is untenable.

The theory of void of Śūnyavādins also is incorrect. The question is whether void is along with witness principle, without witness principle or is it self-evident? The first possibility is invalid because "that which is the witness of void is different from void". The second possibility is ruled out since in the absence of witness principle there cannot be the intelligibility of void. The third possibility is dismissed on the ground that the self-evident entity is *Brahman* in Advaita, which is differently named as void by the Buddhists. Thus, the nihilism of Śūnyavādin is dismissed. The *Taittirīya*[43] and *Chāndogya Upaniṣads*[44] do not reveal void because such a meaning contradicts the prior and later statements in the Upaniṣads. The word *asat* in the Upaniṣadic *mantra* indicates the names and forms in potential state.

The Mādhyamika Śūnyavādin considers ignorance or the bliss-sheath as the Self. Ignorance is divided into three:

1. In the absence of Advaita knowledge, ignorance modifying into the world is taken to be real.
2. The indescribable nature of ignorance is logically established with the support of scriptures by the scholars.
3. For the *jīvanmuktas*, ignorance is a non-existent entity. The words *tuccha, asat* and *śūnya* are synonymous.[45] The ignorance determined as *tuccha* by the *jīvanmuktas* is not taken to be the final goal by the Śūnyavādins. On the other hand, they consider the bliss-sheath of *tuccha* nature to be the Self.

According to Prābhākaras and Naiyāyikas, the Self is not void. If void is experienced then that which experiences void is the Self

43 असद्वा इदमग्र आसीत्। — *TU* 2.7

44 असदेवेदमग्र आसीत्। — *CU* 6.2.1

45 *PD* 6.125-30.

and it should be different from void. If void is not experienced then such a void can never exist. Thus, a Self other than void is to be accepted. For Naiyāyikas, the contact of Self and mind gives rise to knowledge. By the nature of knowledge and quality, the Self is conscious. Self is inert by nature and it becomes conscious due to the qualities like knowledge. Pleasure, pain, desire, dislike, effort, merit and demerit are qualities of the Self. According to Nyāya, Self is bliss-sheath. The consciousness is hidden in the bliss-sheath. It is not known to a non-discriminative person.

Prābhākaras and Naiyāyaikas consider that Self is inert, because Self is devoid of consciousness in deep sleep. In the hidden consciousness that is the bliss-sheath, there is the error of Selfhood. According to them, the nature of Self as eternal knowledge is not in *jīva* but *jīva* possesses non-eternal knowledge. The non-eternal knowledge, according to Advaita, is the intellect in the form of thought in the internal organ. Thus, the Prābhākaras and Nyāya take bliss-sheath as Self. Intellect is taken to be the quality of Self.

The above view of Prābhākara and Naiyāyika is refuted. It is improper to state that the Self is inert due to the absence of knowledge in deep sleep. By the expression that "I had a good sleep, I did not know anything"; it indicates that in deep sleep both bliss and ignorance were experienced. If Self is inert by nature then the remembrance of bliss in sleep will not be possible. As it is remembered, Self is not inert. Other than knowledge that which is inert like pot will be non-eternal. If Self is not of the nature of knowledge then, like pot, Self will be non-eternal. If so, then there will be no desire for liberation and thereby the means to liberation also will be futile. Thus, those who do not enquire into the nature of Self with faith in Vedāntic statements and in the absence of *guru* tradition, and those who involve in knowing the Self by themselves dwell in the nature of the five sheaths and they never come to know *mukhyātmā*, the witness principle. Therefore, the *guru* concludes that the nature of Self is concealed by the five sheaths.

NATURE OF ĪŚVARA CONCEALED BY FIVE SHEATHS

Just as the witness-consciousness nature of *jīva* is concealed by the micro five sheaths, the *guru* says that the macro five sheaths of *Īśvara* conceals the real nature of *Īśvara*. This does not mean that the real nature of *Īśvara* is concealed by the five sheaths. *Īśvara* is beyond concealment and is *nityamukta*. The real nature of *Īśvara* is concealed from the standpoint of *jīva* and, therefore, *jīva* has to engage in the analysis of the nature of the micro sheaths and the Self, and the macro sheaths and the Self. The four features of the Self are Existence, Consciousness, Absolute Peace and Non-duality. The bodies are false, inert, subject to sorrow and are many. The Existence and Consciousness nature of Self is concealed by the false and inert nature of the bodies. Thus, the body falsely manifests as existent and conscious. The *ānanda* and the non-dual nature of Self is overpowered by the properties of the body which is of the nature of sorrow and plurality. This is falsely transferred to the Self which seems to be sorrowful and many. There is mutual error of the five sheaths. Thus, a seeker has to necessarily enquire into the nature of the five sheaths.

The concealment of the nature of *Īśvara* is explained based on Vidyāraṇya's *Pañcadaśī*.[46] The real nature of *Īśvara* is the secondary signification of *tat pada*. Some consider, *antaryāmī* conditioned by the bliss-sheath in the form of *māyā* as the primary meaning of *tat pada* to be the ultimate reality. Some others consider Hiraṇyagarbha, Vaiśvānara, Viṣṇu, Brahmā, Śiva, Gaṇeśa, Devī, Sūrya, etc. sword, crow-bar, fig tree, grass, bamboo, and such objects as the ultimate reality (henotheism). Considering everything as non-different from *Īśvara* is not defective but the objects which serve as the limiting adjuncts are also taken to be *Īśvara*. Hence this view is erroneous. Those who are established in the primary meaning of *Īśvara* are deluded and are caught in the cycle of merit and demerit. They desire to propitiate the various gods to obtain happiness. They reap the results based on

---

46 *PD*, chapters 6-7.

the kind of gods they worship. Since the causal, subtle and gross forms of the world are the bodies of *Īśvara*, by meditating on any form of Him they reap the result.[47] According to Advaita, liberation cannot be attained without knowledge. One who desires for liberation should distinctly study the nature of the five sheaths. To substantiate this it is stated that just as one puts forth effort to separate the cover of a *muñja* grass[48] (long grass with a covering layer) from its *iśīkā* (inner stem of the grass) or stem, the nature of *jīva* and *Īśvara* from the five sheaths should be known distinctly by discrimination (*viveka*). Having pointed out the discriminative process of the five sheaths, now the *guru* uses the method of discrimination to show that the Self is different from the three states of experience and three bodies.

AVASTHĀTRAYAVIVEKA

The *guru* demonstrates the three states of experience and the three bodies as different from the Self. In dream state, the gross body does not manifest, the presence of subtle body is illumined by the Self. In deep sleep, knowledge of subtle body is absent and even though there is absence of knowledge of happiness, on waking up, there is the recollection expressed as "I slept well". The happiness experienced in deep sleep is not due to any object, as in this state the world of plurality resolves. This experience of happiness is the nature of Self, which is self-luminous. During meditation, as a result of *nididhyāsana*, the Self "shines" as it is not concealed by ignorance. The ignorance in the form of causal body does not manifest during meditation. Thus, Self is different from the three states of experience. This is explained herewith.

1. *Waking State* — The states of experience are based on the time principle. The waking state is defined as that state which is different from dream and deep-sleep states, which is the locus of knowledge and impressions resulting from

---

[47] यो यो यां यां तनुं भक्तः श्रद्धयार्चितुमिच्छति ।
तस्य तस्याचलां श्रद्धां तामेव विदधाम्यहम् ॥ — *BG* VII.21

[48] अङ्गुष्ठमात्रः पुरुषोऽन्तरात्मा सदा जनानां हृदये संनिविष्टः । तं स्वाच्छरीरात्प्रवृहेन्मुञ्जादिवेषीकां धैर्येण । तं विद्याच्छुक्रममृतं तं विद्याच्छुक्रममृतम् ॥ — *KU* 2.3.17

sense-organs, experienced in time. In this state, fourteen *tripuṭīs* function. This state has six features:

(a) The all-pervasive *jīva* has its location as the eyes during the waking state,

(b) power is action,

(c) voice is gross (*vaikharī*),

(d) enjoyment is gross,

(e) quality is *sattva*, and

(f) name of the *jīva* in waking state is *viśva*

This waking state does not coexist with dream and deep-sleep states. The falsity of the waking state has been discussed earlier.[49] The Self (*Ātmā*) is the witness-principle in all states and hence *ātmā* is real. This *jīva*, the witness principle, is different from the waking state. Thus, waking world is discriminated.

2. *Dream-World* — The sense-organs resolve during dream state. Without the aid of sense-organs, the mind in the *hita nāḍī* modifies into various (dream) objects due to the impressions gained in the waking world. This state is known as dream-world. Here *jīva*'s

(a) locus is throat,

(b) power is knowledge,

(c) voice is *madhyamā*,

(d) enjoyment is subtle,

(e) quality is *rajas*, and

(f) *jīva* is named *taijasa*.

These are the features of dream state. Dream state is different from other two states. *Ātmā is* witness of dream-world and hence it is different. Thus, dream-world is discriminated.

---

[49] See Section 4.4 of Chapter 4.

3. *Deep-sleep State* — Deep sleep is that state where bliss and ignorance are experienced.
   (a) Locus is the heart,
   (b) power is inertia. The power in inert objects is known as *dravya śakti,*
   (c) voice is subtlest (*paśyantī*),
   (d) enjoyment is bliss,
   (e) quality is *tamas,* and
   (f) *jīva*'s name is *prājña.*

   Deep sleep is different from the other two states. *Ātmā* is witness of the three states of experience. Thus, deep sleep is differentiated as different from the Self.

ŚARĪRATRAYAVIVEKA

The three bodies undergoing three states of experience are also distinct and different from the Self known by the method of *anvaya-vyatireka.* The three bodies are non-pervasive and hence non-eternal. Gross body is the food-sheath, causal body is the bliss-sheath and the subtle body is air, mental and intellect-sheaths. Thus, by discriminating Self from the three bodies, the Self is indirectly discriminated from the five sheaths. Just as the five sheaths are differentiated from the nature of *jīva,* the nature of *Īśvara* is also different from the macro five sheaths.

1. *Gross Body* — The space present prior to the origination of pot and posterior to the destruction of pot is different and distinct from the pot. Similarly, *Ātmā* is present prior to the birth of bodies and posterior to the destruction of the bodies and is different and distinct from the bodies. Like the pot, the gross body is absent prior to its origination and posterior to its destruction hence it is different and exclusive from *Ātmā.* That which pervades more space and time is known as *avyabhicarat. Ātmā* pervading all bodies is one. Like space, *ātmā* is more pervasive. *Ātmā* exists prior and posterior to the bodies. So, *ātmā* is non-

sublatable in all periods of time. *Ātmā* pervades all time. That which exists in a limited space and for some time is *vyabhicarat*. Like the pot, body also is limited by space. Body being subject to birth and death cannot exist in all periods of time. Body exists for some time only. Gross body being limited in space and time is *vyabhicarat*. The finite body and the infinite Self are mutually exclusive. The gross body is not the Self, nor is it an object of Self. But body being a product of five elements is known as elemental. Since Self is different from the body, the characteristics of the body like name, form, class, status and action do not belong to the Self. Thus, it should be known that I am different from the gross body.

2. *Subtle Body* — In the five states — deep sleep, swoon, death, resolution and invalid knowledge — the subtle body resolves into its cause, i.e. ignorance. Thus, the subtle body is *vyabhicarat*. But Self being self-luminous eternally is *avyabhicarat*. Self is of the nature of Existence and being of the nature of Existence, Self is not the subtle body. The subtle body is not related to the Self. It is the effect of non-grossified five elements. Thus, Self is different from the subtle body and its characteristics like doership, enjoyership, pleasure and pain do not belong to the Self. It is witnessed by the Self. Thus, it should be known that I am different from the subtle body.
3. *Causal Body* — Ignorance alone is the causal body. I am not the causal body and it is not mine. The characteristics of causal body, known as, the concealment and projection are also not mine. I am the witness of these features and hence I am different from the causal body.

IDENTITY-KNOWLEDGE EXPLAINED

The *madhyama adhikārī* is not convinced with the knowledge of the Self revealed through the three main discriminative processes. For the sake of conviction in the non-dual nature of *jīva* and

Brahman the analysis is taken up again. The *guru* proceeds to analyse the *mahāvākya* — "Self that is different from the five sheaths is to be known as non-different from *Brahman*". It may be objected as to how can *jīva* be non-different from *Brahman*, since *jīva* is subject to experiences like pleasure and pain in this world, and is subject to travel to heaven or hell based on their merits and demerits? It is answered by stating that the substratal element of consciousness in both *jīva* and *Brahman* alone is real and all other attributes and experiences are unreal. The unreal experiences cannot affect the real Self. The *guru* reminds[50] the *madhyama adhikārī* about the instance that stands as a proof for the incapacity of a false entity to affect the real. The mirage-water cannot fertile the desert land, nor can a rope-snake become poisonous. The scriptures declare *jīvātmā* as non-doer and non-reaper. The experiences of doership and enjoyership are false and hence they do not affect *jīvātmā*. The three states of experience and the three bodies are superimposed on *Brahman* due to ignorance. *Brahman* which is free from all impurities at all times is non-different from *jīvātmā*.

Layacintana

In the teaching so far, the *guru* has attempted to convey the importance of understanding the unreality of bondage to arrive at the identity-knowledge that is the direct means to liberation while living. But even after the instruction of the absolute truth, the *madhyama adhikārī* expresses grief indicating his non-acceptance of bondage as unreal as unravelled by the *guru* earlier.[51] In other words, the *madhyama adhikārī* is in a position to understand *brahma satyam* but is unable to accept *jaganmithyā*.[52] The *guru* attributes the grief of *madhyama adhikārī* as caused by the non-destruction of desire-thought and the absence of rise of *sāttvika* thought in the

---

50 See Section 4.3 of Chapter 4 and 5.1 of Chapter 5.

51 See Section 5.1 of Chapter 5.

52 Or, in other words, the *madhyama adhikārī* could not graduate from *upāsyam brahma* to *jñeyam brahma.*

mind. This means — *citta prasāda* (tranquillity of mind) is that state in which the desire-thought is destroyed by obtaining the desired object without which there tends to be a mental disturbance. On obtaining the desired object, the *ānanda* nature of the Self gets reflected in the *sāttvika* thought that arises in the mind. By this reflected *ānanda* in *sāttvika* thought one considers one is happy. When a desire is not fulfilled, then that desire is not destroyed. The non-destruction of desire-thought does not allow the *ānanda* nature of Self in *sāttvika vṛtti* to get reflected and hence one remains unhappy. The *madhyama adhikārī* desires for liberation. But even after an elaborate teaching, he is unable to destroy that desire, hence the experience of unhappiness.

The *guru*, therefore, adopts another method to impart the identity-knowledge. This method is known as *layacintana* or meditation on the dissolution process that serves as the means to know the existence-status of effect as non-different from cause. Here, the instruction begins from the dissolution of the gross universe. The primary cause of everything is *Īśvara*. The universe as an effect is non-different from *Īśvara*. The nature of world is *Īśvara*. "That *Īśvara* is my nature". The *guru* thus instructs that the resolution of the entire universe in Self is to be meditated upon. The gross universe is an effect of the five elements. In the process of *layacintana*, all the gross elements are to be visualized as of the nature of elements. Like, the product earth is to be resolved into its nature, namely, the earth and so on. Thus, the elementals resolve into their respective element and hence the universe resolves into the five causal elements. The gross universe is the effect of the non-grossified elements. Thus, gross universe resolves into the non-grossified elements. The subtle universe consisting of internal organ, etc. is an effect of non-grossified elements, they are to be visualized as resolving into the non-grossified elements. The internal organ being an effect of the total *sattva* aspect of the five elements are to be visualized as resolving into the *sattva guṇa* of the elements. Similarly, *prāṇa*, an effect of the total *rajas* aspect of the five elements, is to be visualized as resolving into *rajoguṇa* of the elements. Thus, in this visualization, the subtle universe is seen as non-different from the non-grossified elements.

The *layacintana* process is explained further, wherein the ground of resolution of the subtle elements is mentioned. Earth being an effect of water resolves into water and so on, finally, space being an effect of *tamas* aspect of *prakṛti* resolves into *prakṛti*. *Prakṛti* resolves into *māyā*. *Māyā* is also known as *pradhāna*, *prakṛti*, *avidyā*, *ajñāna*, *śakti*, etc. When the universe resolves into the primal matter where everything remains in potential form, it is known as *pradhāna*.[53] When primal matter manifests as the material cause of the universe with *tamas* predominance, that is known as *prakṛti*. Here, the word *prakṛti* represents the material cause of the universe, wherein, *pra* refers to *sattva guṇa*, *kṛ* refers to *rajoguṇa* and *ti* refers to *tamas* with *sattva* and *rajas*. Therefore, *prakṛti* is *tamas* predominant. Just as a magician creates "impossible" things without appropriate space, time, material, etc., there arises an "impossible" desire known as *māyā* in the non-dual unassociated *Brahman*. *Māyā* is known as *ajñāna* since it conceals the nature of *Brahman*. *Māyā* is also known as *avidyā* since it is destroyed by *vidyā*. *Māyā* is known as *śakti* since it remains always dependent on *Brahman* for its existence. If it is argued that *śakti* is different from *Brahman* then such a view contradicts Advaitic tenet.[54] If it is non-different, then, it should be of the nature of *Brahman*. It should not be differently referred to as "power of *Brahman*". The *śakti* of *Brahman* is said to be identity-in-difference.

But the question remains how can mutually opposed attributes have the same locus? The mutually opposed attributes in the same locus advocated by Advaita are different from that advocated by the Bhedābhedavādin. According to Advaita, a real and an unreal entity, which are mutually opposed to each other, can remain in the same locus. For instance, in the cases like the existence of

---

[53] चिदानन्दमयब्रह्मप्रतिबिम्बसमन्विता ।
तमोरजः सत्त्वगुणा प्रकृतिर्द्विविधा च सा ॥ — *PD* 1.15.

[54] *PD* 1.15

"rope-snake", "mirage-water and dry-sand" and "shell-silver". In the same manner, various powers are superimposed on *Brahman*. In reality, *śakti* is non-different from *Brahman* with indescribable relation of identity (*anirvacanīya tādātmya sambandha*). Therefore, in cases of absence of absolute difference, power along with its substratum cannot exist separate from its substratum.[55]

In the *layacintana* process, resolving the material universe into *māyā*, does not mean *māyā* as a second entity other than *Brahman*. In fact, the effect of *māyā*, i.e. the universe, is not a second entity other than *Brahman*. In the case of "rope-snake", the superimposed snake is nothing but the rope; similarly, the destruction of the world is nothing but *Brahman*. There is no world different from *Brahman*. Thus, *Brahman* is eternally non-dual. The inert world along with its cause is to be visualized as resolving into *Brahman*. Then, one should meditate that "I am the non-dual *Brahman*".[56] The *guru* points out that one with a dull intellect (*manda buddhi*, does not refer to the classification of the *adhikārī*s of *Vicārasāgara*) who is unable to understand the *mahāvākya* due to the defects like *pramātṛ doṣa*, etc. can take to this meditation of *layacintana*, gain purity of mind and listen again to the *mahāvākya* which will lead to liberation while living.

Difference Between Knowledge and Meditation

In the course of discussion, the *guru* differentiates knowledge from meditation.[57] Knowledge is *vastu tantra* i.e. knowledge is dependent on the instrument (*pramāṇa*) and object of knowledge (*prameya*). Knowledge is not dependent on desire, faith, injunctions or desire of a human being. Meditation, on the other hand, is dependent on desire, faith and injunctions.[58] "Knowledge

---

[55] *BU* 2.4.7-9.

[56] क्षेत्रक्षेत्रज्ञयोरेवमन्तरं ज्ञानचक्षुषा ।
भूतप्रकृतिमोक्षं च ये विदुर्यान्ति ते परम् ॥ — *BG* XIII.34.

[57] *SV*, pp. 182-83.

[58] ध्यानं चिन्तनं यद्यपि मानसम् तथापि पुरुषेण कर्तुमकर्तुमन्यथा वा कर्तुं शक्यम् पुरुषतन्त्रत्वात्। ज्ञानं तु प्रमाणजन्यम्। प्रमाणं च यथाभूतवस्तुविषयम्। अतो ज्ञानं कर्तुमकर्तुमन्यथा वा कर्तुम् न शक्यम्। केवलं वस्तुतन्त्रमेव तत् न चोदनातन्त्रम् नापि पुरुषतन्त्रम् तस्मान्मानसत्वेऽपि ज्ञानस्य महद्वैलक्षण्यम्।
— *BSŚB* 1.1.4

is dependent on instrument and object of knowledge" is explained — the perceptual knowledge is dependent on the instrument that is the sense-organ — eye and the object of perception is pot. The contact of pot and sense-organ eye gives rise to "pot-knowledge" even without the desire, faith, or persuasion. "Knowledge is not dependent on desire, faith or injunction" is again explained — there is a prohibitive injunction "do not see the moon on the fourth day". Based on this injunction one takes a resolution that "I should not see the moon today". Even though this conviction is made, due to some reason, if the eye contacts the moon then by this contact of instrument and object of knowledge the perceptual cognition of moon does take place. Thus, knowledge is dependent on instrument and object of knowledge and not on desire, faith or injunctions. This is further explained.

Cognition is of three kinds — erroneous cognition (*bhrama-jñāna*), memory cognition (*smr̥ti-jñāna*) and valid apprehension (*pramā-jñāna*). The erroneous cognition is solely dependent on the superimposition on an object (*prameya-adhīna*). Memory-cognition is that which on seeing a similar object or seeing a related object gives rise to a mental-modification based on the past experienced registered object. (*Manovr̥tti* is the *pramāṇa* which gives rise to memory; this is *pramāṇa adhīna*.) The valid apprehension is of two kinds: internal and external. The internal cognition in the form of knowledge of happiness, etc. is said to be dependent on the mind which is the instrument of knowledge and dependent on happiness, etc. which is the object of knowledge, according to Nyāya and Vācaspati Miśra. According to Siddhānta, since the mind is not accepted as the instrument of knowledge in the case of internal cognition, it is said to be dependent on the object of knowledge alone in the form of happiness, etc. Thus, the internal cognition can be said to be as both *pramāṇa-adhīna* and *prameya-adhīna* or only as *prameya-adhīna*. The external cognition, on the other hand, is dependent on the instruments of knowledge like sense-organs and inference, and on the object of knowledge.

The valid apprehension through words that give rise to *Brahman*-knowledge is dependent on the instrument of knowledge in the form of *mahāvākya,* object of knowledge in the form of inner-self and *Brahman,* and the knowledge derived from the secondary signification of the words. In the case of valid cognition of empirical words, some are dependent on the primary meaning of the words and some are dependent on the secondary meaning of the words.

It is thus said that some kind of knowledge is dependent on the object of knowledge only and certain other kind of knowledge is dependent on the relationship between the instrument and object of knowledge or with its related knowledge. The erroneous cognition being the content of knowledge is said to be *prameya* and here the knowability is also possible. Thus, in all cases of knowledge, it is said to be dependent on the object, so it is *vastu-tantra.* Knowledge arises through the instrument of knowledge and hence it is not dependent on desire, faith or injunctions.

Now, meditation as different from knowledge is expounded. Meditation is not dependent on the object but it is dependent on the meditator, i.e. it is *puruṣa-tantra* or *kartṛ-tantra.* Even though meditation also is of the form of mental-modification, then also, it is based on the desire of a person and not dependent on the object. Therefore, meditation though being related to mind is not knowledge but it is an action only. It is a mental action. Meditation is taken up based on desire, faith and injunctions. Meditation on the *śālagrāma* stone as Viṣṇu is believed to yield highest benefit. A person knows the form of Viṣṇu from the descriptions found in the scriptures. When he sees the *śālagrāma* he knows it as a stone only. Then too, having faith in the words of the scriptures and with a desire for the fruit of meditation, he meditates on *sālagrāma* as Viṣṇu. Thus, meditation certainly presupposes injunctions. The meditation performed based on the Vedic injunctions alone is beneficial. Other than the Vedic injunction, performance of meditation by one's own desire, by one's own *saṅkalpa* and meditating on any other kind of object, does not give rise to the desired result.[59] Therefore, only *nididhyāsana* does not have *vidhis*,[60] since it is based on knowledge and *upāsanā* is subject to *vidhi* since it is dependent on the object of meditation. In the case of *Brahman*-knowledge, the *mahāvākya* is the instrument of knowledge and without receiving the teachings of the *mahāvākya* from a *guru* by mere desire one can never gain the direct knowledge.

5.4 Role and Kinds of Meditation

The *guru* explicates various kinds of meditation in order to teach the identity-knowledge to the *madhyama adhikārī*. Meditation is of different kinds. One is *pratīka upāsanā*, i.e. superimposition of one thing on another, like Viṣṇu on *śālagrāma*. The meditation on Viṣṇu as residing in *vaikuṇṭha* with a particular form is not *pratīka* kind of meditation but such a meditation is based on the nature of object of meditation. The knowledge of Viṣṇu as residing in *vaikuṇṭha*, is not directly perceived but is learnt from the scriptures. Thus, meditation is not possible in the absence of faith in Vedic injunctions, and without faith or desire. Injunction is that which makes one act by its statement "meditate on this". Commitment to such a statement is faith. Desire is the modification of *rajas* quality of the internal organ. Meditation is possible by deliberation also. It is a continuous flow of thoughts saturated with the object of meditation. During meditation, when the mind wanders it can be forcibly made to focus on an object. But in the case of knowledge, the moment the mental modification takes place, there is the destruction of the concealment of the object and hence a deliberate effort to stabilize the thought-mode is not required. Therefore, in knowledge there is no such deliberation as in meditation.

AHAṀGRAHA UPASANĀ

So far, having pointed out the difference between knowledge and meditation followed by an explanation of the *pratīka* kind of

---

59 *TUŚB* 1.

60 *BUŚB* 2.4.5.

meditation, now the *guru* introduces another form of meditation known as *ahaṁgraha upāsanā*. Here, it is the meditation on the statement "I am *Brahman*" which is also based on the object of meditation but it is not *pratīka* kind of meditation. In this *ahaṁgraha* meditation, the subject is non-different from the object of meditation. One for whom, on inquiry of Vedānta, direct knowledge does not arise, and who believes in the Vedic statement that declares meditation as an injunction, such a one deliberately engages in *ahaṁgraha upāsanā*. This meditator, who invokes "I am *Brahman*" thought deliberately, successively attains liberation. Even though *Brahman* is the object of meditation, in this case still it is the imagination of the mind. Therefore, the continuous flow of thought related to *Brahman* is an erroneous cognition and it is invalid. Just as a person seeing the radiance attempts to grasp that radiance, but attains the crystal, through *ahaṁgraha upāsanā* one gains *Brahman*-knowledge in course of time and attains liberation.[61] The meditation does not directly give rise to knowledge, but it helps in removing impurities of the mind. With a refined mind, when the *mahāvākya* instruction is heard, there is clarity in that knowledge. Hence, it is figuratively said that *ahaṁgraha upāsanā* gives rise to knowledge. The *madhyama adhikārī* has not yet shown any signs of acceptance of non-duality so the *guru* continues to present other forms of meditation.

AHAṀGRAHA PRAṆAVA UPĀSANĀ

The *ahaṁgraha* meditation in the form of *praṇava*, that is *oṁkāra*, is discussed in *Māṇḍūkyakārikā*,[62] *Kaṭhopaniṣad*,[63] *Praśnopaniṣad*,[64] etc. Śaṅkara deals with this form of meditation in his work titled

---

61 संवादिभ्रमवद् ब्रह्मतत्त्वोपास्त्यापि मुच्यते ।
उत्तरे तापनीयेऽतः श्रुतोपास्तिरनेकधा ॥ — *PD* 9.1

62 *MaK* 1.24-29.

63 एतद्ध्येवाक्षरं ब्रह्म एतद्ध्येवाक्षरं परम् । एतद्ध्येवाक्षरं ज्ञात्वा यो यदिच्छति तस्य तत् ॥
एतदालम्बनꣳ श्रेष्ठमेतदालम्बनं परम् । एतदालम्बनं ज्ञात्वा ब्रह्मलोके महीयते ॥ — *KU* 1.2.16-17

64 एतद्वै सत्यकाम परं चापरं च ब्रह्म यदोंकारः ।
तस्माद्विद्वानेतेनैवायतनेनैकतरमन्वेति ॥ — *PU* 5.2

Pañcīkaraṇa. The Advaitic preceptors consider the propriety of *ahaṁgraha praṇava upāsanā* as it leads to the desire for liberation. The process of this meditation is very briefly presented by the *guru* beginning with the identity of the letters (*akṣaram*) of *praṇava* as identical with the nature of *Brahman*. One should meditate with the thought that "I am *Brahman* non-different from the nature of *praṇava*". The meditator crosses over the ocean of misery (through the enquiry of the *mahāvākya* again). The *guru* finally points out that only a mendicant is eligible to take up this kind of *ahaṁgraha praṇava* meditation. Now, he proceeds to explain the classification of *praṇava upāsanā* to the *madhyama adhikārī* who has not shown conviction with regard to the efficacy of the two types of meditations, viz. *ahaṁgraha upāsanā* and *ahaṁgraha praṇava upāsanā*.

NIRGUṆA PRAṆAVA UPĀSANĀ

In the Upaniṣads, *praṇava upāsanā* is classified into two — *parabrahma praṇava upāsanā* and *aparabrahma praṇava upāsanā*. The attributeless (*nirguṇa*) absolute truth is known as *parabrahma* and the reality with attributes (*saguṇa*) is known as *aparabrahma*. A *parabrahma praṇava upāsaka* is said to attain liberation (through *mahāvākya vicāra*). An *aparabrahma praṇava upāsaka* is said to attain *brahmaloka*. Thus, based on the attributeless and the truth endowed with attributes, *praṇava upāsanā* is twofold.

The *guru* then deals with the sequence of *nirguṇa praṇava upāsanā*. The benefit of *saguṇa upāsanā* is inbuilt within *nirguṇa upāsanā*. If one desires for *brahmaloka* and practises *nirguṇa upāsanā* then one attains *brahmaloka* only. In *brahmaloka*, the meditator enjoys a status equal to Hiraṇyagrabha. Thereafter, the meditator attains liberation by knowledge. But a *nirguṇa upāsaka* who does not desire for *brahmaloka* attains liberation while living. Thus, *nirguṇa upāsanā* is discussed here.

All entities in the form of cause and effects are of the form of *oṁkāra*. Therefore, the entire universe, with form, is *oṁkāra*. In all entities, there are two aspects — name and form. The "form" aspect is non-different from its "name" aspect. In other words, the form is nothing but the name. This is explained (by *anvaya-vyatireka*). Objects that have form are expressed through names. All objects are revealed, grasped and abandoned through names. The "form" alone cannot be expressed without the employment of name. Thus, essentially everything is name. The name remains even after the destruction of form. On the destruction of a pot, clay remains, there is no pot other than clay, but there is clay alone; in the same manner, on destruction of form like the clay, the name remains. Everything is in the form of name.[65]

This is explained further. The effects of clay in the form of pot, bowl, vessel, etc. are nothing but clay. The pot, bowl, etc. are mutually exclusive. Therefore, they are false (*vyabhicāra svarūpatvāt*). Clay that inheres in these vessels is real (*avyabhicāra svarūpatvāt*). In another case of production of many pots from clay, the space contained in these pots is referred to as pot-space pertaining to a particular pot. Even though the same name, i.e. "pot" is used, the space within a pot is not available in the space of another pot. From this angle, the pot-spaces are said to be different and hence they are false. One name "pot" inheres in all pot-forms. Thus, form is also false and it is not different from name. Hence, name is form alone. The name "pot" exists longer than the pot-form, it is said to be real or eternal, which is a figurative expression.

The name-world is not different from *oṁkāra*. *Oṁkāra* is of the nature of all names. That is, name represents a "sound-symbol". All words expressed in the world or in the Veda originate from *oṁkāra*.[66] Effect is of the form of cause. Thus, the sound symbols which are the effects are of the form of *oṁkāra*. The forms of objects are essentially the name. Thus, name is of the form of *oṁkāra* and therefore all forms are nothing but *oṁkāra*. On analysis, it is known that the letter, which is superimposed on *Brahman*, is

---

65 ओमित्येतदक्षरमिदꣳ सर्वं — *MaU* 1.1

66 तद्यथा शङ्कुना सर्वाणि पर्णानि संतृष्णानि एवमोङ्कारेण सर्वा वाक् संतृष्णा। ओङ्कारमेव इदं सर्वम्।
— Quoted in *SV*, p. 186

supported by *Brahman*. As the superimposed object is not separate from the substratum it is said that *oṁkāra* is *Brahman* alone. So, *oṁkāra* is to be meditated as the form of *Brahman*.

The Identity of Brahman and Oṁkāra

One should meditate on *Brahman* as identical with *oṁkāra*. *Ātman* and *Brahman* are primarily non-different (*mukhya-abheda*). *Brahman* or *Ātman* has four *pāda*s as it were. *Pāda* here means parts. The four parts of *Brahman* are Virāṭ, Hiraṇyagarbha, *Īśvara* and the witness-conscious principle, which is the secondary meaning of *tat pada*. Due to the identification with the bodies of all beings, *Īśvara* is known as Virāṭ. Virāṭ is also known as Vaiśvānara, since it manifests in many forms (*vividham rājate*). *Īśvara* is known as Hiraṇyagarbha due to the identification with the subtle universe. As a bestower of results to all beings based on their action, the almighty is known as *Īśvara*. The fourth *pāda* is *Brahman*, the witness consciousness.

The four parts of *Ātman* are *viśva, taijasa, prājña* and the witness-conscious principle which is the secondary meaning of *tvam pada*. Identification with the gross body as "I" in the waking state is *viśva*. In other words, the waker-I is *viśva*. Identification with the subtle body, which is the internal organ, is *taijasa*. The dreamer-I is *taijasa*. The identification of self with deep-sleep state where there is ignorance illumined by self-luminous Self is *prājña*. The fourth *pāda* is *turīya*, the witness consciousness.

Identity of Virāṭ-Viśva-Akāra

Virāṭ/viśva has seven parts — heaven is the head, sun is the eyes, air is the breath, space is the chest, ocean is the bladder, earth is the feet and *āhavanīya* fire is the mouth. Since, Viśva and Virāṭ are non-different, the *Māṇḍūkyopaniṣad*[67] mentions these as parts of Viśva. Viśva has nineteen counters of transaction. They are the five vital airs, five organs of action, five organs of knowledge and internal organ with four functions. These are instrumental in

---

[67] जागरितस्थानो बहिष्प्रज्ञः सप्ताङ्गः एकोनविंशतिमुखः स्थूलभुग्वैश्वानरः प्रथमः पादः ॥
— *MaU* 1.3

gaining various experiences. The gross world is experienced by these organs, since the organs are extrovert. Thus, Viśva is mentioned as *viśvabhuk, jāgrat-avasthā* and *bāhyavṛtti* (*bahiṣprajña*).[68] Each of the organs, which are the means of experience, is presided by a deity. The sense-organ by itself cannot function, being insentient; it functions because of the presence of a sentient deity. The five vital airs with fourteen triads is the face of the Virāṭ. The fourteen features, the deity, and the object together are known as the triad. These fourteen triads and the five *prāṇa* together are the form of Virāṭ, and are the nineteen "faces" of Viśva.[69] Virāṭ is non-different from the world. The first *mātrā* of *oṁkāra* is *akāra* which represents Virāṭ that is non-different from Viśva. The first *pāda* at the macrocosm is Virāṭ and at the microcosm is Viśva. The first *pāda* of *oṁkāra* is *akāra*. These three are non-different since their characteristics are the same. Thus, Viśva with seven *aṅga*s has nineteen "faces".

The Viśva with seven *aṅga*s and nineteen "faces" is said to be present for *taijasa* too but with a difference. The *aṅga*s and *mukha*s of *viśva* are created by *Īśvara*, whereas, the sense-organs, the presiding deities, the triad, the head and other limbs are mind-born. The experiences like pleasure and pain of *taijasa* is subtle in nature. The experiences of the waker's world arise by direct contact of the external world and hence it is known as gross experience. The experience in the dreamer's world is created within the mind and hence it is a subtle experience. Moreover, *viśva* is *bahiṣprajña*, wherein the mind travels outside and reaches the place of the object and *taijasa* is *antaḥprajña*, wherein the mind does not go out. Therefore, sequentially they are known as the external and internal worlds.

Identity of Taijasa-Hiraṇyagarbha-Ukāra

Just as Viśva and Virāṭ are non-different, *taijasa* and Hiraṇyagarbha are non-different. The conditioning factor of both *taijasa* and

---

[68] *MaU* 1.3

[69] *SV*, pp. 188-89.

Hiraṇyagarbha is subtle. To understand the identity of *taijasa* and Hiraṇyagarbha the identity of the second *mātrā* of *oṁkāra*, i.e. *ukāra* is to be known. The second *pāda* of micro is *taijasa* and macro is Hiraṇyagarbha. The second *mātrā* of *oṁkāra* is *ukāra*. The three have the same characteristic, which is of being the second *pāda*. Thus, they are identical.

Identity of Prājña–Īśvara–Makāra

The causal body is the conditioning factor of *prājña* and *Īśvara*. Both *Īśvara* and *prājña* are of the third *pāda*. The third part of *oṁkāra* is *makāra*. The common feature being they belong to the third *pāda* and hence they are identical. This *prājña* is referred to as *prajñānaghana*. The knowledge of waking and dream is dense in deep sleep and there is ignorance alone. Therefore, *prājña* is said as *prajñānaghana*. Just as grains of cooked rice can be made into a *piṇḍa* with water, or the rain-drops falling in slope region become one with the lake-water, the knowledge of waking and dream becomes one in deep sleep. The reflected consciousness in *avidyā* is *prājña-jīva* and along with *kūṭastha* substratum, it is known as *prajñānaghana*. This *prājña*, engulfed with ignorance, experiences *ānanda*, hence it is known as *ānandabhuk*.

Like *viśva* and *taijasa*, there is the description of triad in the experience of *prājña* also. The triad is described as follows:

(a) *adhyātmā* — consciousness, reflected consciousness and *avidyā vṛtti*,

(b) *adhibhūta* — the ignorance of thought-mode and inherent happiness, and

(c) *adhidaivam* — *Īśvara*.

Thus, it can be said as either *viśva-taijasa-prājña* or *bahiṣprajña-antaḥprajña-prajñānaghana*.

Turīya and Amātrā

The mutual difference between *viśva*, *taijasa*, *prājña* is due to the *upādhi* (adjunct). The three adjuncts of *viśva* are the gross, subtle and causal bodies. The two adjuncts of *taijasa* are the subtle and causal bodies. The one adjunct of *prājña* is the causal body. The substratal consciousness of *viśva, taijasa* and *prājña* in reality is unassociated with the adjuncts. The substratum of the three adjuncts is known as *turīya. Turīya* is neither external, nor internal or dense. It is not a sense-organ of action or knowledge or the sense objects. It is not the object of intellect. It cannot be described by words. The fourth *pāda* of micro known as *turīya* and the macro known as *Brahman* are non-different.

The Self has two aspects — real and unreal. The three *pāda*s are unreal and the fourth *pāda* is real. Like the Self, nature of *oṁkāra* is also twofold. The three *mātrā*s are unreal, pervading the three *mātrā*s is the consciousness which is the substratum of existence; illumination and love are real. In the absolute nature, there is no possibility of divisibility in the form of *mātrā* and hence it is known as *amātrā*. The real nature of *oṁkāra* and the real nature of Self are identical. The absolute nature of *oṁkāra* is *amātrā*, which is non-different from *turīya*. This is interpreted differently as *ekacintana*, wherein the three *pāda*s and *mātrā*s resolve into its substratum. This is a second method of *layacintana*.[70]

The *guru* shows the resolution of each *mātrā* into the other and thereby describes a third method of *layacintana* process. The gross effect resolves into its subtle cause. First, at the micro level, *viśva* resolves into *taijasa*; in *oṁkāra*, *akāra* resolves into *ukāra*, and at the macro level the Virāṭ resolves into the Hiraṇyagarbha. Second, *taijasa* resolves into *prājña*, *ukāra* into *makāra* and Hiraṇyagarbha into *Īśvara*. Third, *prājña* resolves into *turīya*, *makāra* into *amātrā*, *Īśvara* into *Brahman*. The absolute nature of *turīya*, *amātrā* and *Brahman* is identical. *Īśvara* and *prājña* which are superimposed on *Brahman* are non-different from *Brahman*.[71] Thus, one should meditate upon *Brahman* as the Self, of the nature of *oṁkāra*, who is fearless, eternally free, non-dual, unassociated, in

---

70 See above in Section 5.3 for the first method of *layacintana*.

71 यत् यस्मिन् कल्पितं तत् तत्स्वरूपमिति न्यायः ।

whom the entire mobile and immobile universe rests. One who meditates on this for a long time unceasingly, the *guru* declares, for such a one, knowledge arises and he attains liberation. Therefore, the *nirguṇa oṁkāra upāsanā* is of higher nature.

As mentioned above, one who knows (meditates) *oṁkāra* is a *muni*. A *muni* is one who takes to *manana*. Therefore, meditation on *oṁkāra* is *manana*. Till now, the *guru* has adopted the analysis of *oṁkāra* based on the *Māṇḍūkyopaniṣad*. The sequence of meditation is also mentioned in the *Nṛsiṁhatāpanīya Upaniṣad* (section 5), which is referred to by Vidyāraṇya in his *Pañcadaśī*.[72] These scriptures declare that the meditation on *oṁkāra* is the secret wealth of the *paramahaṁsa* mendicant and is not meant for those who are extrovert by nature. The meditator attains liberation through knowledge.

So far, *nirguṇa upāsanā* has been discussed and the one who takes up to this kind of meditation without the desire for *brahmaloka* attains *jīvanmukti* through knowledge. The role of *upāsanā* here is to remove obstacles and one takes to *śravaṇa* again or recollects the teaching resulting in clarity. On the other hand, the *guru* says, one in whom the intense dispassion is absent, longs for the result of this world and the other world, and continues to meditate on *oṁkāra*, for such a one, the desire for enjoyment is the obstacle for rise of knowledge. If the meditator dies after developing dispassion for enjoyment in higher worlds, because of the power of meditation, he is reborn in the world in an atmosphere which is conducive, wherein he experiences the fruits of meditation done in past birth and because of the impressions (*vāsanā*) of the practised meditation, he may take to meditation again or to *śravaṇa*, thereby gain knowledge and attain liberation while living. One who has restrained the desire for higher worlds and meditates on the *oṁkāra*, after the fall of the body, reaches *brahmaloka*. There he experiences independently the bliss which is difficult for human, manes and gods to attain. He attains enjoyment equal to

---

[72] *PD* 9.63.

Hiraṇyagarbha, and acquires qualities like *satya-saṅkalpa.*

The *madhyama adhikārī* is unable to understand the identity-knowledge even after the description of the process of meditation described so far, viz., the first method of *layacintana,* the *ahaṁgraha upāsanā* and the *nirguṇa oṁkāra upāsanā* with two other methods of *layacintana* that serve as the means to gain direct knowledge and attain liberation while living. Hence, the *guru* proceeds to explain the path taken by the meditator of *nirguṇa oṁkāra* with a desire to reach *brahmaloka* who attains gradual liberation. We come to know that later the *madhyama adhikārī* resorted to this last mode of teaching and attained *kramamukti.*

5.5 Kramamukti

At the time of death, the subtle body leaves the gross body of *jīva.* Then due to the absence of consciousness (unmanifest) the internal organ and the sense-organs become non-functional, which cannot know anything by itself. The *prāṇa* with *kriyāśakti* is inert and due to the absence of desire it cannot travel anywhere. The meditator is neither aware of anything nor performs any act. The messengers of Yama do not arrive at the end of the meditator's life.

The *deva* identified with fire, at the time of death, separates the meditator from the gross body and leads the *jīva* to its own world. From the world of fire, the *deva* identified with *ahaḥ* (day) lead to their world. Then *jīva* is led by the *deva* identified with *śukla pakṣa,* the *deva* identified with *uttarāyaṇa* and the *deva* identified with *saṁvatsara* (year). Further, the *deva*s identified with *devaloka,* Vāyudeva, Sūrya, Candradeva, Vidyutdeva (in this order) lead to their respective worlds. In the *vidyutloka,* with the features of Hiraṇyagarbha, a divine being (*divya puruṣa*), leads the meditator. This divine being takes *jīva* from *vidyutloka* to *varuṇaloka.* Here Vidyutdeva also accompanies the *divya puruṣa.* This *divya puruṣa* leads *jīva* to *indraloka* from *varuṇaloka.* Here Varuṇadeva follows the *divya puruṣa* to *indraloka.* The *divya puruṣa* guides *jīva* to *prajāpatiloka* followed by Indra. Prajāpati has no entry into *brahmaloka*, the *divya puruṣa* without any follower, leads *jīva* to *brahmaloka*.

The lord of *brahmaloka* is Hiraṇyagarbha. Hiraṇyagarbha is identified with the total micro and macro universes. Hiraṇyagarbha is also known as *aparabrahma* or *kāryabrahma*. *Brahmaloka* is presided by *kāryabrahma*. Based on the maxim of *tat kratuḥ*,[73] since the meditator has *Nirguṇa-Brahman* as the object of meditation, he must attain the same.[74] According to Advaita, *Brahman* is attained only through Vedānta *pramāṇa*, by falsification of duality and rise of non-dual knowledge. Here, the meditator encounters with the obstacle in the form of desire for enjoyment, hence knowledge does not rise, and hence the meditator attains *kāryabrahma*. The meditator, who has reached *brahmaloka*, attains the glories of Hiraṇyagarbha. Other than the function of creation, sustenance and destruction, the meditator attains all the powers equal to Hiraṇyagarbha.[75] This is known as *sāyujya-mukti*. In this manner, the meditator equals to Hiraṇyagarbha, having attained the *saṅkalpa-śakti*, enjoys different benefits, at the time of resolution of *hiraṇyagarbhaloka*, by the rise of Advaita knowledge, he attains *videhamukti*.[76]

Further the *guru* says that just as a *brahma-upāsaka* who meditates on *oṁkāra* attains *brahmaloka* and attains liberation, the other kind of *upāsaka*s also attain the same result. But without the practice of *ahaṁgraha upāsanā*, one does not attain *brahmaloka*.[77] The other kind of *upāsanā* described in the Upaniṣads is *pratīkadhyāna*. Meditation on the black stone (*bāṇa-liṅga*) on the

---

73 स यथाकामो भवति तत्क्रतुर्भवति । — *BU* 4.4.5

74 अथ खलु क्रतुमयः पुरुषो यथाक्रतुरस्मिँल्लोके पुरुषो भवति तथेतः प्रेत्य भवति स क्रतुं कुर्वीत ।
— *CU* 3.14.1

यं यं वापि स्मरन् भावं त्यजत्यन्ते कलेवरम् ।
तं तमेवैति कौन्तेय सदा तद्भावभावितः ॥ — *BG* VIII.6

75 जगद्व्यापारवर्जम् प्रकरणात् असन्निहितत्वाच्च । — *BS* 4.4.17

76 ब्रह्मणा सह ते सर्वे संप्राप्ते प्रतिसञ्चरे ।
परस्यान्ते कृतात्मानः प्रविशन्ति परं पदम् ॥ — *KP* 11.284

77 अप्रतीकालम्बनान्नयतीति बादरायण उभयथादोषात्तत्क्रतुश्च ॥ — *BS* 4.3.15

banks of Narmadā as Śiva, or the *śālagrāma* stones (Gaṇḍaki River, Nepal) as Viṣṇu, is known as *pratīkadhyāna*. This is not *ahaṁgraha dhyāna*.[78] The respective sections of the Upaniṣads discuss the specific result for such kind of meditations and there is no mention of *brahmaloka* for these kinds of meditation. *Ahaṁgraha upāsanā* is meditating oneself as *Saguṇa* or *Nirguṇa-Brahman* and by this meditation alone *brahmaloka* is attained. The above-mentioned path to *brahmaloka* is the *uttarāyaṇa mārga*, also known as *devayāna*, *arcirādi mārga*, etc. The meditator who has attained *brahmaloka* by *deva mārga* and does not return to *saṁsāra* but remains in *brahmaloka*, and by the rise of knowledge, attains *videhamukti*.

For Advaitin, liberation is not possible without the means of knowledge like instruction from a *guru*. In *brahmaloka*, it is said, without the instruction from a *guru*, there is rise of knowledge. The reason is that in *brahmaloka*, there is absence of *rajas* and *tamas guṇas*. It is predominantly *sattva*. Due to the absence of *tamas*, there is no dumbness or laziness. Due to the absence of *rajas*, its effects in the form of desire, anger, etc. and projection are not present. Therefore, there is no concealment or projection and only *sattva* is dominant and thus in *brahmaloka* the primary effect of *sattva guṇa* is knowledge in the form of illuminator.

Earlier, at the time of meditation of *oṁkāra* in the form of *Brahman*, the meaning of *oṁkāra mātrā*s was dwelt upon (Table 5.1).

Table 5.1: The Primary Meaning of Oṁkāra Mātrās

Oṁkāra	*Mātrā*	*Vācyārtha*
Akāra	*Prathamā*	Virāṭ-Viśva conditioned by gross universe and body
Ukāra	*Dvitīyā*	Hiraṇyagarbha-*taijasa* conditioned by subtle universe and body
Makāra	*Tṛitīyā*	*Īśvara-prājña* conditioned by causal universe and body

In *brahmaloka*, the meditator further analyses discriminately, due to *sattva* predominance in the following manner:

[78] मनो ब्रह्मेत्युपासीत। — *CU* 3.18.1; आदित्यो ब्रह्मेति। — *CU* 3.19.1

1. From the angle of gross body, the pure *Brahman* is conditioned as Virāṭ and Viśva. As macro gross body it is Virāṭ and as micro gross bodies it is *viśva*. Without the macro and the micro gross factors Virāṭ and *viśva* are not known. In reality, there is pure consciousness alone. Therefore, the *vācyārtha* of *akāra* is Virāṭ-Viśva, i.e. *Brahman* conditioned by the gross body.
2. In the same way, from the angle of subtle body, the pure *Brahman* is conditioned as Hiraṇyagarbha and *taijasa*. As macro subtle body it is Hiraṇyagarbha and as micro subtle body it is *taijasa*. Without the macro and micro subtle factors Hiraṇyagarbha and *taijasa* are not known. But there is pure consciousness alone. Therefore, the *vācyārtha* of *ukāra* is Hiraṇyagarbha-*taijasa*, i.e. *Brahman* conditioned by the subtle body.
3. Similarly, from the point of causal body, the pure *Brahman* is conditioned as *Īśvara* and *prājña*. As total causal body (*māyā)* it is *Īśvara*. As individual causal body (*avidyā*) it is *prājña*. Without the total and individual subtle factors *Īśvara* and *prājña* are not known. But there is pure consciousness alone. Therefore, the *vācyārtha* of *makāra* is *Īśvara-prājña,* i.e. *Brahman* conditioned by the causal body.

When an entity is seen from different angles, it is not the absolute nature of the entity. That entity which is seen without any divisions is self-evident and is of the absolute nature. Just as a certain person from the angle of father is a son, from the angle of grandfather is grandson, is not the absolute nature of the person, but the humanness alone is the absolute nature of the human; in the same way, from the angle of gross, subtle and causal conditions the *viśva, taijasa* and *prājña* are not absolute characteristics, but they are *mithyā*. Consciousness alone is the reality.

The *guru* further explains the process of discrimination. Consciousness is devoid of all kinds of duality. The difference like *viśva* and Virāṭ is based on the *upādhi*. The gross universe is the conditioning factor of Virāṭ. The gross body is the conditioning factor of *viśva*. Though the difference is based on total and individual gross factors, by nature differences like *viśva* and Virāṭ are not present. In the same way, differences like Hiraṇyagarbha and *taijasa* are based only on the *upādhi*. The subtle universe is the conditioning factor of Hiraṇyagarbha. The subtle body is the conditioning factor of *taijasa*. Though the difference is based on total and individual subtle factors, by nature differences like Hiraṇyagarbha and *taijasa* are not there. Likewise, differences like *Īśvara* and *prājña* are based on the *upādhi*. The causal universe is the conditioning factor of *Īśvara*. The causal body is the conditioning factor of *prājña*. Though the difference is based on total and individual causal factors, by nature differences like *Īśvara* and *prājña* are not there. If the conditioning factors are dissolved there is no difference at all. By giving up these factors, there remains the consciousness alone without any difference. Moreover, even with the presence of non-self, there is no plurality in the consciousness. The non-self like body and world appears due to ignorance. It is not absolute. Therefore, the non-self in the form of world along with consciousness is different and is unassociated. The secondary signification of the *oṁkāra*, by which it is arrived that the inner self is of the nature of *Brahman* that is eternally free, free from modifications, unassociated, is free from all duality is known to the meditator in *brahmaloka*. Therefore, the meditator residing in *brahmaloka*, does not return to mortality but with this knowledge attains *kaivalya videhamukti* during the resolution of the *kāryabrahma*. This is known as *kramamukti*.

IDENTITY OF OṀKĀRA-MAHĀVĀKYA VICĀRA

Now the *guru* reconciles the Advaitic position who claims that liberating knowledge cannot arise without the analysis of *mahāvākya*. It is shown that the analysis of *oṁkāra* is non-different from the *mahāvākya* analysis (Table 5.2).

Table 5.2: The Analysis of Oṁkāra

Omkāra	*Vācyārtha*	*Lakṣyārtha*
Akāra	Gross + Consciousness	Consciousness — gross factor
Ukāra	Subtle + Consciousness	Consciousness — subtle factor
Makāra	Causal + Consciousness	Consciousness — causal factor

The *oṁkāra vācyārtha* is consciousness with name and form factors, and the *oṁkāra lakṣyārtha* is consciousness without any conditioning factor. Thus, the meanings of *oṁkāra* and *mahāvākya* is identical. Therefore, by the analysis of the *oṁkāra* there is Advaita-knowledge. The dialogue of the *guru* with the *madhyama adhikārī* is concluded who is said to have embraced the path of meditation and attained *kramamukti*.

5.6 Teachings to Manda-madhyama Adhikārī

The state of *manda-madhyama adhikārī* is discussed in the seventh *taraṅga* of *Vicārasāgara*. He is a seeker of Truth and develops dispassion towards worldly pleasures. However, since his dispassion is not intense he does not yearn to gain *Brahman*-knowledge. In his pursuit of solace, he develops a desire to practise meditation and seeks the advice of the learned ones to enlighten him on the nature of *deva*, the object of meditation. To his utter dismay, he comes across five different schools of theology who hold their own deity as primary. Each school presents its deity as the only object of meditation.

MEDITATE ON VIṢṆU

The Vaiṣṇava tradition proclaims that Vāsudeva is the chief god and creator of all the scriptures. Viṣṇu is worshipped by Śiva and other gods. He wields conch and discus, lotus and mace, and is the protector. He possesses attractive form and is a repository of compassion. Viṣṇu knows the minds of all his devotees and fulfils the wishes of his devotees. Śakti, Gaṇeśa, Sūrya, Śiva and others only implement the command of Viṣṇu. Thus is described in the Purāṇas. The entire world has originated from Viṣṇu. He removes the sorrows of all beings. He has assumed many forms and redeemed devotees from sorrow. Therefore, Viṣṇu alone is to be meditated upon. Even though Śiva is a devotee of Viṣṇu, Śiva is not to be meditated. He is inauspicious who smears ashes, holds *ḍamaru*, wears elephant skin, skull garland, etc. His son Gaṇeśa is also of the same category. Gaṇeśa is the lord of *gaṇas*; He is a combination of human and animal. Devī is also inauspicious and Sūrya always roams restlessly like *alātacakra*, causing day and night. The meditators of Sūrya will also be constantly moving about. Therefore, the other gods are to be abandoned and one should serve Viṣṇu always. The means to worship Viṣṇu are mentioned in *Nāradapāñcarātra*.

MEDITATE ON ŚIVA

The Śaiva tradition claims that Śiva is superior to all gods. Śiva fulfils the desires of all his devotees. He bestows riches to everyone and he accepts only ashes. In order to remove differences he adorns himself with skin and skull. He remains naked to indicate that dispassion alone is the means to *ānanda*. He grants *sāyujyamukti* to one who dies in Kāśī. They are freed from sorrows of rebirth and enjoy the *ānanda* equal to Śiva. Śiva is superior since he was worshipped by Viṣṇu at Rāmeśvara. Purāṇas may glorify different deities, they are figurative expressions, Śiva alone is superior. The purport of *Mahābhārata* as explained by Appayya Dīkṣita is described here — Aśvattāma employed *nārāyaṇa-āgneya astra* wherein the armies were killed but Pāṇḍavas did not die. He deserted the chariot and reprimanding *Dhanurveda* and its teacher went to the forest. Vyāsa speaks to Aśvattāma "Do not degrade scripture and teacher. Kṛṣṇa and Arjuna were Nara–Nārāyaṇa *ṛṣi*s. By the intense meditation of Nara–Nārāyaṇa on Śiva, Śiva blocked the power of the missile that was released to kill the Pāṇḍavas." Thus, the glory of Śiva is described in *Mahābhārata*. Appayya establishes that all texts on Viṣṇu reveal Śiva as superior. Śiva is also known as Mahādeva, meaning the supreme most. Moreover, the word Śiva means auspiciousness.

Other than Śiva all gods are inauspicious. The means of worshipping Śiva is described in *Pāśupatatantra*. Śiva alone is to be meditated upon.

MEDITATE ON GAṆEŚA

Gaṇeśa is superior to Śiva. While Śiva prepared to vanquish the three cities of the demons, he was unsuccessful since he did not worship Gaṇeśa. He then prostrated his son Gaṇeśa and then won over the demons. Thus, Gaṇeśa is the supreme lord. *Gaṇeśa Purāṇa* mentions that all gods originated from the trunk of Gaṇeśa. Thus, Gaṇeśa alone is to be meditated upon.

MEDITATE ON DEVĪ

Devī is superior to all because without *śakti* the gods are equal to dead bodies. One who meditates on *śakti* will attain power. The different powers possessed by gods and those seen in the world are expressions of Devī. Devī expresses in two forms, one as the power in all things that is instrumental in bringing an effect, this is the general cause of *śakti* and the other is Devī with eight arms possessing specific power. Devī is formless and just as the powers are varied, in the same manner the formed powers are also many. Such a formed *śakti* is Kālī who is the primary deity. Māheśvarī, Vaiṣṇavī, Śaurī, Gāṇeśī, etc. are also primary. This is declared in *Devī Bhāgavata*. It says, the foremost devotees of Devī are Śiva and Viṣṇu. The result of meditation is assuming the form of the meditated object. Śiva and Viṣṇu by the power of meditation gain the form of the meditated object. Thus, they are the primary meditators. The Upapurāṇas proclaim that devotion to Devī is superior most and the method of worship is also mentioned. Thus, Devī alone is to be meditated upon.

MEDITATE ON SŪRYA

Sūrya alone is the illuminator of everything. In the absence of Sūrya, the entire creation will be engulfed by darkness. Other luminaries borrow light from Sūrya. All activities are based on time. Sun is one, but is referred to as past, present and future since it illuminates the three periods. Sun is seen as *sūtrātmā*. Varied things originate from sun. Sūrya has two aspects — one with form and other without form. The formless light pervades the entire name and form. It is the substratum of the entire universe. Sūrya with form is that light which is experienced during dawn. Moon and stars are part of sun. Between these two forms, the formless light is to be known and the light with form is to be meditated upon. These two forms are described in Vedānta as *nirguṇa* and *saguṇa*. Sūrya alone is the superior deity and by meditating on Sūrya, darkness is destroyed. Thus, Sūrya alone is to be meditated upon.

The above five schools of meditation dismiss each other by bringing out the greatness of their respective gods. The Smārta sect does not differentiate these gods. According to the Smārtas, all gods are equal. Thus, the view of Smārta contradicts the above five views.

MUTUALLY CONTRADICTING PHILOSOPHICAL SYSTEMS

The *manda-madhyama adhikārī* is perplexed with regard to the object of meditation. He tries to find an answer in the orthodox philosophical systems. He finds their views to be mutually contradicting. The Sāṁkhya system does not accept the existence of *Īśvara*. It arrives at the nature of liberation through the analysis of *puruṣa* and *prakṛti*. In Yoga system, *Īśvara* is accepted but liberation is said to be through *samādhi*. Thus, there is a contradiction between the views of Sāṁkhya and Yoga. The basic principles of Nyāya and Vaiśeṣika are different and they provide liberating knowledge by the analysis of the material world. In Pūrva Mīmāṁsā, again the existence of *Īśvara* is denied and they hold that human goal is happiness born of performance of action. The Uttara Mīmāṁsā establishes non-duality after the negation of duality that is accepted in other systems. Thus, all the philosophical systems seems to hold mutually contradictory ideas. Thus, the *manda-madhyama adhikārī* could not find a solution in the philosophical systems too. In this situation, he meets his son, the *kaniṣṭha adhikārī,* a *jīvanmukta* now and seeks clarification with regard to the valid source of knowledge related to one object of meditation.

PURPORT OF PURĀṆAS

Now, the questions in the mind of the *manda-madhyama adhikārī* can be given as follows:

1. What is the object of meditation described in varied Purāṇas?
2. How to arrive at the valid system of philosophy?

The *kaniṣṭha adhikārī* gives the answer for the first question in two stages. First, he retains the difference between the five *deva*s described above but shows the non-difference in the result of meditation. From this standpoint, he explains the *nindā-stuti* (censure-eulogy) method adopted in varied Purāṇas for the sake of meditation. In the second stage of the answer, he differentiates the *kāraṇabrahma* from *kāryabrahma* (explained in the sequel) and reconciles the position of the Purāṇas. As the answer to the second question, he explains the philosophical teachings of Uttara Mīmāṁsā alone as valid.

At the outset, the *kaniṣṭha adhikārī* clarifies that one should meditate on *kāraṇabrahma* and not *kāryabrahma.* The five *deva*s described in different Purāṇas refer to one *Īśvara* alone. Each Purāṇa propitiates a particular deity. The purport in each Purāṇa is to develop the practice of meditation on the primary god described and the censure of other deities does not suggest giving up of meditation on other forms. But in a given context, the eulogized deity alone is to be meditated upon, this is the idea. In *Viṣṇu Purāṇa,* the reason for taking to the practice of meditation (on Viṣṇu) is adopted by the method of censure of other gods and eulogy of Viṣṇu. Likewise, the objective is the same in *Śiva Purāṇa,* etc. where the respective deity is eulogized and others are censured. In any case, it does not convey the idea of giving up of meditation of a particular deity. By censure of a *deva,* if it suggests giving up of meditation, then one can never take to the practice of meditation since all *deva*s are censured in different Purāṇas in different contexts. Thus, the censure of some deities in a context is to highlight the predominance of a particular deity and it is not conveying the idea of giving up of meditation on the censured deities.

The *kaniṣṭha adhikārī* gives an example to explicate his above contention. The Vedas prescribe performance of Agnihotra twice — before and after sunrise — in the statement *udite juhoti anudite juhoti*. While describing *udita homa, anudita homa* is censured. In the context of *anudita homa, udita homa* is censured. If because of this censuring the very Agnihotra is given up then one will give up the performance of Agnihotra both the times. Therefore, the censuring of one, in the context of another, is for the glorification of the subject in a particular context. In the same way, the censuring of other gods in a context is to glorify one god as supreme. The idea is not to criticize other gods.

RESULT OF MEDITATION

The *kaniṣṭha adhikārī* then points out that, however, the benefit of meditation of any of the five deities highlighted above is the same, i.e. attainment of *brahmaloka*. After enjoying the pleasures of *brahmaloka* one is said to gain *videhamukti* (through *kramamukti*). The Purāṇas state that a meditator on Viṣṇu, reaches *vaikuṇṭhaloka* and not *brahmaloka*, then too, since the meditator is eligible for *videhamukti*, the *upāsaka* through *devayāna mārga* reaches *brahmaloka*. *Brahmaloka* appears as *vaikuṇṭhaloka* for a Viṣṇu *upāsaka* and as *śivaloka* for a Śiva *upāsaka* and so on. The route to *brahmaloka* is known as *devayāna mārga*. Therefore, the meditators eligible to gain *videhamukti* reach *brahmaloka*. Thus, the result of meditation on any of the five deities described above is the same.

RECONCILIATION OF THE PURĀṆIC TEACHING

Here, if it is argued that the names and forms of the five deities described above are different but *Īśvara* is known to be one only, then how can one *Īśvara* appear in many forms? It is replied as follows: From the transcendental angle, there are no names or forms, but for the sake of meditation the names and forms are imagined. Therefore, in one *Īśvara* alone there is the appearance of many names and forms due to *māyā*.

He explains further that each deity, viz. Viṣṇu, Śiva, etc. in a context, refers to either *kāraṇabrahma* or *kāryabrahma*. The Consciousness conditioned by *māyā* is said to be *kāraṇabrahma* and Hiraṇyagarbha who is an effect of *Īśvara* is also referred to as *brahma* (*kāryabrahma*). Thus, the words Viṣṇu, Śiva, etc. can refer to either the *kāraṇabrahma* or the *kāryabrahma*. From this standpoint, various names of deities are synonymous, at times referring to the *kāraṇabrahma* or *kāryabrahma*. It is like the word *saindhava* that may mean "salt" or "horse" in a given context.

In this second stage of the answer, the *kaniṣṭha adhikārī* reconciles the position of the Purāṇas. He reinforces that one should meditate on *kāraṇabrahma* and not *kāryabrahma*. In the Vaiṣṇava Purāṇas, the word "Viṣṇu" refers to *kāraṇabrahma*. The other gods refer to *kāryabrahma*. The other Purāṇas also should be known in this manner. Thus, in all the Purāṇas the names referring to *kāraṇabrahma* and *kāryabrahma* are different. The idea is that the *kāraṇabrahma* is to be meditated upon and the *kāryabrahma* is to be given up. Thus, all Purāṇas refer to one *kāraṇabrahma* alone. The purport of the Purāṇas is to highlight the practice of meditation on *kāraṇabrahma*. The Purāṇas, therefore are not mutually contradictory.

ROLE OF VARIED NAMES AND FORMS

In the sequel, the *kaniṣṭha adhikārī* explains the role of varied names and forms of deities described in the scriptures. The forms are the result of modification of *māyā* and transfiguration of Consciousness, hence meditation on forms (*kāryabrahma*) is said to be given up. But, when these forms are understood as Consciousness conditioned by *māyā* then they refer to *kāraṇa-brahma* and hence should be taken up for meditation. Thus, the essential teaching of the scriptures is to sublate the respective names and forms and meditate on *kāraṇabrahma*. Though the forms, which are effects, are false and the cause alone is real, the scriptures describe forms for a dull intellect who can concentrate only on described forms. On development of firm concentration, the scriptures elevate the seekers to meditate on the cause by giving up the effects.

KĀRAṆABRAHMA UPĀSANĀ

Now, the *kaniṣṭha adhikārī* gives the method of meditation on *kāraṇabrahma*. The cause of the universe should be meditated upon as one endowed with omniscience, omnipotence, omnipresence, etc. The purport of the scriptures is not to focus on the meditation of forms. Though many forms are described in the scriptures for the sake of meditation, they are meant as *upalakṣaṇa* for *kāraṇabrahma*. This is explained through the following example —

In the instance, *kākavatdevadattagṛham* (the crow in Devadatta's house) is *upalakṣaṇa* (incidental feature). The crow sitting on the terrace for some time is a distinguishing factor that differentiates Devadatta's house from all other houses. But the crow does not serve as the distinguishing factor all the time. In the same way, in *kāraṇabrahma*, some time there is an assumption of forms with eight arms, etc. and since it differentiates from other forms it is known as *upalakṣaṇa*. The benefit of *upalakṣaṇa* is that it gives rise to the knowledge of the nature of a specific entity alone. In the example, with the help of a crow, one comes to know of Devadatta's house and it does not serve any other purpose. Similarly, the description of different forms in the scriptures is specifically meant to indicate the formless causal *Brahman* for the sake of meditation, and they do not serve any other purpose.

UTTARA-MĪMĀṀSĀ ALONE IS VALID

Now, the *kaniṣṭha adhikārī* resolves the position of the orthodox philosophical systems seen as mutually contradictory by the *manda-madhyama adhikārī*. He shows that the teachings of Uttara-Mīmāṁsā alone is non-contradictory to the Vedas. The other five schools being contradictory to the Vedic teaching are said to be invalid. He says that some *manda* seekers follow other systems with regard to those teachings that are non-contradictory to the Vedas. This partial acceptance of certain systems is to be thwarted. The creator of the Vedas is *Īśvara,* wherein there is no scope for delusion, doubt, negligence, misleading, etc. The founders of other systems are human beings wherein there is scope for delusion, etc. The *kaniṣṭha adhikārī* differentiates the omniscience of *Īśvara* from that of the omniscience acquired by the founders of the philosophical systems. The omniscience of *Īśvara* is natural, hence *Īśvara* is *yukta-yogī* whereas, the omniscience of sages and others are acquired through meditation, etc. and hence they are *yuñjāna-yogī.* He points out that the teachings of the Veda given out by *yukta-yogī Īśvara* alone gains more validity when compared to the teachings of *yuñjāna-yogīs.*

From this, the *kaniṣṭha adhikārī* arrives at a maxim as that teaching which is based on the Veda alone is valid and the teaching contradicting the Veda is invalid. Applying this maxim, he states that the five schools of philosophical systems are invalid since they are clearly contradicting the Vedas. On the other hand, Uttara-Mīmāṁsā does not contradict the Vedas in any respect and hence it is always valid. He cautions that some people follow other systems with respect to those teachings that do not contradict the Vedas. This is partial acceptance of non-contradictory portions of other systems with the Veda. The *kaniṣṭha adhikārī* condemns this approach too. He says that even, for instance, the Jaina teaching of non-violence is in keeping with the Vedic teaching then also it should be given up since it said to be *vedabāhya.* Likewise, he says that Buddha's teachings are subject to defect like *vipralabdhi*[79] and it should be given up, even though Buddha is worshipped as an incarnation. Thus, in all aspects the Uttara-Mīmāṁsā alone is to be followed since it does not contradict the Vedas.

He further points out that the teachings of Veda Vyāsa in Uttara-Mīmāṁsā are to be studied by the seekers of liberation. Though there are many commentaries to it, one should study only the commentary of Ādi Śaṅkarācārya since it alone is in keeping with the Vedas. Thus, the *kaniṣṭha adhikārī* instructs on the validity of Uttara-Mīmāṁsā alone.

---

[79] *Vipralipsā* = desirous to deceive.

The *guru* had mentioned to the *kaniṣṭha adhikārī* that the purport of all scriptures is the non-dual knowledge.[80] Here, to the *manda-madhyama adhikārī*, the *kaniṣṭha adhikārī* cautions to avoid the other schools of thought and follow only the non-dual system. In a certain case, a sick enemy regains health when stabbed by a knife, due to the gushing out of toxic blood. Here, his killer becomes his saviour. In the same way, one may think that by following any teaching, other than the scriptures, if somehow the mental refinement is gained then one may attain liberation said in the Vedas. This is not possible and this is explained through the maxim *andhagolāṅgūla nyāya*.

The maxim *andhagolāṅgūla nyāya* is explained as follows: a certain rich man's son adorned with jewels was kidnapped into the forest by thieves. They snatched his ornaments and tied his eyes and took him to another place. A deceiving person approached the son and asked him to hold the tail of the intoxicated bull. The son in pain, believing the words of this person, held the tail of the bull and never got released. In the same way, the sense-objects in the form of thugs, tie the eyes and kidnap into the *saṁsāra* forest and abandon the seeker of knowledge. Then the Bhedavādins and other schools deceive and create interest in other systems and state that their system alone is valid. A *manda* seeker, having faith in these words, follow those systems but is caught up in the repeated cycles of births and deaths. The *kaniṣṭha adhikārī* reiterates that the study of other systems should be given up and one should follow the teachings of Uttara-Mīmāṁsā alone. The *manda-madhyama adhikārī* is said to have practised *kāraṇabrahma upāsanā* and attained *brahmaloka*.

The above dialogue reminds us of the possibility of flexible pedagogical measures in Advaita that values any kind of seeker who yearns to realize the Truth. The first part of this chapter dealt with the teaching imparted to the *madhyama adhikārī* in the fifth *taraṅga* for whom the following were the pedagogical measures:

---

[80] See Section 3.1 of Chapter 3.

1. The notion of duality as an obstacle to the recognition of non-dual knowledge was revealed by pointing out the reproach of duality in scriptures and through the story of minister Bharchu. The refutation of duality was also analysed through the arguments as found in the third *taraṅga.* The falsity of bondage and liberation was shown through the dream of a king.
2. The ontological variations were explained through the analysis of the three orders of reality.
3. The process of creation was revealed by the analysis of the nature of *māyā* and its effects in order to arrive at the discriminative method to reveal the Self.
4. Nature of Self was examined by the methods of five-sheaths discrimination, witness of the three states of experience and three-bodies discrimination.
5. Identity-knowledge was explained through the method of *layacintana.* The difference between knowledge and meditation was pointed out.
6. Various kinds of meditation were elaborated upon as an aid to arrive at non-dual knowledge later.
7. The practice of meditation leading to *brahmaloka* and attainment of *kramamukti* through *oṁkāra-mahāvākya vicāra* by the *madhyama adhikārī* was elaborately described.

   The final part of this chapter described the state of (Śubhasantati as) *manda-madhyama adhikārī* as found in the seventh *taraṅga* of *Vicārasāgara.*
8. The nature of object of meditation was revealed by the *kaniṣṭha adhikārī* by differentiating the *kāraṇabrahma* from *kāryabrahma.*
9. The purport of the Purāṇas and the validity of the teaching of Uttara-Mīmāṁsā were elaborately discussed.
10. The *manda-madhyama adhikārī* is said to have attained *brahmaloka.*

6

On the Nature of Liberation (Mokṣasvarūpaprakaraṇa)

In this final chapter of the present study, we shall deal with the nature of liberation according to Advaita as discussed in the text *Vicārasāgara*. Here again we have pooled in the contents of discussion with regard to liberation occurring in different *taraṅgas* of the text that are presented in a particular sequence.

1. The definition of liberation, nature of *Brahman* as *ānanda*, the nature of sense pleasure as a reflection and the attainment of *ānanda* as figurative, etc. are elaborately discussed (*taraṅgas* 2, 4 and 1).
2. The nature of *jīvanmukti* is described and the views of the Samādhivādin related to liberation are refuted with a mention of the difference between *nididhyāsana* and *samādhi* (*taraṅgas* 7 and 1).
3. The *prārabdha* of an enlightened person and the questions regarding the rise of desire based on *prārabdha* and the status of *karma* and *upāsanā* performed by a *mukta* are also discussed (*taraṅgas* 7 and 6).
4. The various concepts of *videhamukti* and the absolute view of *nityamukti* are briefly examined (*taraṅga* 7).
5. Finally, this chapter closes with an account of the "kind" of liberation attained by the *adhikārīs* of *Vicārasāgara* (*taraṅga* 7).

6.1 Definition of Liberation

In the context of establishing the *prayojana* of *Vicarāsāgara* in the second *taraṅga*, liberation is defined as "the destruction of the world along with its material cause, namely, ignorance and subsequent attainment of *Brahman*". Liberation, thus defined, consists of two components, one is destruction of ignorance and the other is attainment of *Brahman*. Here, an opponent refutes the possibility of both these components that form the definition of liberation.

SELF-IGNORANCE IS THE CAUSE OF SORROW

Objection: The destruction of the world with its material cause is impossible as no one desires to annihilate the world along with its primal cause. One, who is subject to the three kinds of miseries, discriminatively, desires to remove the miseries but never desires to destroy the world. The three kinds of miseries are:

1. *Ādhyātmika* — sufferings due to fever, disease, hunger, thirst, etc.,
2. *Ādhibhautika* — fear from external environment, and
3. *Ādhidaivika* — fear of supernatural powers.

Liberation is the removal of sufferings caused by these three factors and hence the remedy is as follows. The problem from the first factor (*ādhyātmika*) can be removed by *Āyurveda*. There is a direct experience of removal of hunger by consumption of food, in the same manner, pain caused in the body can be removed by appropriate solution as prescribed in the science of medicine and thus, without destruction of the world with its primal cause, freedom from sorrow is achieved.[1] This is the objection with regard to the first part of the definition of liberation.

Advaitin: According to Advaita, the root cause of all kinds of sorrow is primal ignorance and its effects in the form of the world,

[1] In the text *Vicārasāgara* the solution offered by the opponent to ward off the second and third kind of miseries is not dealt with. The same is not relevant in the present study and hence not analysed.

without destroying which, any other method proves futile. One may resort to medicines for cure from pain; even then it is not the ultimate solution since there is the experience of recurrence of pain. For some, disease is removed by medication but for some it is not. Thus, medicine as a solution to get rid of pain is not definite in all cases. Moreover, the one who is cured now with the medicine may be afflicted by disease in future again. Thus, the solution of medication to remove sorrow is not absolute. Absolute destruction (*ātyantika nāśa*) is that which is destroyed and does not recurr again. Since medicine cannot remove disease completely, but it afflicts again, solutions of such kind in thousands will not remove sorrow completely. But, destruction of the cause of all sorrows will remove all sorrows completely. Thus, by the removal of cause one is not affected by sorrow again. Hence, everyone desires to destroy the root cause of sorrow.

Just as one afflicted by disease wishes to regain health, knowing the prescribed disciplines, gives up unhealthy habits and destroys the cause of disease, one who wishes to get rid of sorrow totally, follows the means, knowing the Vedāntic teaching as instructed by the teacher, and destroys the cause of sorrow. This is revealed in the Upaniṣad[2] where Nārada, an exponent in all arts and sciences, longed to cross the ocean of sorrow. The scriptures declare that the only means to remove sorrow is by the knowledge of the Self. The ignorance and its effect, i.e. the world of perception seen as different from *Brahman* is said to be the cause of all sorrow. On removal of the world, with its cause, as instructed in the scripture, sorrow is completely annihilated.[3] Thus, removal of sorrow in the form of destruction of the world along with its cause is desired by all, which is the first part of the definition of liberation.

Objection: It is known that every desire presupposes a prior experience. That is, only if one has experienced a thing in the

---

[2] तरति शोकं आत्मवित् । — *CU* 7.1.3

[3] नेति नेति । — *BU* 2.3.6

past, can the same thing be desired to be experienced in the future too. In the case of removal of sorrow, a person do not desire to annihilate the world along with its root cause, by the rise of *Brahman*-knowledge, since one has never had such an experience in the past. So, such a desire for the removal of sorrow does not exist.

Advaitin: One cannot definitely formulate the nature of desire as that which is nurtured, determined by a prior experience. If it is so, then one can desire for the past eaten food in the present time, that being a desire caused by prior experience. But such a desire cannot be entertained by anyone. On the other hand, there is desire for a similar kind of food which was experienced in the past. Thus, this argument, that prior experience is a necessity for rise of desire is untenable.

The desire of the seekers to annihilate the world by the knowledge of the substratum is explained. Just as the rope is the substratum on which the "snake" gets superimposed, *Brahman* is the substratum on which the world along with its root cause is superimposed. In rope and *Brahman*, the substratum part of the superimposition is of the same class. In rope-snake instance, the sublation of "snake" is non-different from the direct knowledge of the substratum, rope. This prior experience of removal of an erroneous cognition by a seeker helps in understanding the *Brahman*-substratum. Thus, the removal of the root cause with its effects equated to the knowledge of the substratum is desired by the seekers.

BRAHMAN IS ĀNANDA

Objection: The second part of the definition of liberation, that is the attainment of *Brahman*, is also refuted, as not desired by anyone. One can desire for something experienced or known earlier. The seekers of liberation do not have prior experience of *Brahman*. If one knows *Brahman*, such a one is not a seeker, since knower of *Brahman* is liberated. The liberated one is not a seeker since he does not desire for knowledge. Due to absence of an aspirant, the definition of liberation according to Advaita is futile.

Advaitin: The above objection is untenable. Happiness is favoured by everyone and hence everyone desires for happiness. *Brahman* being eternal, infinite, and of the nature of *ānanda*, is actually sought by everyone. Moreover, if a general rule is said to be, that which is experienced in the past alone is desired, then past unfavourable experiences like disease and the sorrow experienced thereby, also has to be desired for. This is not so. One wishes for favourable prior experienced happiness and its means. The sense-pleasures reflect the *ānanda* nature of *Brahman* which is experienced by all. Similar to the sense pleasure is the original eternal infinite non-dual *Brahman-ānanda* which is desired by all.

SENSE PLEASURE IS NOT ĀNANDA

Objection: In fact, everyone desires for sense pleasure only. One who practises penance, desires for pleasure of the higher world, so gives up pleasures of this world and takes to intense painful austerities. Thus, either in this world or in the other world, everyone desires for sense pleasure only. Liberation, according to Advaita, does not deal with sense pleasure that is sought by all. Also, from Brahmā to a blade of grass, everyone engaged in sense pleasure is subject to attachment and bindings, therefore, no one would take to means like sense control, mind control, withdrawal, etc.

Advaitin: It is improper to conclude that all seek sense pleasures only. If so, then how is that everyone equally aim for happiness? If it is said that one seeks pleasure only through the sense objects, then one will not desire for the happiness obtained during deep sleep or in meditation, since sense objects are absent during deep sleep[4] and meditation. Thus, it has to be understood that all seek happiness equally but not sense pleasures alone. Moreover, one is aware of gradation in sense pleasures.[5] The natural inclination is

---

4 यत्सुषुप्तौ निर्विषय आत्मानन्दोऽनुभूयते ।
श्रुतिः प्रत्यक्षमैतिह्यमनुमानं च जाग्रति ॥ — *VC* 107

5 *TU* 2.8.

to attain an eternal, infinite, ungraded *ānanda*, which is said to be the nature of Self. Liberation, according to Advaita, is the knowledge of the Self which is of the nature of *ānanda*. A discriminative person analyses the nature of sense pleasures in stages as described below:

1. Sense pleasures are non-eternal, since it is experienced by the contact of sense-organs and objects. The sensual pleasure while experiencing is connected with some kind of pain. At the end of the sensual pleasure one experiences grief.[6] Even while experiencing the sense pleasures, one is unhappy with the thought that "this highest pleasure will perish". Thus, one engaged in sense pleasures is under the grip of sorrow. This sorrow cannot be redeemed by any kind of worldly solutions. One who tries to seek solution in the world also cannot totally remove sorrow. Even though one may succeed in removing sorrow, it recurs.
2. The second stage of discrimination is that, as long as one identifies with the body, sorrow cannot be eliminated.[7] Body is the result of *karma*, i.e. *puṇya* and *pāpa*. By the application of *anvaya-vyatireka*, one understands that the body is subject to pleasure and pain.
3. The body which is the result of *puṇya* and *pāpa* cannot be destroyed without total cessation of *puṇya* and *pāpa*. This is the third stage of discrimination. By the exhaustion of *prārabdha* the present body can be destroyed, but the results acquired through countless past births will result in future birth.
4. That *puṇya* and *pāpa* cannot perish without the destruction of attachment and hatred is the discriminative knowledge

[6] विषयेन्द्रियसंयोगाद्यत्तदग्रेऽमृतोपमम्।
परिणामे विषमिव तत्सुखं राजसं स्मृतम्॥ — *BG* XVIII.38

[7] न वै सशरीरस्य सतः प्रियाप्रिययोरपहतिरस्त्यशरीरंवाव सन्तं न प्रियाप्रिये स्पृशतः।
— *CU* 8.12.1

at the fourth stage. Even by the exhaustion of *puṇya* and *pāpa* that resulted in the present body, one engages in action, due to the predominance of likes and dislikes and reaps either *puṇya* or *papa*. Thus, in the absence of the total cessation of attachment and hatred, *karma* cannot be completely destroyed.

5. Attachment and hatred cannot be removed without the destruction of their means, namely, likes and dislikes.

6. That likes and dislikes are based on the notion of duality is the discriminative knowledge at the sixth stage. If one sees everything as different from the Self, then there rises the notion of likes and dislikes. If it is known that nothing is different from the Self, then there will be no means for likes and dislikes. The nature of the Self is neither the means to pleasure nor pain. It is of the nature of *ānanda* and there is the impossibility to know the nature of Self as *ānanda* through any means. It emerges from this that the notion of favourable and unfavourable things arises only during the vision of plurality. The notion of likes and dislikes cannot be eliminated without eliminating the notion of difference.

7. The seventh stage is the discriminative knowledge that the notion of duality is the result of ignorance of Self.[8] Thus, the cause of sorrow is Self-ignorance.

8. In this final stage of discrimination, it is clearly known that Self-ignorance is removed only by Self-knowledge, both being opposed like darkness and light and not by any other means (*karma*, *upāsanā* or any other knowledge). Ignorance of an entity is removed by the direct knowledge of that entity, like the ignorance of rope, in case of rope-snake, is removed by the direct knowledge of rope.

---

[8] यत्र हि द्वैतमिव भवति तदितर इतरं जिघ्रति। — *BU* 2.4.14
यदेव जाग्रद्भयं पश्यति तदत्राविद्या मन्यते। — *BU* 4.3.20
यत्र वा अन्यदिव स्यात् तत्र अन्योऽन्यत् पश्येत्। — *BU* 4.3.31

Therefore only, by the direct knowledge of Self, one attains *Brahman* of the nature of *ānanda*.

SENSE PLEASURE IS A REFLECTION

In relation to this, the *uttama adhikārī* questions, if *Brahman* is Self which is of the nature of *ānanda* then one should not be experiencing happiness caused by sense object contact. Since one experiences happiness caused by sense object contact, it would amount to say that Self is not of the nature of *ānanda* and one may have to conclude that *ānanda* experienced in the Self is the result of sense object contact.

The *guru* clarifies that enjoyment through external object is desired by one who is ignorant of the nature of Self. The mind of such a one, who desires for sense pleasure, is restless. In a wavery mind, the *ānanda* nature of Self does not manifest. By the attainment of the desired object, the mind is at rest (*sāttvika vṛtti*) for a moment. The thought is internal (*antarmukha*) wherein the *ānanda* nature of Self manifests. In such a case, the person is experiencing the reflection of the original *ānanda*, but unknowingly, out of delusion expresses that, "I attained happiness through the sense object". In reality, there is no happiness in an inert object.[9] The *guru* further explains that just as a disturbed mind does not register an object in front, similarly a disturbed mind, in which *rajoguṇa* is predominant, there is the absence of reflection of the *ānanda* nature of Self. As in the case of a mirror that is in motion, the reflection of face is unclear, similarly in a mind predominant with *rajoguṇa*, even though the *sat* and *cit* nature of Self are reflected, the *ānanda* nature of Self does not get reflected.

MECHANISM OF REFLECTION

The mechanism of reflection of *ānanda* in the mind is described here. When the mind desires for a liked object there is the rise of

---

[9] एतस्यैवानन्दस्यान्यानि भूतानि मात्रामुपजीवन्ति । — *BU* 4.3.32

एषोऽस्य परमानन्दो योऽखण्डैकरसात्मकः ।
अन्यानि भूतान्येतस्य मात्रामेवोपभुञ्जते ॥ — *PD* 15.2

desire-thought (*icchā vr̥tti*) and it is a disturbed mind with *rajas vr̥tti*. On attaining the object, there is the thought-mode in the form of knowledge (*jñāna vr̥tti*), that the object desired is attained, which results in the thought mode of experience (*viṣaya anubhava vr̥tti*). This is known as *sāttvika vr̥tti*, in which the *ānanda* nature of Self gets reflected.[10] It may also be explained as, on obtaining the object, the mind experiences tranquillity (*śānti vr̥tti*) is *sāttvika vr̥tti* in which the *ānanda* nature of Self gets reflected.[11] The reflection of *ānanda* in the sentient mind is said to be *viṣayānanda* or *pratibimbānanda* or *leśānanda*.

If sense object is a source of happiness, a person who enjoys a certain object, later desires for another object, should continue to receive the happiness experienced from the previous object. But the intensity of happiness experienced through the first object diminishes. In the desire for another object, there is a mental disturbance, and in such a mind, the *ānanda* nature of Self does not get reflected.

DIMINISHING NATURE OF SENSE PLEASURE

The *guru* further gives an instance to reveal the nature of sense pleasure. If it is said that sense object is the source of happiness then in the case of arrival of the son after a long time, one should experience the same intensity of happiness. It is not so. This is explained — the dear son after a long time arrives home, and on seeing the son, the father is extremely happy at the first moment. The father should experience the same level of happiness, as the son who is the cause of happiness, is near. But this does not happen so. The happiness arising from the sight of the son is enjoyed and

---

[10] In an empirical cognition, the mind goes out through the sense-organ, say, the eye, and reaches the place of the object and assumes the form of the object thus resulting in *vr̥ttivyāpti*. *Caitanya* is all-pervasive. In the cognized object there is *viṣayākāravr̥tti* and *viṣaya avacchinna caitanya* in which there is the *ānanda aṁśa*. The *ānanda aṁśa* in the *viṣaya avacchinna caitanya* reflects in the *viṣayākāra sāttvikavr̥tti*.

[11] काचिदन्तर्मुखा वृत्तिरानन्दप्रतिबिम्बभाक् ।
पुण्यभोगे भोगशान्तौ निद्रारूपेण लीयते ॥ — *PD* 3.9

the happiness experienced at every successive moment through the same sense object, namely, the son (here), begins to diminish. Thus, it is said that on obtaining an object, at that particular moment, the mind is undisturbed. In that undisturbed mind, the *ānanda* nature of Self gets reflected. What one experiences is nothing but the reflected happiness. Then one desires for other objects and mind is disturbed again. In that disturbed mind (*rajoguṇa*) the *ānanda* nature that was reflected seizes and even though the son is present, in this case, that happiness which was experienced at the first moment does not get repeated. Also, if the sense object is the source of happiness it must give happiness to all, this is not so. Therefore, sense object is not the source of happiness.

Further, by the support of secondary scriptures (Smr̥ti)[12] it is explained that the shadow planet (Rāhu) is not recognized, but is known only when there is an eclipse, where moon is the means of recognizing the shadow planet. Similarly, the Self which is devoid of experience is recognized as the subject in the presence of an object.

EXPERIENCE OF SENSE PLEASURE BY A MUKTA

The *uttama adhikārī* questions whether an enlightened person desires for sense objects and in that case is there the reflection of happiness from sense object contact. The *guru* confirms here that in an empirical pursuit, an enlightened one also is extrovert but with the knowledge that the happiness gained from sense object and the *ānanda* nature of Self is non-different. The mind can entertain only one thought at one moment. While the thought pertaining to the waker's world is invoked, the thought of dream-world is absent and in dream-world the waker's thought is absent. Similarly, when the liberated person entertains thought in the form of *ātmā*; at that time thought related to *anātmā* does not arise. When he engages in the *anātmā* thought; at that time *ātmā* thought does not arise.

---

12 अदृश्यो दृश्यते राहुर्गृहीतेन यथेन्दुना ।
तथाऽनुभवमात्रात्मा दृश्येनात्माऽवलोक्यते ॥ इति स्मृतेः । — Quoted in *SV* p. 77

Even though in one internal organ, which is the locus of different kinds of thoughts, in which simultaneously two kinds of thought — a general and a particular — may arise, then also two "particular" kinds of thought cannot arise. Just as a person carrying the money in a box does not remember it while holding the box and engaging in other activities. But at the time of transaction, the person remembers the presence of money in the box. In the same manner, when a *mukta* is engaged in external objects at the time of *vyavahāra,* the knowledge of Truth subsides. At the end of a *vyavahāra*, once again the *mukta* gets established in the Reality. So, a *mukta* also engages in worldly pursuit like an ignorant one. If the *mukta* always entertains thought of True Self, then such a *mukta* cannot even eat food. Therefore, both an ignorant and an elightened one are extrovert at the time of worldly pursuit.

The *guru* then points out the difference between an ignorant one and a *mukta.* An ignorant one is always extrovert since such a one seeks sense pleasure only. But an enlightened one is extrovert without being attached to the external objects and engages in activities and derives graded pleasures just like an ignorant one. Also, the knowledge that — "the happiness originating from the sense object contact is the reflection of Self which is of the nature of happiness. The reflected happiness is non-different from the *ānanda* nature of Self. Such a happiness derived from the sense object is only a reflection" — is known to the enlightened one. Thus, even at the time of sense pleasure, the enlightened one is established in True Self. On the other hand, an ignorant one does not know that the sense pleasure is the *ānanda* nature of the Self alone. In reality, both an enlightened and an ignorant one "experiences" *ānanda* nature of Self but the ignorant one has deluded knowledge that the source of happiness is the external object. Morever, even at the time of sense pleasure, the enlightened one is aware of:

1. The defect of external object;
2. the false nature of the objects;

3. the consequence of experience of sense enjoyments as sorrow; and
4. the reflected happiness as non-different from the *ānanda* nature of Self.

APPARENT ATTAINMENT OF ĀNANDA

In the first *taraṅga* while establishing the *prayojana* of the text *Vicārasāgara,* the Advaitic position is presented as one is of the nature of *ānanda* and on gaining *Brahman*-knowledge, it is figuratively expressed as one has "attained" *ānanda*. Since the Self, i.e. *Brahman* is of the nature of eternal *ānanda* one need not strive to gain happiness. For instance, in rope, the "snake" is non-existent at all times, but on knowing the substratum it is said "this is rope"; hence the "snake" is said to be "removed". In the same way, due to delusion one sees bondage in the Self. This bondage or sorrow is always absent in the Self and on the knowledge of the substratum Self, sorrow seems to be removed. Therefore, even though bondage is eternally absent, it is said to be removed and even though Self as the nature of *ānanda* is eternally present, it is as though attained.[13] Thus, attainment of *ānanda* and removal of sorrow are only figurative. Just as a poor person is not aware of the treasure hidden beneath the floor of his house, but walks above it brooding over his poverty, even when everyday (in deep sleep) one resolves into the Self, one grieves not knowing the *ānanda* nature of the Self.[14]

APPOSITION OF DESTRUCTION OF IGNORANCE AND ATTAINMENT OF ĀNANDA

It was mentioned that the definition of liberation is the removal of ignorance and attainment of *ānanda*. The removal of ignorance is non-existent (*pradhvaṁśa abhāva*), and attainment of *ānanda* is existent, both refers to the same locus, that is, liberation. The existent and non-existent entities are mutually opposed to each

[13] नित्यप्राप्तस्य प्राप्तिः । — *SV*, p. 23

[14] *CU* 8.3.2.

other and contradictory characteristics cannot coexist simultaneously in the same locus. Therefore, the said definition is incorrect. Such an argument is raised in the first *taraṅga* and it is shown that in the case of liberation as defined in Advaita Vedānta, such a contradiction does not arise.

"The absence of a thing is the substratum."[15] Based on this reasoning it is said that the Self is the substratum of absence of bondage, hence Self is of the nature of absence of bondage. Removal of ignorance and its effects is the form of substratum that is *Brahman* consciousness.[16] Just as the superimposed snake is of the nature of its substratum, viz. rope alone,[17] the superimposed names and forms are of the nature of substratum, the consciousness principle. There is nothing other than consciousness.[18] Therefore, removal of ignorance is equated with *Brahman* which is the substratum of the superimposed perceived world. *Brahman* is the self-evident entity and hence is a positive entity. Therefore, removal of ignorance is positive in nature. Here, there is the coexistence of non-existent ignorance and existent *ānanda* which is non-contradictory.

6.2 Jīvanmukti

The *guru* restates that liberation is the removal of Self-ignorance by Self-knowledge and defines *jīvanmukti* as one who is established in the Self as *Brahman*-consciousness with the knowledge that world is an appearance.

Having taught the highest truth to the three seekers, the *guru* describes the life of a *jīvanmukta* in the seventh *taraṅga* of

---

15 अभावस्य अधिकरण रूपत्वात् ।

16 यस्मिन् अधिकरणे यः अभावः उच्यते तत् अधिकरणं तस्य अभावस्य स्वरूपं भवति ।

17 The erroneously perceived snake has rope as its substratum. On knowing that "this is rope", the rope-knowledge destroys the "snake" at that very moment. Therefore, the destruction of "snake" and the knowledge of the substratum, that is the rope, are conditioned by the same moment. Thus, the removal of "snake" is nothing but the substratum, rope.

18 आरोपितप्रतियोगिकप्रध्वंसस्य प्रतियोग्यधिष्ठाने भासमानस्य अधिष्ठानमात्रत्व नियमात्।
— *SV*, p. 23

Vicārasāgara. He says that just as the dry leaves move by the course of the wind, due to *prārabdha* the enlightened one acts differently. A *mukta* at times travel in vehicles like chariot, horse and elephant, and sees wonderful places. At times, he walks barefoot. His sleeping place, seat, etc. are not the same. At times he eats good food, at times without eating, he resides in the mountain caves, lies on the hardest rock and spends the night. At times thousands of people worship him. At times he is criticized by the *karmī*s as *ubhayaloka-bhraṣṭa* (neither *jñānī* nor *karmī*). The residual *puṇya* of the *mukta* reaches those who praise him and the residual *pāpa* goes to those who censure him.[19] Thus, the activities of a *mukta* are not governed by code of laws. For the knower of Truth, there is no possibility of delusion, doubt, etc. At any time, at any place there is nothing to be accomplished since in him difference, delusion, fear, etc. are completely destroyed. The enlightened has the direct knowledge of *Brahman-Ātman*, as non-dual and self-luminous, which is gained from the primary source of knowledge, the Vedas.

JĪVANMUKTA NOT GOVERNED BY LAWS

Objection: It is improper to say that an enlightened person is not governed by the laws. The guideline to conduct oneself in the prescribed stage and status of life is enjoined in the scriptures. A *jīvanmukta* should adhere to the injunctions of the scriptures. The enjoinments prescribed for a renunciate are taken to be the factors governing the life of a *jīvanmukta*. A *jīvanmukta* cannot involve in ephemeral activities. He should withdraw from the sensory world and concentrate on the prescribed symbol. This restrains the mind from wandering in the empirical world. In order to attain a single pointed concentration, a *jīvanmukta* should take to the means of *samādhi* and free himself from performance of activities. The absorption in the chosen symbol and the negation of the external

---

19 ये ज्ञानिनं स्तुवन्ति भजन्ति अर्चयन्ति तान्प्रति ज्ञानिकृतं आगामि पुण्यं गच्छति। ये ज्ञानिनं निन्दन्ति द्विषन्ति दुःखप्रदानं कुर्वन्ति तान्प्रति ज्ञानिकृतं सर्वागामि क्रियमाणं पदवाच्यं कर्म पापात्मकं तद्गच्छति।

— *Tattvabodha*, p. 75

world are said to be the states of *samādhi*. Thus, a *mukta*, eliminating the projection and delusion of the world, remains in the ocean of *ānanda*.

Answer: The above view is untenable. According to Advaita, an enlightened person is not governed by rules to perform any action. The cause of action is ignorance, its effects give rise to plurality, delusion produces likes and dislikes, all of which are absent in a *mukta*. What remains is only *prārabdha*, which is the cause of action in a *mukta*. The *prārabdha* varies and hence the action of a *mukta* is different. But no rule as such is enjoined for *mukta*s.

Objection: Even though there is absence of enjoinment of obligatory duties, a *mukta* is instructed to refrain from performance of prohibited actions.

Answer: This cannot be so, since a *mukta* engages only in the minimum action of appeasing hunger, thirst, etc. Prior to *Brahman*-knowledge, through the fourfold qualifications, dispassion was developed by knowing the intense defects of sense objects in the form of sorrow through birth, death, old age, disease, etc. This quality of dispassion is intense in a *mukta* who has falsified the world by *Brahman*-knowledge. By the strength of the direct knowledge of Self, a *mukta* has the conviction of the falsity of the non-self objects and reality is not superimposed on the non-self world. Due to this intense dispassion, attachment is not produced. Attachment is the root cause for *pravṛtti*. In a *mukta*, attachment is impossible and hence he cannot take to action. Action in the form of sustenance of the body is performed without developing attachment and this again depends on *prārabdha*.

SAMĀDHIVĀDIN

According to the Samādhivādin, since the nature of the mind is unstable, it has to be quietened through the means of meditation and a *mukta* should ever remain in *samādhi* so that he does not engage in any activity (*pravṛtti*). The impressions of withdrawal are invoked, by negating the extrovert impressions, because of which a single-pointed concentration of the mind is attained and this is said to be *samādhi*.[20] The cause of sorrow is the operation of the triad in the form of knower, known and instrument of knowledge. A *jīvanmukta* should abandon this triad and remain in *samādhi*.

Savikalpa and Nirvikalpa Samādhi

There are two kinds of *samādhi*: *Savikalpa* and *Nirvikalpa*.

1. *Savikalpa* — The knower, known and the object of knowledge are perceived as non-dual *Brahman*. This state of modal thought in the mind is known as *savikalpa samādhi*.

   Savikalpa is of two types:

   (a) the thought-mode with the words "I am *Brahman*" (*śabdānuviddha*); and

   (b) the flow of thoughts without any words (*śabda-ananuviddha*).

   Savikalpa is the means to *nirvikalpa*. The plurality perceived in *savikalpa* is the appearance of the causal *Brahman*. As in the case of perceiving the clay, in the clay products, here too plurality is non-different from *Brahman*.

2. *Nirvikalpa* — Remaining in the thought-mode of non-dual *Brahman* without the perception of the triad is known as *nirvikalpa samādhi*. Here, the presence of triad is not perceived. As the case of salt dissolves in water is known, but the same is imperceptible, here too the difference is imperceptible.

---

[20] व्युत्थानसंस्कारतिरस्कारेण निरोधसंस्कारप्रकटनेन च सहान्तःकरणस्यैकाग्रतापरिणामः समाधिः ।
— *SV*, p. 330

निर्विकारतया वृत्त्या ब्रह्माकारतया पुनः ।
वृत्तिविस्मरणं सम्यक् समाधिर्ज्ञानसंज्ञकः ॥ — *AB* 124

अथातो संप्रवक्ष्यामि ध्यानं संसारनाशनम् ।
अथातो संप्रवक्ष्यामि समाधिं भवनाशनम् ।
— *Jābāla Darśana Upaniṣad* 9.1 and 10.1

Suṣupti and Nirvikalpa Samādhi

In *suṣupti* (deep sleep), there is causal ignorance wherein the mind is resolved and hence thoughts are absent. In *nirvikalpa samādhi*, the mental modification in the form *Brahman* is present. The thought-mode of *Brahman* evoked in *savikalpa* is retained in *nirvikalpa*. The presence of mind with thought-mode is imperceptible in *nirvikalpa*. There is the remembrance of the happiness enjoyed during *nirvikalpa samādhi* and this indicates the presence of thought-mode in subtle form. In the total absence of mind, in *nirvikalpa samādhi*, the body identification should fall, as in deep sleep, but this does not happen. Mind is present in its subtle form during *nirvikalpa samādhi*.

Nirvikalpa samādhi is also of two kinds:

(a) *Advaita-bhāvanā* — the mental modification in the form of Advaita *Brahman*; and

(b) *Advaita-avasthā* — in the intense *advaita-bhāvanā* stage the mental modification of *Brahman* attains tranquillity. It is the state where mental modes are absent. As the water particles disappear in a hot iron plate, the mind enters into a higher state from *advaita-bhāvanā* to *advaita-avasthā*. The seven stages of *samādhi* are:

1. *Śubha icchā* — one who possesses virtues and noble qualities.
2. *Vicāraṇa* — one who has taken to listening and retrospection of the Vedāntic statements.
3. *Tanu mānasī* — one who meditates on the Vedāntic statements.
4. *Sattvāpatti* — one who gains direct knowledge. Such a one is known as *Brahmavit*.
5. *Asaṁśaktiḥ* — one who reduces the latent impressions or habitual notions, who meditates and dissolves the state of concentration by oneself. Such a one is known as *brahmavitvara*.

6. *Padārtha bhāvanī* — one who further reduces the latent impressions and can come out of *samādhi* by putting forth effort. Such a one is known as *brahmavitvarīyān*.
7. *Turyaga* — one who nullifies the latent impressions and enters into a state of *samādhi* which cannot be disturbed by oneself or by others. Such a one is known as *brahmavariṣṭha*.

Suṣupti and Advaita-avasthā Samādhi

In deep sleep, the mind and its mental mode resolve into the causal body or ignorance and in *advaita-avasthā samādhi*, the mental mode resolves into self-luminous *Brahman*. In deep sleep, ignorance and happiness are experienced. In this *samādhi*, there is the illumination of the unconcealed *Brahman ānanda*. The resolution of the mind into the luminous *Brahman*-consciousness is impossible since *Brahman* is not the material cause of the mind. An effect resolves into its material cause. In the example cited earlier, the water particles do not resolve into the hot iron plate as the hot iron plate is not the material cause of water particles. The material cause of water is fire. It is figuratively mentioned that water particles resolve into the hot iron plate. In the same manner, during *samādhi*, *rajas* and *tamas* are completely destroyed, the thought-mode resolves into the causal body, which is its material cause. It is figuratively said that thought resolves into *Brahman*-consciousness.

Obstacles to Nirvikalpa Samādhi

There are four obstacles to *nirvikalpa samādhi*:

1. *Laya*: The mind withdraws naturally due to tiredness or sleep. The absence of mental mode results in sleep wherein *Brahman* is concealed. In such a case, an attempt is to be made to deliberately evoke the thoughts. This is known as *citta-sambodhana* (waking up). The obstacle in the form of *laya* is caused by tiredness or sleep.
2. *Vikṣepa*: Just as a sparrow frightened on seeing a cat enters

into a safe place that is devoid of any danger and unable to find shelter in this place, the sparrow flies out and experiences sorrow or death, seeing the world as the cause of sorrow, the mind objectifies the non-dual *ānanda* and withdraws. But since the inner consciousness is extremely subtle, the mind unable to remain stable does not experience the consciousness-*ānanda*. The mind wanders again becoming extrovert. This extrovert mind is said to be affected by the obstacle known as *vikṣepa*. The nature of *ānanda* cannot be experienced in an unstable mind. Therefore, even when the mind was withdrawn, it could not modify into the mental mode of *Brahman*. To overcome this obstacle of *vikṣepa* one should practise to control the mind by analysing the defect of the external world.

3. *Kaṣāya*: The mind is subjected to defects in the form of attachment, hatred, etc. This is known as *kaṣāya*. It is of two kinds: (i) *External*: attachment or hatred centred on external objects like wealth, house, etc. This is a hurdle that obstructs one from entering into *samādhi*. (ii) *Internal*: remembering the problems of the past or imagining problems of the future time. These two obstacles do not allow one to take to *samādhi*. This is a hurdle that obstructs one during *samādhi*. The five stages of experience of the internal organ are.

   (a) *kṣepa*: it is a *rajas*-predominant extrovert mind involved with the world, body or scriptures. *Lokavāsanā*: an intense obsession of being praised by others without censure. *Dehavāsanā*: attempting to get rid of diseases or demerits or impurities in gross, subtle bodies, seeking gem, *mantra*, medicines, pilgrimage, etc. for merit to remove all sufferings completely, or else improvising the nourishment, beautifying, earning merits, such an obsessed impression is *dehavāsanā*. *Śāstravāsanā*: study of all scriptures to grasp the meaning and then to follow — this obsessive impression is *śāstravāsanā*.

(b) *mūḍhatā*: it is a *tamas*-predominant mind which expresses in the form of sleep, tiredness or negligence.

(c) *vikṣepa*: the restrained thought in meditation at times becomes extrovert.

(d) *ekāgrata*: The identity of a past and a present thought is single-pointedness. The mind is not devoid of thoughts but is sustained in the thought of *Brahman*. The past and present thoughts have *Brahman* as the object of meditation.

(e) *nirodha*: It is the incessant stream of thought-flow gained in the previous stage. The first two stages do not lead to meditation. The last three stages are conducive for meditation.

4. *Rasāsvāda*: A meditator "experiences" *Brahman-ānanda*. The *vikṣepa* kind of obstacle is destroyed at this stage. The absence of sorrow yields experience of happiness. It is like a person carrying a heavy bundle, is in pain and when the person shrugs off the bundle he is at ease. This happiness or pleasure is not a result of sense object contact. By getting rid of the load, he expresses "I am happy". In the same way, on removal of *vikṣepa*, which is the cause of sorrow, there is the experience of happiness which is known as *rasāsvāda*. If one is contented with this happiness, then further travel into *Brahman-ānanda* without adjuncts is impossible. One remains, experiencing a conditional happiness. Thus, the experience of *ānanda* as a result of destruction of sorrow, which is known as *rasāsvāda*, in *samādhi* is an obstacle.

   Rasāsvāda also could be described as the transition from *savikalpa* to *nirvikalpa*. While *savikalpa* is experience of happiness with adjuncts, *nirvikalpa* is experience of happiness without adjuncts. Thus, the experience of happiness either by removal of *vikṣepa* or through *savikalpa* is known as *rasāsvāda*. *Rasāsvāda*, which is of two kinds, is to be given up, since both the kinds are obstacle to *nirvikalpa* experience of *ānanda*. Thus, in *nirvikalpa*, these four obstacles have to be diligently avoided to gain the experience of *ānanda* in meditation. This is known as *jīvanmukti* and one who engages in such a practice is known as a *jīvanmukta*. This is the contention of the non-Advaitic schools of thought. While Advaita Vedānta recognizes the role of *samādhi* as a means to *citta ekāgratā*, *samādhi* is not seen in relation to *mukti*. This idea of Samādhivādin is refuted.

Refutation of Samādhivādin

The above-mentioned contention that an enlightened one refrains from action and takes to meditation based on the Vedic injunction is untenable. A *jīvanmukta* is free from injunctions. The lifestyle of a *jīvanmukta* is unfettered. On gaining the non-dual *Brahman*-knowledge, the knower of *Brahman* is non-different from *Īśvara*. Veda is said to be a manifestation of *Īśvara*. Such a Veda cannot command *Īśvara* or a *mukta* who is non-different from *Īśvara*. That, a *jīvanmukta* requires injunction for withdrawal too is untenable. A *jīvanmukta* is described as *niraṅkuśa*,[21] one who is not subject to enjoinments or prohibitions.

Nididhyāsana and Samādhi

It is important to note the difference between *nididhyāsana* and *samādhi* here, as explained in the first *taraṅga*. After the cessation of duality thought, the incessant flow of *brahmākāra-vṛtti* is known as *nididhyāsana*. The result of *nididhyāsana* is *samādhi*. Thus *samādhi* is part of *nididhyāsana* and need not be attained by distinct means. Like a branch of a tree that is bent and naturally lies low without any effort, in the same way, without self-effort, in the knowledge generated by *aham brahmāsmi* there is the absence of non-self and the presence of Self thought, this is known as *samādhi* (*sākṣātkāra vṛtti*). On the other hand, with self-effort, like a branch that is not

---

21 साङ्कुशा विषयैस्तृप्तिरियं तृप्तिर्निरङ्कुशा ।
कृतं कृत्यं प्रापणीयं प्राप्तमित्येव तृप्यति ॥ — *PD* 7.252

bent and can be bent by effort, in the same way, attaining the incessant thought-flow of Self by putting forth effort is known as *nididhyāsana*. At the end of *nididhyāsana, brahmākāra vṛtti* is withdrawn by effort. The word *samādhi* means absence of illumination of triad which is known as *nirvikalpaka samādhi*. By the word *nididhyāsana* the triad is present in the form of meditator, meditated object and process of meditation, and it is known as *savikalpaka samādhi*.[22]

6.3 On Prārabdha of a Mukta

According to Advaita, the cause of bondage is ignorance. The effect of ignorance is duality which gives rise to delusion in the form of favourable and unfavourable experiences. On gaining the Self-knowledge, ignorance and its effects get destroyed and a *jīvanmukta* is free from all kinds of limitations. The continuity of the life is dependent on *prārabdha karma*. The cause of action in a *jīvanmukta* is due the operation of *prārabdha*. It is varied in individuals and hence the response of a *jīvanmukta* is also varied. The conduct of a *jīvanmukta* does not fall under codified laws.

One of the fourfold qualifications to enquire into the Vedāntic statement is dispassion that is developed by analysing the defective nature of the sense objects. Even after the rise of knowledge, this dispassion is intense since the Self-knowledge dismisses the non-self world as false. A *jīvanmukta,* though interacts in this world, does not pose reality to the non-self world. The action of a *jīvanmukta* is based on *prārabdha*. On sublation of "snake" delusion by "rope" knowledge, the reminiscence of "snake" experience continues in the form of fear, etc. This experience of fear, etc. is overcome in due course of time. In the same manner, even after the removal of ignorance, the material cause of the world, the prior non-self experience may continue in the mind of a *jīvanmukta*.

---

[22] ताभ्यां निर्विचिकित्सेऽर्थे चेतसः स्थापितस्य यत् ।
एकतानत्वमेतद्धि निदिध्यासनमुच्यते ॥ — *PD* 1.54

वृत्तीनामनुवृत्तिस्तु प्रयत्नात्प्रथमादपि ।
अदृष्टासकृदभ्याससंस्कारसचिवाद्भवेत् ॥ — *PD* 1.57

It is like the released arrow from the bow imagining to be a tiger in front, but on understanding that the animal is a cow, though the intention is not to kill the cow, the released arrow cannot be stopped.[23] The released arrow terminates when the speed is lost. Similarly, *prārabdha* is destroyed only by exhaustion and not otherwise. Thus, even though *Brahman*-knowledge is attained, *prārabdha* causes experience of the world.

A *jīvanmukta* is aware of the defects in sense objects and hence cannot engage in action. But, contrarily, it is said that an enlightened one, engages in activity, knowing the defects of the sense objects. Just as due to unhealthy habits one is afflicted by a disease and even when one is aware of the results caused by the disease, still, one takes to such unhealthy habits, and it is due to *prārabdha*, in the same manner, a *jīvanmukta* engages in activity with the knowledge of sensory limitations which is attributed to *prārabdha*. This is explained in terms of three types of *karma*:

1. *Sañcita* — It is the unfructified past accumulated results of actions of countless births. In a granary the grains are filled from the top but to consume, the grains are collected from the bottom; similarly the fresh results of actions get accumulated as even the results of acquired actions fructify. *Sañcita karma* accumulated over many births is that action manifesting in the witness-consciousness conditioned by the internal organ with the concealment power of ignorance. *Sañcita karma* is destroyed by the Self-knowledge
2. *Āgāmī* — The actions performed in the current human body fructifies over a period of time. Just as one sows the seeds in the present, expecting yields in future, so also the actions performed now give results in future, and it is known as *āgāmī*. On the rise of *Brahman*-knowledge, the doership, etc. are destroyed and hence *āgāmī karma* is absent.

---

23 व्याघ्रबुद्धया विनिर्मुक्तो बाणः पश्चात्तु गोमतौ ।
न तिष्ठति छिनत्त्येव लक्ष्यं वेगेन निर्भरम् ॥ — *VC* 452

3. *Prārabdha* — The fructified results experienced in the current body giving rise to experiences of pleasure or pain manifesting in the projection power of ignorance is *prārabdha*. The activities of a *jīvanmukta* are based on *prārabdha*, which is destroyed only by exhaustion. That a *jīvanmukta* is subject to fructified results is proclaimed in the *Bhagavad-Gītā*.[24]

EXHAUSTION OF PRĀRABDHA

One may argue on the exhaustion of *prārabdha karma* in the following manner. There are different types of *prārabdha karma*. Based on the general *prārabdha* one attains a particular body. The specific *prārabdha* is the cause for origination of many other bodies. If a person attains knowledge being in the very first body, even then the enlightened person should take to many other bodies. This is so because *prārabdha* cannot be destroyed by knowledge, but has to be exhausted through experience.

Such an argument is dismissed by Vedānta *ekadeśī*. An enlightened person assumes as many bodies as required to exhaust *prārabdha* and since he has already attained knowledge, on the exhaustion of the final part of *prārabdha*, he attains *videhamukti*.

This contention of *ekadeśī* is refuted by Advaita Siddhānta. The scriptural statements declare the non-travel of *prāṇa* of a *mukta* and the resolution of senses and mind here itself.[25] Without the aid of *prāṇa*, one cannot attain another body. Therefore, the view that a *mukta* assumes another body for exhaustion of *prārabdha* is untenable. When the result of *karma* is to be reaped in many bodies, then it is said that, the knowledge is gained only in the last birth, and not in prior births. *Brāhmaṇa-hatyā*, etc. is one action, but results in many experiences like suffering in hell, becoming a dog, fox, snake, etc. This is said in Smṛti, Purāṇas, etc. Scripture also says that in a particular month, if one worships the Lord on the full-

---

[24] सदृशं चेष्टते स्वस्याः प्रकृतेर्ज्ञानवानपि ।
प्रकृतिं यान्ति भूतानि निग्रहः किं करिष्यति ॥ — *BG* III.33

[25] न तस्य प्राणाः उत्क्रामन्ति । — *BU* 4.4.6; अत्र ब्रह्म समश्नुते । — *BU* 4.4.7

moon day, one will gain wealth and in the next seven births will be born as a brāhmaṇa. Thus, many births caused by one *karma* in the form of *prārabdha* is an obstacle for final release.

Even if one does *sādhanā*s, in the form of *śravaṇa*, etc. there would still be the *prārabdha*-obstacle, and knowledge would not rise. This obstacle is known as *āgāmī pratibandha*. Therefore, it is said that knowledge rises in the last body, wherein the *prārabdha* has been exhausted in the previous births and the obstacle is removed. The *śravaṇa*, etc. undertaken in many births, germinate in final birth and hence the performed *sādhanā*s are not redundant. *Prārabdha* of (*jaḍa*) Bharata[26] was the cause for three births. Even if the *sādhanā sāmagrī* is present, he could not gain the knowledge. In the third birth, he gained knowledge without instruction, because of the *sādhanā*s undertaken in previous births.

PRĀRABDHA AS AN OBSTACLE

Prārabdha that has to be exhausted through several bodies is an obstacle to the rise of knowledge. Dull intellect, attachment to sense objects,[27] displaced logic and contradictory ideas[28] are the obstacles of the present (*vartamāna pratibandha*). The obstacle of the past (*bhūta pratibandha*) is the remembrance of son, wife, wealth, etc. even after renunciation. The future obstacle (*āgāmī pratibandha*) is the desire for the experience of *brahmaloka*, etc. or the experience of residual *prārabdha* of the past birth.[29] Just as attachment towards sense object, a dull intellect,[30] and an inclination towards dualistic statements of the scriptures, are obstacles to the rise of knowledge, the *vilakṣaṇa prārabdha* or the residue *prārabdha,* which is the cause of many births, is an obstacle to the rise of knowledge. The

---

[26] *BP* 5.

[27] अशास्त्रीयमपि द्वैतं तीव्रं मन्दमिति द्विधा ।
कामक्रोधादिकं तीव्रं मनोराज्यं तथेतरत् ॥ — *PD* 4.49

[28] *BG* XVIII.33-35.

[29] *PD* 9.32-46.

[30] मेधावी पुरुषो विद्वानूहापोहविचक्षणः ।
अधिकार्यात्मविद्यायामुक्तलक्षणलक्षितः ॥ — *VC* 16

obstacles as a result of *prārabdha* have to be exhausted and only after the exhaustion of *prārabdha*, the obstacles are destroyed and in the final birth, knowledge arises.

As in the case of Vāmadeva and other sages, even when *śravaṇa*, etc. were done in the past birth, knowledge was not gained because of the strength of residual *prārabdha* that had to be exhausted through several births. In the case of Vāmadeva, the *śravaṇa*, etc. done in the past birth produced knowledge in the womb itself. Thereafter, there is no association with the body. Thus, the action of a *mukta* in the present body is dependent on *prārabdha*. It is performed only for the sustenance of the body and is not instigated by attachment or hatred. Hence, a *mukta* is free from all kinds of actions.

THREE KINDS OF PRĀRABDHA

Prārabdha is divided into three kinds as *manda*, *tīvra* and *tīvratara*. The *manda prārabdha* consists of feeble merit, wherein one has to put forth more effort to gain a favourable result; with a feeble demerit and with less effort an unfavourable result can be avoided. In the *tīvra prārabdha*, the merit and demerit are of medium nature, hence less effort is to be put forth to gain favourable result and more effort to avoid unfavourable result. The *tīvratara prārabdha* has intense merit and intense demerit. Due to intense merit one enjoys favourable results, without much effort to gain them, but one cannot avoid unfavourable results that occur due to intense demerit. It is improper to say that one cannot avoid *prārabdha* and hence human effort is futile since the compensatory actions mentioned in the scriptures like medicine, *mantra*, *yoga*, etc. will become invalid. The direct compensatory actions too will be futile. Thus, *prārabdha* and human effort are like the two wheels of a chariot.

FIVE EXPRESSIONS OF PRĀRABDHA

Based on the grades categorized as *uttama*, *madhyama*, *kaniṣṭha*, *adhama* and *adhamatara*, *prārabdha* is of five kinds.

1. *Uttama Prārabdha* — a predominantly withdrawn life due to dispassion from birth to death, like Śuka, Vāmadeva, Sanaka and others.
2. *Madhyama Prārabdha* — a life of *pravṛtti* prior to knowledge and a life of *nivṛtti* on gaining knowledge, like Yājñavalkya.
3. *Kaniṣṭha Prārabdha* — a predominantly action-oriented life, like Janaka.
4. *Adhama Prārabdha* — a life of *nivṛtti* prior to knowledge and a life of *pravṛtti* on gaining knowledge, like Śikhidhvaja, Rahūgaṇa[31] and Priyavrata.[32]
5. *Adhamatara Prārabdha* — a life of *kāmacāra, kāmavāda, kāmabhakṣa,* like Dattātreya and others.

THREE MODES OF EXHAUSTION OF PRĀRABDHA

There are three modes of exhaustion of *prārabdha.*[33] The actions of a *jīvanmukta* can be based on desire, without desire, or on others desire. A *jīvanmukta* may desire to take to action, may remain without a desire to act or act to fufil other's desires. In all the cases, a *jīvanmukta* acts selflessly. The condition for exhausting desire is produced by *prārabdha* and without desire, exhaustion of fructified results is not possible.

1. In the case of Yājñavalkya, the exhaustion of *prārabdha* is found in two stages. First, he was engaged in activities without any disinterest and later developed disinterest so as to renounce the worldly pursuits.
2. Janaka, known for his spirituality had to exhaust *prārabdha* in administering the kingdom. Though he did not develop disinterest to renounce everything neither did he develop hatred.
3. Vāmadeva developed disinterest in action at an early stage and renounced. He never took to activity.

---

31 *BP* 5.10-14.

32 *BP* 5.1.

33 *PD* 7.152-62.

4. Śikhidhvaja engaged in more activities after knowledge.

Thus, the enlightened ones got involved in various activities even after gaining knowledge. The various responses do not imply that their level of knowledge is different. They all enjoy the same state of liberation gained through knowledge.[34] Their actions vary since their *prārabdhas* are varied. By the reduction of activities, the happiness gained through liberation is manifold and by taking to actions the happiness, based on liberating knowledge, weakens.

ON PRĀRABDHA-PRAUḌHIVĀDA

The position of Advaitin with regard to the *prārabdha karma* in an enlightened one is explained from different perspectives. One way of explanation of *prārabdha* in a *mukta* is by stating that the incomprehensible direct knowledge of *Brahman* identity dismisses *māyā* as non-existent and thereby *prārabdha karma*, etc. are impossible. It is also argued that even if an indescribable phenomenal reality of *māyā* is accepted then too *prārabdha* is not possible.[35] On the rise of knowledge, *prārabdha* is not destroyed, says Śaṅkara.[36] At the same time, he questions the existence of *prārabdha* in the case of a *mukta*.[37]

Moreover, according to Dṛṣṭi-sṛṣtivādins and Ekajīvavādins of Advaita School, the world is non-existent like dream and shell-silver, since knowledge destroys its root cause, viz. ignorance along with which *prārabdha* also dissolves. Thus, we find varied views related to the nature of *prārabdha* in a *jīvanmukta* according to Advaita presented from various perspectives. The root cause of *karma* is *māyā*, according to Advaita and *māyā* is described in three different ways in the scriptures.[38] Based on the

---

34 कृष्णो भोगी शुकस्त्यागी नृपौ जनकराघवौ ।
वसिष्ठः कर्मकर्ता च त एते ज्ञानिन समाः ॥ — Quoted in *SV*, p. 338

35 *AB* 90-97.

36 *VC* 451-52.

37 *VC* 459-67.

38 *SV*, p. 325; *PD* 6.128-30

understanding of the concept of *māyā*, a seeker extends his understanding with regard to the nature of a *mukta*. However, here we consider that the action of a *mukta* is based on his *prārabdha*.

Śaṅkara in his *Aparokṣānubhūti*,[39] *Vivekacūḍāmaṇi*[40], etc. mentions that on the rise of *Brahman*-knowledge, a *mukta* not only burns *sañcita* and *āgāmī* but also *prārabdha karmas*. If this is so, then actions like eating will be impossible. Hence, the statement of Śaṅkara is to be understood in the light that from the point of view of a *mukta*, there is no relation between action and its results. Thus, negation of all actions includes negation of *prārabdha* also. This does not dismiss, the experience, in case of a *mukta*. The *sañcita* of a *mukta* is destroyed by knowledge. There is no relation with the *āgāmī karma* and *prārabdha* is destroyed only by exhaustion. Therefore, a *mukta* takes to action because of his *prārabdha*.

NATURE OF DESIRE OF A MUKTA

The *kaniṣṭha adhikārī* questions the possibility of rise of desire based on *prārabdha* in case of a liberated person even though scriptures declare that an enlightened person does not have desire. The *guru* clarifies that an ignorant person is bound by desires and considers them to be the attributes of Self. Whereas, even when the desires, etc. arise, a *mukta* knows that they are not the attributes of the Self but they are the modifications of the mind. Since, a *mukta* does not see desire, etc. as attributes of the Self, the scriptures declare that they are free from desires, etc. Thus, even though a *mukta* engages in activities, he is a non-doer.[41] This is declared in *Gītā*[42] that a *mukta* engages in activities but he knows "I am not the doer".

---

[39] *AB* 90-99.

[40] *VC* 453-463.

[41] स न साधुना कर्मणा भूयान्नो एवासाधुना कनीयान् । — *BU* 4.4.22

[42] नैव किंचित्करोमीति युक्तो मन्येत तत्त्ववित् ।
पश्यन्शृण्वन्स्पृशञ्जिघ्रन्नश्नन्गच्छन्स्वपञ्श्वसन् ॥
प्रलपन्विसृजन्गृह्णन्नुन्मिषन्निमिषन्नपि ।
इन्द्रियाणीन्द्रियार्थेषु वर्तन्त इति धारयन् ॥ — *BG* V.8-9

A *mukta* knows that "I am unassociated, free from modifications, of the nature of consciousness *Brahman*". From the absolute angle, he is a non-doer. From the empirical angle, he is a performer and enjoyer. He exhausts *prārabdha karma*. Even though *mukta* experiences because of *prārabdha*, he is not attached to such experiences. Attachment is not caused by sense-organs. Sense-organs present the objects objectively. Neither is *ātmā* the cause of attachment. *Ātmā* illumines the perceived objects and itself remains unaffected. The mind has the capacity to discriminate the qualities and defects of objects. Hence mind develops attachment towards the desired objects. This kind of attachment does not rise in the mind of a *mukta*. The mind of a *mukta* is serene and withdrawn. According to the scriptures attachment itself is an indication of ignorance.[43]

Objection: If there is no attachment in the case of a *mukta* then he cannot engage in any activity like consuming food. Then *prārabdha* cannot be exhausted. Based on the universal law of *karma*, a *mukta* also have to exhaust *prārabdha*. Thus, for the sake of exhaustion of *prārabdha* one should accept the rise of desire in the mind of an enlightened person.

Answer: This cannot be so. A *mukta* who is devoid of any desire, experiences the rise of desires due to *prārabdha*. But this desire of a *mukta* is non-binding and hence its dissolution does not require the teachings of Vedānta. This non-binding desire is under the control of the *mukta* and it is unaffecting since it is weakened because of falsification, like a roasted seed. Such a desire of a *mukta* cannot bring about *saṁsāra*. For the bare sustenance of the gross body he eats, in keeping with the injunctions and does not consume food that are prohibited. Moreover, since a detached *jñānī* has falsified the objects, the desires arising from these false objects do not affect him. Just as a tight rope-walker or a stick-walker walks or dances on the rope/stick but his mind is stable and alert, or just as a woman who carries pot with milk on her

[43] रागो लिङ्गमबोधस्य चित्तव्यायामभूमिषु। — *NS* 4.67

head engages in gossip with friends but is alert with regard to the milk-pot on her head, the mind of a *mukta* may be engaged in activities based on *prārabdha* but he is ever alert with regard to the nature of the Self. Moreover, the sense-organs of a *mukta* can engage itself without attachment. A *mukta* remains in the nature of the Self; he does not develop intense attachment, since he knows that these are false experiences. At times (mind will have *rāga-dveṣa* to some extent), a *mukta,* under the grip of *prārabdha,* may experience imbalance of mind like an elephant during the flow of rut but the power of discrimination dormant like a sleeping lion, wakes up the *mukta* immediately and detects the defects, balances the mind, freeing it from extreme emotions at the mental level itself.

A *mukta* need not act to accomplish anything. An ignorant person alone engages in action. He considers that there are things other than oneself to be accomplished and hence they should be attained with effort. One who firmly knows that there is nothing to be accomplished nor is there a desire to become someone else, there is serenity and no fascination for any objects, such a one is liberated. *Jñānī* does not "perceive" anything other than Him (Existence–Consciousness–Absolute Peace) and hence a *jñānī* does not engage in performance of action.[44]

NATURE OF KARMA AND UPĀSANĀ OF A MUKTA

The *kaniṣṭha adhikārī* seeks clarification about the performance of *karma* and *upāsanā* by a *jīvanmukta*. He asks that if a *jīvanmukta* gives up performance of action then will he incur demerit? So, a *mukta* has to continue the performance of action and meditation. The *guru* clarifies that, generally, by the non-performance of noble actions (*śubhakarma*) one does not incur demerit[45] but only by the

---

[44] योगयुक्तो विशुद्धात्मा विजितात्मा जितेन्द्रियः।
सर्वभूतात्मभूतात्मा कुर्वन्नपि न लिप्यते॥ — *BG* V.7

[45] कथमसतः सज्जायेतेति। — *CU* 6.2.2;
नासतो विद्यते भावो नाभावो विद्यते सतः।
उभयोरपि दृष्टोऽन्तस्त्वनयोस्तत्त्वदर्शिभिः॥ — *BG* II.16

performance of a prohibited action one reaps demerit. Therefore, giving up of action does not result in acquisition of demerit. In the case of a *mukta,* no kind of demerit is incurred.[46] That is, a *mukta* is aware of the fact that both merit and demerit have the internal organ for their support and hence not real and it is only due to ignorance they get manifested falsely. This false projection of the merits, etc. due to ignorance is absent in a *mukta.* Thus, the *guru* says, giving up of noble actions and performance of improper actions do not produce demerit in the case of a *mukta.*[47]

To the question that a *mukta* may have to perform action and meditation to enjoy the liberation gained, the *guru* explains that knowledge is of two kinds — mediocre (*manda*) and firm (*dr̥ḍha*). *Manda jñāna* is a knowledge riddled with doubts and *dr̥ḍha jñāna* is the knowledge devoid of doubts. One with firm knowledge has no actions to be performed. The knowledge without doubt that rises in the mind destroys ignorance completely. By the repeated study of scriptures, the *brahmākāravr̥tti* rises and it is not the result of performance of action or meditation. *Karma* and *upāsanā* are useful to purify and maintain the balance of mind and in such a mind there is the rise of knowledge. The mind of a *mukta* is free from demerits and fickleness. Ignorance is the cause of likes and dislikes through which demerit and fickleness arise. This ignorance is destroyed by knowledge alone. Thus, in a *mukta* demerit and fickleness are absent and hence *karma* and *upāsanā* are purposeless.

Objection: Likes and dislikes are natural characteristics of the mind. A *jīvanmukta*'s mind is also subject to attachment and hatred. This results in imbalanced mind, and for the stability of the mind a *mukta* has to practise meditation. The fickleness in the mind of a *mukta* may not affect *videhamukti* but in an imbalanced mind the

---

46 अनन्वागतं पापेन। — *BU* 3.7.22

47 पुण्यानि पापानि निरिन्द्रियस्य निश्चेतसो निर्विकृतोर्निराकृतेः।
कुतो ममाखण्डसुखानुभूतेः ब्रूते ह्यनन्वागतमित्यपि श्रुतिः॥ — *VC* 503

हयमेधसहस्राण्यथवा कुरुताद्ब्रह्महतिलक्षाणि।
परमार्थविन्न पुण्यैर्न च पापैः स्पृश्यते विमलः॥ — Quoted in *SV*, p. 275

ānanda nature of Self does not get reflected. An unstable mind is opposed to *jīvanmukti*.

Answer: For a *mukta*, a balanced mind and an imbalanced mind, both are falsified by the rise of *Brahman*-knowledge. Also, a *mukta* performs action and withdraws from action based on *prārabdha*. *Prārabdha Karma* varies from person to person that includes a *mukta*. (1) Like the enlightened ones as Janaka and others, *prārabdha* is meant for exhaustion. Such a one with an inclination for exhaustion of the result of action due to *prārabdha* puts forth effort. (2) Like Śuka, Vāmadeva and others *prārabdha* enhances withdrawal. Such a one rejoices in *jīvanmukti ānanda* (*śāstrānanda*) and is disinterested in other kinds of enjoyments.

For the sake of *ānanda*, due to *jīvanmukti*, one engages in *brahmākāravr̥tti* that arise by the study of Vedānta (*vicāra*) and not *upāsanā*. In a stable mind, along with *brahmākāravr̥tti*, there is the reflection of *brahmānanda*. *Brahmākāravr̥tti* is always possible only by the analysis of Vedānta and not by *upāsanā*. The instability of the mind of a *mukta* also gets destroyed only by the analysis of the Vedānta. So, a *mukta* does not take to *upāsanā* for the sake of maintaining a balanced mind. It is thus clear that one with a firm knowledge does not take to *karma* and *upāsanā*.

The *guru* then elucidates the two types of enlightened persons as *dr̥ḍha jñānī* and *adr̥ḍha jñānī*, who are not eligibile to perform *karma* and *upāsanā*. An *adr̥ḍha jñānī* further takes to *manana* and *nididhyāsana* and not to action and meditation. He is not engaged in any other activity other than *manana* and *nididhyāsana*.[48] A *dr̥ḍha jñānī* takes to *manana* and *nididhyāsana* not as a commandment but to enjoy the *ānanda* of *jīvanmukti*.[49] Pointing out to the role of means to liberation, the *guru* says that one who does not have the knowledge of the Highest should listen to the scriptural statements (*śravaṇa*), one who has doubts should eliminate it by the process

---

[48] लिङ्गाच्च । — *BS* 4.1.2.

[49] शृण्वन्त्वज्ञाततत्त्वास्ते जानन् कस्माच्छृणोम्यहम् । मन्यन्तां संशयापन्ना न मन्येऽहमसंशयः ॥ विपर्यस्तो निदिध्यासेत् किं ध्यानमविपर्ययात् । देहात्मत्वविपर्यासं न कदाचिद्भजाम्यहम् ॥ — *PD* 7.260-61.

of reasoning (*manana*) and one who faces the obstacle of contradiction should recollect the teaching in order to assimilate its essence (*nididhyāsana*). The injunction of *śravaṇa*, etc. is for such kind of seekers. A *mukta,* who does not have ignorance, doubt or habitual notion, is not bound by any such injunction.

Further, the *guru* classifies seekers into three grades and mentions that none of them is bound to take to action and meditation. The first category is the *uttama jijñāsu* who has not gained the knowledge but whose desire for liberation is intense; such a one should take to *śravaṇa*, etc. and not to *karma* and *upāsanā*. The second category is the *manda jijñāsu* who desires for liberation but has not completely detached himself from the clutches of sensual pleasures. Such a one also need not take to action or meditation but to *śravaṇa* that will give the result of pure and tranquil mind. On the other hand, it is said that if such a one gives up *śravaṇa* and takes to *karma* and *upāsanā* there will be a spiritual downfall (*ārūḍhapatita*).[50] Thus, *dr̥ḍha jñānī, adr̥ḍha jñānī, uttama jijñāsu* and *manda jijñāsu* are not bound to perform action and meditation. One who has desire for knowledge but has inclination for worldly pleasures does not take to *śravaṇa*; such a person is eligible for *niṣkāma karma* and *upāsanā*. One who desires only for worldly pleasures and is not interested in *śravaṇa* is an extrovert, and such a one should take to *sakāma karma*. Thus, a *mukta* is not eligible for *karma* and *upāsanā* since they are opposed to knowledge.

Moreover, *karma* and *upāsanā* are not opposed to *dr̥ḍha bodha* but only to *manda bodha.* A performer of action performs with an attitude that "I am doer, sacrifices are performed by me, sacrifices result in heaven". A meditator's attitude is "I am a meditator, meditating on a deity". These two notions place at distance the statement "everything is *Brahman*" (*sarvam khalvidam brahma*). Thus, *karma* and *upāsanā* are opposed to knowledge. Even if a *jñānī* knows that the Self is unassociated then also he engages in physical

[50] उपेक्ष्य तत्तीर्थयात्राजपादीनेव कुर्वताम्। पिण्डं समुत्सृज्य करं लेढीति न्याय आपतेत्॥ — *PD* 9.130

activities like consuming food or engages in activities like protecting the kingdom as in the case of Janaka. It may be noted that, in such cases, knowledge is not opposed to action. That is, when for an enlightened one, the Self as unassociated is known, then even in the presence of action, the knowledge is not opposed to action. Since the realized one engages in activity with the knowledge that "all activities rest on body, etc. and the action along with body, etc. are not related to the Self". Thus, the action (*pravṛtti*) of a *mukta* is withdrawal (*nivṛtti*).[51]

The action of a *mukta* is a mere semblance (*ābhāsa*) that is not opposed to knowledge. Whereas, in the case of a *manda bodha* even though the action is *ābhāsa*, it is opposed to knowledge because the knowledge is riddled with doubts. Prior to *manda bodha*, one should perform action and meditation and not posterior to *manda bodha*. Just as the protection of the mother bird is needed for the eggs to open up and not after the eggs are hatched, prior to the rise of knowledge, *karma* and *upāsanā* are to be done; not after the rise of knowledge. If *karma* is performed after the rise of knowledge, then the *manda bodha* gets destroyed.[52] Thus, a *jñānī* need not perform anything for the sake of liberation.[53]

6.4 Videhamukti

In the seventh *taraṅga* the concept of *videhamukti* as described in Advaita is analysed from two different standpoints — that of a *jīvanmukta* and a *kramamukta*. *Videhamukti* in the case of a *jīvanmukta* is further presented in two different ways. First, it is described as, on the rise of *Brahman*-knowledge, the material cause in the form of ignorance is destroyed and its effects, namely, the

---

[51] जगत्सत्यत्वमापाद्य प्रारब्धं भोजयेद्यदि । तदा विरोधि विद्याया भोगमात्रान्न सत्यता ॥ यदि विद्याऽपह्नुवीत जगत्प्रारब्धघातिनी । तदा स्यान्न तु मायात्वबोधेन तदपह्नवः ॥ — *PD* 7.177-79; मायामयः प्रपञ्चोऽयमात्मा चैतन्यरूपधृक् । इति बोधे विरोधः को लौकिकव्यवहारिणः ॥ अपेक्षते व्यवहृतिर्न प्रपञ्चस्य वस्तुताम् । नाप्यात्मजाड्यं किं त्वेषा साधनान्येव काङ्क्षति ॥ मनोवाक्कायतद्बाह्यपदार्थाः साधनानि तान् । तत्त्वविश्नोपमृद्नाति व्यवहारोऽस्य नो कुतः ॥ — *PD* 9.88-90.

[52] *bālapakṣi nyāya.*

[53] *BGŚB* 3.18.

world and the reflected consciousness are sublated. Even then, as long as *prārabdha* remains, so long, even the sublated body, world and the reflected consciousness continues to appear. At the cessation of *prārabdha* they do not appear and this is said as *videhamukti* attained by a *jīvanmukta*. Second, it is explicated that on the total cessation of ignorance by knowledge, the material cause of the gross and the subtle bodies, posterior to the exhaustion of *prārabdha*, completely resolves into its substratum, namely, the consciousness. This is said to be the *videhamukti* of a *jīvanmukta*.

The point to be noted here is that in the seventh *taraṅga*, *videhamukti* is not presented in its conventional sense as described in the Advaita School that defines *videhamukti* as the fall of the physical body after exhaustion of *prārabdha* and absence of rebirth. Here, it is shown that *videhamukti* is the destruction of ignorance while living because on destruction of ignorance the world and the bodies are falsified, in other words, destruction of ignorance from the standpoint of a *mukta* is absence of body, which is seen as *videhamukti*.

A *kramamukta*, who takes to *devayāna mārga* to reach *brahmaloka*, is eligible for *videhamukti* after the experience of pleasure in the *brahmaloka* as a result of meditation. A *jīvanmukta* may choose to give up the happiness of liberation and take to actions based on *prārabdha*. In the same line of argument, it cannot be said that a *jīvanmukta* chooses to give up *videhamukti* and travel to higher worlds on fall of the mortal body, because:

(a) the scriptures declare that the subtle body of a *jīvanmukta* does not travel. So, travelling to higher worlds in case of a *mukta* is not possible.

(b) Giving up of *videhamukti* is not possible since, as mentioned earlier, the complete cessation of ignorance, the material cause, by knowledge, resolves into the substratal consciousness. Thus, in the absence of the material cause there cannot be another birth, which is *videhamukti*.

One may argue that the residue of primal ignorance that is destroyed may rise again and *videhamukti* will remain unattained. This is untenable since such a residue is not possible as, on the rise of knowledge, ignorance is completely destroyed. The ignorance destroyed by *pramāṇa* can never occur again, and hence the absence of *videhamukti* is impossible. Moreover, the certainty of *videhamukti* is declared wherein it is said that even if one does not desire for *videhamukti* it is inevitable.[54]

In the seventh *taraṅga* there is a further analysis of the nature of oneness as a result of *videhamukti* by presenting two alternatives. The question is whether the non-difference of Self attained with *Īśvara* or with *Brahman*, the Pure Consciousness. The answers as examined in the Advaita school of thought are presented.

1. In *videhamukti*, one attains *satya-saṅkalpa*, etc. is the view of Jaimini.[55]
2. *Videhamukti* does not include attaining such virtues like *satya-saṅkalpa* is the view of Auḍulomi.[56]
3. Siddhānta is that both the above views are tenable.[57]

According to some, *videhamukti* is the non-difference "attained" with *Īśvara*. Some consider that an enlightened person becomes one with *Īśvara* and attains divine virtues. From the transcendental angle, *Īśvara* is pure consciousness. Pure consciousness or *Brahman* is free from attributes. Being attributeless, there are no virtues like *satya-saṅkalpa* in *Īśvara*. Similarly, even in the case of a bound *jīva*, *jīva* is essentially the pure consciousness as seen from the angle of absolute reality. Due to ignorance, this is not known and hence *jīva* experiences doership, etc. But, for *Īśvara*, there is no appearance of the world or experience of

---

54 देहात्मज्ञानवज्ज्ञानं देहात्मज्ञानबाधकम्।
आत्मन्येव भवेद्यस्य स नेच्छन्नपि मुच्यते ॥ — Quoted in *SV*, p. 339

55 ब्राह्मणे जैमिनिरुपन्यासादिभ्यः। — *BS* 4.4.5

56 चितितन्मात्रेण तदात्मकत्वादित्यौडुलोमिः। — *BS* 4.4.6

57 एवमप्युपन्यासात् पूर्वभावादविरोधं बादरायणः। — *BS* 4.4.7

bondage. Thus, *Īśvara* is always unassociated, attributeless and pure consciousness. Thus, when it is said that *videhamukti* is oneness with *Īśvara* it only means it is oneness with the pure consciousness, *Brahman*.

If it is argued that non-difference from *Īśvara* is not the same as non-difference from *Brahman*, then the non-difference between *Īśvara* from pure *Brahman* can never be established. *Īśvara* can never be described as eternally pure. From this angle, *Īśvara* will be inferior to *jīva* and will be always bound. This is *reductio absurdum*. To avoid the above fallacy, the nature of *Īśvara* is to be understood in the following manner. In the case of *Īśvara*, the power of concealment is inoperative. So, knowledge through instruction is not expected. Since there is no concealment, there is no delusion. Thus, *Īśvara* is eternally omniscient and free. *Māyā* and its effects do not affect *Īśvara*. *Īśvara* is ever unassociated and pure. Hence, it is declared that the non-difference from *Īśvara* is nothing but non-difference from pure consciousness. Based on the following example, it is arrived that there is oneness with *Īśvara*. On the destruction of a pot in a room, the pot-space is said to have merged with the room-space and not with the total-space. In the same manner, the body is destroyed in the world created by *Īśvara*. The entire universe is the cosmic body of the lord. The subtle body of the *mukta* does not travel out of the universe at the time of *videhamukti*. Thus, it is said that there is non-difference with *Īśvara*. The non-difference between pot-space and room-space can be expressed as the non-difference between the pot-space and the total-space, since the room-space is non-different from the total-space. Here too, *mukta* is non-different from *Īśvara*. That *Īśvara* is pure *Brahman* alone. Thus, it is said that the *mukta* attains the pure *Brahman*. From the angle of an enlightened one, prior to *videhamukti* the entire world did not exist but there is only *Brahman*. Therefore, *mukta* merges with *Brahman* alone. The enlightened one alone attains pure *Brahman*. From the standpoint of an ignorant person, prior to *mukti* world appears. Such a one understands that a *mukta* merges with *Īśvara*.

NITYAMUKTI

From the standpoint of a *jīvanmukta*, ignorance and its products are non-existent. A *mukta* knows that the world is like sky-lotus (Ajātivāda) for which there can be no creator. There is no witness-principle since object of witness is non-existent. The object of knowledge is illumined by the knower. By negating the objects, body, etc. the knowerhood is also negated. The status of the witness principle is from the standpoint of witnessed objects, i.e. one is said to be an observer from the standpoint of observed objects. Thus, the states of a witnesser and an observer are relative. If there is bondage, then liberation in the form of freedom from bondage is to be explained. But, according to Advaita, there is neither bondage nor liberation. Similarly, there is neither ignorance nor knowledge (*vṛttijñāna*). This world and the other worlds are non-existent, thus to obtain such worlds neither action nor meditation need to be performed. Prior to Self-knowledge one is of the nature of non-dual *Brahman*. But there is the notion that "I am the performer and the experiencer", which is a false identification. One engages in various means in vain to attain happiness and to get rid of sorrow. One who approaches a *guru* as a result of ripening of various past merits receives the instruction of Vedānta. Hearing the Vedānta words one understands that "I am not a doer or enjoyer but I am of the nature of *Brahman*". Therefore, there is nothing to be accomplished. This is the result of Vedānta *śravaṇa*. Advaita Vedānta, thus, is not meant to "attain" *Brahman* since one is *Brahman* by nature, which is eternally accomplished.[58]

6.5 On Liberation of the Adhikārīs

However, we close with an account of the "state" of each *adhikārī*s — *uttama*, *madhyama*, *manda-madhyama* and *kaniṣṭha* — as a result of listening to the teaching as found in the seventh *taraṅga* of *Vicārasāgara*.

[58] सिद्धस्य वित्तिः सत एव सिद्धिः स्वप्नोपमानाः खलु सिद्धयोऽन्याः ।
स्वप्नः प्रबुद्धस्य कथं नु सत्यः सति स्थितः किं पुनरेपि मायाम् ॥ — *SD* 37

Uttama Adhikārī: Scriptures point out that on the rise of Self-knowledge, the enlightened one continues to live in the physical body and this state is known as *jīvanmukti*. After the fall of the body, the vital air resolves into its material cause and does not travel. The *uttama adhikārī*, who is a *jīvanmukta*, sheds the body and "attains" *videhamukti*.

1. A *jīvaṅmukta* may not depart in a specific time (*uttarāyaṇa* or *dakṣiṇāyana*) or place but is ever free.
2. A *jīvanmukta* may resolve in a sacred place or an unclean place but is ever free.
3. A *jīvanmukta* may not pass away in a specific posture but is ever free.
4. A *jīvanmukta* may depart with the thought on *Brahman* or may groan in physical pain, but is ever free.[59]

Thus for a *jīvanmukta*, rules related to place, time or posture prior to death are not prescribed. As the fall of body has no specifications, the rise of knowledge does not require specific place or time. One may argue, if this is so, then why did Bhīṣma, a *mukta*, waited for an appropriate time to shed the body. It is said that, Bhīṣma and others are *ādhikārika puruṣa*.[60] They desired to reveal the greatness of meditation and hence waited for the specific time. Vasiṣṭha, Bhīṣma and others have assumed many births. *Prārabdha* of an *ādhikārika puruṣa* continues till the end of the *kalpa*. Without the dissolution of *kalpa*s, they do not attain *videhamukti*. Within that *kalpa*, they may assume any birth according to their desire. They are not deluded ones but are *jīvanmukta*s. Their life is meant to serve as an instruction for others.

Madhyama Adhikārī: One, who resorts to meditation as an end to gain liberation, should shed the body in appropriate time and place.

---

[59] नीरोग उपविष्टो वा रुग्णो वा विलुठन् भुवि । मूर्च्छितो वा त्यजत्वेष प्राणान् भ्रान्तिर्न सर्वथा ॥ दिने दिने स्वप्नसुप्त्योरधीते विस्मृतेऽप्ययम् । परेद्युर्नानधीतः स्यात्तद्वद्विद्या न नश्यति ॥ प्रमाणोत्पादिता विद्या प्रमाणं प्रबलं विना । न नश्यति न वेदान्तात् प्रबलं मानमीक्ष्यते ॥ — *PD* 2.106-08.

[60] यावदधिकारमवस्थितिराधिकारिकाणाम् । — *BS* 3.3.32

1. The result of meditation is attained on meditating upon the same *devatā* at the time of death, which he practised throughout his life.
2. The meditator should remember the *devatā* and also the *mārga* through which he is to attain the meditated lord's place. Remembrance of the *mārga* is an *aṅga* of meditation.

The *madhyama adhikārī*, who took to the path of meditation, attained *kramamukti*.

Manda-Madhyama Adhikārī: Also reaches *brahmaloka* that was attained by Sanaka and others since they took to the meditation of *kāraṇabrahma*. It is said that in their death, there is no requirement of adherence to a "proper" place or time.[61] Whether it is day or night, southward or northward direction, pure or impure place, by the strength of *upāsanā*, all the paths lead to *brahmaloka*.[62] In the case of *madhyama adhikārī*, who was also a meditator, there was the need for a proper place and time for his death, because of his meditation without (*karma*) *yoga*. It is said that one who has committed to the Lord completely, like the *manda-madhyama adhikārī*, such a meditator need not have "proper" place or time of death.

Kaniṣṭha Adhikārī: The *kaniṣṭha adhikārī* who was established in the non-dual knowledge ruled the kingdom with great commitment. He was detached and remained in *Brahman*-knowledge. At the exhaustion of *prārabdha*, he attained the eternal abode that is the non-difference between *kūṭastha* and *paramātmā*. Even though *kūṭastha* is non-different from *paramātmā*, then too, due to *upādhi* there is difference. The resolution of *upādhi* destroys the difference. Thus, *kaniṣṭha adhikārī*, a *jīvanmukta*, attained *videhamukti*.

---

61 *BS* 4.2.20.

62 *BSŚB* 4.2.21.

Conclusion

A GLIMPSE into the Sanskrit *Vicārasāgara* with its novel approach of presenting the knowledge of Advaita to different kinds of aspirants has facilitated in understanding the various pedagogical measures adopted to impart the knowledge of Reality.

Pedagogical Difficulty

In a critical examination of the dialogue between the *guru* and the *adhikārī*s we do find some lacunae in discerning a well-defined *adhikārī*, the basis of classification of an *adhikārī* and the reason for employment of a particular pedagogy to impart the knowledge to an *adhikārī*. The text *Vicārasāgara* aspires to present the entire range of pedagogy and the various concepts of Advaita with an endeavour to reach all kinds of aspirants. This itself has posed the difficulty of understanding the author and thereby the trans-creator. The difficulty of learning the pedagogy as a distinct means in the field of education of philosophy from the text *Vicārasāgara* is done away with the present study. This is overcome by concentrating on the end result (liberation) of the dialogue as a clue to derive the pedagogical measures.

Pedagogical Novelty

The novel approach in *Vicārasāgara* can be enumerated as focusedly addressing an *adhikārī* in separate chapters, introducing the dialogue through a narration, providing alternatives in every stage of understanding of a seeker, amalmagating the use of parables and anecdotes to convey the philosophical thought, substituting the remote means in keeping with the ability of the seeker, and encouraging through various methodological support in gaining the primary objective declared in the scriptures, i.e. liberation.

Table 1: Pedagogical Concerns shown to the Four Adhikārīs

Pedagogy	*Uttama Adhikārī (Tattvadṛṣṭi)*	*Kaniṣṭha Adhikārī (Tarkadṛṣṭi)*	*Madhyama Adhikārī (Adṛṣṭi)*	*Manda-Madhyama Adhikārī (Śubhasantati)*
Reality	Did not question the knowledge that "*Brahman* is real".	Revealed by the method of analysing *sat, cit, ananda*	Revealed by the methods of discrimination, viz. (a) *pañcakośa viveka*, (b) *avasthātraya viveka*, and (c) *śarīratraya viveka*	Revealed by graduating from *kāryabrahma* to *kāraṇabrahma*
Falsity	By examining *anirvacanīya khyāti*	By the method of Dṛṣṭi-sṛṣṭi-vāda	Through parables	Not attempted
Identity	By the method of four-space and four-consciousness identity, *citcāturvidyā*	Through the linguistic analysis of the *mahāvākya*	By the method of *layacintana* and equation of *oṁkāra* and *mahāvākya*	By meditation on *kāraṇabrahma*
Result	*Jīvanmukti, videhamukti*	*Jīvanmukti* — ruled the kingdom for some time and attained *videhamukti*	*Kramamukti* by the analysis of *oṁkāra* and *mahāvākya* in *brahmaloka*	*Brahmalokaprāpti* (no mention of *kramamukti*)

Pedagogical Concern

The ultimate aim of the present study is fulfilled, i.e. to highlight the concern of the preceptors to educate every kind of seeker that is exhibited by the employment of various pedagogical devices. By the analysis of the contribution of Niścaladāsa and Pītāmbar as in the Hindi *Vicārasāgara* and the identification of the contribution of VB as in the Sanskrit *Vicārasāgara*, the study has justified the pedagogical concern shown by the author, commentator and the trans-creator. A special note on the concern demonstrated by VB as the trans-creator is highlighted. We shall conclude the pedagogical concern shown to the four *adhikārī*s in *Vicārasāgara* as represented in Table 1.

Appendix 1

Definitions Culled from Sanskrit Vicārasāgara

तरङ्ग १

1. विघ्नध्वंसानुकूलव्यापारविशेषः **मङ्गलम्**।
2. परमप्रेमास्पदीभूतनिरतिशयानन्दः **सुखम्**।
3. त्रिकालाबाध्यं कूटस्थसत्यम् **नित्यम्**।
4. अनन्याधीन प्रकाशरूपं चिन्मयं **स्वप्रकाशम्**।
5. देशकालवस्तुपरिच्छेदशून्यं अनन्तं निरतिशयमहत् **व्यापकम्**।
6. विवर्तोपादानकारणं **अधिष्ठानम्**।
7. वृत्तिप्रतिफलितचिदाभासविषयत्वं **फलव्याप्तिः**।
8. केवलवृत्तिविषयत्वं **वृत्तिव्याप्तिः**।
9. माया तत्कार्यरहितत्वात् **निर्मलम्**।
10. अविद्याचित्संयोगः **कालः**। कालो मायात्मसंबन्धः सर्वसाधारणात्मकः इत्युक्तेः।
11. अलक्ष्ये लक्षणस्य सत्वम् **अतिव्याप्तिः**।
12. लक्ष्यैकदेशासत्वम् **अव्याप्तिः**।
13. लक्ष्यसामान्यासत्वम् **असम्भवः**।
14. प्रतीतिकालमात्रसत्ताकं कल्पितं **मिथ्या**।
15. यत् यत्र कल्पितं नैव तत् ततः अधिष्ठानात् अतिरिच्यते।
16. विषयेभ्यो बुद्धिं यो नियच्छति सः एव **धीरः**।
17. स्वज्ञानमनु स्वविवेकविज्ञानमनन्तरमेव मुमुक्षुं बध्नाति वेदान्तविचारं प्रवर्तयति इति **अनुबन्धः**।
18. **मलं** नाम पापम्। **विक्षेपो** नाम चित्तचाञ्चल्यम्।
19. हंसस्य नीरक्षीरविवेचनवत् आत्मानात्मनोः दृढतर वेदान्तार्थविचारेण स्वरूपविवेचनं **विवेकः**।
20. **वैराग्यं** नाम सर्वविषयतित्याजयिषा इच्छासामान्याभावो वा।
21. विषयदोषदृष्ट्यात्मकाङ्कुशेन मनोरूपमातङ्गस्य स्वायत्तीकरणं **शमः**।
22. दोषदृष्टिपूर्वकं शास्त्रचिन्तारूपकशाघातेन तत् शब्दादिविषयरूप विषममार्गेभ्य इन्द्रियरूपहयानां स्ववशतापादनं **दमः**।

23. यस्य त्वीश्वराचार्यवेदवाक्यादिषु पूज्यत्वग्रहेण प्रेमातिशयरूपा निरतिशयभक्तिः संजायते तस्यैव वेदशास्त्राचार्यादिषु **श्रद्धा** जायेत।

24. लक्ष्ये ब्रह्मणि चित्तैकाग्र्यं **समाधानम्**।

25. त्यक्तेऽपि विषये कथञ्चित्पुनः प्राप्ते पूर्वानुभवजनितवासनावशात् पुनरिच्छानुदयो वैराग्यस्य फलीभूतावस्था **उपरतिः**। अप्राप्ते विषये दोषदृष्टिपूर्वकमिच्छानुदयो वैराग्यम् इति भेदः।

26. चिज्जडयोरुपलभ्यमान-कारणकार्यत्वाधिष्ठान-आरोपितत्व दृग्दृश्यत्व-साक्षिसाक्ष्यत्वादि स्वरूपस्य शास्त्रानुसारि विचारणमेव **शोधनम्**।

27. यज्ञादिनिखिलकर्माणि तत्साधनवित्तदारपुत्रादीनि च निश्शेषं यः सन्न्यस्यति सः एव ज्ञाने **उत्तमाधिकारी**।

28. **श्रवणं** नाम युक्त्या षड्विधतात्पर्यलिङ्गैर्वेदान्तवाक्यानामद्वितीये प्रत्यगभिन्नब्रह्मणि तात्पर्यनिर्णयानुकूलचेतोवृत्तिविशेषः।

29. **मननं** नाम प्रत्यग्ब्रह्मैक्यसाधक तद्भेदबाधकयुक्तिभिः सदाऽद्वितीय-ब्रह्मात्मैक्यानुसन्धानम्।

30. भेदप्रत्ययानन्तरित ब्रह्माकारप्रत्ययप्रवाह एव **निदिध्यासनम्** उच्यते।

31. यदौपाधिकं न भवति तन्मिथ्या न भवति।

32. यत्र यत्र उपाधिनिबन्धनो भेदः तत्र तत्र मिथ्यैव सः।

33. जीवात्म-परमात्म-स्वरूप-प्रतिपादकवाक्यम् **अवान्तरवाक्यम्**।

34. जीवात्म-परमात्मैक्य-प्रतिपादकवाक्यं **महावाक्यम्**।

35. अस्ति ब्रह्म इति ज्ञानं **परोक्षम्**।

36. अहमेव ब्रह्म इति ज्ञानं **अपरोक्षम्**।

37. आरोपित-प्रतियोगिक-प्रध्वंसस्य प्रतियोग्यधिष्ठाने भासमानस्याधिष्ठान-मात्रत्वनियमात्।

38. नित्यप्राप्तत्वेप्यविद्ययाऽप्राप्तत्वभ्रमः।

39. यस्य वस्तुनो येन सह संबन्धो भवति तस्य तद्विषयेप्युपयोगोऽस्ति।

40. यस्य येन संबन्धो नास्ति न तस्य तद्विषये उपयोगोऽस्ति।

तरङ्ग २

41. आत्मानमधिकृत्य वर्तमानं स्थूलसूक्ष्मशरीरम् **अध्यात्मम्**। ततो जायमानं दुःखादिकम् **आध्यात्मिकम्**।

42. स्वशरीरादिसङ्घातव्यतिरिक्तं सत् यत् चक्षुरिन्द्रियगोचरं तत् **अधिभूतम्**। ततो

जायमानं दुःखादिकम् **आधिभौतिकम्**।

43. स्वशरीरादिसङ्घातव्यतिरिक्तं सत् यत् चक्षुरिन्द्रियागोचरं तत् **अधिदैवम्**। ततो जायमानं दुःखादिकम् **आधिदैविकम्**।

44. निवृत्तस्य पुनरपि कदाचिदप्यनुत्पत्तिरेव **आत्यन्तिकी निवृत्तिः** इत्युच्यते।

45. निश्शेषदुःखध्वंसपूर्वक नित्यनिरतिशयसुखस्यैव **मोक्षरूपम्**।

46. विषयजन्यं सुखं वस्तुतः सुखस्वरूपमपि विषयोपाधिसंबन्धात् दुःखमेव भवति सर्वदा।

47. यद्विषयकमज्ञानं भवति तदज्ञानं तद्विषयकापरोक्षज्ञानेनैव निवर्तते।

48. स्थूलसूक्ष्मकारणात्मकशरीरत्रयविलक्षणं पञ्चकोशविलक्षणं च स्वस्वरूपं अखण्डाद्वितीयस्वयंज्योतिस्स्वभावानन्दघनब्रह्मरूपेण यः साक्षादपरोक्षी करोति करतलामलकवत् स एव **मुक्त** इत्युच्यते।

49. यन्मिथ्या न तदधिष्ठानादतिरिच्यते।

50. अन्तःकरणस्य वृत्त्याश्रयत्वान्न तत् स्वाश्रितवृत्तेर्विषयीभवितुमर्हति।

51. कर्तृत्वभोक्तृत्वादिरूप संसारिविशेषणानां यो विशेष्यांशः स एव **साक्षी** इत्युच्यते।

52. यद्वस्तु स्वसमीपस्थं वस्त्वन्तरं व्यावर्तयति अपि तु स्वयं तेन न संबध्यते स **उपाधिः** इत्युच्यते।

53. स्वात्मना सहैव वस्तुनोऽवभासकं **विशेषणम्** इत्युच्यते।

54. न केवलः साक्षी सुखदुःखादीन् भासयति किन्तु वृत्तिद्वारैव।

55. ज्ञानस्य ह्येषः स्वभावः यत् स्वविषयीभूतवस्तुनिष्ठाज्ञानतत्कार्याध्यास-निवर्तकत्वमिति।

56. भ्रमज्ञानविषयीभूत मिथ्यावस्तु तद्विषयकभ्रान्तिज्ञानं च **अध्यास** इत्युच्यते।

57. भ्रान्तिज्ञानविषयीभूतमिथ्यासर्पादिः **अर्थाध्यासः**।

58. तादृशमिथ्यार्थज्ञानं **ज्ञानाध्यासः**।

59. यो भ्रान्तिदशायां प्रतिभाति यदभावे भ्रान्तिरेव न स्यात् स एव सामान्यांशः **आधारः** इति उच्यते।

60. यो भ्रान्तिदशायामपि न भाति यद्भाने भ्रान्तिनिश्शेषं नश्येत् स एव विशेषांशः **अधिष्ठानं** इति उच्यते।

61. पुरुषप्रवृत्तिमधिकृत्य यद्वेदेन विधीयते तत् **विहितम्**।

62. वेदेनैव यत्प्रतिषिध्यते तत् **प्रतिषिद्धम्**।

63. प्रवृत्तिनिवृत्त्यर्थं वेदोक्ता एव क्रियाः **कर्माणि** इत्युच्यते।

64. पापपरिहारार्थं विहितं कर्म **प्रायश्चित्तम्**।

65. फलार्थं विहितं कर्म **काम्यम्**।

66. वेदेन अनिषिद्धं अविहितं च सदरागद्वेषतः कृतं गमनागमनशौचादि स्वाभाविकं सर्वप्राणिसाधारणं कर्म **उदासीनं** इति कथ्यते।

67. अवश्यानुष्ठेयकर्मणो विस्मरणं सत्यामपीच्छायामननुष्ठानं वा **प्रमादः**।

68. यस्याननुष्ठानात्प्रत्यवायः श्रूयते अनुष्ठानाच्च पुण्यापुण्यफलाभावः यच्च न नित्यमेव विहितं किन्तु यत्किञ्चिन्निमित्तमधिकृत्यैव विधीयते तत्कर्म **नैमित्तिकम्**।

69. यद्येन जायते नान्येन तत्तस्य **फलं** इत्युच्यते।

70. कर्मैव मोक्षसाधनमिति प्रतिपादकमतस्य शास्त्रे **ऐकभविकवाद** इति प्रसिद्धः।

71. पूर्वपूर्वसजातीयवस्तुज्ञानजन्यसंस्कार एव उत्तरोत्तराध्यासहेतुः।

72. सर्वत्र हि तत्तदनुभवाहितसंस्कार एवाध्यासत्वावच्छिन्नं प्रति नियमेन कारणं भवति।

73. तत्तद्वस्तुज्ञानजन्यसंस्कारोप्यन्तःकरणे एव वर्तते।

74. यस्य वस्तुनोऽध्यासो भवति तत्सजातीयवस्त्वनुभवाहितसंस्कारोऽध्यासहेतुः। न तु विजातीयवस्त्वनुभवाहितसंस्कारः।

75. अहंकारादिनिखिलानात्मवस्तुजातं तज्ज्ञानञ्च **बन्ध** इत्युच्यते।

76. दृष्टिर्नाम अविद्यावृत्तिरूपं ज्ञानम्। तादृशज्ञानकाल एव विषयाणामुत्पत्तिरिति यो वादः स एव **दृष्टिसृष्टिवादः** इति शास्त्रेषु कथितः।

77. पूर्वशरीरस्थितजातिरेव शरीरान्तरेप्यनुवर्तनीयेति न नियमः।

78. **आत्मा** व्यापकः प्रत्यक् विषयी चिद्रूपः। **जातिस्तु** परिच्छिन्ना पराचीना विषयात्मिका जडा च।

79. अन्तःकरणस्थाज्ञानस्य विक्षेपहेतुभूतशक्तिनिष्ठशुभाशुभकर्मजन्य-संस्काररूपादृष्टं **प्रमातृ दोषः**।

80. चैतन्ये स्वातिरिक्तप्रमाणाभावात् स्वस्वरूपमेव प्रमाणम्। तदाश्रितऽविद्या **प्रमाण दोषः**।

81. आन्तरत्ववस्तुत्वरूपधर्माभ्यां चैतन्यप्रपञ्चयोः सादृश्यं सिद्धम्। अयं च **प्रमेय दोषः**।

82. सर्वत्र व्याप्य वर्तमानमखण्डचैतन्यं **सामान्यम्**। अन्तःकरणवृत्यारूढचैतन्यं **विशेषात्मकम्**।

83. अधिकदेशकालवर्ति यत्तत्सामान्यस्वरूपमिति न्यूनदेशकालवर्ति यत्तद्विशेषस्वरूपमिति च लौकिकपदार्थानां विवेकः।

84. फलाभिसन्ध्यनभिसन्धिपूर्वकं कृतवतोरुभयोरपि कर्मावश्यं फलं ददात्येव ।

तरङ्ग ३

85. यः साङ्गवेदाध्यायी तदर्थज्ञो जीवब्रह्मैक्यविषयकदृढतरनिश्चयात्परिनिष्ठितात्म-साक्षात्कारवान् स एव **गुरुः**।

86. वेदान्तग्रन्थप्रवृत्तिसंपादकं साधनचतुष्टयरूपं तत्संपत्तिरेव **शिष्यस्य लक्षणं** भवति ।

87. **पञ्चभेदखण्डनयुक्तयः**

घटाकाशमठाकाशभेदवत् जीवेश्वरभेदोऽविद्या मायारूपोपाधिजनितत्वात् कल्पितः।

नानाघटाकाशभेदवत् जीवानां परस्परभेदः आभाससहितान्तःकरण-रूपोपाधिजनितत्वात् कल्पितः।

जीवजडभेदः साभासान्तःकरण निराभासनामरूपमायोपाधिजनितत्वात् कल्पितः।

ईश्वरजडभेदः साभासमाया नामरूपमायोपाधिजनितत्वात् कल्पितः।

रज्ज्वारोपितसर्पदण्डादिभेदवत् जडानां परस्परभेदो नामरूपमायोपाधिजनितत्वात् कल्पितः।

88. ईश्वरसेवाऽदृष्टफलमात्रहेतुः। सद्गुरुसेवा तु दृष्टादृष्टोभयफलहेतुः।

89. धर्माधर्मोत्पत्तिद्वारा फलहेतुर्यो भवति सोऽदृष्टफलहेतुरिति धर्माधर्मोत्पत्तिं विनैव साक्षात्फलहेतुर्यो भवति स दृष्टफलहेतुरिति च उच्यते।

90. ईश्वरसेवा धर्मोत्पत्तिद्वाराऽन्तःकरणशुद्धिरूपफलहेतुर्भवति अत एव ईश्वर-सेवाऽदृष्टफलहेतुः। सद्गुरुसेवा तु धर्मनिरपेक्षा आचार्यप्रसादमात्रेणोपदेशात्मक-फलहेतुर्भवति। तस्मात् दृष्टफलहेतुः सद्गुरुसेवेत्युच्यते।

तरङ्ग ४

91. अनिर्वचनीयस्य सर्पादेः प्रतीतिः स्फुरणमभिवदनञ्च **अनिर्वचनीयख्याति-**रित्युच्यते।

92. अविद्यावृत्तिद्वारा यद्यत् साक्षी प्रकाशयति तत् तत् **साक्षिभास्य**मित्युच्यते।

93. उपादानकारणसमस्वभावकोऽन्यथाभावः **परिणामः**।

94. अधिष्ठानविषमस्वभावकोऽन्यथाभावो **विवर्तः**।

95. न ह्येकं कल्पितं वस्तु कल्पितवस्त्वन्तरस्याधिष्ठानं भवेत्।

96. यस्मादावरणं जडमनाश्रित्य तदधिष्ठानचैतन्यमेवाश्रयति।

97. अन्तःकरणजन्यवृत्तिज्ञानं अखण्डं ब्रह्म विषयी करोति।

98. स्वकारणेन सहैव कार्यस्य निवृत्तिः **आत्यन्तिकी निवृत्ति**रित्युच्यते।

99. साक्षिचैतन्यमेव वृत्त्युपहितचैतन्यम् इत्युच्यते ।

100. घटादिरूपः **विषयः**। चिदाभाससहितवृत्तिरूपं घटादिविषयकं **ज्ञानम्**। चिदाभाससहितान्तःकरणरूपो **ज्ञाता** एतत्त्रयमपि साक्षी प्रकाशयति ।

101. यावन्ति ज्ञानानि जायन्ते तानि सर्वाण्यपि प्रमातारं साक्षिणं वा आश्रित्य जायन्त इति नियमः ।

102. वृत्त्युपहितचैतन्यस्थाविद्यायास्तमोगुणांशः **सर्पस्योपादानकारणं** तस्या एव सत्त्वगुणांशः **सर्पज्ञानस्योपादानकारणम्** ।

103. यद्यन्मिथ्यावस्तु तत्सर्वं स्वाधिष्ठाने कल्पितं भवति ।

104. यद्वस्तु यस्याज्ञानाद्भाति तद्वस्तु तस्य ज्ञानात् निवर्तत इति नियमः ।

105. जीवत्वापादकं विशेषणं यत् तदधिष्ठानस्य **कूटस्थ** इति नाम ।

106. कूटस्थसहितचिदाभासो **जीव** इति कीर्त्यते ।

107. यस्य प्रतिबिम्बोऽन्यत्र प्रतीयते स एव **बिम्ब** इत्युच्यते ।

108. अधिष्ठानादपृथग्भूतं सत् यदधिष्ठानमावृणोति तदेव **आरोप्यं** इत्युच्यते ।

109. रूपवत एव पदार्थस्य रूपविशिष्टे एव पदार्थान्तरे प्रतिबिम्बोदयः इति नियमो नास्ति ।

110. रजस्तमोगुणाधिक्यादेवाविद्या स्वप्रतिबिम्बितजीवरूप चिदाभासांशस्यावरणं करोति ।

111. यद्वत्सु स्वव्याप्यापेक्षया व्यापकं स्वव्यापकापेक्षया व्याप्यं च भवति तत् **आपेक्षिकव्यापकं** इत्युच्यते ।

112. यद्वस्तु सर्वापेक्षया व्यापकं भवति तन्निष्ठव्यापकत्वं **निरपेक्षव्यापकत्वं** इत्युच्यते ।

113. **ब्रह्मशब्दः** स्वरसतो लक्ष्यार्थमेव प्रायशो बोधयति क्वाचित्कतया तु वाच्यार्थमपि ।

114. **ईश्वरशब्दस्तु** वाच्यार्थमेव प्रायशो बोधयति लक्ष्यार्थं तु क्वाचित्कतया ।

115. वस्तु नास्तीति प्रतीतिहेतुभूता शक्तिः **असत्वापादिकेति** ।

116. वस्तु न भातीति प्रतीतिहेतुभूता शक्तिः **अभानापादिका** इति च उच्यते ।

117. यस्य वस्तुनो येन वस्तुना सह सदाऽभेदसंबन्ध अस्ति तस्य वस्तुनस्तेन वस्तुना सह **मुख्यसामानाधिकरण्य**मुच्यते ।

118. यस्य हि वस्तुनः स्वरूपनाशपूर्वकं येन वस्तुना सहाभेदो जायते तस्य वस्तुनस्तेन वस्तुना सह **बाधायां सामानाधिकरण्य**मुच्यते ।

119. कार्यत्वावच्छिन्ननिष्ठकार्यतानिरूपितकारणताशालि यत् तत् **साधारणकारणम्** ।

120. कार्यत्वातिरिक्तधर्मावच्छिन्ननिष्ठकार्यतानिरूपितकारणताशालि यत् तत् **असाधारणकारणम्** ।

121. यच्छरीरं यस्य सुखदुःखादेर्हेतुर्भवति तच्छरीरं तदीयपुण्यपापजन्यमिति न्यायः।

तरङ्ग ५

122. समसत्ताकयोर्निवर्त्यनिवर्तकभावदर्शनात्।

123. ब्रह्मप्राप्तिस्तु न वेदान्तश्रवणफलं ब्रह्मणः स्वस्वरूपतया नित्यप्राप्तत्वात्।

124. ज्ञानरूपान्तःकरणवृत्त्युदयकाल एव विषयावरणभङ्गस्य सिद्धत्वात् वृत्तिस्थैर्यसंपादनस्य नास्त्युपयोगः।

125. यत्र यद्वस्तु अन्यदृष्ट्या प्रतीयते तत्र तद्वस्तु परमार्थतो नास्ति।

126. यस्य वस्तुनो यद्रूपमन्यदृष्टिं विना स्वत एव प्रतीयते तदेव तस्य पारमार्थिकं स्वरूपम्।

तरङ्ग ६

127. विषयेण सहेन्द्रियाणामन्तःकरणवृत्तेश्च संबन्धः **प्रत्यक्षज्ञाने हेतुः**।

128. यस्य वस्तुन उत्पत्तौ देशकालादिरूपो यावान् सामग्रीकलाप अपेक्षितस्तावन्तं सामग्रीकलापं विनैवोत्पद्यमानं वस्तु **मिथ्या** इति अभिधीयते।

129. यत् यद्विवर्तभूतं तत् तत्स्वरूपमेव भवति न ततोऽतिरिच्यते।

130. यद्वस्तु अविवेकादुत्पद्यते विवेकाच्च नश्यति तद्वस्तु रज्जुसर्पवन्मिथ्या।

131. यदनित्यं वस्तु तज्जडमिति नियमः।

132. यद्वस्तु कदाचिद्भवति कदाचिच्च न भवति तदागमापायि भवति।

133. युक्ति अभावः एव **विनिगमनाविरह** इत्युच्यते।

134. मायाधिष्ठानचैतन्यं माया तत्र चैतन्याभासः इत्येतत् त्रयं मिलित्वा **ईश्वरः**।

135. अविद्यांशाधिष्ठानचैतन्यं अविद्यांशः तत्र चैतन्याभासः इत्येतत् त्रयं मिलित्वा **जीवः**।

136. उपाधेः प्रतिबिम्बपक्षपातित्वमिति नियमः।

137. यया यया प्रक्रियया जिज्ञासोर्बोधो भवेत्सा सा प्रक्रिया तस्य तस्य समीचीनाऽभिप्रेता।

138. आत्मनोऽन्यत् सर्वमनित्यमिति नियमः।

139. सर्वप्रतीतिविषयः आत्मा आनन्दरूपो भवति।

140. **अवच्छेदवादे** मायाविशिष्टचैतन्यमीश्वर इत्युच्यते। अविद्या विशिष्टचैतन्यं तु जीव इति।

141. **आभासवादे** मायया आभासेन च विशिष्टं चैतन्यमीश्वर इति वर्ण्यते। आभाससहिताविद्याविशिष्टं चैतन्यं जीव इति च।

142. **आभासवादे** आभाससहिताविद्यायाः आभाससहितमायायाश्च भेदोऽस्ति। तथैवावच्छेदवादे अविद्याया मायायाश्च भेदोऽस्ति।

143. **बिम्बप्रतिबिम्बपक्षे** अज्ञानगतचैतन्यप्रतिबिम्बो जीवः। बिम्बचैतन्यमीश्वरः। चैतन्यस्य स्वरूपतः नास्ति भेदः। एकस्मिन्नेव चैतन्ये जीवत्वेश्वरत्वे कल्पिते।

144. पूर्वरूपं त्यक्त्वा अन्यरूपप्राप्तिः **विकारः**। स एव विक्रिया **परिणाम** इति चोच्यते।

145. अपरोक्षभ्रान्तेरपरोक्षज्ञानेनैव विरोधः परोक्षज्ञानेन न विरोधः इति नियमः।

146. स्वमाहात्म्यप्रकटनाय वादः **प्रौढिवादः**।

तरङ्ग ७

147. **जीवन्मुक्तिलक्षणं** प्रपञ्चप्रतीतिपूर्वकं प्रत्यक्ब्रह्मचैतन्यनिष्ठत्वम्।

148. **विदेहमुक्तिलक्षणं** प्रपञ्चप्रतीतिशून्यत्वे सति प्रत्यक् चैतन्यात्मना वर्तनम्।

149. यतो ज्ञानेन निःशेषाज्ञाननिवृत्तौ प्रारब्धभोगानन्तरं स्थूलसूक्ष्मशरीराकारपरिणतस्य मूलाज्ञानस्य स्वाधिष्ठानचैतन्ये निःशेषप्रविलय एव **विदेह मोक्ष** इति कथ्यते।

150. बन्धभ्रान्त्यभाव एव सशरीरस्य ज्ञानिनो **जीवन्मुक्ति**रित्युच्यते।

Appendix - 2[1]

Contents of Hindi Vicārasāgara

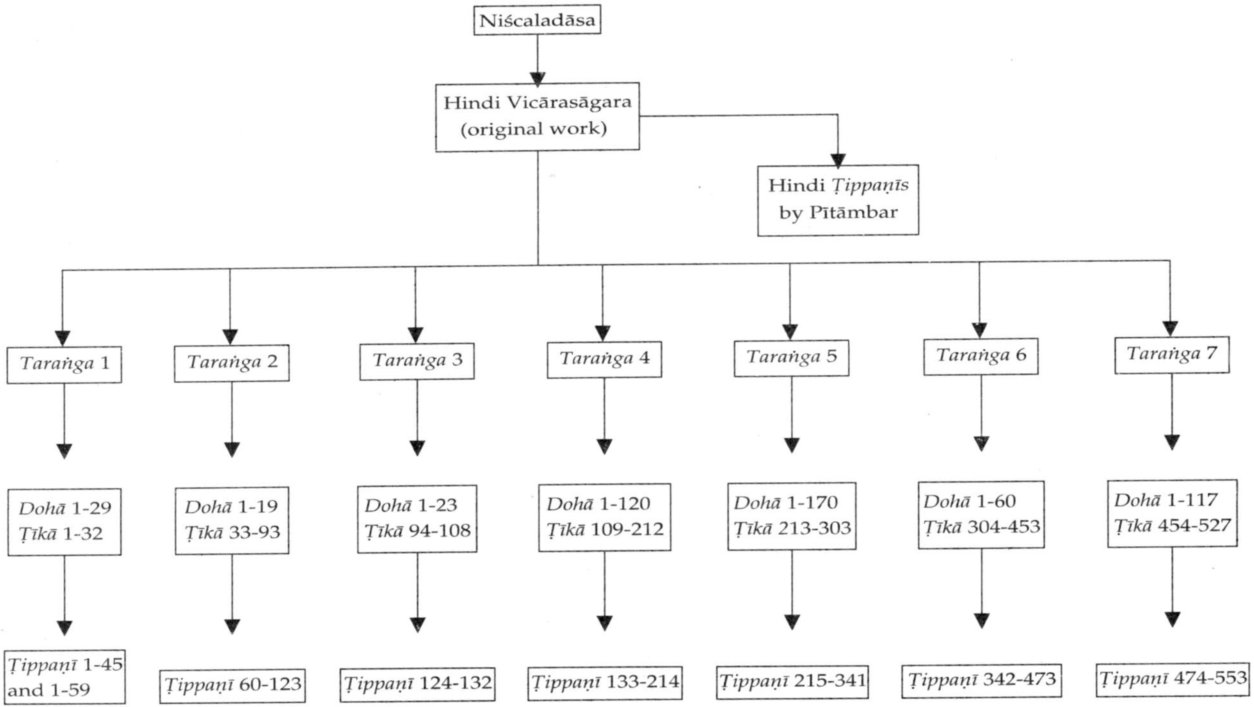

[1] See *HV*.

Appendix - 3[1]

Contents of Sanskrit Vicārasāgara

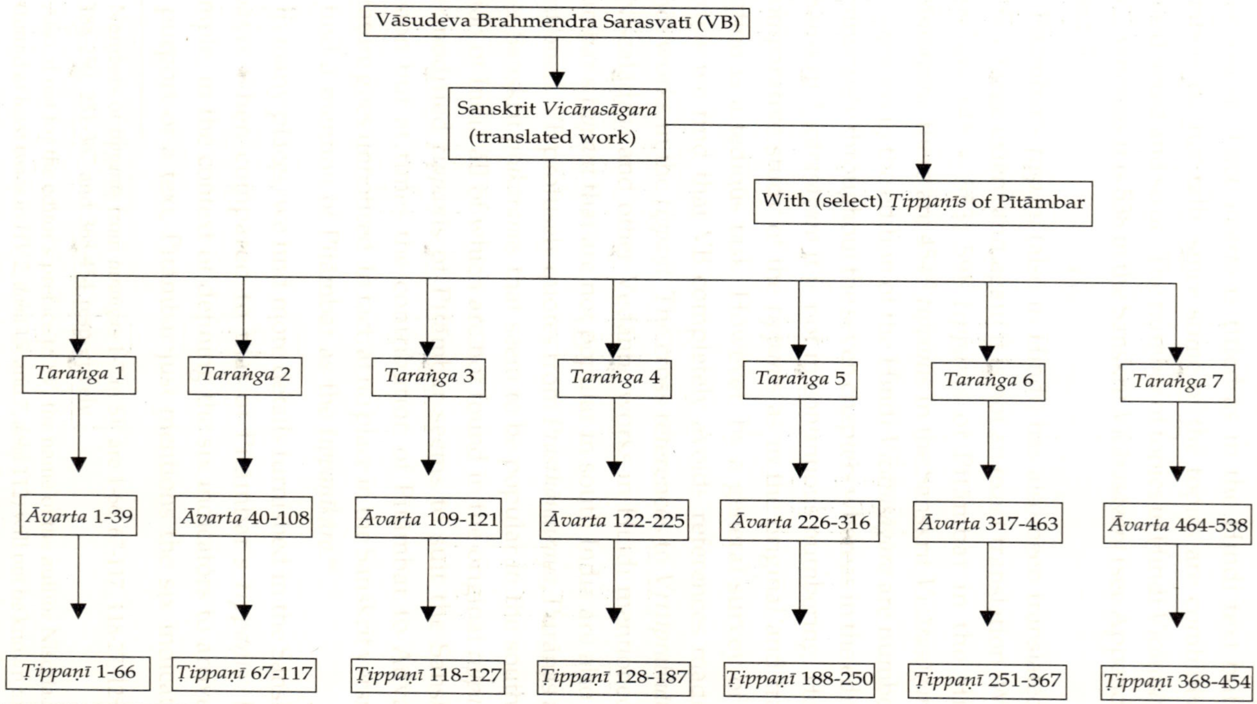

---

[1] See *SV*.

Bibliography

Books

Advaita Sabha, 1946, *Advaitākṣaramālikā*, Sri Kamakoti Granthavali Series No. 20, Kumbhakonam: Sri Kamakoti Kosasthanam.

Allen, Michael S., 2013, *The Ocean of Enquiry: A Neglected Classic of Late Advaita Vedānta*, Ph.D. Dissertation, Harvard University.

Balasubramanian, R., 1983, *A Study of the Brahmasiddhi of Maṇḍana Miśra*, Chaukhambha Amarabharati Studies, vol. X, Varanasi: Chaukhambha.

Bhuvaneshwari, S., 2013, *A Treatise on Advaita Vedānta: English Translation of Vicāracandrodaya of Pandit Pitambar*, Delhi: D.K. Printworld.

Chakraborty, Nirod Baran, 2008, *A Dictionary of Advaita Vedānta*, Kolkata: The Ramakrishna Mission Institute of Culture.

Dasgupta, Surendranath, 2006, *A History of Indian Philosophy*, vols. 1-2, Delhi: Motilal Banarsidass.

Farquhar, J.N., 1920, *An Outline of the Religious Literature of India*, Delhi: Motilal Banarsidass.

Gupta, Anand Swarup, ed., 1971, *Kūrma Purāṇa*, Varanasi: All India Kashiraj Trust.

Haragovind Sastri, ed., 2001, *Manusmṛti with Kullūkabhaṭṭa's Manvārtha-muktāvalī*, Kashi Sanskrit Series No. 114, Varanasi: Chaukhambha.

Jagadisa Sastri, ed., 2006, *Jābāladarśanopaniṣad, Upaniṣad Saṁgraha*, Delhi: Motilal Banarsidass.

Joshi, Veneemadhava Shastri, B., 2008, *Vidyāraṇya's Contribution to Advaita*, Delhi: Parimal Publications.

Kamal, R., 1980, *The Philosophy of Advaita as Expounded by Niścaladāsa with Special Reference to His Vṛttiprabhākara*, Unpublished Thesis, Department of Philosophy, University of Madras.

Kar, Bijayananda, 1978, *The Theories of Error in Indian Philosophy*, Delhi: Ajanta Publications.

Karmakar, K.D., ed., 1962, *Vedāntakalpalatikā*, Poona: BORI.

Kishoredas, 1992, *Vicārasāgara* (Modern Hindi), Bombay: Śrī Sādhubelā Udāsīna Āśram.

Krishnamurthi Sastri, S.R. and N. Veezhinathan, eds., 1973, *Appayya Dīkṣita's Śāstrasiddhāntaleśasaṁgraha with the Commentary Kṛṣṇālaṁkāra of Acyutakṛṣṇānanda Tīrtha*, Secunderabad: Śrīmad Appayya Dīkṣitendra Granthāvalī Prakāśana Samiti.

Layak, Satyajit, 1990, *An Analysis of Dream in Indian Philosophy*, Sri Garib Dass Oriental Series No. 99, Delhi: Sri Satguru Publications.

Madhavananda, tr., 2000, *Vedānta Paribhāṣā of Dharmarāja Adhvarīndra*, Calcutta: Advaita Ashrama.

Mahadevan, T.M.P., ed., 2003, *Preceptors of Advaita*, Chennai: Samata Books.

———, 2006, *The Philosophy of Advaita*, Bharatiya Kala Prakashan.

Mishra, Umesh, n.d., *Dream Theory in Indian Thought*, Allahabad University Studies.

Munilal, 1924/2013, *Adhyātma Rāmāyaṇa*, Gorakhpur: Gita Press.

Naulakha, R.S., 1964, *Shankara's Brahmavada*, Kanpur: Kitab Ghar.

Niścaladāsa, 1994, *Śrīvicārasāgara* of Niścaladāsa, with Pitambar's *Vṛttiratnāvalī*, and *Pañcadaśī Nāṭakadīpa Ṭīkā*, Bombay: Khemraj Sri-krishnadas.

Panicker, Sisupala V., 1995, *Vedāntakalpalatikā: A Study*, Sri Garib Dass Oriental Series No. 188, Delhi: Sri Satguru Publications.

Pītāmbar, 1981, *Vicāracandrodaya*, Bombay: Vrajavallabh Hariprasad Bhagirath, 9th edn.

Pratap, K., 1983, *Śravaṇa Manana Nididhyāsana: As Triple Means to Mokṣa*, Tirupati: T.V. Press.

Ramachandra, Sastrigal V.S., 1977, *Advaitic Import of All Darśanas*, Bombay: Bharatiya Vidya Bhavan.

Ramaṇa, 1997, *Saddarśanam*, tr. Svarupananda, Tiruvannamalai: Sri Ramanasrama.

Revathy, S., 1990, *Three Little Known Advaitins*, University of Madras.

Sarasvatī, Saccidānandendra, 1968, *Viśuddhavedāntasāra*, Holenarasipuram: Adhyātmaprakāśakāryālaya.

Sadānanda, 2002, *Vedāntasāra*, tr. Nikhilananda, Kolkata: Advaita Ashrama.

Śaṅkarācārya, 1996, *Aparokṣānubhūti*, tr. Vimuktānanda, Calcutta: Advaita Ashrama.

———, *Commentaries* to *Īśa, Kena, Kaṭha, Praśna, Muṇḍaka, Māṇḍūkya, Taittirīya, Aitareya, Chāndogya, Bṛhadāraṇyaka, Bhagavad-Gītā, and the Brahmasūtras* (Several Editions).

———, 2001, *Haristuti, "In Adoration of the Self: The Haristuti of Śaṁkara with the Commentary Haritattvamuktāvalī of Svayamprakāśa Yati"*, ed. N. Veezhinathan, Chennai: The Adi Sankara Research Centre.

———, 2008, *Pañcīkaraṇam*, ed. Shambusunugajanana, with six commentaries, Chaukhambha Rajamata Granthamala No. 18, Delhi: Chaukhambha Orientalia.

———, 1993, *Tattvabodha*, Bombay: Central Chinmaya Mission Trust.

———, 1991, *Vākyavṛtti*, tr. Chinmayananda, Bombay: Central Chinmaya Mission Trust.

———, 1978, *Vivekacūḍāmaṇi*, tr. Mādhavānanda, Calcutta: Advaita Ashrama.

Sarma, R.N., 1988, *Mīmāṁsā Theory of Meaning*, Delhi: Sri Satguru Publications.

Sarma, Thangaswami, R., 1980, *Advaita Vedānta Literature: A Bibliographical Survey*, Madras Sanskrit Series No. 36, University of Madras.

———, 1995, *Bhāratīya Darśaneṣu Pratyakṣa Pramāṇa Vimarśaḥ*, The Adyar Library General Series, vol. 13, Madras: The Adyar Library Research Centre.

———, 1996, *Mīmāṁsā Mañjarī*, New Delhi: Indian Council of Philosophical Research.

Satprakashananda, 2005, *Methods of Knowledge according to Advaita Vedānta*, Kolkata: Advaita Ashrama.

Shastri, J.L., ed., 1999, *Śrīmad Bhāgavata Mahāpurāṇa* with Śrīdhara Svāmin's *Bhāvārthabodhinī Ṭīkā*, Delhi: Motilal Banarsidass.

Sinha, Jadunath, 1971, *Problems of Post-Śaṅkara Advaita Vedānta*, Calcutta: Sinha Publishing House.

Srivatsava, L.K.L., 1990, *Advaitic Concept of Jīvanmukti*, Delhi: Bharatiya Vidya Prakashan.

Sastri, Ve., Subrahmanya, 1982, *Khyātitattvasamīkṣā*, Trichi: Advaita Sabha.

Sundararama Aiyar, K., 1923, *The Vedānta: Its Ethical Aspects*, Srirangam: Sri Vani Vilas Press.

Sundaram, P.K., 1984, *Advaita Epistemology*, Madras Philosophical Series No. 11, University of Madras.

Sureśvara, 2002, *Bṛhadāraṇyakopaniṣad Bhāṣyavārttikam*, with the Commentary *Śāstraprakāśikā* of Ānandagiri, vols. 1-2, ed. S. Subrahmanya Sastri, Advaita Grantha Ratna Manjusha, Ratna 23 and 30, Varanasi: Mahesh Research Institute.

———, 1988, *The Naiṣkarmyasiddhi of Sureśvara*, ed. R. Balasubramanian, Madras University Philosophical Series No. 47, Radhakrishnan Institute for Advanced Study in Philosophy, University of Madras.

Giri, Svayamprakasha, tr., 1999, *Sūta Saṁhitā of Skanda Purāṇa with Tātparyadīpikā of Mādhavācārya*, vols. 1-2, Varanasi: Dakshinamurti Math Publishers.

Vāsudeva Brahmendra Sarasvatī, 1932, *Brahmānhikam: A Book Containing Valuable Selections on Advaita Philosophy*, Mayuram: Ananda Sagar Publications.

———, 1926, *Śāstrasiddhāntaleśatātparyasaṁgraḥ*, Madras: Hindi Prachar Press.

———, 1986, *Vicārasāgara (Sanskrit)*, ed. Pañcāpageśa Sāstrigaḷ and Kalyāṇasundara Sāstrigaḷ, Mayilāḍuthurai: The Vāsudeva Brahmendra Saraswathi Swāmigal Library Committee.

Vātsyāyana, 2007, *Kāmasūtra* with *Jayamaṅgala Ṭīkā*, ed. Devadatta Sastri, The Kashi Sanskrit Series, 29, Varanasi: Chaukhambha Sanskrit Sansthan.

Veezhinathan, N., 1985, *The Saṁkṣepaśārīraka of Sarvajñātman*, Radhakrishnan Institute for Advanced Study in Philosophy, Madras University Philosophical Series No. 18, University of Madras.

Vidyāraṇya, 1998, *Dṛg Dṛśya Viveka: An Inquiry into the Nature of the 'Seer' and the 'Seen'*, tr. Nikhilananda, Calcutta: Advaita Ashrama.

———, 1984, *Pañcadaśī* with *Padadīpikā* of Ramakrishna, Harajivandasa Sanskrit Granthamala 22, Varanasi: Chaukhambha Amarabharati Prakashan.

Vijayanarayanamishra, ed., 1992, *Lakṣmīdhara's Advaita Makaranda with Svayamprakāśa's Ṭīkā*, Varanasi: Sampurnanada Sanskrit Visvavidyalaya.

Warrier, Krishna, A.G., 1981, *The Concept of Mukti in Advaita Vedānta*, University of Madras.

Yati, Rāmacandra, 1936, *Mahāvākyaratnāvalī*, 7th edn., Mumbai: Nirnaya Sagar.

Articles

Advayananda, 2004-05, "Tat Tvam Asi", Part I-IX, *Tapovan Prasad*, Chennai: Central Chinmaya Mission Trust.

Balasubramaniam, R., 1988, "The Liberated-in-Life", *Voice of Śaṅkara*, **12**(4) and **13**(1): 33-44.

Bhatt, S.R., 1974, "The Concept of Māyā", *Indian Philosophical Quarterly*, **11**(1): 65-71.

Bhuvaneshwari, S., 2008, "Bondage Is an Error: Based on Niścaladāsa's Vicārasāgara", *Voice of Śaṅkara*, **33**(1): 79-96.

Chari, V.K., 1990, "The Limits of the Meaning of a Sentence", *Brahmavidya*, **54**: 42-53.

Devadoss, T.S., ed., 1992, "Special Number on Śrī Śaṅkara", *Indian Philosophical Annual*, **21**.

Devasenapati, V.A., ed., 1976, *"The Concept of Consciousness"*, part 1, *Indian Philosophical Annual*, **11**.

Elayath, Neelakantan K.N., 1988, "The Advaita Theory of Meaning", *Brahmavidya*, **52**: 94-104.

Javadekar, A.G., 2000, "The Message of the Māṇḍūkya Upaniṣad: A Phenomenological Analysis of Mind and Consciousness", *Indian Philosophical Quarterly*, **XXVII** (1&2): 187-93, January-April.

Jayashanmukham, N., 1992, "The Waking Life and Its Conquest: A Teaching of Advaita Vedānta", *Brahmavidya*, **56**: 47-55.

———, 1997, "The Mission of the Original Vedānta", *Journal of Indian Council of Philosophical Research*, **XV**(1): 65-73.

Kanthamani, A., 2001, "What Is to Be a Witness Consciousness (Sākṣin)", *Indian Philosophical Quarterly*, **XXVIII**(1): 1-13.

Mahadevan, T.M.P., 1976, "Vedāntic Meditation and Its Relation to Action", *Indian Philosophical Annual*, **8**: 215-26.

Malkani, G.R., 2004, "The Principle of Inexplicability in Philosophy", *Voice of Śaṅkara*, **29**(2): 77-87.

Mishra, Ganeswar, 1975, "Sankara's Doctrine of Adhyāsa: Difficulties of Propositional Symbolism", *Indian Philosophical Quarterly*, **11**(3): 225-36.

Mishra, Satya Deva, 1969, "The Theory of Appearance in Śaṅkara Vedānta", *Indian Philosophical Annual*, **5**: 272-90.

Nayak, G.C., 1995, "Understanding Śaṅkara Vedānta", *Journal of Indian Council of Philosophical Research*, **XIII**(1): 71-82.

Rao, Prabhakara M., 1997, "A Critique on Brahman-Realization", *Journal of Indian Council of Philosophical Research*, **XIV**(2): 71-82.

Revathy, S., 1992, "Śruti and Arthāpatti in Respect of Avidyā", *Brahmavidya*, **56**: 99-115.

———, 2001, "A Note on the Definition of Valid Knowledge According to Dharmarāja", *Voice of Śaṅkara*, **26**(1): 88-93.

Sastri, S.R., Krishnamurti, 1976, "On the Role of Karma-Sanyāsa in Advaita", *Voice of Śaṅkara*, **1**(2): 168-76.

Sastri, V.R., Kalyanasundara, 2003, "Jīva Is Brahman Itself, not Different from It", *Voice of Śaṅkara*, **28**(2): 73-79.

Sastry, Kutumba, 1992, "On Tātparya-liṅgas", *Voice of Śaṅkara*, **17**(1): 72-84.

Sen, Brinda, 2001, "A Note on Some Identity Sentences of Nyāya and Advaita Vedānta", *Indian Philosophical Quarterly*, **XXVII**(1&2): 195-201.

Shah, K.J., 1974, "A Note Towards the Discussion of Śaṅkara's Theory of Error", *Indian Philosophical Quarterly*, **11**(1): 1-8.

Sharma, A.D. and S.K. Shukla, 1997, "Pramāṇa Saṁplava and Pramāṇa Vyavasthā", *Journal of Indian Council of Philosophical Research*, **XIV**(2): 83-98.

Sundaram, P.K., 1974-75, "Akhaṇḍārtha", *Indian Philosophical Annual*, **10**: 183-87.

Tiwari, D.N., 2000, "Advaitic Critique of Experience", *Indian Philosophical Quarterly*, **XXVII**(1&2): 133-50.

Veezhinathan, N., 1968, "The Problem of Method in Advaita", *Indian Philosophical Annual*, **4**: 232-40.

———, 1976, "The Locus and Content of Modal Ignorance in Advaita", *Indian Philosophical Annual*, **8**: 282-94.

———, 1978, "On the Identity of Māyā and Avidyā", *Voice of Śaṅkara*, **3**(3): 295-308.

Sastry, Goda, Venkateswara, 2007, "Falsity of the World", *Voice of Śaṅkara*, **32**(1&2): 111-32.

Warrier, Krishna A.G., 1980-81, "The Logic of Nivrtti in Advaita", *Brahmavidya*, **XLIV-XLV**: 229-40.